Nearly Famous

Famous

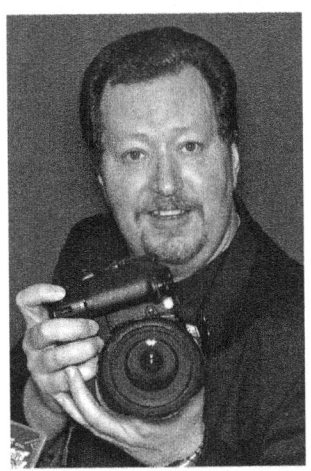

My Autobiography

Wayne Paulo

Published By

PHOTO-STOCK INTERNATIONAL

www.photo-stock.co.uk

Cover Photograph and Artwork,
Designs, Illustrations and Editing: Danielle Paulo
www. p3visuals.com
All Photography by: Wayne Paulo
(Unless otherwise credited in the Photographic Index)
Copyright © www.waynepaulo.com
Picture Editing: Estelle Paulo
Song Lyrics and Titles: Copyright © Wayne Paulo
Published by: Storm Music
www.waynepaulo.com/StormMusic.html

First edition published in 2009 by Photo-Stock International
www.photo-stock.co.uk

Copyright © Wayne Paulo, 2009

Contents

Acknowledgements

There are far too many people to mention individually, though a few of you have made it in to this collection of additional head shots. So just in case I have missed someone out in the pictures or book, through memory lapse!

Thank you all!

For the fun and interesting times we had together and for allowing me to take your pictures along the way.
For those I haven't photographed yet, please be patient!

If your photograph didn't make it into the book, I probably couldn't find room or a nice enough picture of you in time for the publication!

A Special Thank You
To Pete and Chris for house sitting while we were away on our travels, hedge trimming and feeding the goldfish!
And especially to all my family, friends, contacts, contributors and anyone who helped make this book possible without realising!

If you didn't make it into this book, don't worry, there is always the next one. Only one criteria, you have to be photographed by me!

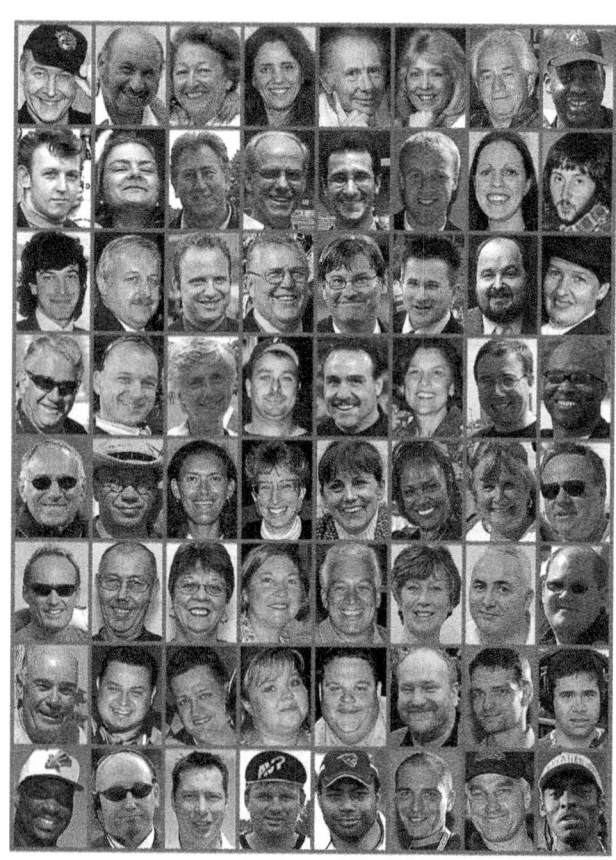

Foreword

I'm not sure if I should be writing this or not. Is it traditional for somebody else to say something good about you in the foreword? I don't think I will take the chance. I should also point out it is not a sex expose. It's not about the time I smoked Ganja but didn't inhale! Or even the time I was arrested for insobriety. Here and there it may appear sad, but it does have some very funny moments. I'm sure it does, at least to me!

I have to be honest, I didn't really expect to be writing a book never mind my life story. I started it because a lot of friends over the years have said what an interesting life I've led and it would make a good book. Some even suggested that they would like to write it themselves, so I am actually writing it in spite of them as they haven't turned up yet. I hope they weren't joking, they all have a wicked sense of humour. Well let's hope they are right and you enjoy my adventures so to speak.

Given my early education it is a wonder I could write this at all, but with the wonders of modern science, computers of course, I was encouraged to start writing. That, and with the help of my wife for over 36 years Estelle and daughter Danielle to proof, approve and then even design it.

I didn't believe anybody should ghost write this book either, it is the truth as I remember it, is it over dramatised? I don't think so, am I biased and perhaps a little misled in my personal opinions, yes I'm sure, but that is exactly what it is, my life story, and here and there my personal opinions. It may be that I'm wrong with my perceptions, but they are written as they were perceived at the time without any liable intent, better get that in just in case. It could all be an expression of my feelings, well who knows!

I have known a lot of educated people and journalists in my time, oops, that came out wrong! It's a photographer journalist thing. I'm sure they and you will find this book grammatically incorrect, perhaps even the odd spelling mistake, but it's my words in my book and I have the right to do it how I deem fit, can you visualise me actually getting off my soap box around about know or should that be now!

Let us move on. I have tried to keep it in sequence, but my change of direction and careers overlapped. Often it's quite hard, so I have put it together how I think it fits best.

There will be some people mentioned and I apologise in advance for those that are not, you'll know who you are, the good, the bad or the indifferent!

The most important people in my life are my family, Estelle, Danielle and without any doubt my Mum, without whom this book would have not been possible. I dedicate it to them and her, who bless her, is no longer with us, there is even a poem I wrote for her funeral.

Evelyn,
She was ever so humble, but always proud,
she was kind and caring, but seldom loud.
Devoted to her family, Loving mother to her son,
remembered here for all she has done.
Internationally renowned, a circus star,
but she was always aware of who you are.
Once more remembered, for what has become,
with loving memories, now she has gone.

Wayne Paulo 20/02/02

Throughout my younger life I have thought of myself as quiet, shy and modest, yet if I was to ask anybody today they would say the opposite. Estelle, will probably die laughing at that statement alone!

But in the environment that I was brought up in and progressed to, then compared with, the people I have met and worked with throughout my life, I really was, I was the quietest and most modest person I knew.

Another thing, I can't write about everything or everyone. Why? Well because I'm a photographer not a writer, I need lots of space for the pictures!

By the way, I looked up the word famous in my dictionary, it read "known to or recognised by many people", hey what do you know? Drop the 'Nearly', I am famous and didn't even know it!

Seriously though, the question is not really, "Was I famous?", but what was it that made me what I am today and did I perhaps achieve some fame along the way? Only you can decide. So here we go.

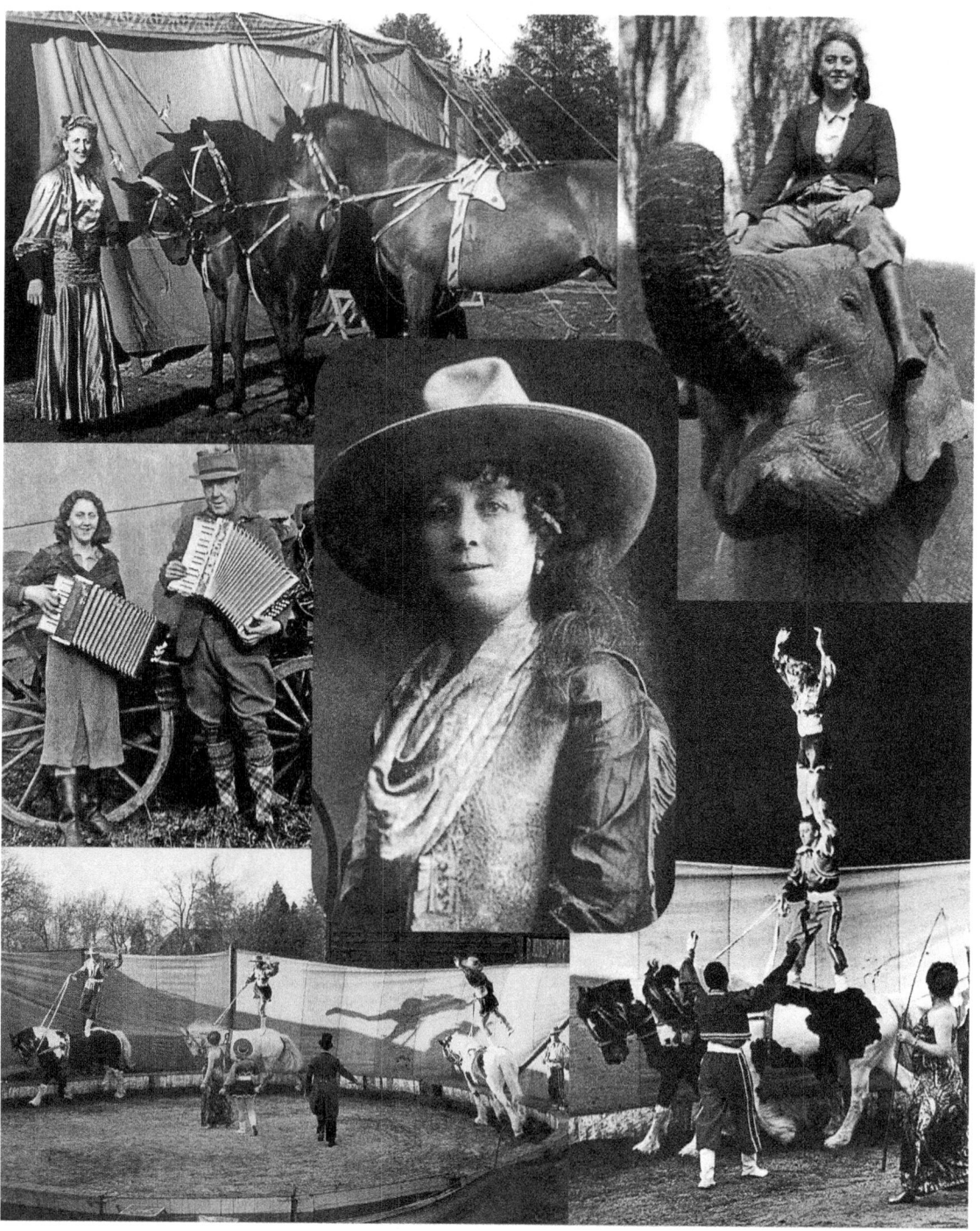

NEARLY FAMOUS

In the beginning

I was born into the famous Paulo's Circus family in March 1949, in a small 12 foot (4m) trailer at their winter quarters in Stanwell Moor near London, England. I think now it might actually be part of a runway at Heathrow Airport.

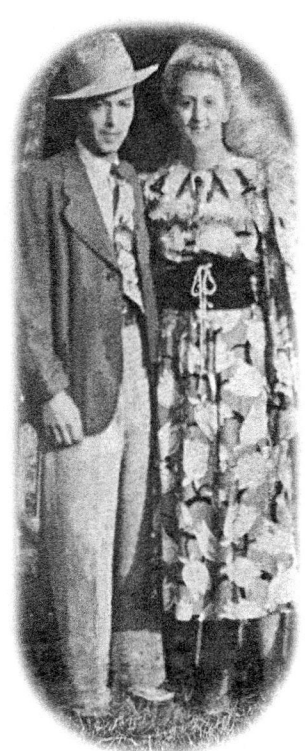

Coming from a long line of equestrian performers, it's not surprising I could ride a horse before I could walk, but hey, all you have to do is sit on a horse, right? Wrong. In my family, riding meant vaultage, jumping on and off horses while they were in motion and standing up on the horses backs as they went around the circus ring. We were known as Bareback Riders, the term was used because the horse had no saddle for you to hang on to and not because we didn't wear a shirt!

I'm pretty sure I wasn't quite up to that standard in those very early years, especially given the horses were about 15 and 16 hands tall, which for those of you who aren't aware is quite high. My recollections from my baby years are none existent, but I have seen the pictures of me and my family in action and heard the stories, according to mum I was nearly born on a horse, literally!

From my vague early memories I had what 'I' would call a normal child's up bringing. I was always falling off horses (a lot), wondering off regularly to explore the exotic animals (usually from the wrong side of the cage). I once even had a radiator fall on my toes breaking them, and I cried for days. I recall I nearly drowned some kittens trying to see if they could swim. I know how sad!

Actually I'm a Pisces so I seem to be drawn to water a lot. At the bottom of the road where my home, a trailer, was situated, two rivers met creating an island and a great whirlpool. I fell in once and was very lucky to be dragged out as opposed to being dragged under! Another recollection I have with water was on tour with my mother in Scandinavia. I actually got into a small rowing boat and untied the rope that was holding the boat at the river side. I think I was quite proud of myself with this new adventure, as I slowly started to drift away from the shoreline, I'm pretty sure I had a change of heart, as it started to dawn on me I was in the boat alone and this was a rather deep fast flowing logging river. Again, I was rescued by a fast acting cousin, Evelyn I think, who managed to reach out to the rope and pull the boat back to shore and safety.

From a very early age I always thought my Father was a Cowboy and my Mother was a Native American Indian!

I know it sounds bizarre for a child born just outside London, but at that age it was a childhood dream to be a Cowboy and ride horses. All I had seen were pictures of him, a Cowboy in the full outfit, the hat, the boots, the saddle, on a rearing horse and my mother used to say this is your dad and she was often in costume for the circus act dressed as a Native American Indian!

My Mother bless her, was a very beautiful young woman and extremely brave back in that era, she ran away to get married, then split up with her husband, and then had me to somebody else! In those days it didn't matter what kind of background you came from it was still frowned upon.

I guess my father came along on his beautiful horse called Gipsy, he swept her off her feet and I was the result of that romantic period, at least that is what I would like to think!

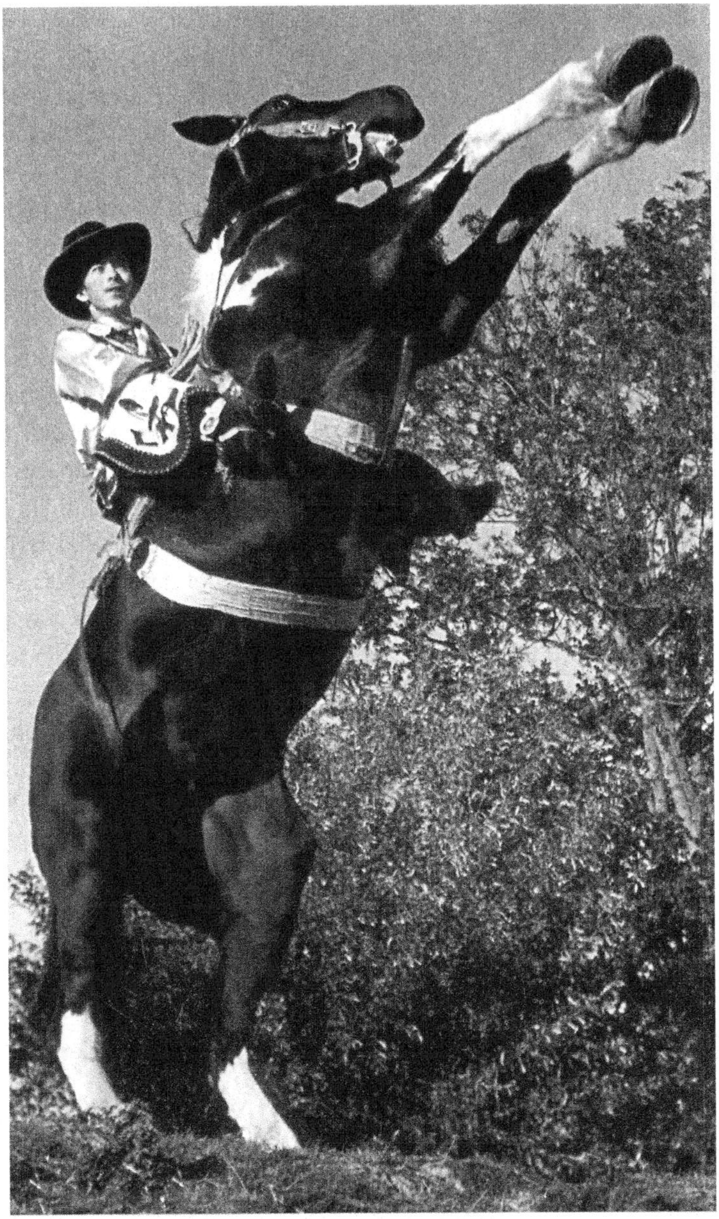

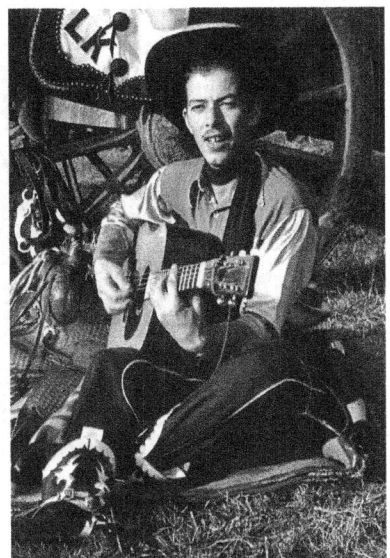

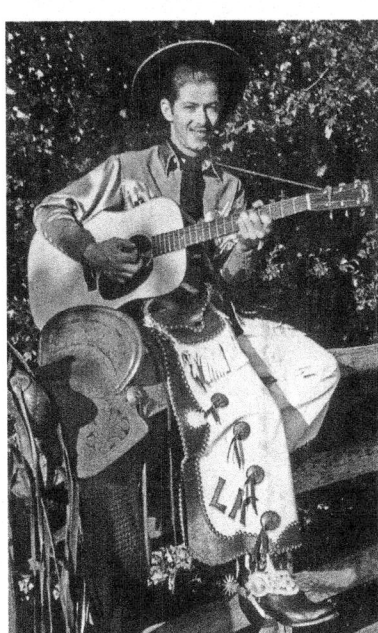

"My father was a cowboy and my mother was an Indian!"

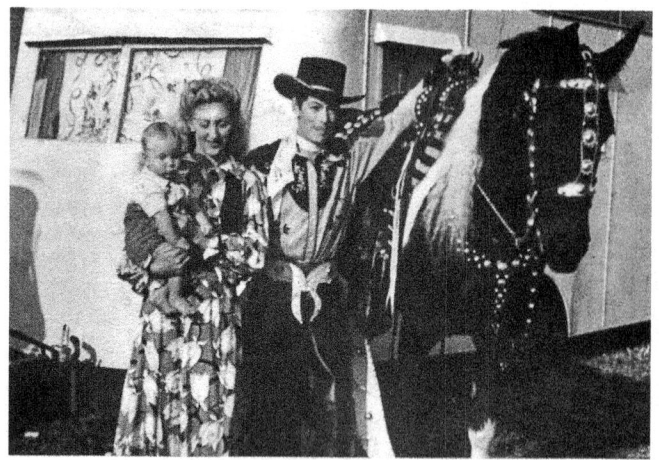

Of course my mother wasn't really a Native American Indian, she was born in the Scottish Borders. However I later learnt that my father was a Canadian Cowboy from the Winnipeg area. I was told his grandfather was in the cavalry and his grandmother was a full blooded Native American Indian, so perhaps it really is in my blood after all.

I have tried to trace my family history on that side, but without much success. I guess I will never know why he didn't stay, it wasn't something my mum ever wanted to discuss and with respect to her, you didn't ask that kind of question back in those days, as I got older it didn't seem to matter.

Anyway, she continued to perform all kinds of different acts in 'Paulo's Circus', which was owned by my grandmother, mum was a very versatile and talented performer. My so called dad went on to perform touring around the world under the name 'Lance King'. I believe he worked in Paris at a place called 'The Crazy Horse Saloon,' which seems appropriate. The point is, he wasn't there for me as a child, unfortunately I still don't know why he didn't hang around!

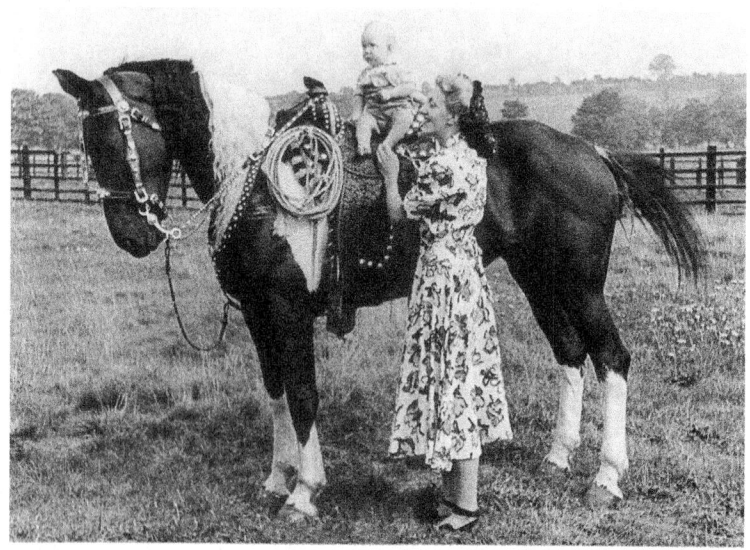

NEARLY FAMOUS

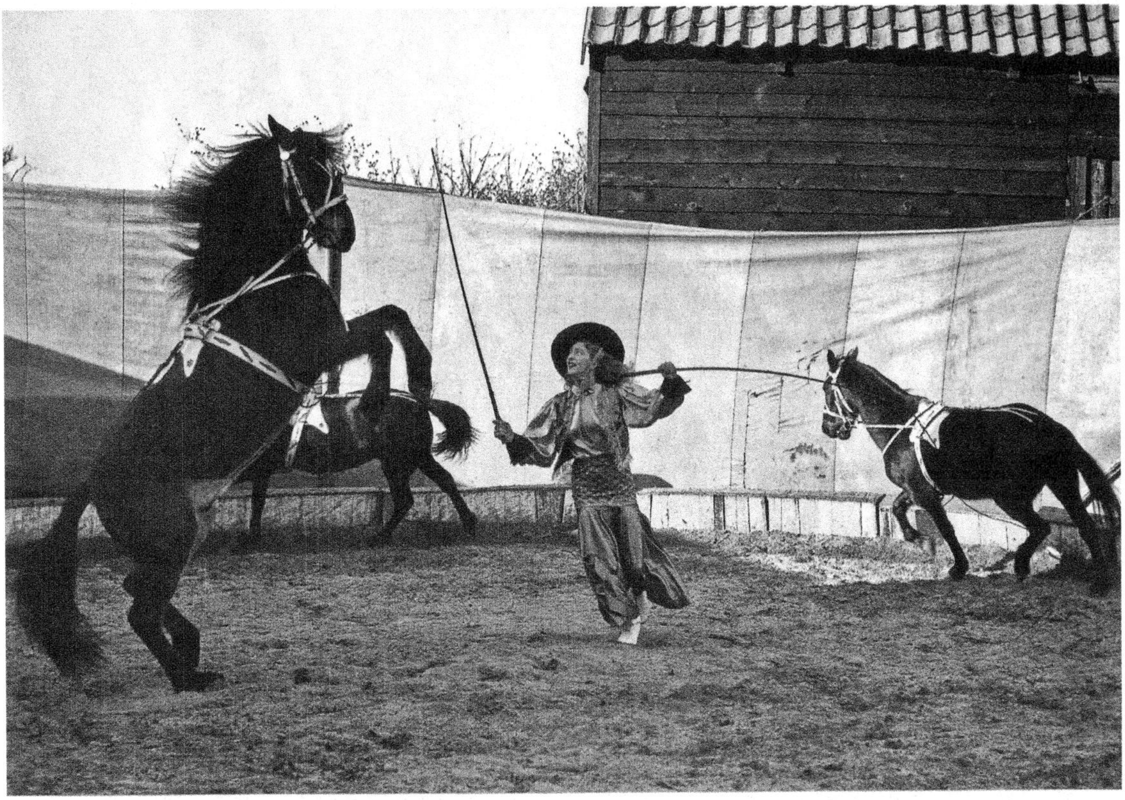

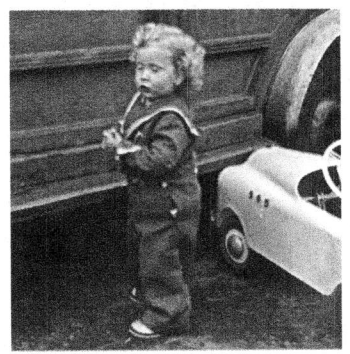
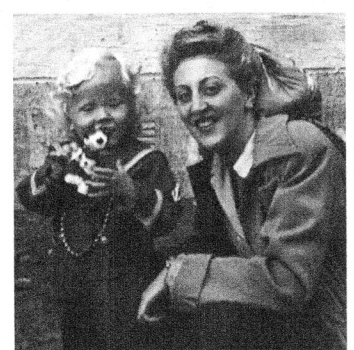
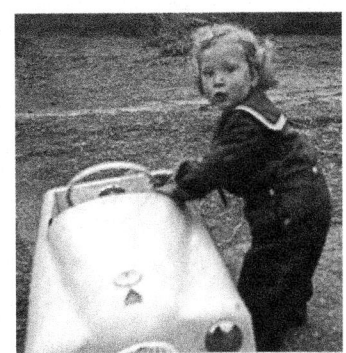

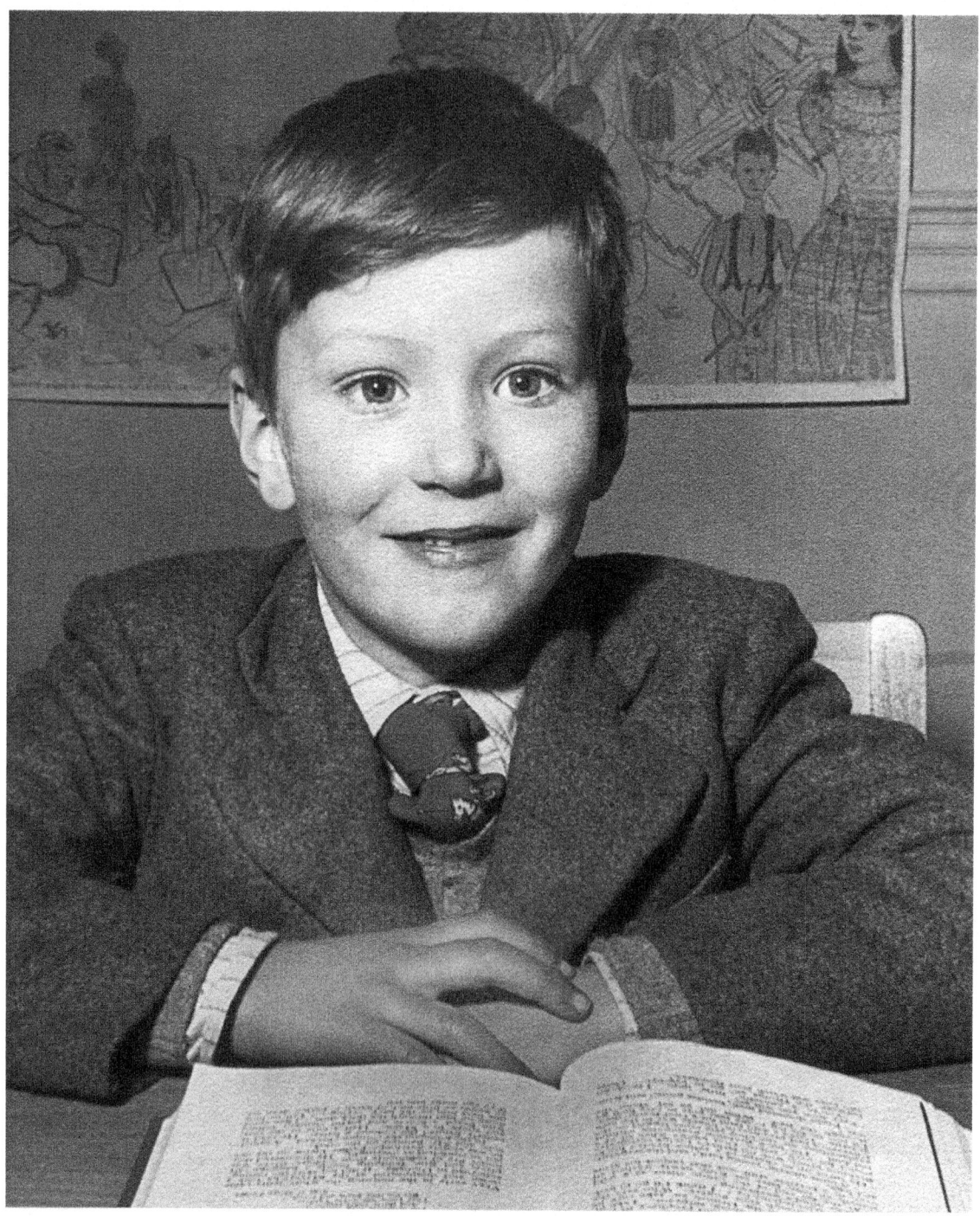

Education - if you can call it that!

School was always a disaster for me, my earliest recollection was perhaps my first day at school. I remember we went to an enormous place, it was like a Gothic mansion, with very high ceilings and very intimidating, just walking into the place gave me the willies (not sure if I can say that). I remember going up some stairs to a classroom, whether I did something wrong or perhaps I was just in the wrong classroom I don't remember, I probably stood up and told them my father was a Cowboy and my mother was an Indian and got in trouble straight away. Anyway, I was sent to see the headmaster in his room downstairs, unfortunately I didn't know where he was and panicked. I went down the stairs and straight out the front door, into the woods in the surrounding grounds and that's where I stayed!

"Huckleberry Finn had nothing on me!"

I went there every school day for the next two weeks. Adventure training and Huckleberry Finn had nothing on me, and of course I played Cowboys and Indians (Native American). It was inevitable that I would eventually be seen or missed by somebody at school, they may have split on me, or perhaps my mum just thought I was always coming home in too much of a mess. I don't really recall, but one day from my lookout post in the woods, through the trees, I saw my mum heading into the school grounds and I knew the gig was up!

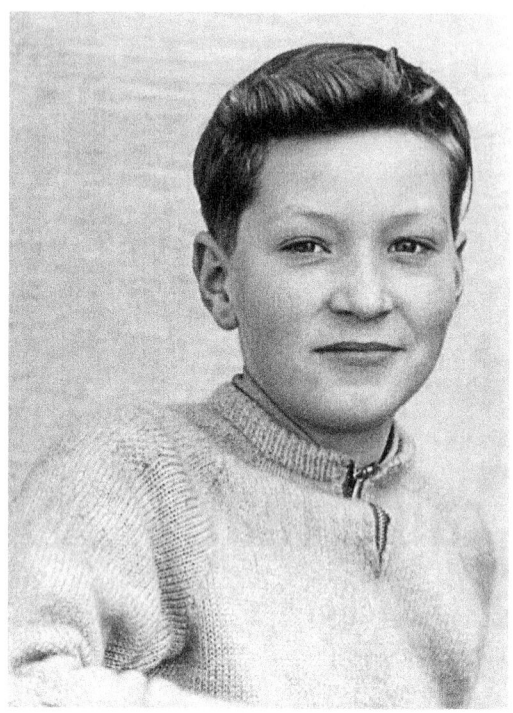

It was probably around about this time when I gave up smoking. Yes smoking. I was about six years old I think. I used to play with an older friend, who's mother was a housekeeper for a well to do member of the British Military, I only knew him as the 'Major'. He had a liking for circuses and we used his grounds for winter quarters. As kids we would often be at his place playing in the gardens and as we got more adventurous we ended up climbing through the windows into his house. We discovered the study and also discovered cigarettes in there, naturally curious we left with a handful on a couple of occasions! It only took a couple of trips before we were caught, footprints on the window ledge were a give away, our punishment was to be made to smoke a rather large cigar until we felt ill. It worked for me but my friend who shall remain nameless went on to smoke fifty a day and still likes a good cigar!

It was no wonder then that my mother sent me off to stay at Gracie Fields Home for orphaned children when she had to travel with the circus. They seemed like dark days to me, a strict Matron and early morning walks to Sunday school every week, regimental style living and always in bed by 6pm. I remember crying alone regularly, bed wetting and whooping cough, mostly I just hated going to school. I felt deserted and totally alone.

I was homesick so much so, that I once stole pages of maps out of a geography book from school and planned an escape. I was convinced I could walk home to my mum and the circus, well it was only about 250 miles I could do it in a week. It's perhaps not so funny that sometimes small things can seem natural to a grown up, yet can be so intimidating and such a horror to a small boy, especially if he is in a new and different environment.

"I once stole pages of maps and planned my escape!"

Like a lot of small boys of the time, I started collecting military Dinky toys, I had a complete and great collection, enough for a whole battle scene. I could reenact the 'Normandy Beach Invasions' from World War II, I had that many tanks and troop carriers in mint condition and was proud of it. Playing with them was everything to me at the time, that's what kept me sane. Hey I was only young and very impressionable. One day our Matron decided to do a collection for needy children and asked us all to donate some toys, so I routed through my box, I just assumed my older and broken ones would do, wrong. Matron declined to accept them and decided to give away half my prized military collection instead. Yes, wow! Are kids impressionable, I'll say, to this day I hoard things!

The only bright and bizarre lightness I remember from those times, was one sunny Sunday afternoon playing croquet on the lawn with bird sounds and buttercups, on a beautiful summer's day in the rolling downs of Peacehaven in the South of England. It was almost surreal but I know it happened, I was there!

Before I leave the schoolboy chapters, I want to reflect on the most important things I'd learnt. There must have been something I'm sure! I know I did learn a couple of things, map reading and swimming. The latter coming when I went to a new school on my travels and was told it was learn to swim day. I went along that early winter morning to the outside pool, I do miss those school issue woolly swimming trunks. Being a none swimmer and my earlier experiences with water, I was reluctant to go in, the teacher forced me to jump in and see what I could do, well the water was that bloody cold I jumped in swam across and got out the other end as quick as I could, it earned me a 25 yard swimming certificate. Well there you have it then, some kids learn nothing, and others learn very quickly!

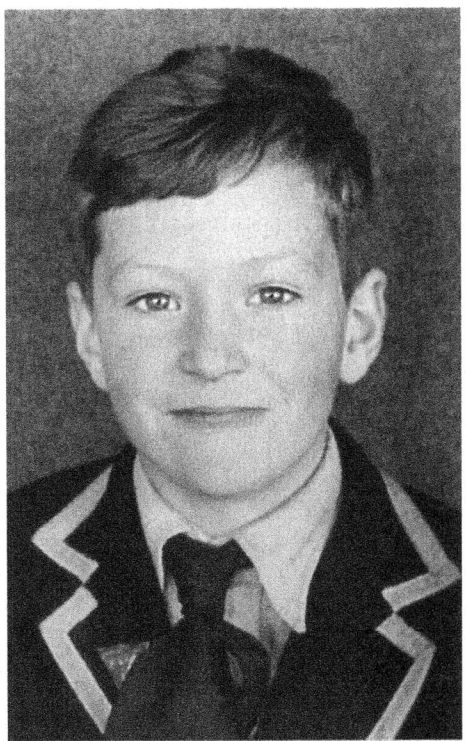

There was one other thing I vaguely remember, I had started learning to play the trumpet, that was enough to get me into the school assembly one morning playing with the band, now don't laugh, I managed to busk through one Hymn and then started to pass out! In all the excitement of my first public musical performance I had forgotten to breath between the notes. I blamed it on the hot weather at the time, strangely I still pass out today when I try to play the trumpet, it must be my age now!

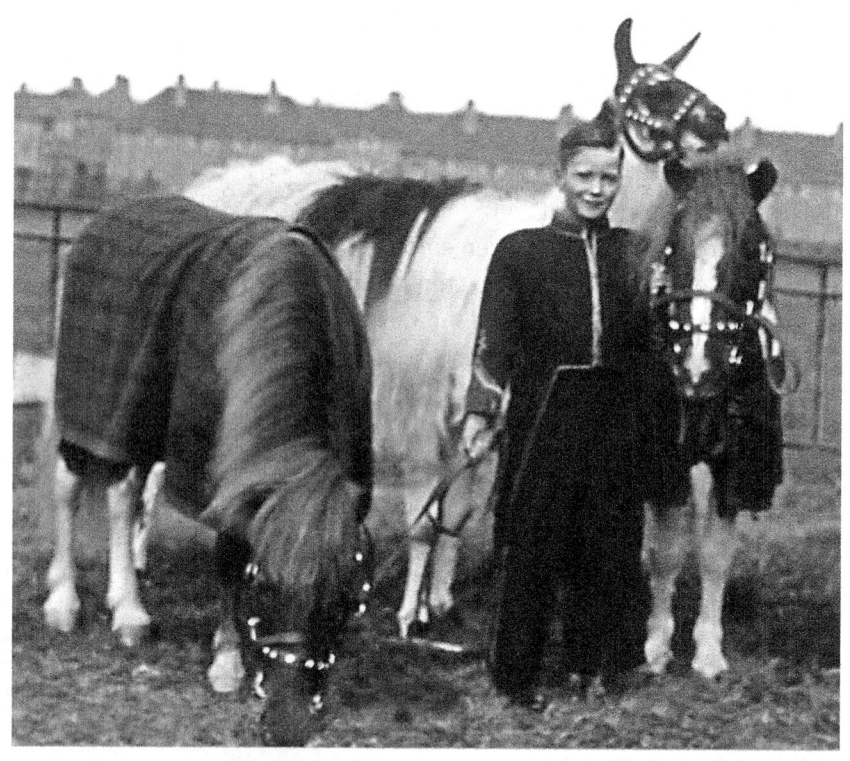

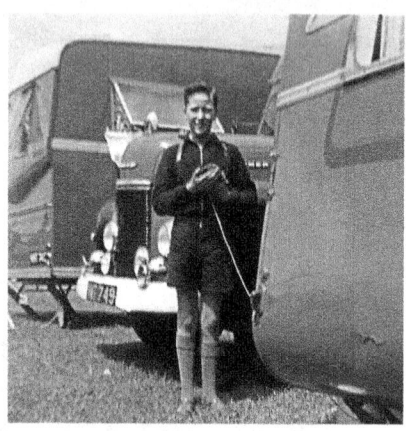

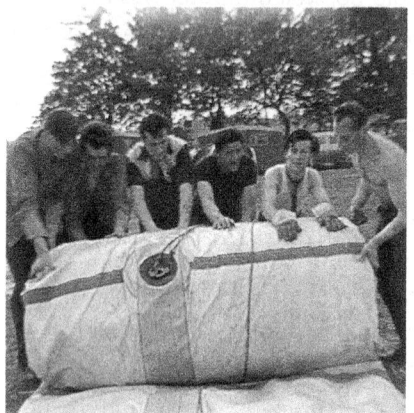

NEARLY FAMOUS

Return to the circus

Eventually, after what seemed a life time, though I'm sure it was only a couple of years, my mum finally let me join them on tour, they were with the famous Bertram Mills Circus. The family troupe toured with them from 1956 until 1960 appearing as 'The Mohawks', it was without doubt Europe's finest circus of the time.

It was utopia for a small boy, a huge travelling circus, live exotic animals, helping out with build ups and pull downs (that's the term used for the putting up and pulling down of the big top and tents) lots of new towns and adventures every week, but of course there was always a down side, new schools to go to for only a week at a time. Fortunately for me there was never enough time to actually start any lessons. Mostly I was the entertainment for the rest of the kids, a novelty visitor, a circus boy!

"Mostly I was the entertainment, for the rest of the kids!"

I used to love travelling with the show, and I even made my first official appearance at Bertram Mills, leading the animal menagerie of llamas and ponies in the parade at the start of the show.

It was here my Mum bought me my first camera, a Coronet, it was one step up from a Box Brownie but for me it was my first foray into photography. Little did I know then it would be a career for me later in life, unfortunately only a few pictures remain from that period but even then you could see potential.

I also spent one summer season with my aunt Emily, she owned and ran Gilbert's Circus which was resident at Chessington Zoo. I

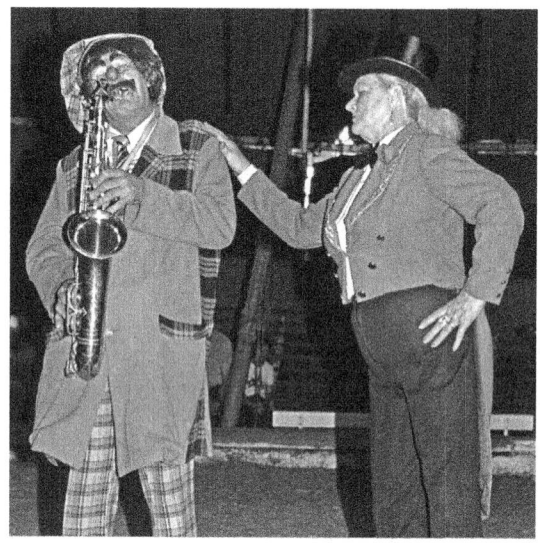

guess that was my wildlife period, playing with animals, particularly in the beaver pen. There was an island surrounded by a moat and I could just jump on to it, when the zoo was closed, it was great fun. Fortunately I never left any cage doors open, at least I don't think anything escaped during that period. Eventually I got caught so that was stopped and I went back to doing what I did best, falling off the ponies. I always got the smallest one when my cousins and I went riding, with their short legs, the ponies that is, they have to trot like greased lightning to keep up with the big horses when they went galloping off. I think it was fun, well everyone else used to laugh. In fact my cousins still laugh about it when I see them now!

As the years progressed and I grew up I always felt I led a normal life, yet I was constantly reminded I was a circus boy. Children and teenagers are very unforgiving and I was always treated slightly different, sometimes bullied, sometimes admired, but often left in silence to go my own way. In the end I learnt very little at the vast array of schools I went to, far too many for too short a time, only the school of life taught me how cruel people could be.

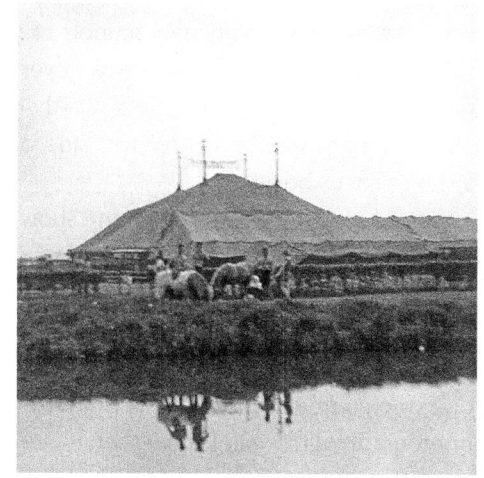

Lonely Circus boy

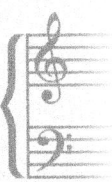

I was a lonely circus boy and I grew up all alone.
I went to school from town to town but always on my own.
A jolly life but a hard life with a trailer for a home.
No one knows my suffering being all alone.

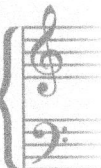

Through the years I grew to know your never on your own,
with a mother who looks after you and always brings you home.
There was a time when far away strange and all alone,
With my mother and faith in her I knew I'd soon be home.

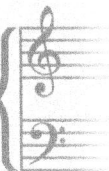

And now the years have past I've a wife and child of my own,
I sit here and remember the times I was alone.
My mother too is long gone now and no longer at my home.
But I'll always have my faith in her and never be alone.

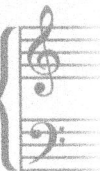

Circus boy, circus boy, just a lonely circus boy.

Lyrics by Wayne Paulo

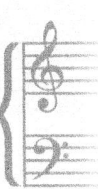

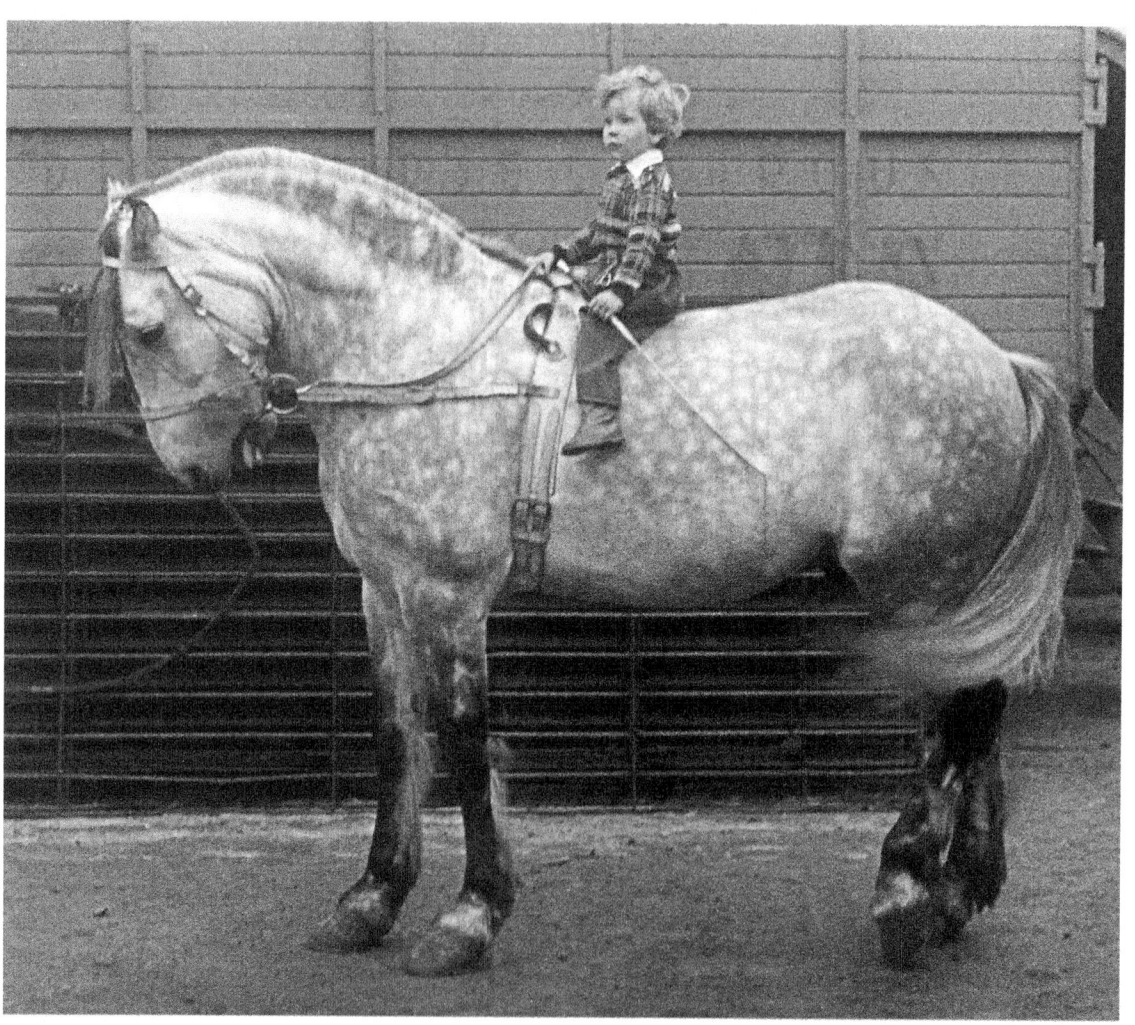

NEARLY FAMOUS

Performer in training

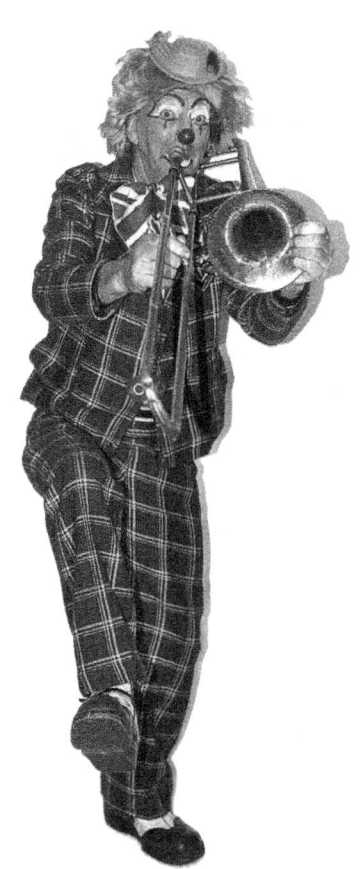

As a child I looked good on a horse, but being a teenager for me was about learning to be a circus performer, a bareback rider, a juggler and an acrobat. The acrobat was the first to go, I just couldn't get the hang of falling on my head after a round off and backward somersault. For some reason I couldn't get past that pain barrier, if it hurt, it hurt!

Most of all I just wanted to be a musical clown, well that was a change from a Cowboy or an Indian. My uncle Frank had given me an old trumpet, yes the one I mentioned earlier, I moved on from the Hymns and I would practice 'Cherry Blossom Pink' in the centre of the circus ring. I must have driven people mad at the time, yes it took quite a while, but it was a beautiful sound in that haunting echoing atmosphere when I eventually got it right!

I'm pretty sure those daunting tones have been used as background soundtracks in a couple of circus documentaries, or perhaps it was just another young boy's dream!

At thirteen I got out of school altogether when we toured Italy with Circo Casserteli, but my memories from that beautiful country are just of feeding and looking after animals and carrying gallons and gallons of water for the horses, every day, seven days a week. Water wasn't on tap, every new location was a challenge to find the

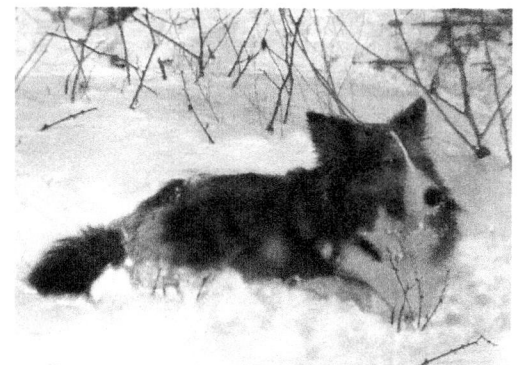

nearest source. I seemed to have spent most of the time building up tent stables at the crack of dawn and taking them down in the middle of the night and then we would drive to the next town, come wind, rain and snow, yes snow, heavy snow, even in Italy!

For those years my mother and I lived in the front end of a horse box about 9 ft by 6 ft (3m x 2m) and for several years with nothing more than each other and a homemade crystal radio set for company. My life in real terms was always cleaning horses and mucking out the stables, that was the real circus life for me!

I did eventually get a beautiful pet of my own, a Shetland Sheepdog and most of my fun time was taken up with her 'Lassie'. Although a pet and not a circus animal I took pleasure in teaching her the basics of sit, stay, rollover and fetch. She was my best friend and the love of my life for a couple of years, until sadly she got run over following me to work and died.

I guess around about this time could be called my doggy period. Not only did I have my own, but for one summer season at the Pavilion Theatre Circus in Rhyl I was the dog assistant for my cousin David Rosaire and his Perky Peeks. His wife had become pregnant

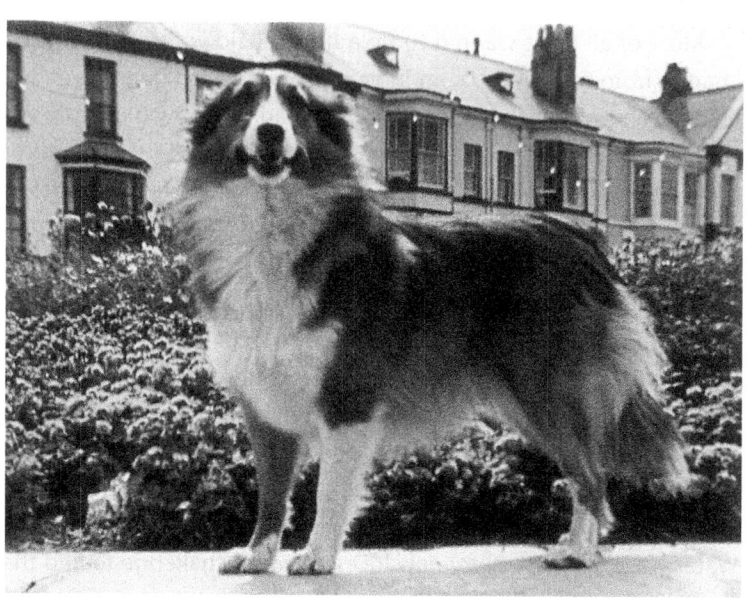

NEARLY FAMOUS

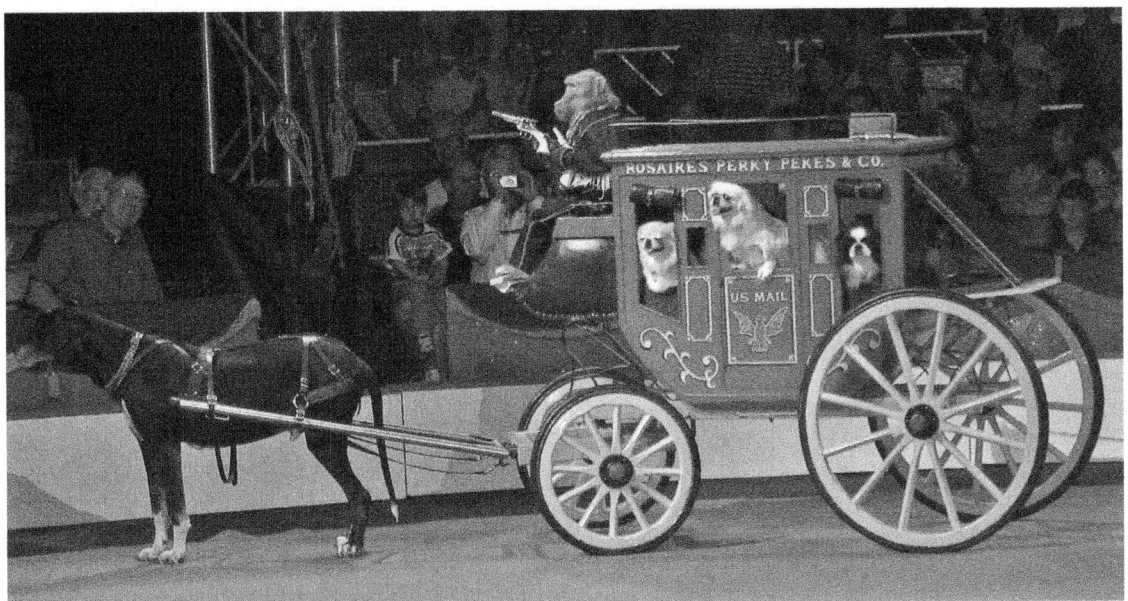

and couldn't assist him so he needed help. I would help in the ring as the Pekinese dogs went through their routines, even helping Dave chase one of the funny mischievous ones as part of the act. It was another chance under the spotlights and a little bit of fame for one glorious summer. When Dave's son was born he called him Wayne. I guess I did a good job then!

Dave now lives with his family in Sarasota in the USA and still performs today across the States and in the Sarasota State Circus. His son Wayne has also gone into the entertainment business but his four legged stars are of the pig variety!

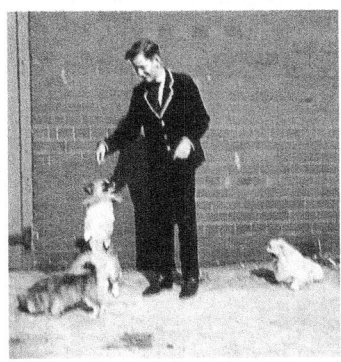
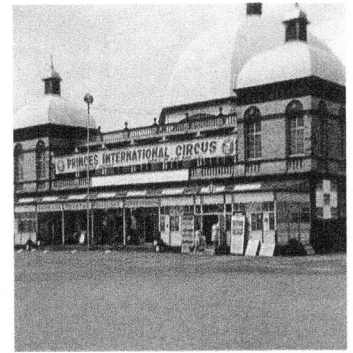
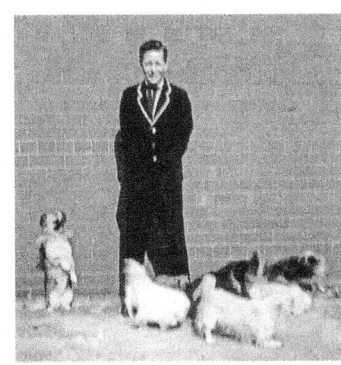

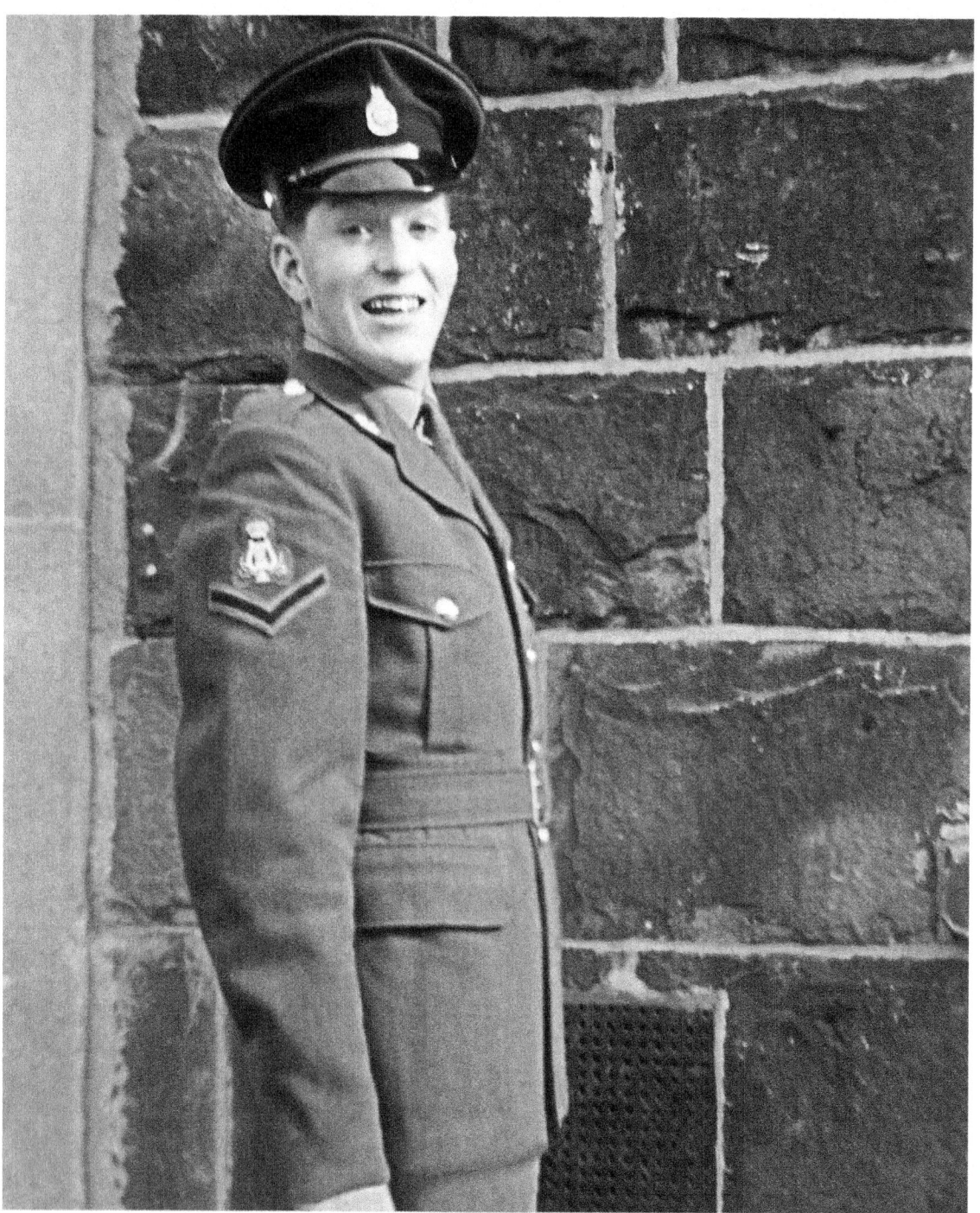

NEARLY FAMOUS

Soldier Boy

It's little wonder I was developing an urge to leave the circus, in fact I think I have might have an exclusive being the only boy that wanted to run away from the circus rather than to it!

I was 16 when my family were appearing at the Tower Circus in Blackpool. I was still looking after the horses and now working as one of the ring boys in the show to earn extra money, there was very little money in working for your own family, especially if you were only the groom and not one of the performers.

When the British Army came to town to do a display, a friend of mine said he was going to join up, he asked did I want to come along, it seemed the perfect opportunity. Tempted, I first went for an interview to join the band of the Royal Horse Guards, obviously with my horse skills I thought it would be easy. As a straight cavalry soldier it might have been, but because I wanted to be in the band, it wasn't to be. Unfortunately for me they wanted skilled musicians and I couldn't busk the 1812 Overture or read music quick enough. Well the 'Tune a Day' book one didn't actually give me the musical qualifications I needed, even though I blew a mean 'Cherry Blossom Pink'!

Not to be deterred, I went along to the junior soldiers regimental band at Fulwood Barracks in Preston and much to my surprise I was

"The only boy that wanted to run away from a circus!"

accepted into the Lancashire Regiment as a junior bandsman for the Prince of Wales Volunteers.

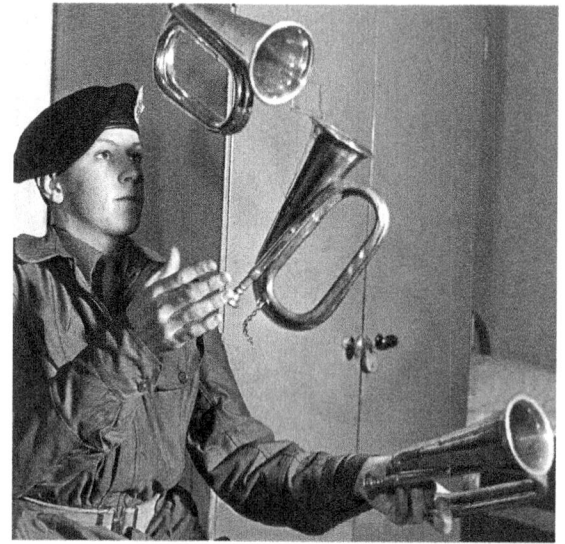

It was a great development time in my life. With my background I was also a minor celebrity, the local paper in Preston photographed me juggling bugles, and then I even made it into the Sunday Nationals, (there's that fame creeping in) I don't know how you missed me!

At last I had some regular schooling in education and music. I improved to 2nd cornet in the band eventually playing in the Liverpool Military Tattoo.

In just a year I picked up enough education and trumpet playing that has served me reasonably well through life since. I also attained the rank of Lance Corporal with potential, I was told, for much better things.

I represented my company at the Battle of Waterloo remembrance ceremony in Belgium and was in the paper again. Though stopping the bus to throw up after sampling a few pints of the local beverage on the way was a little embarrassing. I'm sure it was just travel sickness!

The Army was also good for my sporting career, I took up cross country running, though it might have been the hot baths and excused duties in the mornings that helped convince me to do it, but it was certainly not my favourite sport. Despite that I represented the Company in the Army cross country championships. I came 2nd in our company and 10th overall, of course in true Brit style it's not the winning, it's the competing that matters!

I also captained the Basketball team, a sport I really did love, I would play anytime and anywhere. It paid off and I earned MVP honours on the way, my commanding officer was convinced I would have made the senior Army team.

But unfortunately, once again I found myself looking for maps. It was perhaps the strict military regime again, the not being able to do what you want when you wanted to, you just couldn't get on a bus

NEARLY FAMOUS

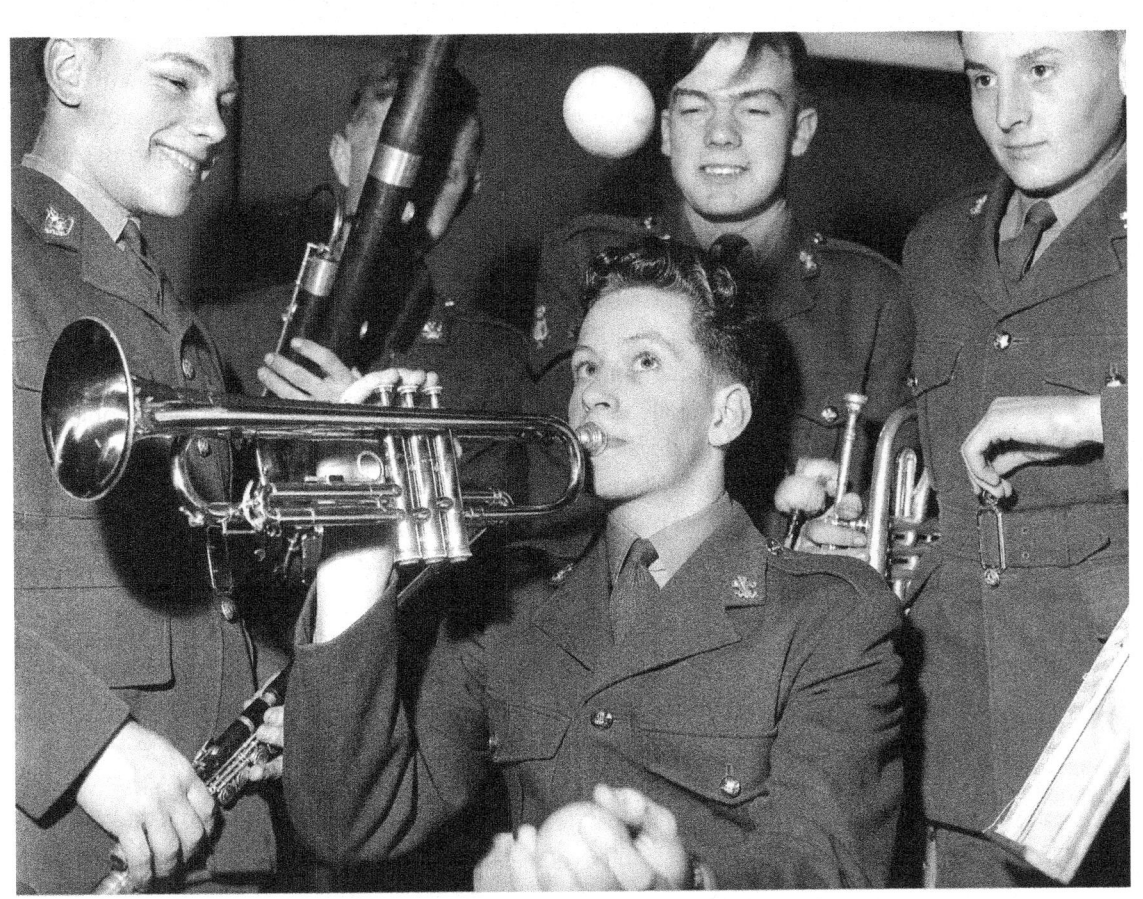

and leave. When problems at home developed it made me a little homesick, which in turn led me to going AWOL (that is the military term for going absent without leave).

There was trouble at the circus, my cousin had run off to get married (I spot a theme here) and they were one short in the act. It was an excuse to go home, I asked for leave and was refused, so I packed my bag and went over the wall!

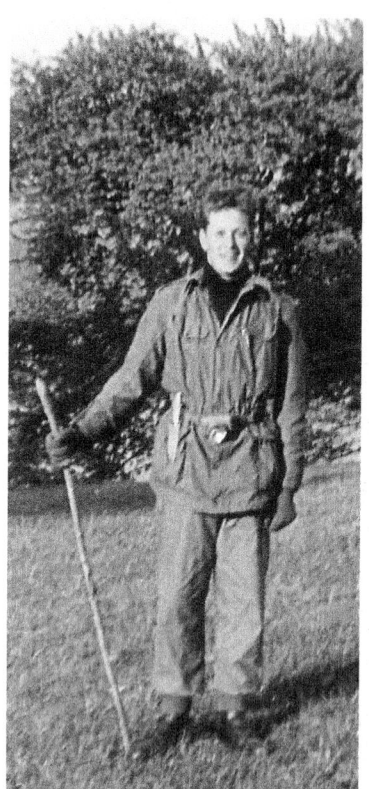

I hadn't done my military training for nothing, I was a new man, nobody saw me leave as I crawled through the grass at night across the fields and away. I went about five miles on foot and decided it was too conspicuous by night, so I sneaked into a farmers barn and slept in the straw for a few hours. At the crack of dawn I started off again, then as I tried to hitch a lift down the motorway a police car drove past. Duh!

Just my luck, I may have looked a little suspicious as I ran up the embankment, jumped a fence and ducked into a housing estate. I was really fit now, I could have been a Marine, except I could only swim 25 yards remember? I didn't want to break in anywhere or get arrested for trespass so I just sat on a doorstep. That's where they caught me and my Army kit bag, it was a real give away. One phone call was all it took and they returned me to the barrack guardhouse for the next few hours.

Fortunately, the irrational behaviour from an otherwise exemplary soldier was enough for my Commanding Officer, he realised I really did need a compassionate leave pass and I was on a train heading south, home to the circus later that day.

The whole episode was also enough for me to realise I wanted out and a small fee was all it took, just in case you were wondering you could buy yourself out of the Army as a junior soldier, my CO asked me to rethink it and not to leave but I had made up my mind. I received my discharge papers with the comments "I am sorry to lose a junior soldier of his potential" I was quite proud of that and perhaps a little emotional. I'm sure I would have had a successful career in the Army but I don't know of any famous 2nd Cornet players do you? And where does the English basketball team stand in the World ranking today? Mmm... Exactly!

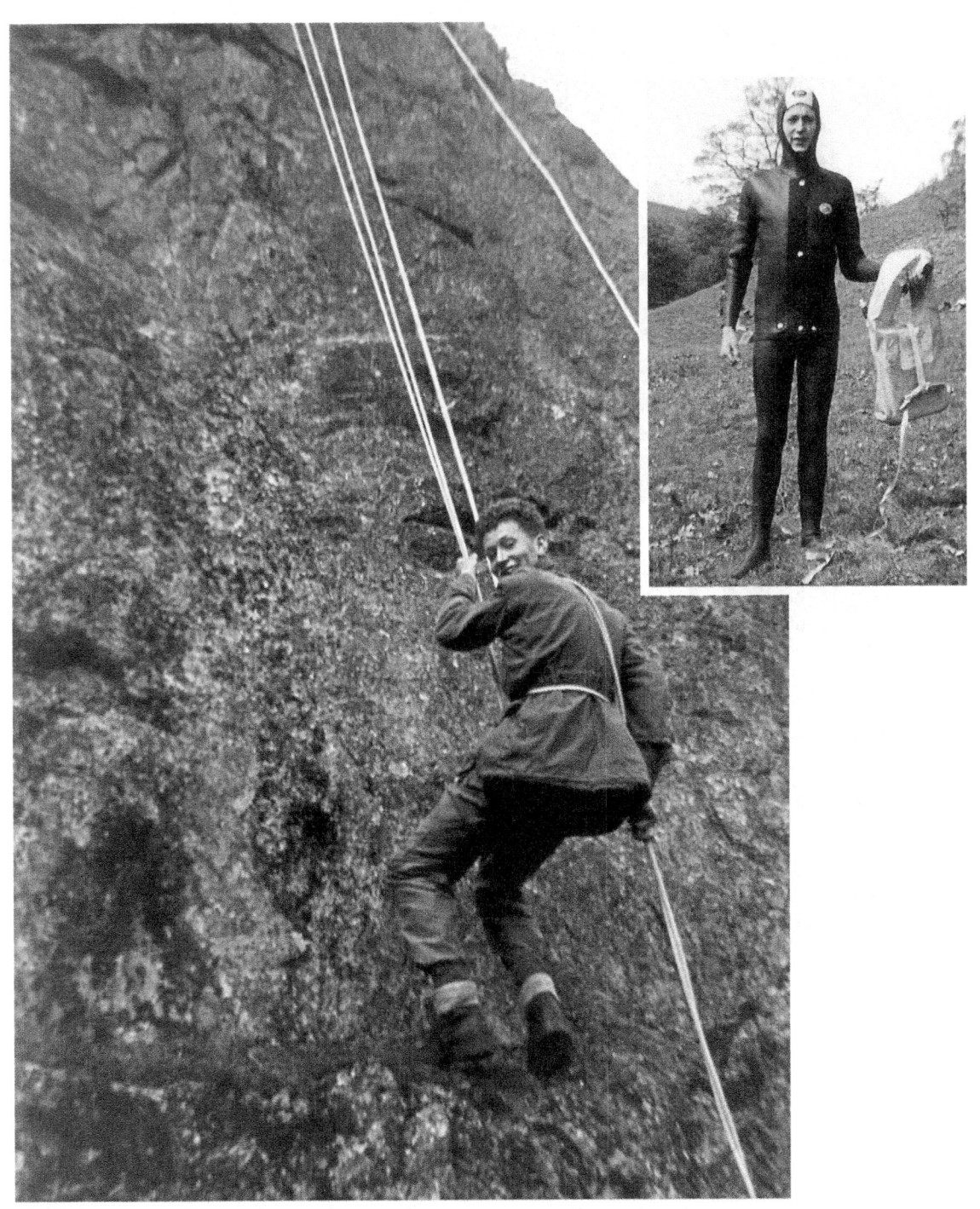

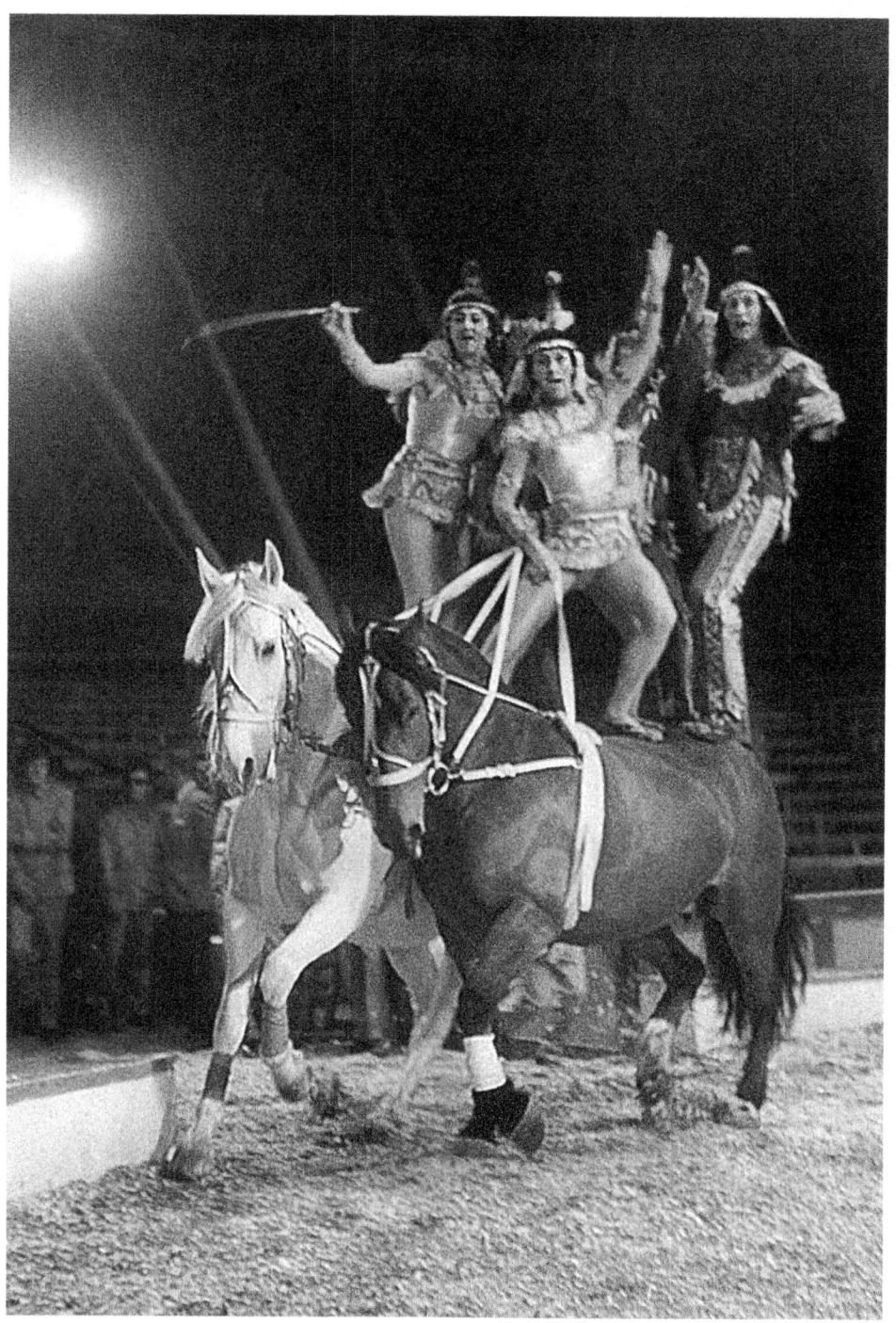

NEARLY FAMOUS

Winds of change, a performer at last

I went back to the family's winter quarters in Ascot to start training as a bareback rider in 'The Mohawks' troupe, I also had to find a temporary job working to earn some money, that's what circus folk did between touring shows. I worked on the famous Royal Ascot race course digging drainage ditches, repaired ice cream trolleys, drove a dumper truck and picked mushrooms, delivered hay, straw and oats to the local stables and carried coal bags to most of the houses in Ascot, eventually landing a regular job as a fork lift driver at a local factory for quite a while. It wasn't until I ended up collecting horse manure from the police stables in London that I realised I had gone full circle, back to mucking out, a stable cleaning specialist!

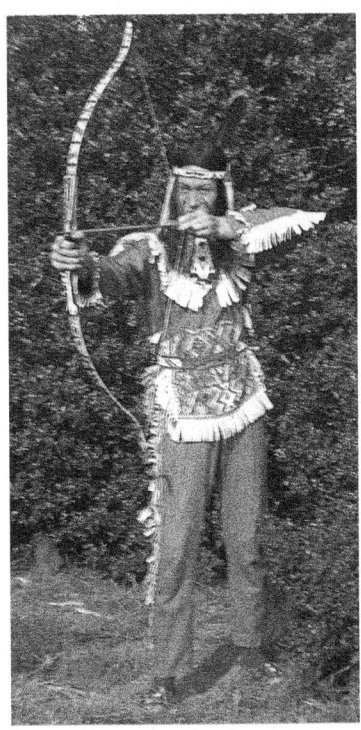

I made my official riding debut at the famous Blackpool Tower Circus 1966 in the days when it was the best in Europe, with animals galore. I was finally a bareback rider in The Mohawks troupe, one of the top horse riding acts in the country. Dressed as Native American Indians, we would go through our trick riding routines, jump up's and vaultage, six family members balancing on the back of two horses twice a day. Could this be my future? My breakthrough in life. Well actually no!

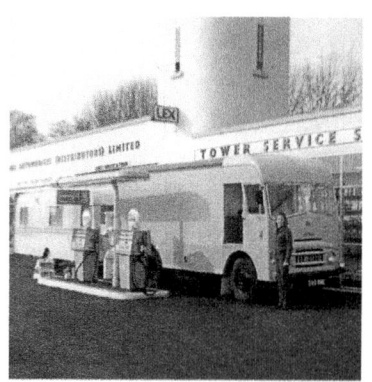

By day I was still a groom and mucking out specialist, by night I was an anonymous bareback rider masquerading as an Native American Indian, though I always felt it was part of my heritage.

It lasted all of three years. In 1967 we travelled to Sweden and Norway and toured with Circus Scott a Scandinavian circus.

Touring through Scandinavia was a great time and place for a teenager, I made many friends and partied a lot. When we travelled it was always overnight, I drove a truck all through 'The land of the midnight sun' a beautiful country.

Mum and I were still sharing the front end of a truck 6 x 9 ft (2 x 3m) with bunk beds and little else, but I guess as a teenager I was mostly out and didn't get a lot of sleep. Well you don't need it when you are young do you? Hey, I knew friends who had houses with lounges and whole bedrooms to themselves, that was a real novelty to me!

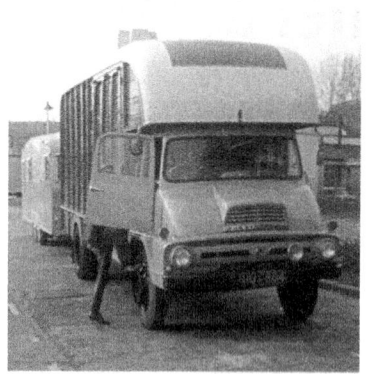

After that season we went back to Ascot for the winter and I know I spent it removing nails from second hand wood acquired from the old Ascot Race course. I have a lot of painful memories of that place, on three separate occasions I stood on nails that went right through my shoes into my foot. I don't know which was more painful, the nail or the tetanus injections in hospital!

In 1968 we purchased an estate car and a small 14 foot caravan (trailer), a home at last. We went on tour with Cirkus Sarrasani, travelling Germany, Denmark and Holland, but friction was building, typical family squabbles I guess. My cousin and her husband had returned to the act for the Scandinavian tour, we fought a little and of course it created an atmosphere. Well, he had married the bosses daughter and acted like he was the boss, as a teenager that didn't sit too well with me, so we were always falling out, as families do.

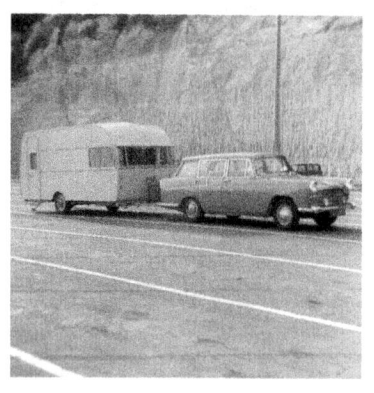

I know I wasn't that bad as a performer, in the act I carried out my routines with poise, style and efficiency. I wasn't the star turn but then I didn't want to be, just glad to be in the act. I made no mistakes at least not when the show was on. I did commit a cardinal sin in rehearsals once, whilst running up to the horse as it went around the circus ring carrying my family, it was approaching the open part of the circular ring fence, the ring doors. I ran gracefully across the ring

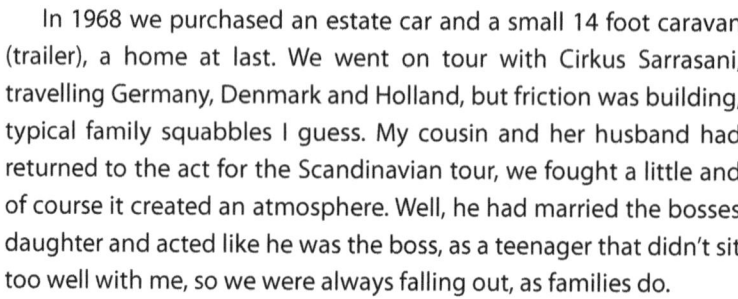

like a Cheetah, rising into the air like a Springbok Antelope jumping, turning into a ballet like jeté, then the beautiful dapple grey mare saw me coming. I swear, when she looked up through her flowing mane there was a twinkle in her eye, then in a flash, she was gone out the door. My life flashed before me as I came down like a ton of bricks in a heap on top of my mum, uncle, auntie and cousin. I had never been so close to my family, especially when I suggested it might make a good finish to the act. Call me Mr Popularity!

Then one day at the end of a show performance, a real petty mistake in positioning for a bow led to an argument with my uncle, I was branded as a trouble maker and asked to leave. Nothing I could say at the time would appease the situation despite my mother defending me. As I was the rebellious youth they decided I should leave, my mum bless her stood by me as always, she decided they were wrong, so on principal we both left at the same time!

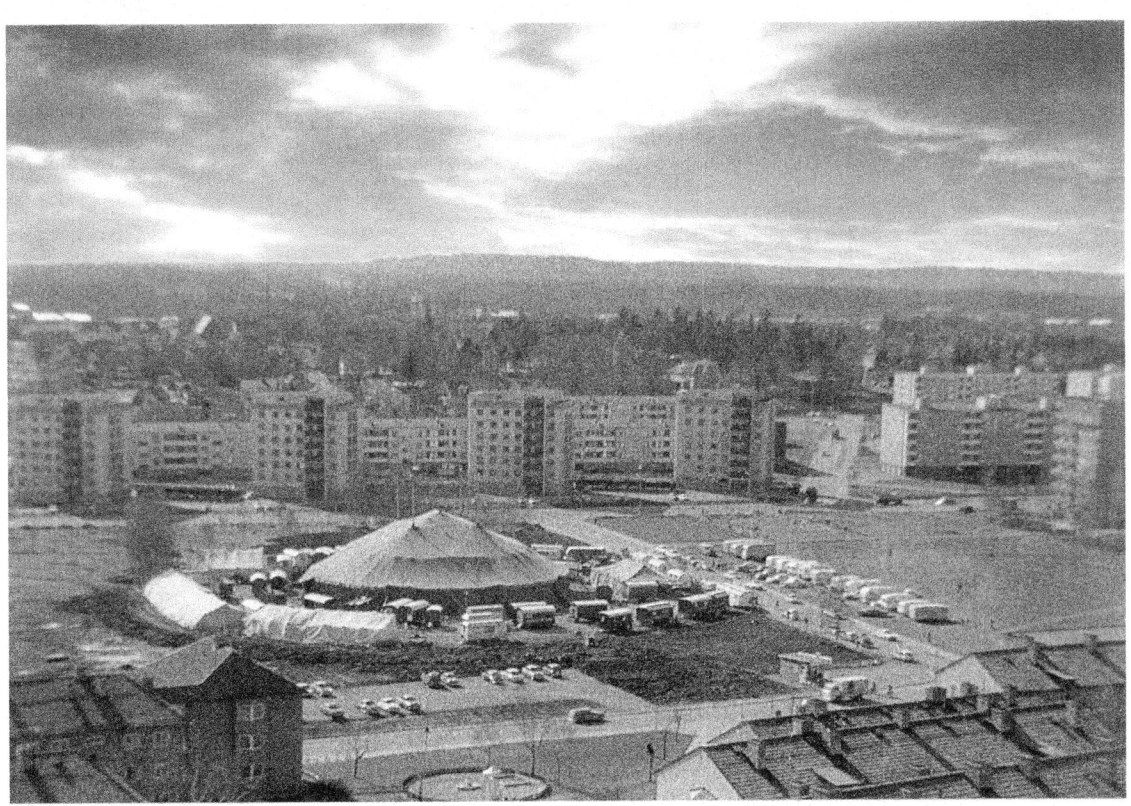

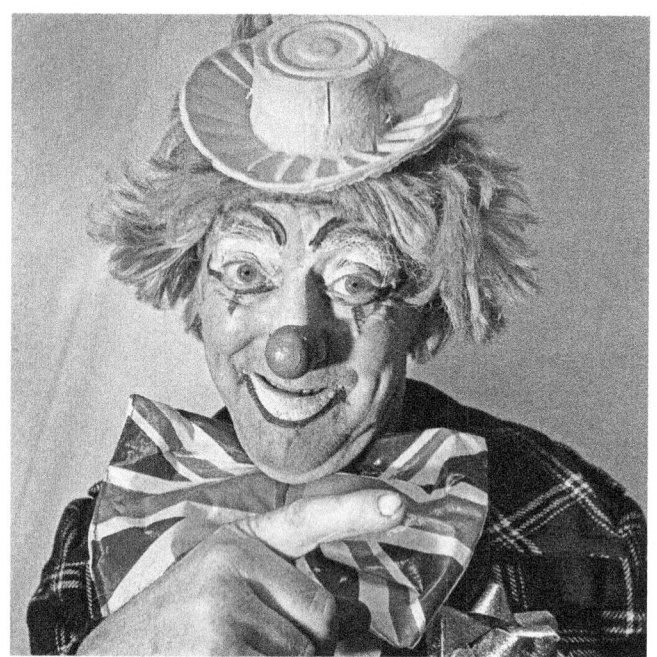

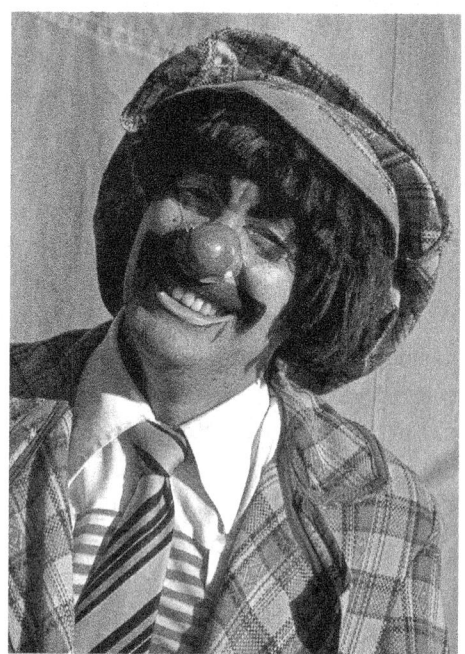

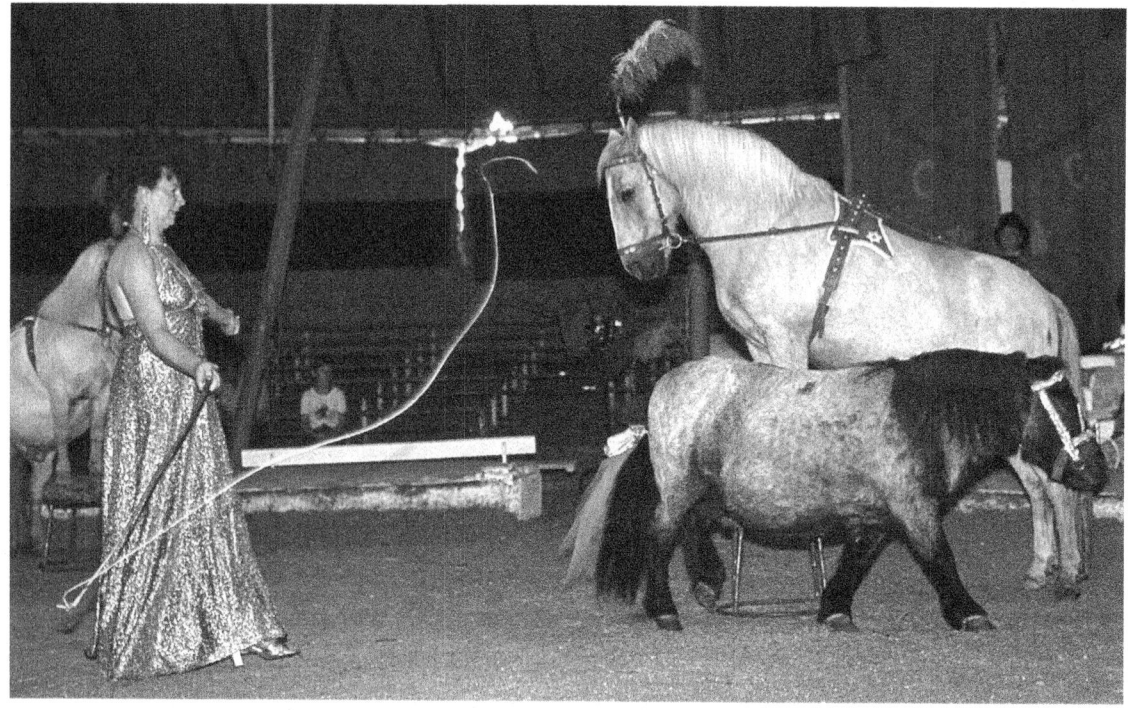

NEARLY FAMOUS

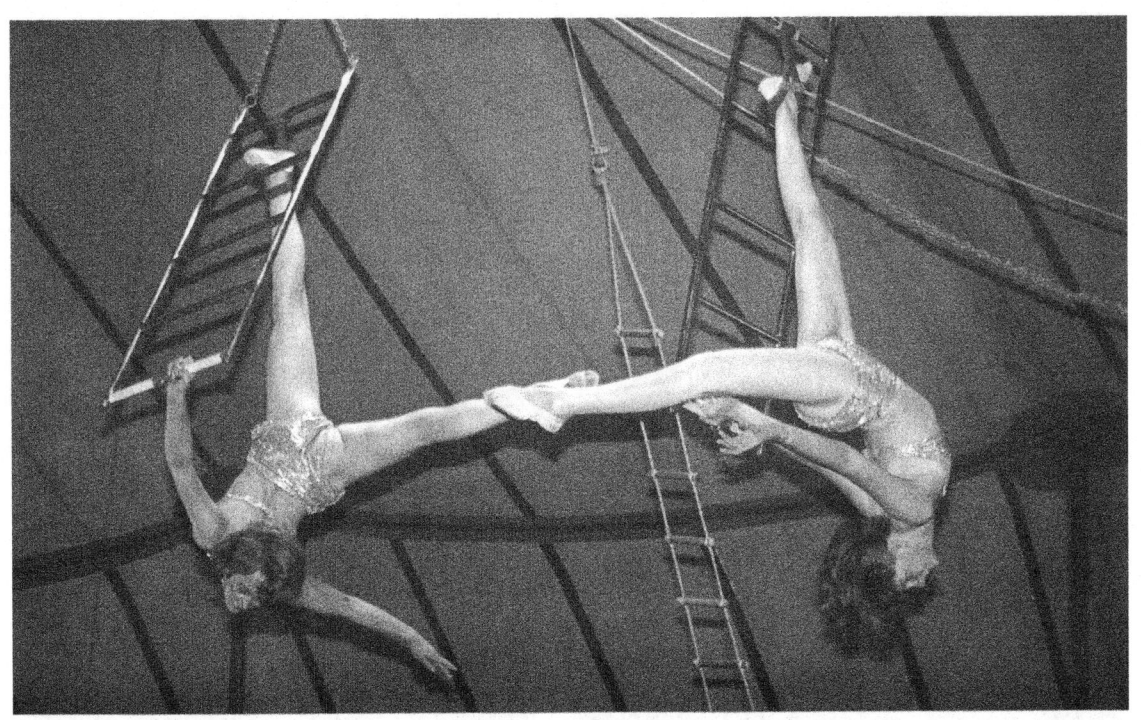

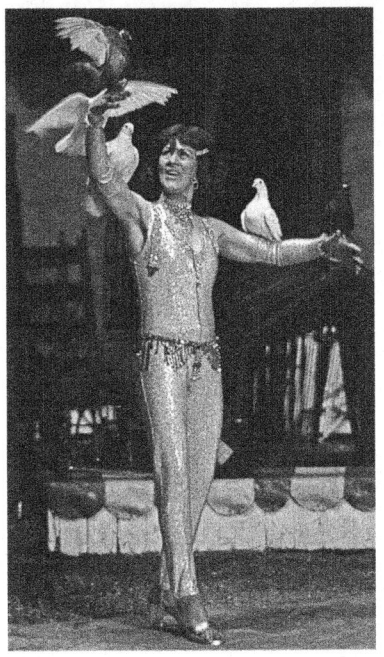

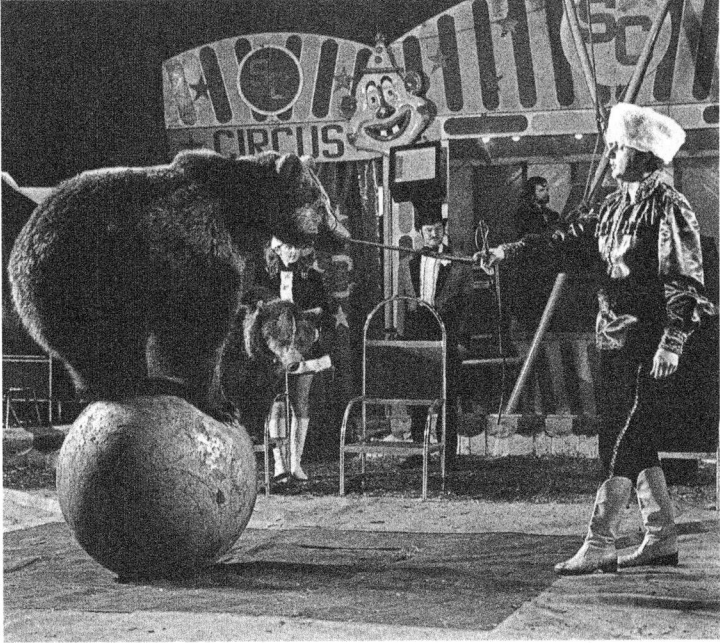

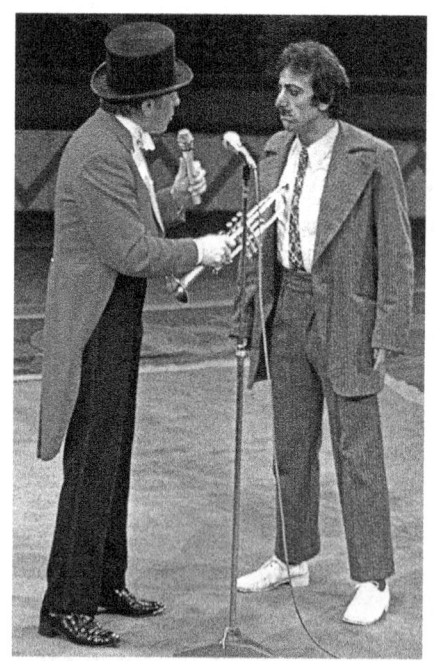

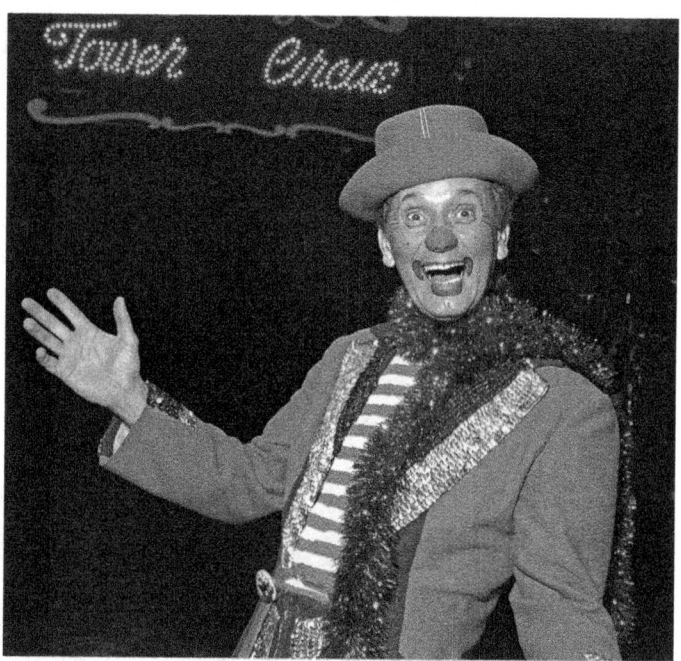

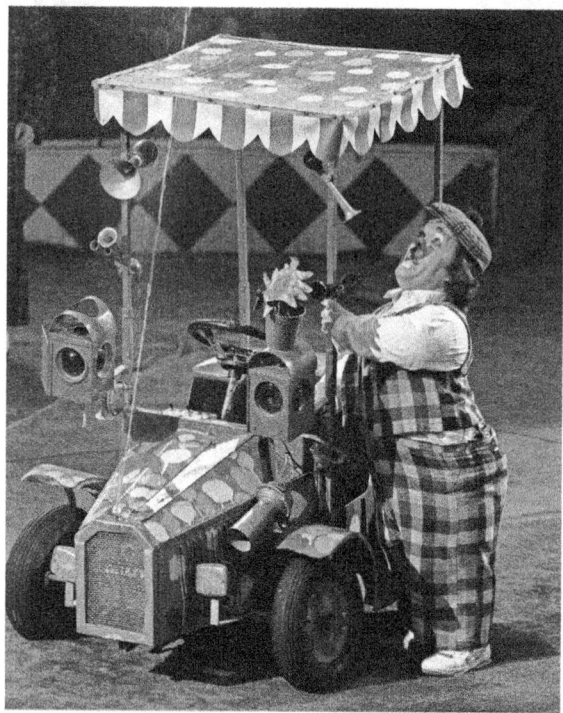

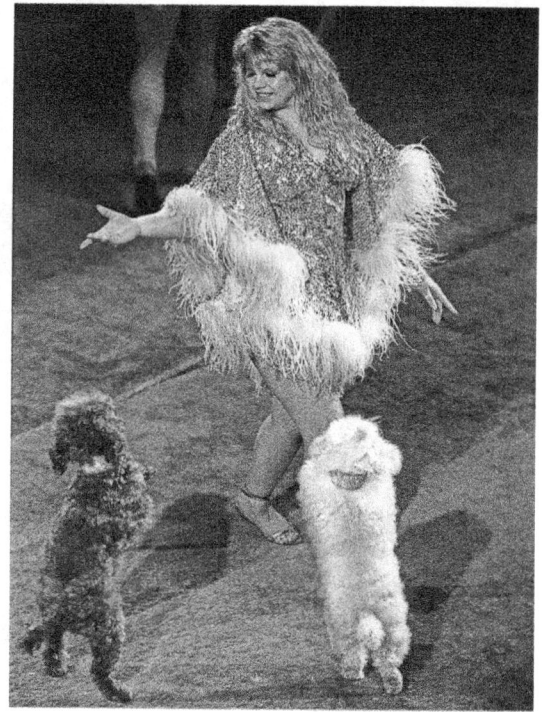

NEARLY FAMOUS

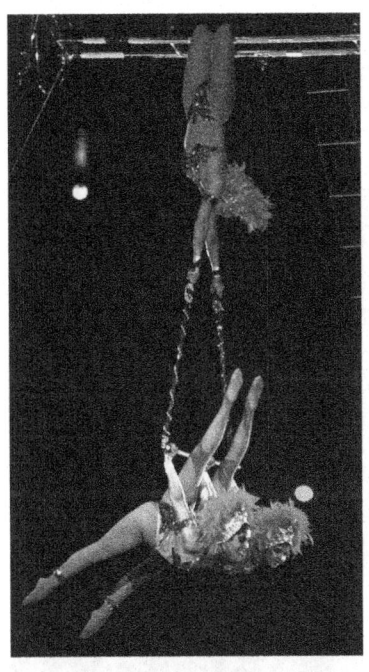
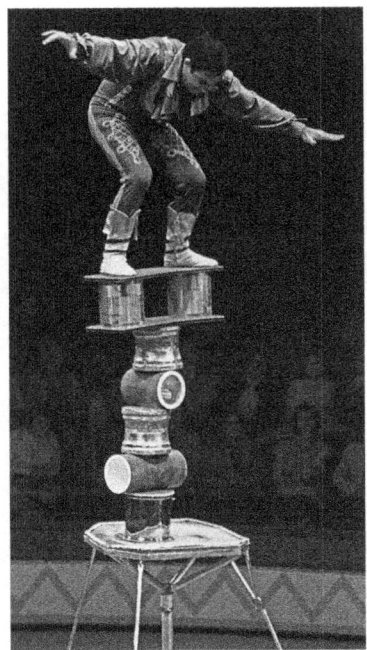
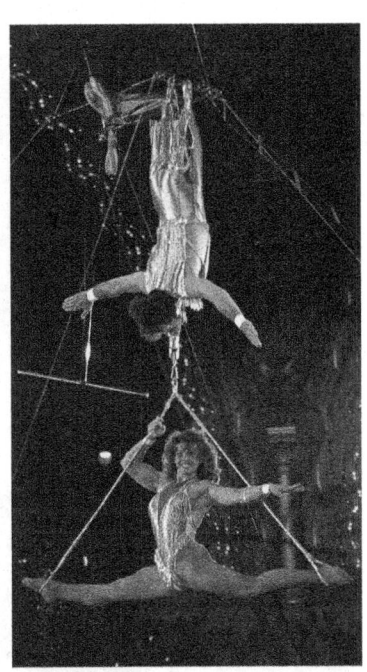
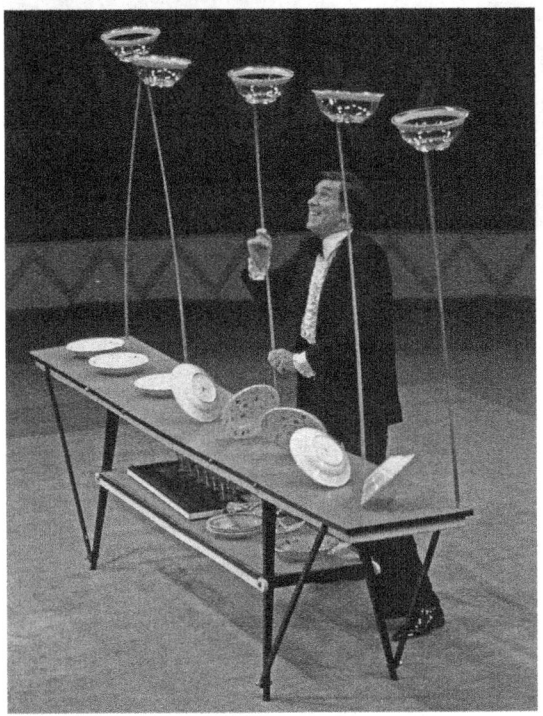
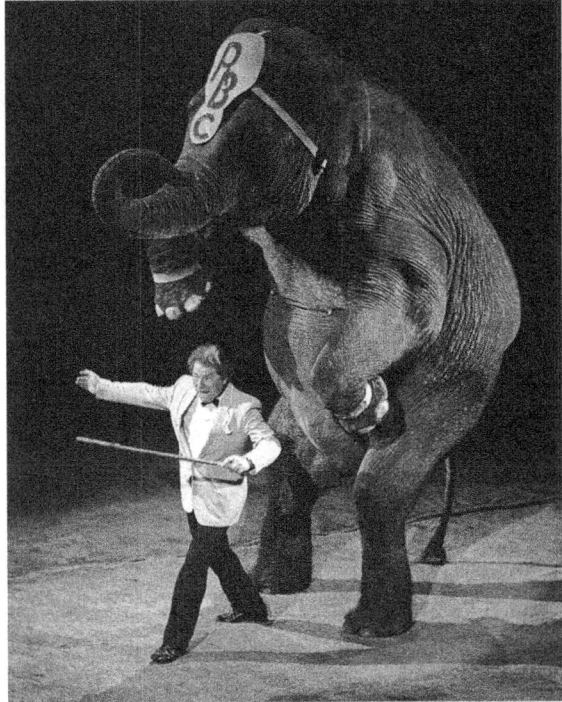

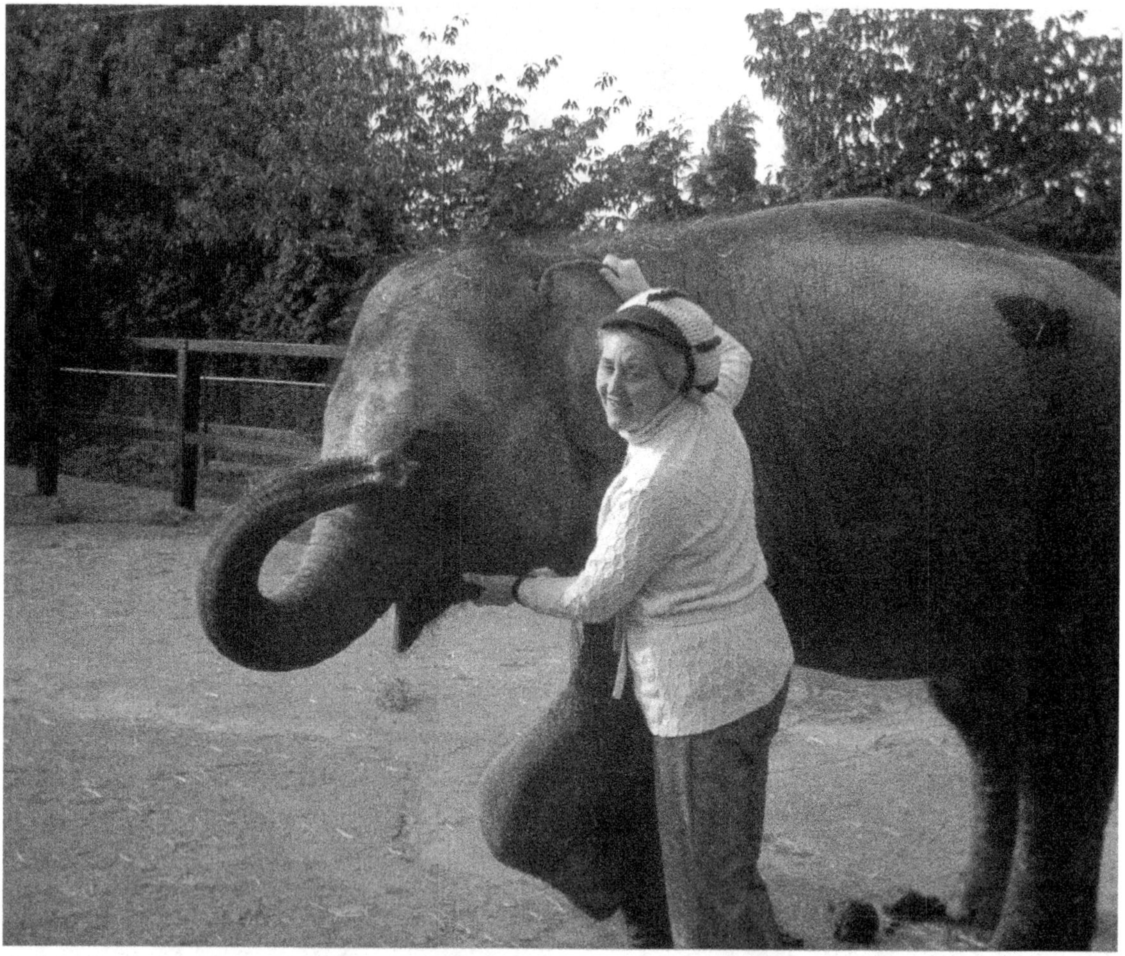

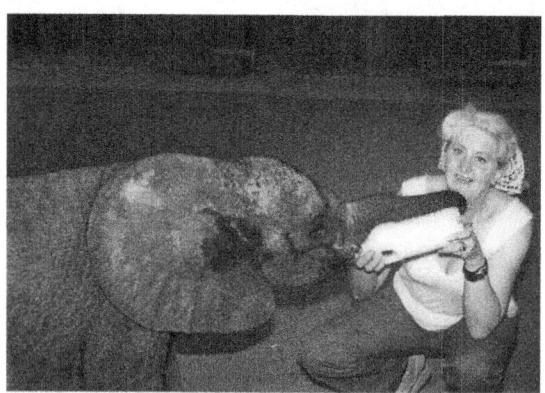

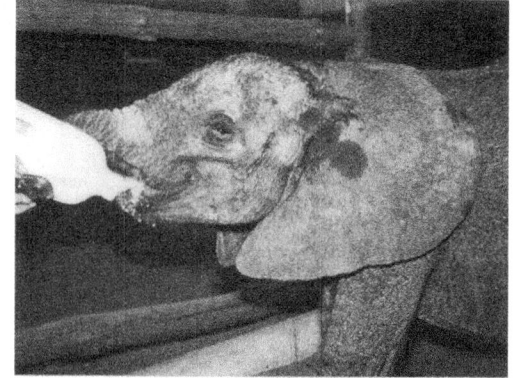

NEARLY FAMOUS

A change in direction - moving on

From then on things changed even more dramatically. Mum went on to be the manager at pets corner in Chessington Zoo and continued to be a deserved celebrity in her own right. She regularly appeared on television with the zoo's baby elephant Bella and various other animals, making the national press on numerous occasions, even featuring in a movie!

I spent that Christmas vacation season clowning around, literally, as a stooge in a comedy car clown act belonging to 'Spider Austen' a famous English clown, and a cousin, I think I am related to everyone that is in the circus somehow. Anyway, I was asked to help them out in Spain and we appeared in the capital Madrid. I used to be dragged out of the audience as a spectator and would then avoid all attempts by two clowns to throw water over me, drenching themselves as they went through the routine. It wasn't a career move and it wasn't long before I was on my own again, but at least for the time being I was earning better money for a change, well for that Christmas. What do I remember from that trip, barmy days at the movies watching cartoons in Spanish and pickled octopus with a beer at the Tapas bar.

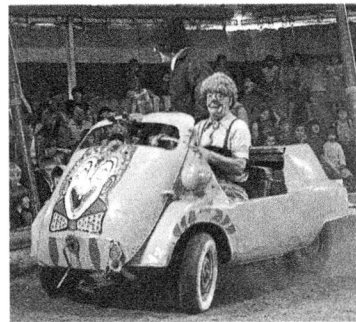

When I came back from Spain my Mum was at the Liverpool Empire where the headliner, popular entertainer and comedian Charlie Drake, needed some pigeons for a sketch. She was looking

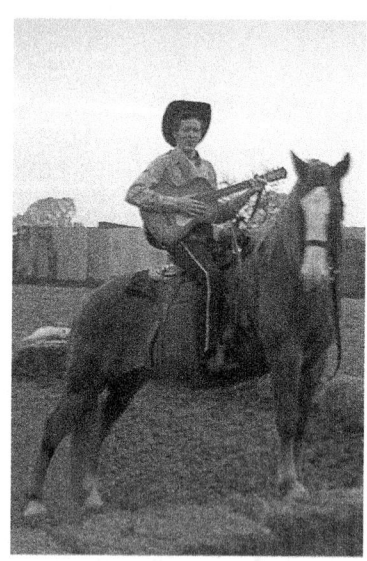

after them for another cousin June Witney, she did such a good job of looking after things Charlie Drake asked her to become his personal dresser for the Pantomime. I spent a few weeks with her before moving on. Funniest thing I remember was trying to copy my Beatles records onto a cassette recorder I could carry around with me. I used a live microphone, playing back the records on an old gramophone. I was in the dressing room with the pigeons and if you listen to the breaks between tracks on my recordings you can hear coo, coo, coo!

For the summer season I headed back to the Mecca of British entertainment, Blackpool, in an Austin Cambridge estate car and a 14 ft (4m) caravan that would be my home for the next few years!

I arrived in Blackpool, no work no money and no horse. Sorry I forgot to mention that I'd thought about being a singing 'horse riding Cowboy' like my Dad. Perhaps I could star at the 'Crazy Horse Saloon' in Paris. It sounded like a great idea, touring with just me and my horse. So I gave it a try, well at least for the demo Super 8 movie I made. I sent it to an agent and didn't hear from him again, he didn't return the movie so I always thought there was still a chance, but it probably got lost in the post. Then the Spanish job came up as a clown and that was that!

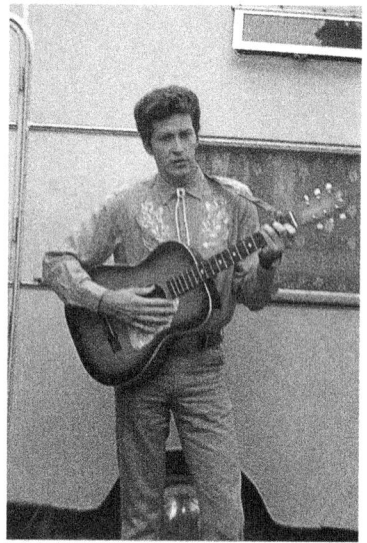

Where was I? I went down to the Tower Circus and got a job working the spotlights. The money was poor, but while I was there a friend heard there was a job going and suggested I should go down to the Ashton Pavilion, a Theatre in St Annes. I went down and was taken on straight away as the Resident Stage Manager. I had enough experience in show business for the lighting set ups and the strength of youth to change the scenery three times a week for the repertory companies that came in!

It gave me a job and a title with regular money, for at least a summer season, with time to think of what I would do in the off season. Now as a Stage Manager at least I had enough credibility to get invited to a few party's in town, I could even join the showbiz ten pin bowling league. I hooked up with a well known circus act, 'The Castors', of course I would, wouldn't I? Toly M, Eddy and Charly, great guys. I'm pretty sure we won the league that year, well why wouldn't we, four handsome guys and a mean set of bowls!

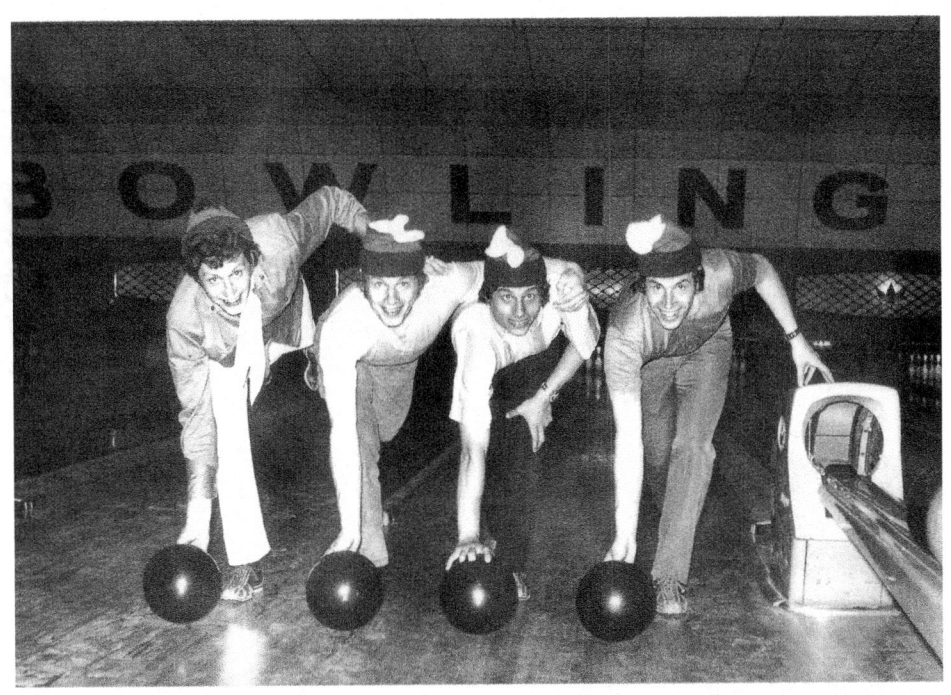

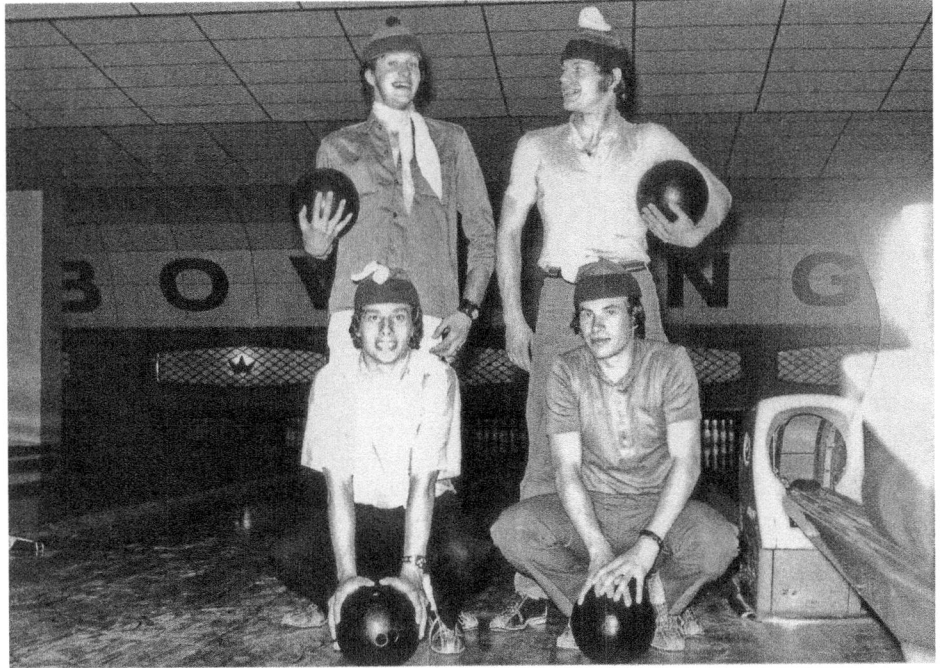

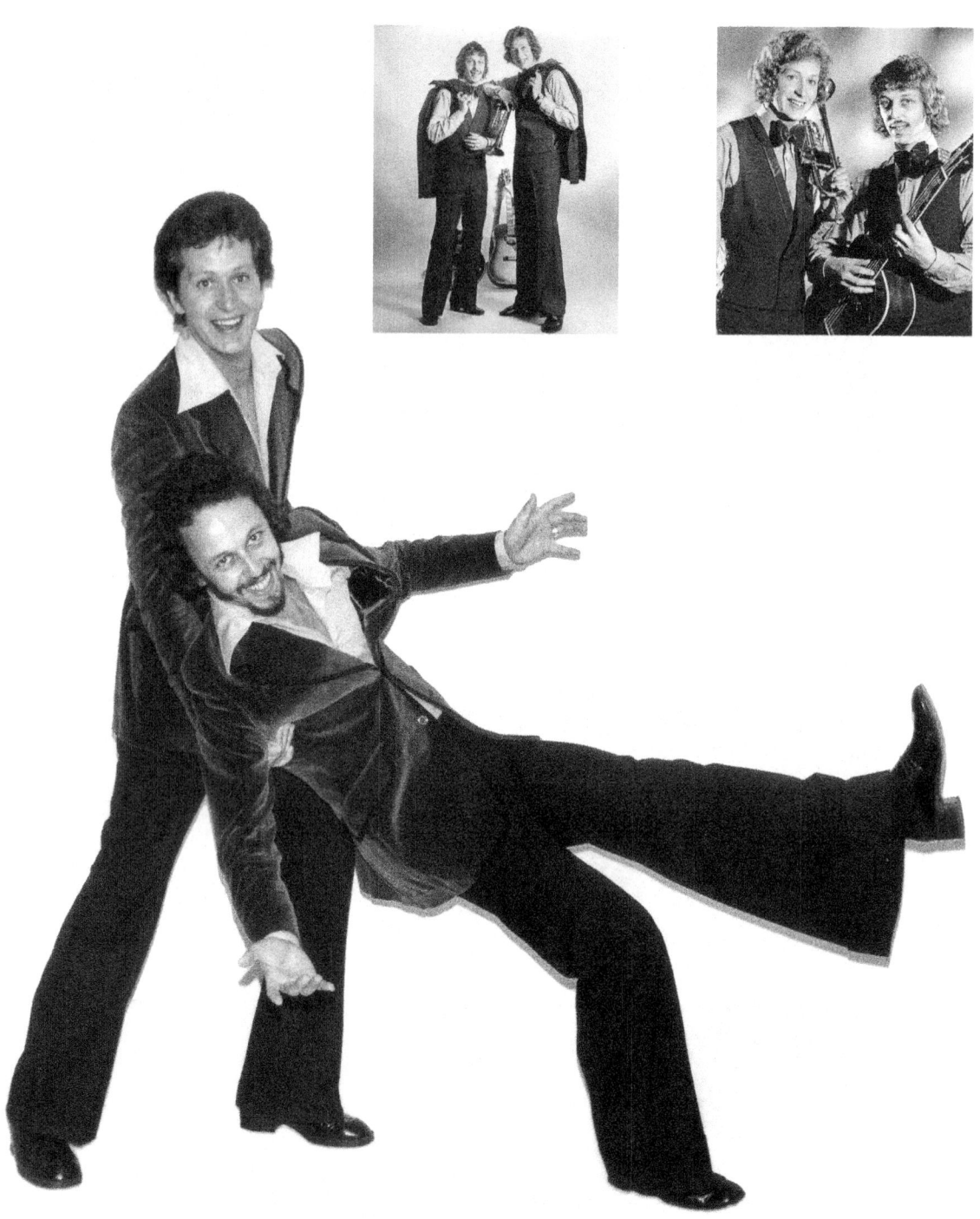

NEARLY FAMOUS

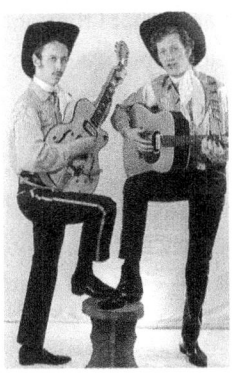
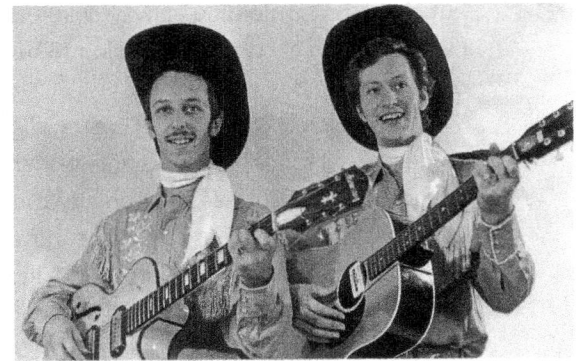
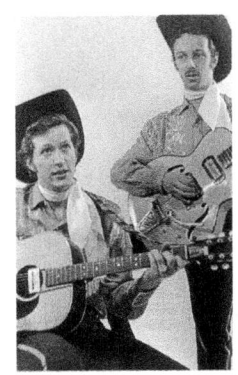

Musical career

I used my spare time wisely, well sort of. I was in a fun seaside town, the mecca of British entertainment. If I was going to sing about the Honky Tonks and Bars I had to at least try some, didn't I?

So there I was practising my singing with an old beat up guitar 'Ole MacDonald had a farm' etc. etc. 'Tune a day' book one, hey didn't that teach me the trumpet? Yes it did, well it taught me the guitar chords too, and for that I will be forever grateful, but it was never really enough, even with the harmonica I was struggling. Still I kept up the trumpet and I knew I could always blast a mean half dozen tunes, all I needed was an old circus tent or an Army band!

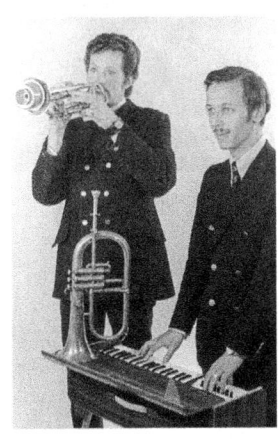

One day I walked into a coffee bar in Blackpool and started a conversation with a guy called Lenny Harris, it started as a suggestion of guitar lessons and ended up as a whole new career as one half of the double act 'The Paulo Brothers'.

Lenny had a natural gift for lead guitar and could harmonise with my singing. I told him with his talent and my looks all we needed was an agent and we could be famous, and I believe we nearly made it!

To be honest our cabaret career nearly ended the first night out. I had worked out two spots for us, one singing Country & Western songs and for the other I drew on my former skills. No not horse riding

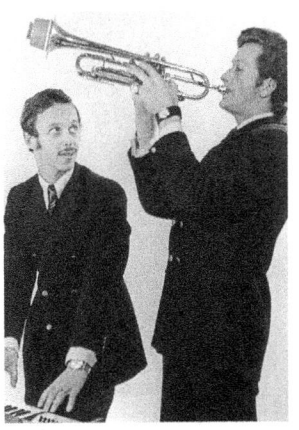

but clowning, something I always wanted to do and what I thought I would become. I was finally going to be a musical clown, a dream come true. Oh boy was I wrong!

In our defence, I would offer, we travelled to one of the notoriously hardest areas for experienced entertainers to work never mind two young guys doing their first comedy routine, sorry, clown act and Country singing, also not one of the most popular styles of music in England in those days, though I'm glad to see it has changed a bit, but I think it's too late for me now, maybe!

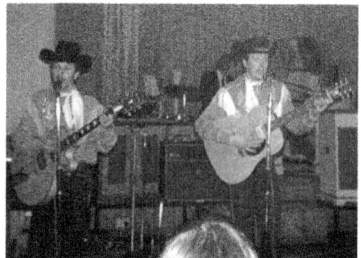 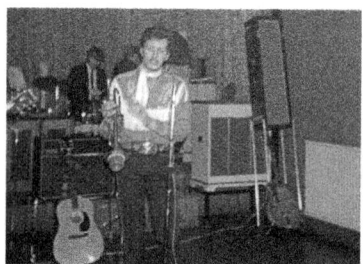 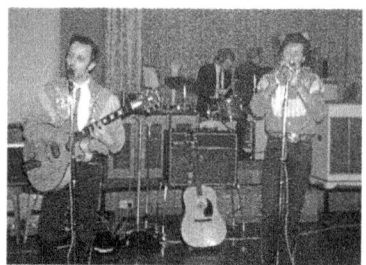

I will try and paint the picture. For the opening of our first spot I was on the trumpet and Lenny accompanied me on a Bon tempi Organ (that's pretty much a kiddies organ), the sound was less than inviting, an argument then pursues between me and Lenny as part of the act. I shoot Lenny by mistake (yes I said shoot) and then I do a dead and alive routine (only acting) taken straight from circus clowning, but in a dinner jacket, does this make sense so far? Well the gun went off (a starting pistol actually with a discharge chamber on the top of the barrel) and I peppered the front row of the audience with hot ash from the discharge chamber, (I guess I could have been arrested just for that these days, but hey. Our audiences were tough!) I started to try and carry Lenny off and if you have ever seen this routine you might appreciate the comedy, his hands and legs goes up and down and my face gets slapped a few times etc. when I eventually picked him up the audience shouted, "get him off and don't bring him back"!

"Get him off and don't bring him back!"

We were already driving back the 200 miles home before the audience started their second house of Bingo, no second spot and no money. Had I been on my own, my cabaret period would have

NEARLY FAMOUS

ended right there, but it was a long very slow drive back with a car and trailer in tow!

We had time to work through the mistakes, which was pretty much everything we did in the comedy spot. So we decided to just be a singing musical duo, we would do a spot featuring our talents. It worked, and it worked well, we sang, Lenny played lead guitar, I played some rhythm guitar and occasional trumpet. We added to that our own very individual personalities and there you have it 'The Paulo Brothers' were reborn, doing some pop and dance numbers in our cabaret set and Country & Western at other times. Eventually we knew enough C&W to actually tour the English circuit, we went from strength to strength over the next six years.

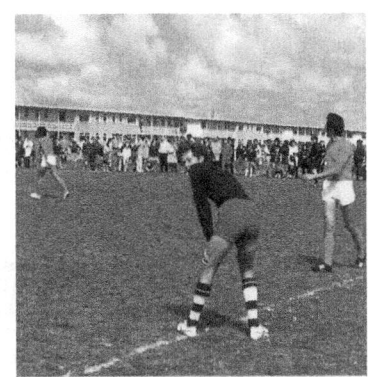

In our first summer season we worked as blue coats at the Pontins Holiday Camp Blackpool, it was a 24 hour entertaining job, always having to smile and work with an audience. It has been a good training ground for a lot of big stars and was just what we needed, an invaluable experience, it also gave us a small but regular income. We worked with people all day, from breakfast until after show time, it developed our communication skills, Bingo calling, dancing, sing-a-longs, soccer training and life guard! Yeah that swimming certificate came in handy after all!

We did a bit of everything, then at the weekends we were allowed to go out working our own act, travelling to the social and working men's clubs around the county to earn and learn more, by the end of our first year we were seasoned veterans.

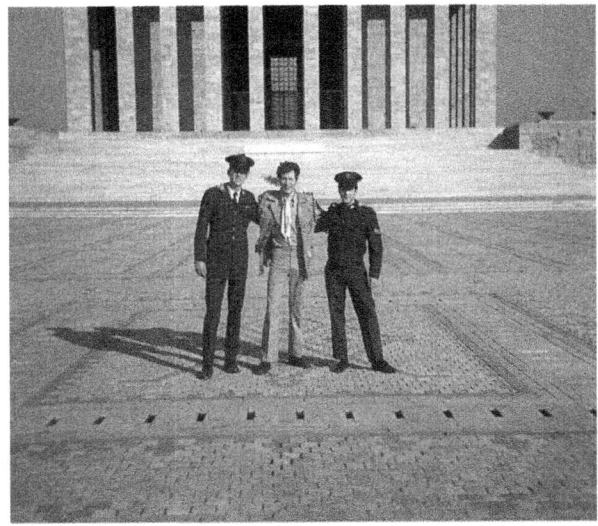

We toured England, Scotland and Wales working our cabaret act in clubs of all sizes, co starring and sometimes even starring in our own shows. We toured American bases in Germany, Turkey and Italy, twice. Even headlining some of the locations. One stint was with Al T Kossy a comedian with a mean sense of humour, even with his travelling partners as we were later to find out!

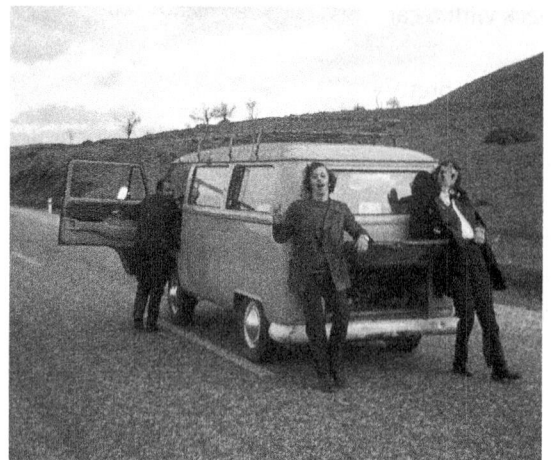

We drove through Belgium to Germany, where the show met up in Frankfurt, and then onwards, until we had covered thousands of miles on the tour. That's a lot of kilometres, travelling through the old communist countries, Yugoslavia, Bulgaria, in a small classic Volkswagen van, all the way to Turkey. It was crazy, driving that little van in some hair raising situations, on some occasions there was only one other alternative, we just had to get out and push!

After driving through the night on and on, taking it in turns, none stop, we were exhausted and just wanted a bed to sleep in. Finally when we arrived at our hotel in Turkey, Al called us into his room, threw back the covers of his bed, there in the bed were three huge dead bugs, we still think he planted them but we never really knew and we weren't prepared to take a chance, so we went back to the van and slept in there!

It was a bizarre tour, on one occasion we were in Turkey's capital city Ankara in an American forces NCO's club. It was in a basement, and there were rumours of terrorists blowing the place up. We were a bit nervous, but Al just said if they throw a Molotov cocktail in here we'll drink it before it goes off!

We laughed it off then, but we heard that they really did try to

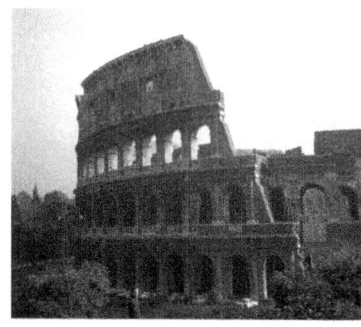

blow the place up some time later. They were tough trips and often scary, planes and bus trips like something out of an Indiana Jones movie. Once, we were going up a mountain road in fog, our driver just put his trust and our lives in Alla's hand and pulled out to overtake a large truck, the fog was like pea soup but he pulled out anyway and we just made it. Then we travelled on to bases in Italy and Sicily.

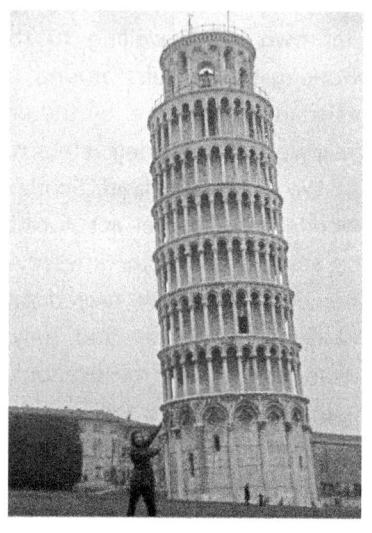

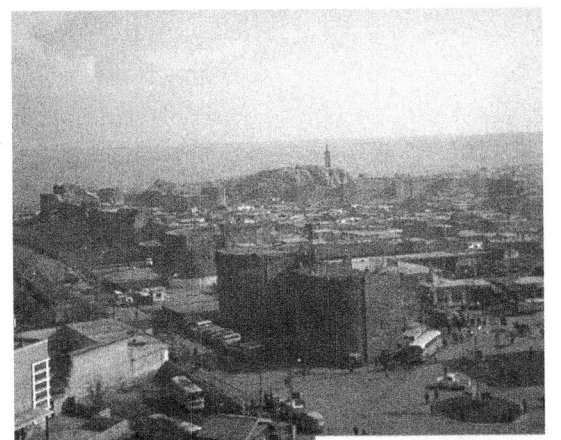

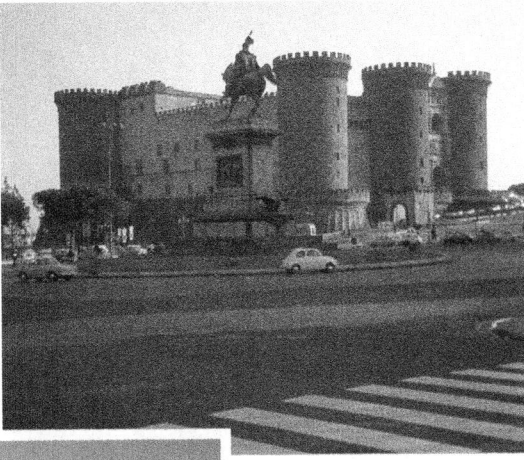

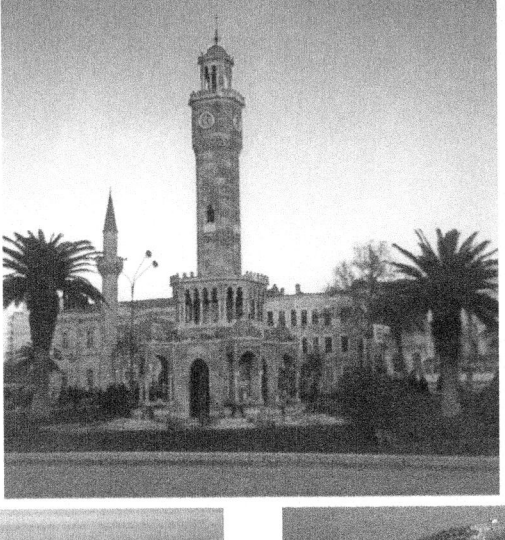

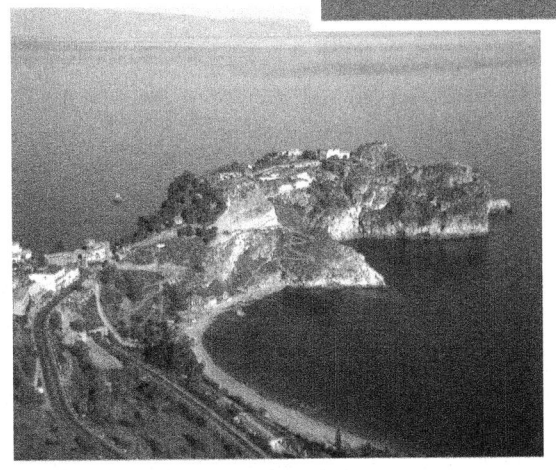

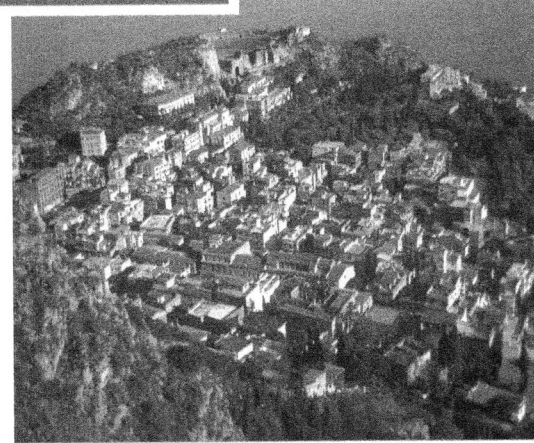

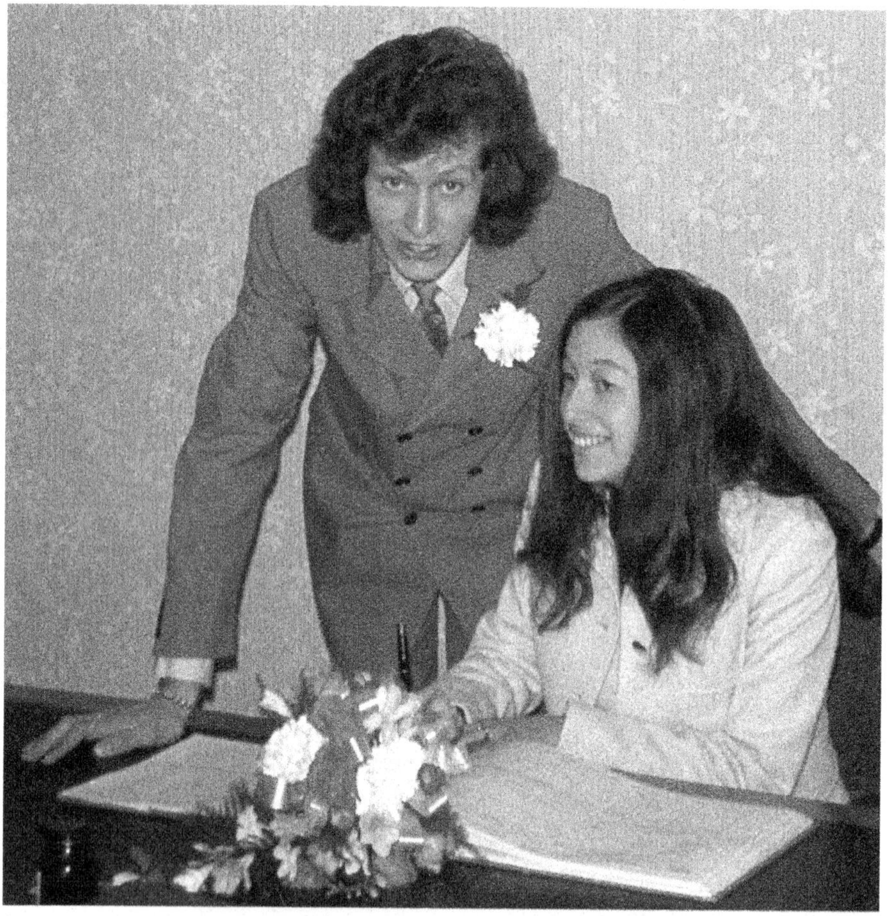

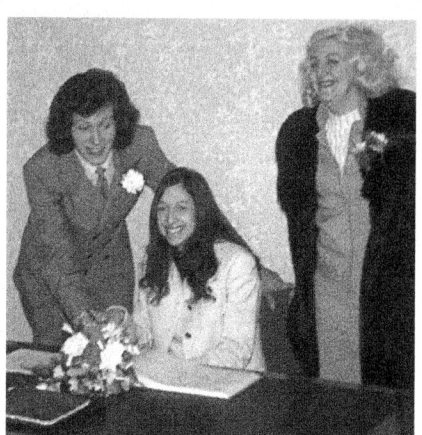

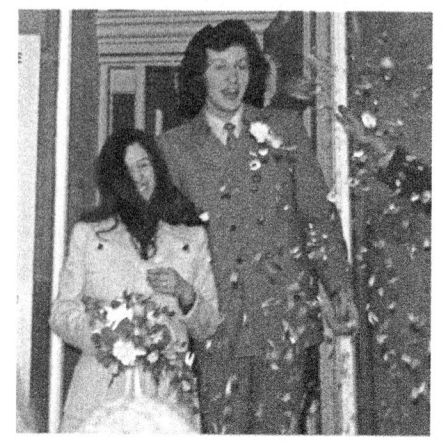

NEARLY FAMOUS

Meet the wife

She hates to be called that. When I first met Lenny I also met another partner in life his sister Estelle, we courted in secret for about two years, why, because our family backgrounds in life and in religion were so far apart, if they found out it would be frowned upon, and sure enough it was!

That said, she had a great family, they looked after me, fed me and let me park my trailer in their yard, her father was the closest I had been to having a real father and to me it felt like how a father should be. However it was inevitable that we would eventually get caught out seeing each other, too many doors and windows squeaking at night!

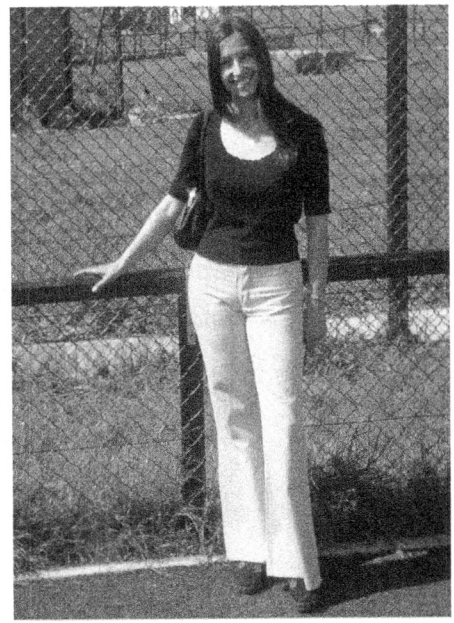

When he found out we were courting he asked me to leave, I felt really sad like it was my own family kicking me out. It was fortunate that gigs came in and we went on another tour of American bases for a month, it let the air settle for a bit, a tiny bit, at least until Estelle told him she was going to marry me!

We were married on my return from Turkey, a month after writing the following lyrics (*Show me the way to your heart*).

Didn't I mention my song writing yet?

Show me the way to your heart

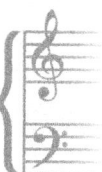

Show me the way to your heart
and I'll show you the way to mine
Show me the way to your heart
or is it such a great big crime

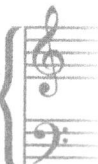

Lead me astray with your emotions
your laughing, crying and your smile
Lead me astray with your emotions
the way you do it all the while

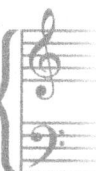

Take me into your arms
and I'll take you with me today
Take me into your arms
and I'll take you far far away

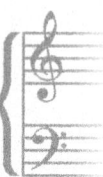

Walk me to my silver lining
with all the warmth of your heart
Walk me to my silver lining
and our love will never ever part

Lyrics by Wayne Paulo

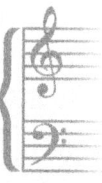

We managed to get a larger resident trailer and stayed on a farm on the outskirts of Blackpool, I carried on giging and things started to slightly pick up financially.

I have to tell you one little story about the farm. I invited a friend and his wife out to visit us one night, as it was going to be dark when he arrived, I had given him directions through the farm, explicit I thought!

It was getting late and I started to worry, no signs of him, then all of a sudden there was a knock on the door. I opened the door in my pyjamas, funny place for a door! Only joking. Now you have to imagine this scene, from the trailer door I am looking down into a dark rainy abyss, a figure in a light suit and what might have been a cream coloured raincoat walked forward with pleading eyes and a look of horror on

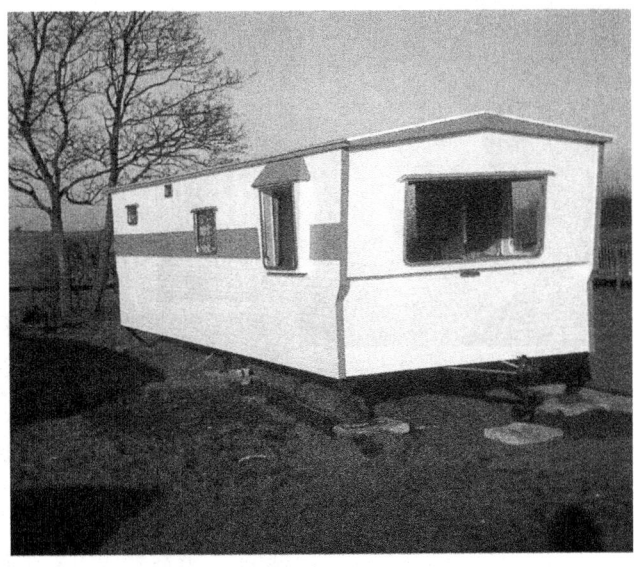

his face, looked up at me and said in a voice full of anxiety "Wayne! Wayne! What have you done to us?" Then his wife peeped out from behind him looking like a drowned rat and said "look at us" They were covered from head to toe in Cow Sh@*!

"Wayne! Wayne! What have you done to us!"

Well obviously he had misread the directions. Did he not hear the cows when he opened the gate? It's still so funny now, as he explained how he went over two fields, got the car stuck in the mud and his wife had to get out and start pushing the car, as the wheels spun the Cow pats started to fly. I'm sorry I can't write anymore the tears are running down my legs. Where is the camera when you need it!

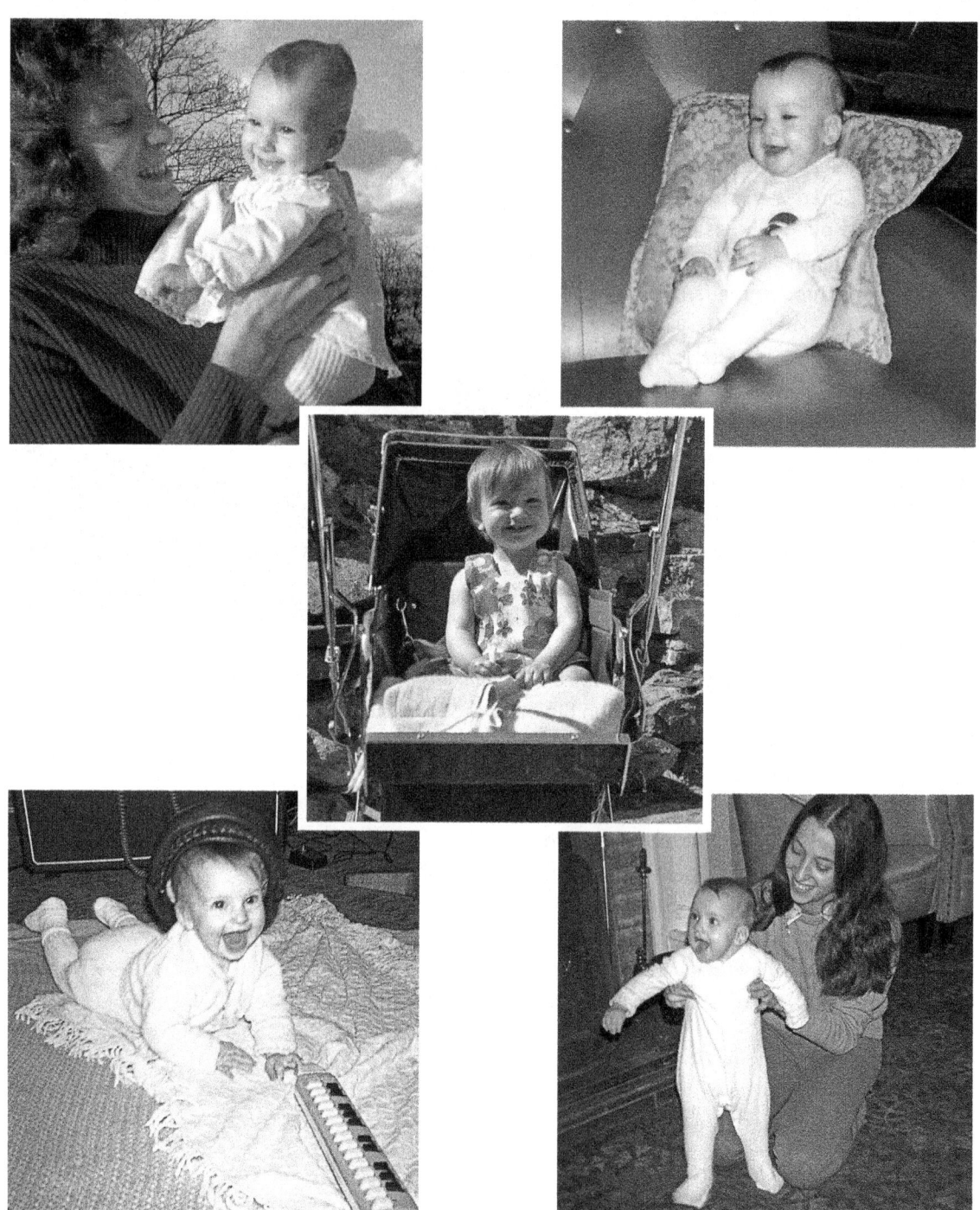

Little surprises!

The next time we went away was for a summer show in the Channel Islands, Estelle came too, I didn't want to leave her on her own this time, especially as she was pregnant. Our daughter Danielle was later born in St Helier Jersey at the local hospital.

Early one Saturday morning Estelle woke me to say she thought the baby was on its way and we rushed to the nearby hospital. When we arrived the nurse asked if I would like a cup of tea while waiting and I went off to the toilet. When I returned I was already a father, in fact I was told Dani was nearly born in the bath. Estelle told me later that the nurse had insisted she had a bath prior to the delivery, Estelle's reply was "I haven't got time for a bath the baby's coming!", at which point the nurse ran off to get the Matron, apparently, leaving Estelle with one foot in and one foot out of the bath. They both returned and the Matron agreed she should go to the delivery room straight away, so she then had to 'walk' to the delivery room! Blimey UPS don't have that much confusion with a delivery. Apparently it all happened so quick that she just popped out. The baby that is not Estelle, imagine that? Well maybe not. I didn't even get my cup of tea. What kind of day was that for an Englishman!

"I thanked them for the applause and told them it was my pleasure!"

During the show that night the compere announced to the audience that I was the proud father of a 5 lb 12 oz daughter called Danielle. I think I was still in shock, I thanked them for the applause and just told them it was my pleasure!

It was a barmy summer for us both, we carried Dani, yes we called her that, unless she was naughty then it would be the full title Danielle Paulo. It could have been worse, at the time, I was mad on the cartoon character Scooby Doo and if the baby had been a boy, it was definitely going to be called Scooby. So where was I? We carried Dani in a little papoose, walking all over the Island sightseeing, we nearly had to leave her at the Zoo when the Gorilla became curious and took a liking to her!

Dani's arrival also changed attitudes toward me when Estelle's family came over to see the baby and we eventually all made up.

Everyone else said the marriage wouldn't last. But hey, we are still together thirty six years later and we have managed to prove them wrong. Estelle has always said "better the devil you know" and I just know nobody else would put up with me this long!

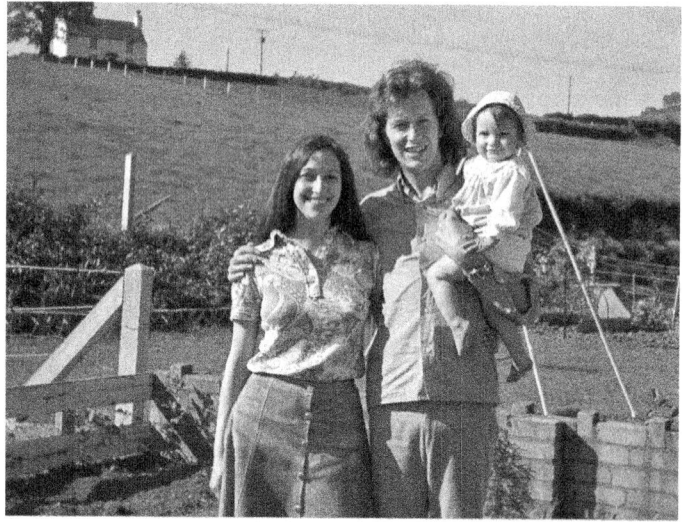

Well I continued to compose and write songs and here is another set of lyrics on the right, (The Wonders of a Child), I wonder where I got that idea from!

After finishing the summer season we landed a six week show on a Cunard cruise ship in the Caribbean, too good to miss and a great opportunity we thought at the time, even though I would have to leave Estelle and my new daughter at home, not to mention I was a bit prone to motion sickness.

Though it sounded a great gig it didn't quite turn out that way!

The wonders of a child

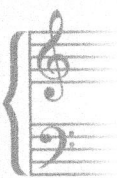

Here I sit and wonder, of baby's little cry,
of parting and sweet sorrow, lest I should go and die,
of the world around me, what children grow to be,
If she'll grow to love, a father such as me.

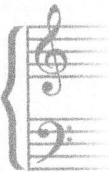

Now for her mother so dear, close to us at heart,
a mother to us both, who frets when we're apart,
When our child is older, if by chance she'll sing,
my wife and I will wonder, of the joys a child can bring.

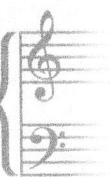

We sit here and we wonder, what she will grow to be,
could she fill our dreams, of things we want to see.
Sometimes she plays softly, others times she's wild.
Makes you sit and ponder, the wonders of a child.

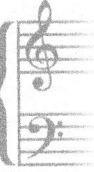

Lyrics by Wayne Paulo
(Danielle was one year old)

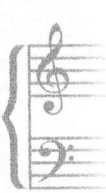

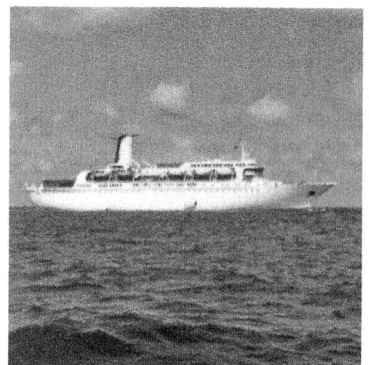

After the first couple of cabaret shows they wanted to fire us and send us home. It turned out that my Louise Armstrong trumpet tributes and Lenny's guitar solos over the back of his head, were also the same little stints that the backing band performed in their own cabaret spot. Certainly a conflict and jealous rivalry arose, it also got deeper when we discovered they were trying to get rid of the booking agent and we were going to be the fall guys!

However we weren't going lightly, we were under contract and had done nothing wrong. We offered a compromise, "Put us in a room to perform on our own, and we will see if it works. We will let the people decide!". Well they did, They put us in the cocktail bar on the first night of departure at 6pm and they kept it quiet, with no announcements. Fortunately we didn't keep it quiet, well we weren't born yesterday we were veteran performers now, we spread the word ourselves, setting up in the corner of the cocktail lounge with our own mike system and two guitars, we went back to our roots and started our Country hour special. When the Captain and Cruise Director walked through it was packed, not surprisingly we stayed on for the rest of the tour until the end of our contract. I have to admit with a little bit of smug satisfaction.

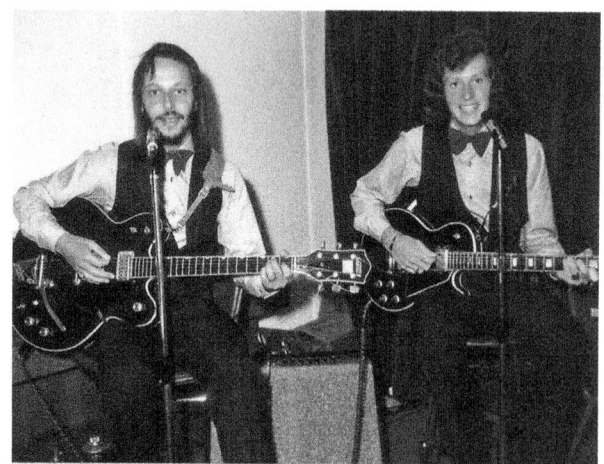

Unfortunately, I think due to the change of circumstances, us no longer being the main cabaret spot onboard, it didn't feel the same, there was always something missing, we needed that buzz. Then friction started to brew and spread to me and Lenny. We weren't doing what we were best at, the cabaret act and expressing ourselves, we started arguing over rehearsals and new songs. We just kept away from each other when we weren't working. I started to spend more time just sitting on the top deck on my own. Well it stopped me getting sea sick, and there I was again with my lonely songs! (Tears in the ocean).

Tears in the ocean

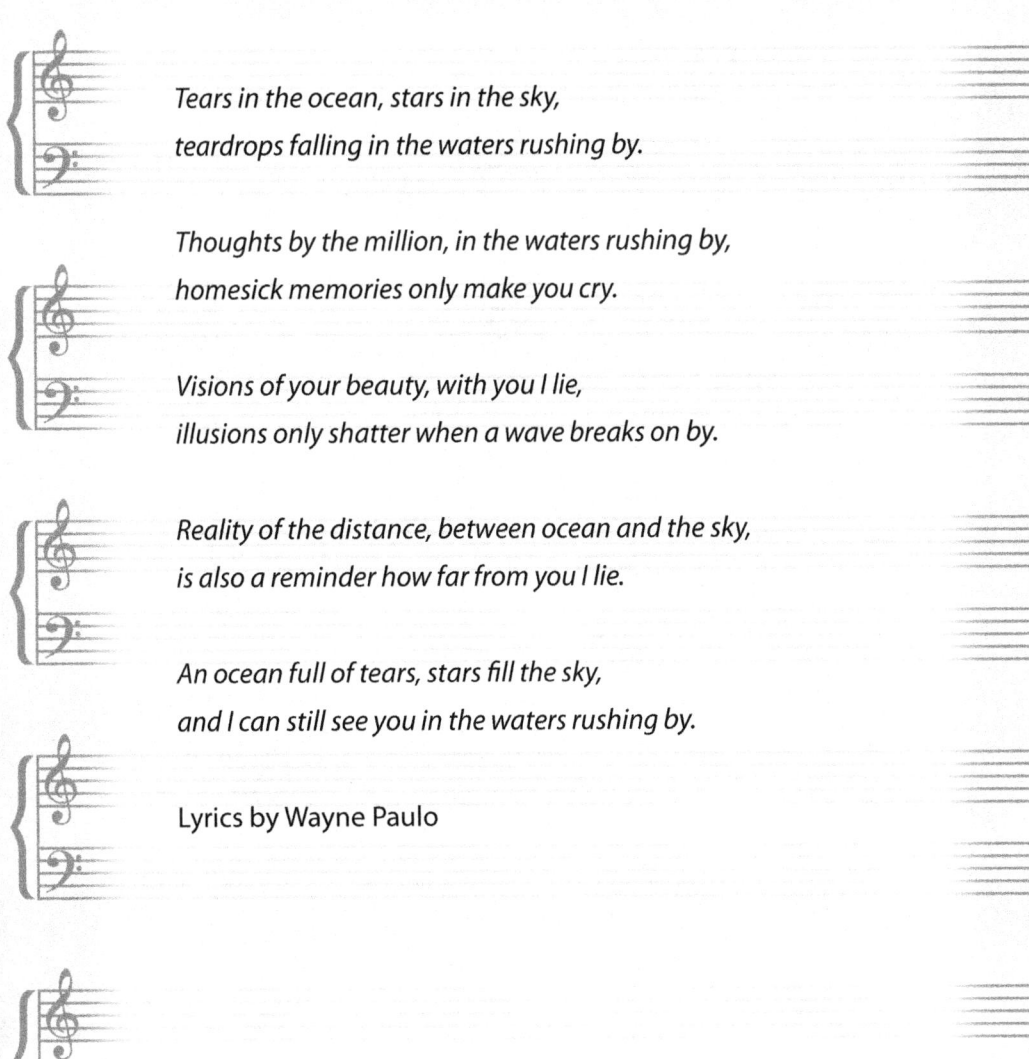

Tears in the ocean, stars in the sky,
teardrops falling in the waters rushing by.

Thoughts by the million, in the waters rushing by,
homesick memories only make you cry.

Visions of your beauty, with you I lie,
illusions only shatter when a wave breaks on by.

Reality of the distance, between ocean and the sky,
is also a reminder how far from you I lie.

An ocean full of tears, stars fill the sky,
and I can still see you in the waters rushing by.

Lyrics by Wayne Paulo

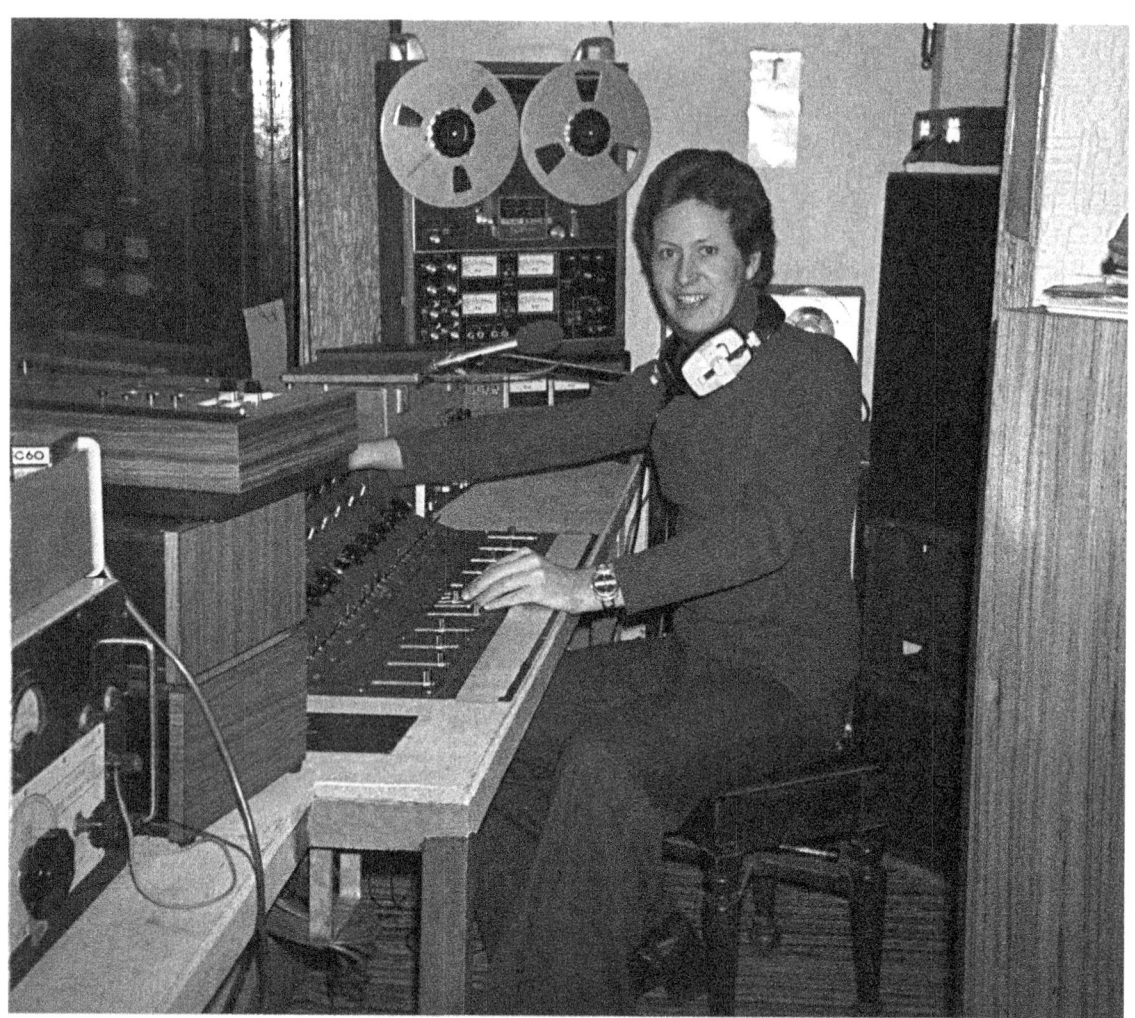

Recordings, the birth of Tiny's Studio

Most of my career changes have crossed over and my song writing, the recording studio, record label and music publishing experience were no exception!

I had started writing lyrics for songs in 1968 before I could play the guitar, I just figured they would come together somehow further along the line. First I just filled a book full of lyrics and hummed the tunes, then as I progressed to guitar chords I would write them down under the lyrics. Eventually I had to record them, there were too many to remember!

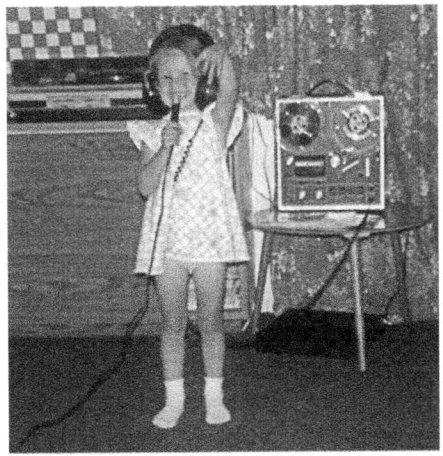

In the beginning I recorded them with a small mono cassette player just to keep the tunes. When I progressed to a reel to reel tape recorder my first studio was born. It was a wooden outhouse, a shed about the size of a small toilet, actually a lot smaller, it still had all my garden tools in it, guitars, a trumpet and an amplifier!

Still the lyrics kept coming and I kept singing, on my all in one super duper Akai recording machine! Seen here with Dani in this picture.

It blows your mind if you think of the machinery we started on, it would be another 15 years before computers would enter my life and change things again!

Back to the studio, this all started while I was still with Lenny and after a while I was able to convince him we should build our own recording studio, we could record local bands and produce our own records to sell in the clubs. Maybe it was to stop me moaning or writing, or just the bad tapes I kept playing to him, over and over again. I would write songs all night long, on road trips and in hotels everywhere, some were really bad. I guess I wore him down or he saw the benefits, actually I'm kidding a bit here, I know he wanted to record his own songs and guitar playing as well. So basically we had no option. Thousands of egg boxes and tons of carpeting felt

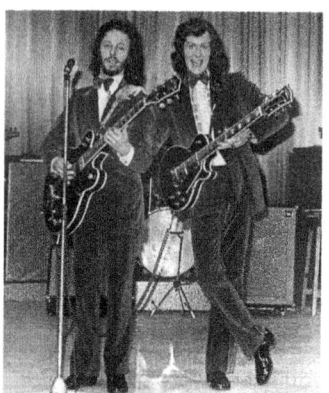 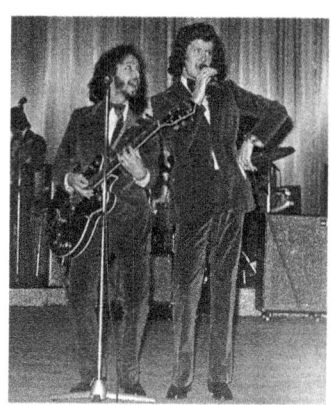

later, 'Tiny's Recording Studio' was born in the basement of Lenny's parents place, a small hotel on Blackpool's sea front. It was fortunate for us we had somewhere to put it, that was sound proofed and quite good. Well it was when we'd finished. Contacts in the industry led us to buy a second hand valve mixing console that was used to record Acker Bilk's 'Stranger on the shore', (even our studio had famous links), along with a 4 track TEAC tape machine. We started to record local bands and set up a recording service for songwriters, it would earn money to pay for the equipment and we became extremely proficient sound engineers, building from scratch a 16 into 8 mixing console and I mean from scratch including all the woodwork and frame, I'm sure Lenny claims he was the carpenter!

We went on to produce a series of records for acts to sell in the clubs they worked, as record producers we created the Storm Records label and combined that with Storm Music as Publishers. It looked and sounded good in principal, but we poured any money we made back into the equipment, so logically it was never going to make us any money and succeed, barely enough to break even!

We even produced a single release for ourselves to sell in the clubs we played at. That was a vinyl record for all you kids out there, it was way before CD's had been invented. All original tracks, Pretty Little Smile, Jungle Fever, Varda and Tiny's Song. There might even be an odd one hanging around out there somewhere, it should be quite an exclusive now if you have one, and just in case the tax man is reading this, we didn't sell that many, maybe a few hundred!

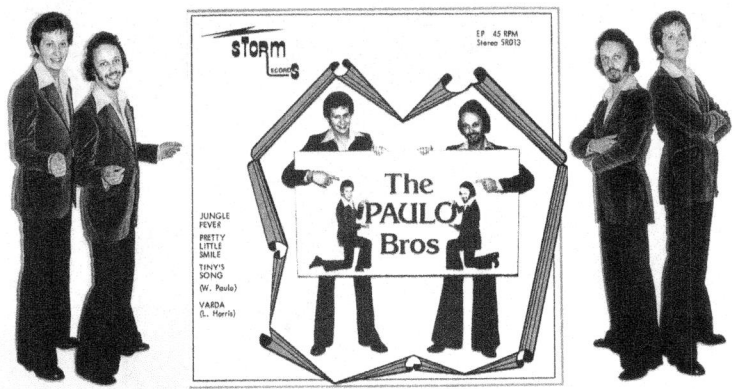

Estelle and I even went over to Cannes for the music industries annual event Midem, as publishers we would try and place groups and songs with Record companies. We produced a lot of original work in the studio those days with the help of, Nigel King, Chris Downton and John Imeson, some featuring Tony Andrews original songs performed by the Imeson group themselves. Despite a close interest by some, it just didn't happen, everyone thought disco pop would never sell. We were always ahead of our time!

Eventually the recordings came to a halt, it wasn't going to be, technology was moving too fast for us, and in those days it was an arm and a leg to pay for the next stage up in the recording industry.

Groups were now starting to use the next generation in tapes, 8 track cassette recorders in their bedrooms and stopped using the pro studios. Not only that, but our regular job as the dynamic duo the Paulo Brothers was also coming to an end!

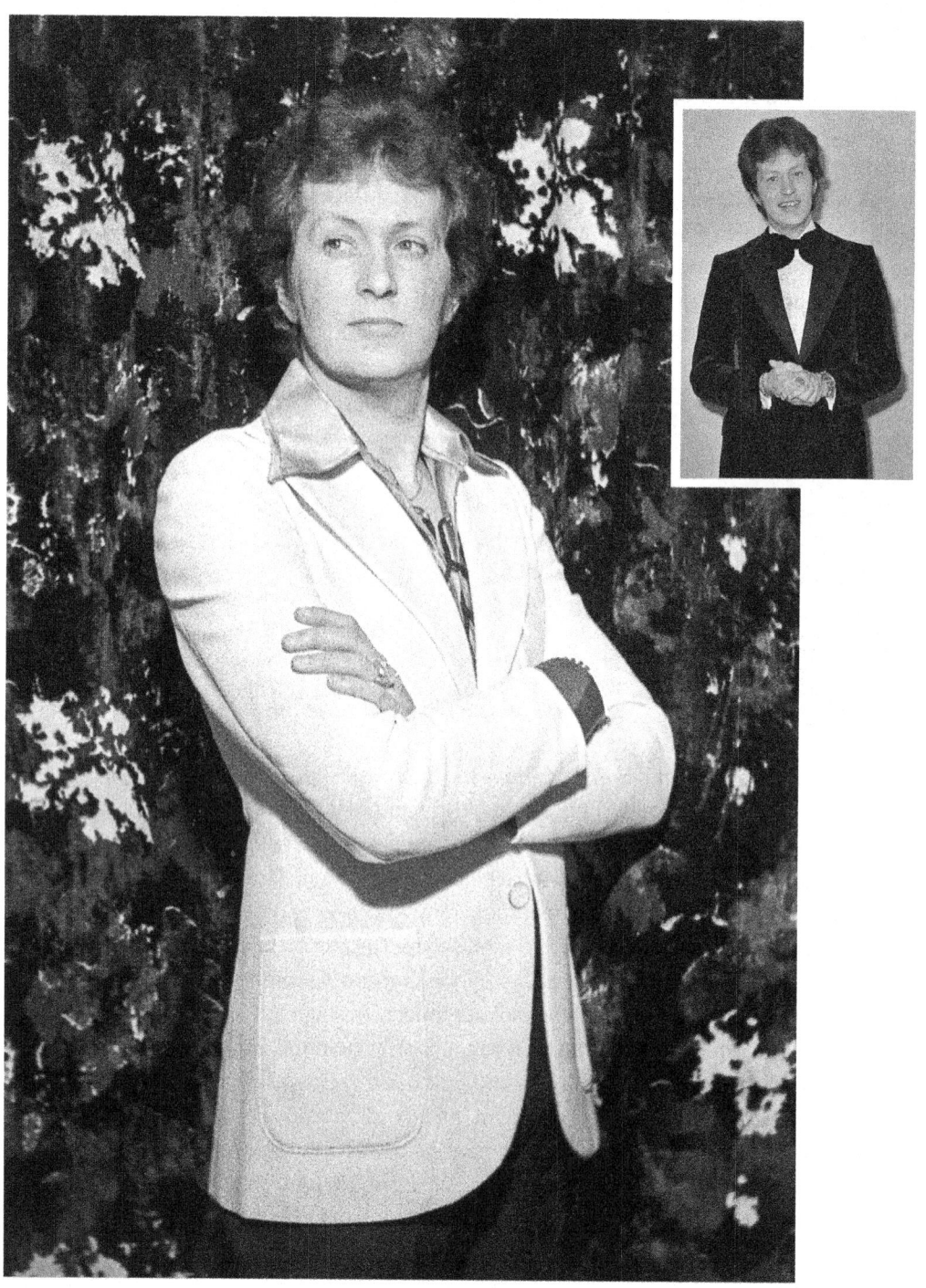

NEARLY FAMOUS

This is not the end not even ...

As a double act on stage Lenny and I were pretty good, but off stage there was more and more friction, differences of opinion which created a lot of arguments. We were working on the cruise ship I mentioned earlier in the Caribbean when Lenny told me this was the end, it would be our last gig together!

Despite the atmosphere and arguments we had been having, it came like a bolt out of the blue. It hit me hard, it wasn't just losing the act, the mutual bond we had created over all those years, on the road trips fighting through all the adversary together, the good times and bad, now it was all over in a flash. I had lost more than the act, to me it felt like I had lost a brother!

I put a brave face on as any male would, but musically I never really recovered from that. Though I did manage to carry on for another three years as a solo artist, even headlining in my own small shows and compering in summer seasons, but it was never quite the same.

"I opened up as a singing trumpet playing Gorilla!"

I introduced juggling into the act and opened up as a singing trumpet playing Gorilla. Yes I said Gorilla, I had the complete head to toe costume, I was the king of the swingers. I would enter the stage from the audience side, terrifying them as I crept up behind them in the dark. I remember once a woman ran off into the toilets screaming. I followed her to the door, then I knocked on it and she screamed, the more I knocked the more she screamed and the more the audience laughed, I milked it for all it was worth!

If you can't picture that, you'll never visualise how I got out of the costume on stage to the tune of the 'Stripper', I know, bizarre! I then went into 'King of the road', a bit of 'Amarillo', Johnny Cash and Chuck Berry, I finished it off nicely with the old trumpet Louis Armstrong

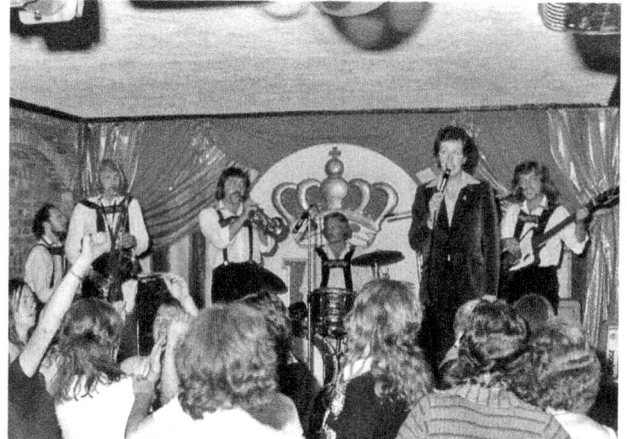

style and the audience clapping to 'O when the saints go marching in'. When I think back, there were some funny nights.

The progression to compere first took me into a German Beer Kellar, it's amazing how the things I have picked up in life have helped me along the way. During my circus days touring Germany I learnt some of the language, so when a German speaking compere was required in Blackpool I applied and got the job, all together now, "In Munchen State ein Hoffbraus house, ein swie suffer...". Free beer at last!

But as competent live backing musicians got less and less in the clubs it became a real struggle for me on my own, well this was before Karaoke and when backing tapes were frowned upon!

When one backing 'musician', I use the term loosely, the organist, stopped playing during a song because he couldn't read the music, and I asked what was wrong, he said the music was wrong, I said it wasn't I had been playing it for nine years, his response was "well you bloody well play it then"! He actually used stronger words than that but either way I knew it was time to give up.

By the way, that song was 'Amarillo', it may have revitalised Tony Christie's singing career but it helped end mine!

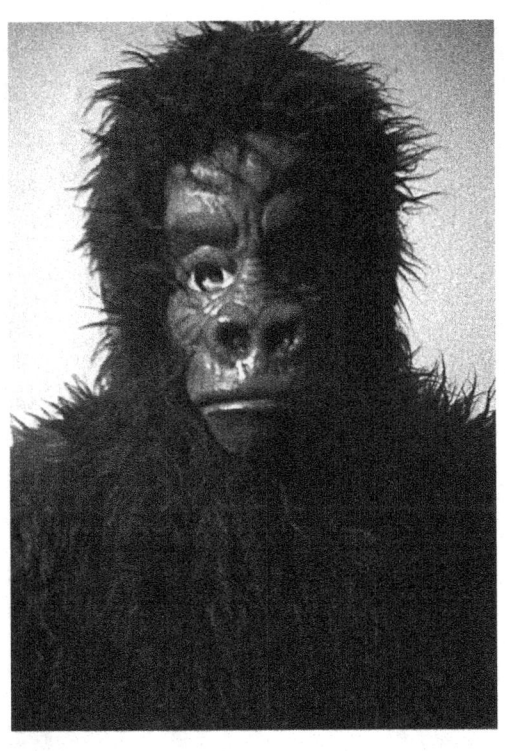

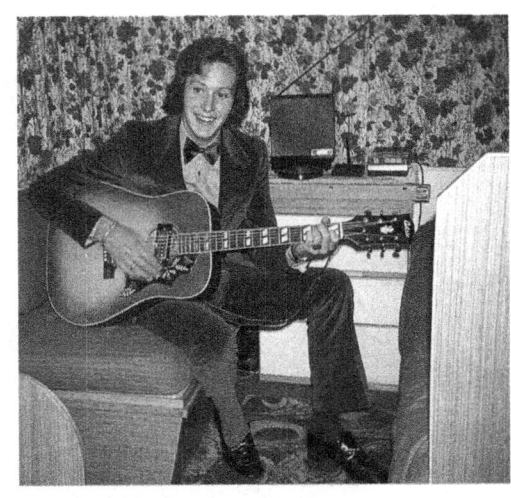

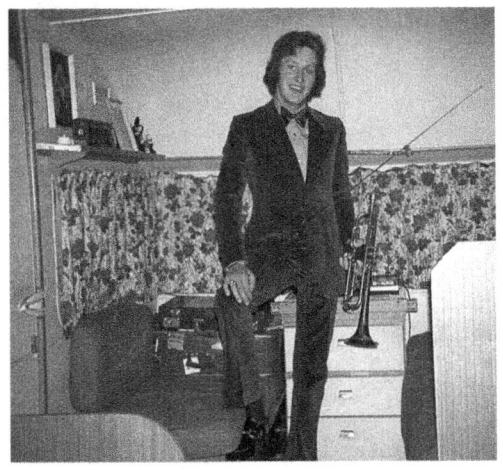

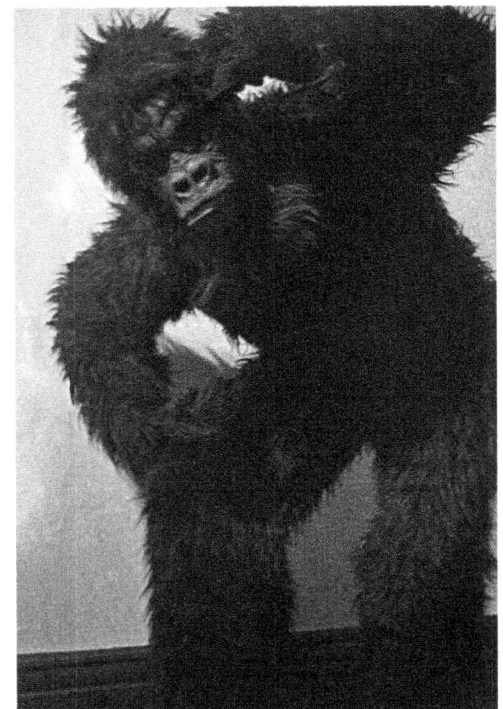

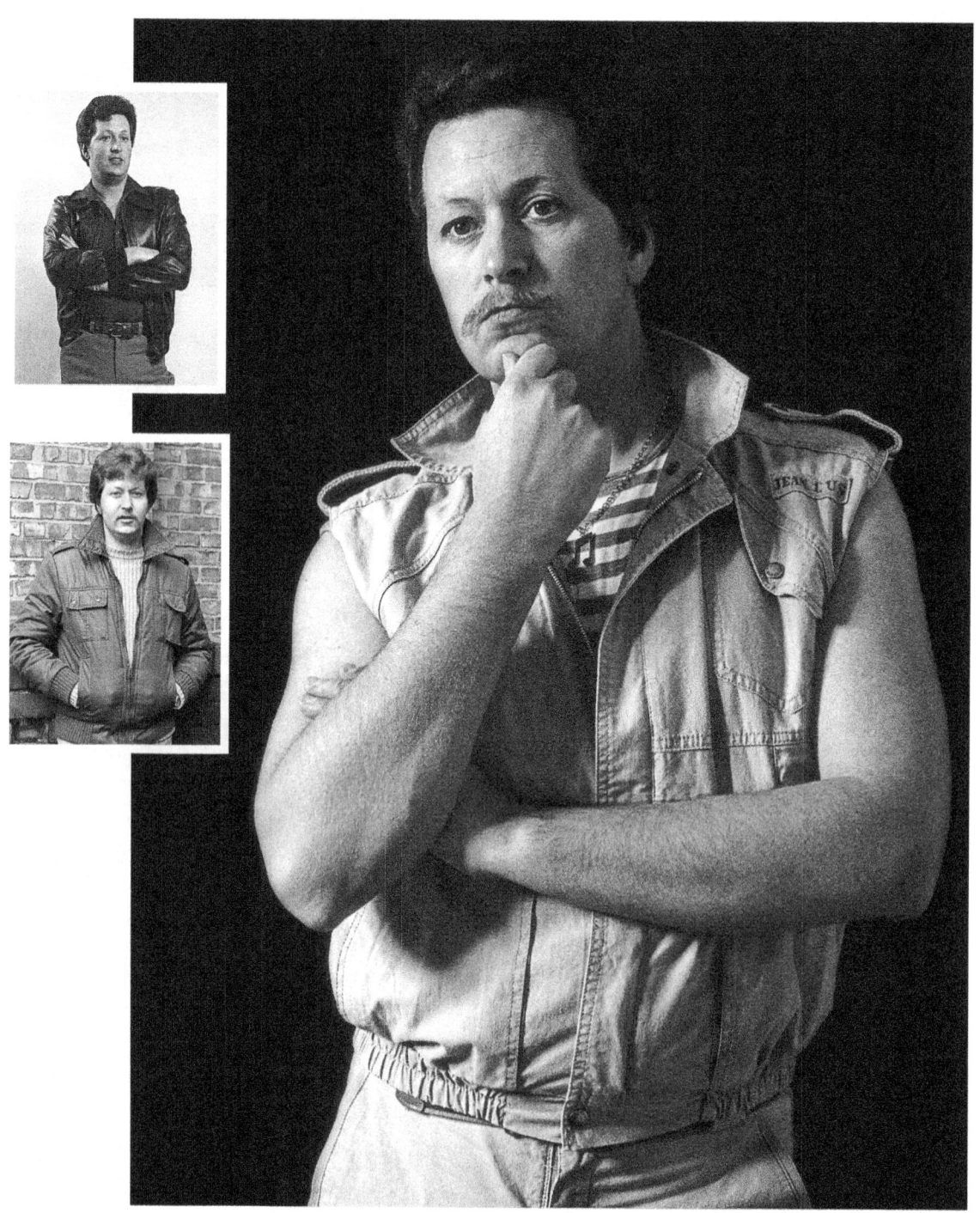

NEARLY FAMOUS

The actor in me

We would have starved then but for my Television career. Yes Ha Ha I was an actor. Fortunately I had previously become an Equity member, badgered into it by the local union rep when we set up the The Paulo Brothers act. We were encouraged at the time into bit parts and supporting artist work for Granada TV. As my singing career faded away I pursued more work through my agent Pan Artists, it would help keep the wolves from the door and eventually it helped pay for my first trips to the USA!

Acting as I did (well that's what they call it), I have met and worked with hundreds of great actors, Jeremy Irons, Michael York, Rod Steiger and the charming Jeremy Brett to name but a few.

People are always asking me, what are these stars like in person? Well, when I played the Adjutant in the multi-award winning Brideshead Revisited alongside Jeremy, we waited together between scenes, had polite conversation and he appeared quiet and friendly. Michael was courteous and amicable to pose for a picture when I asked, and Rod was beyond belief, he talked to me like we were pals. On one occasion I was trying to get his picture as he came off the set, he saw me and I thought he would be mad and I would be in trouble, he asked "are you trying to take my picture?" embarrassed I said yes, he just stopped what he was doing and posed for me!

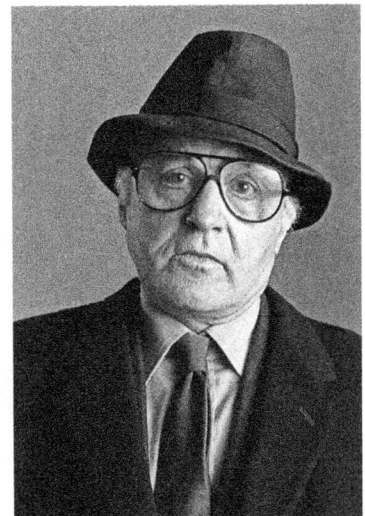

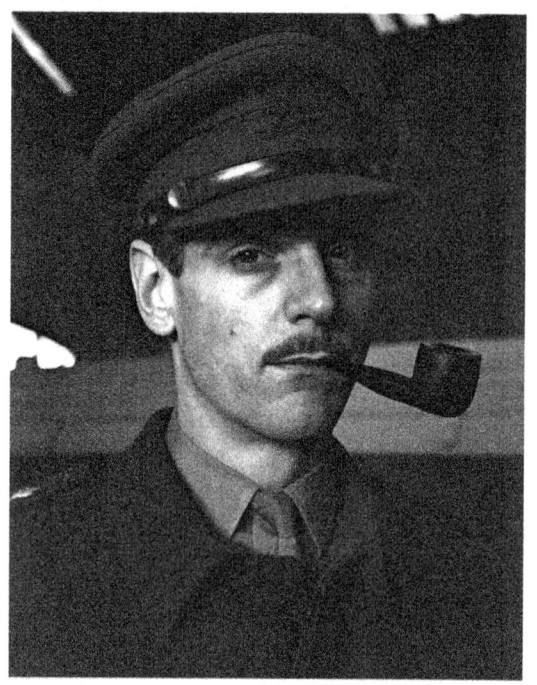

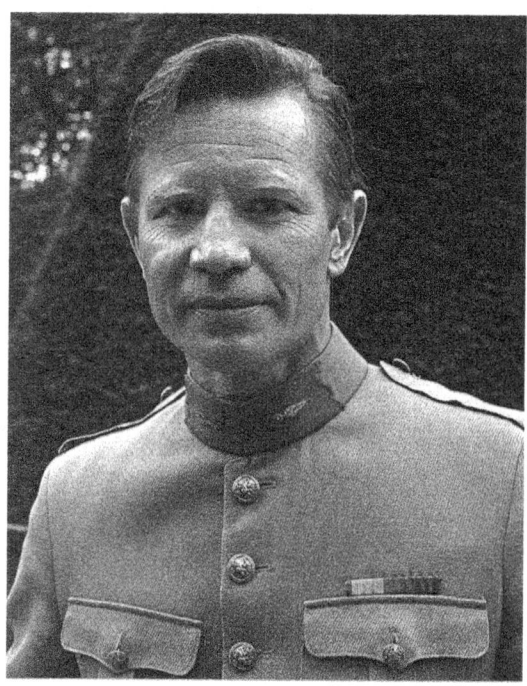

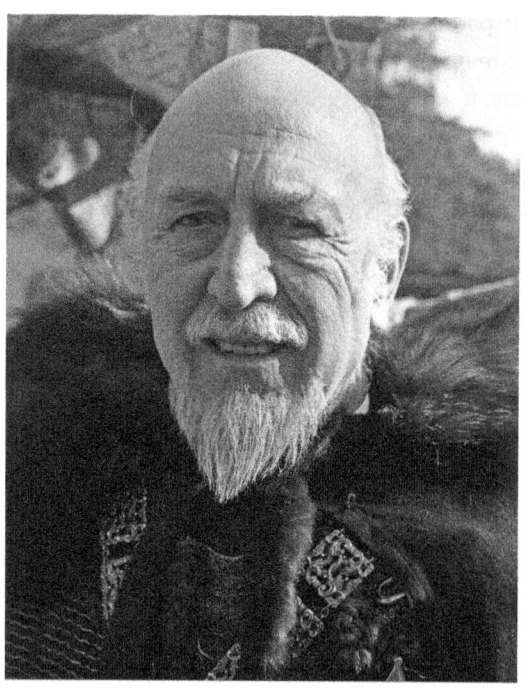

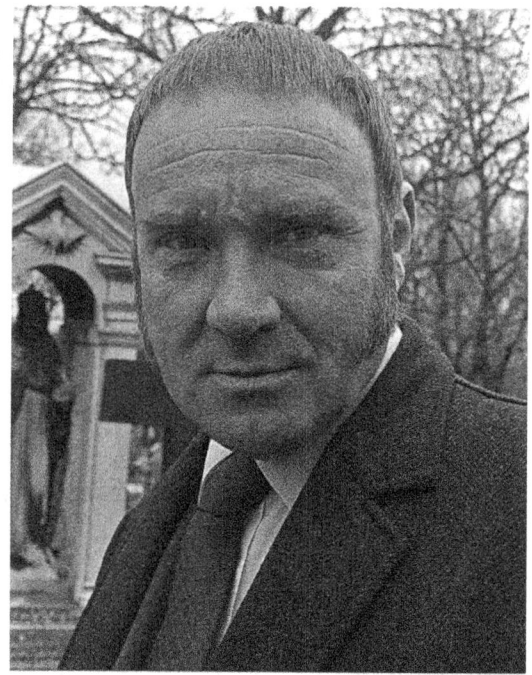

NEARLY FAMOUS

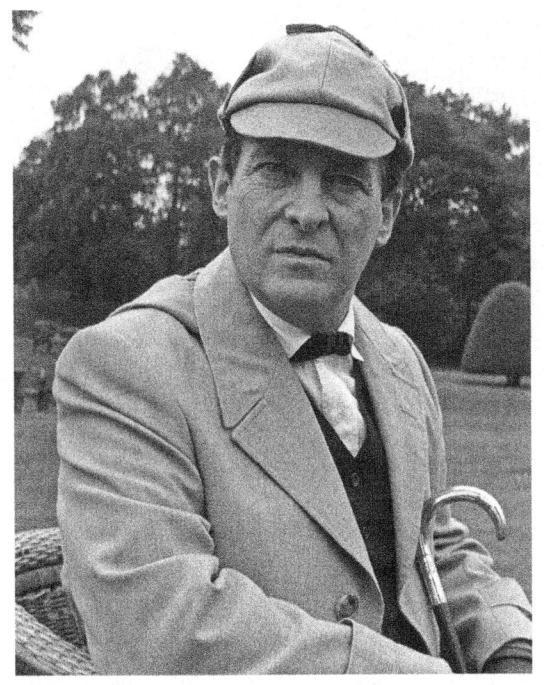
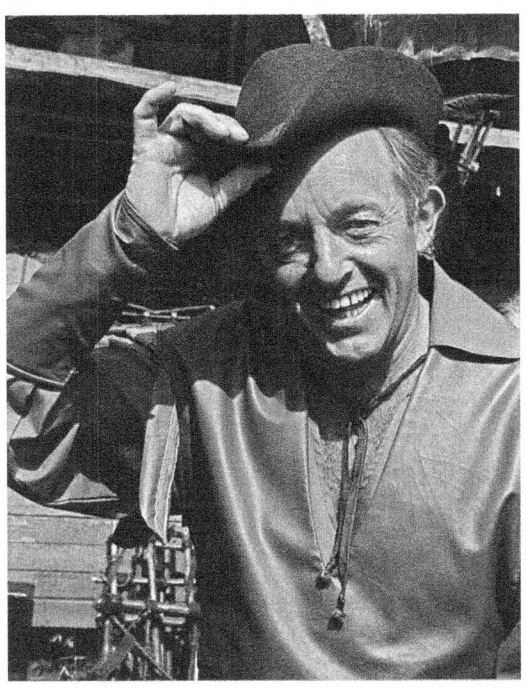
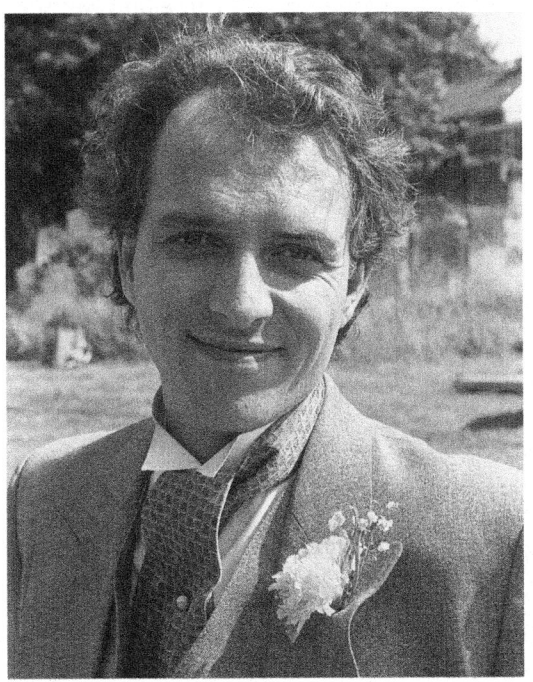
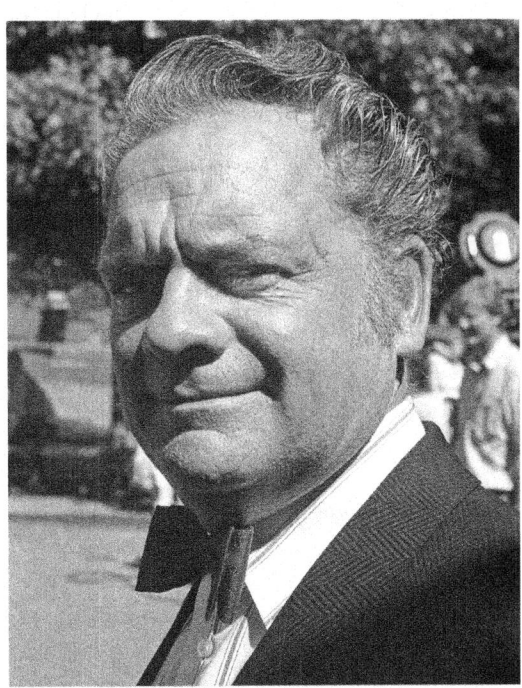

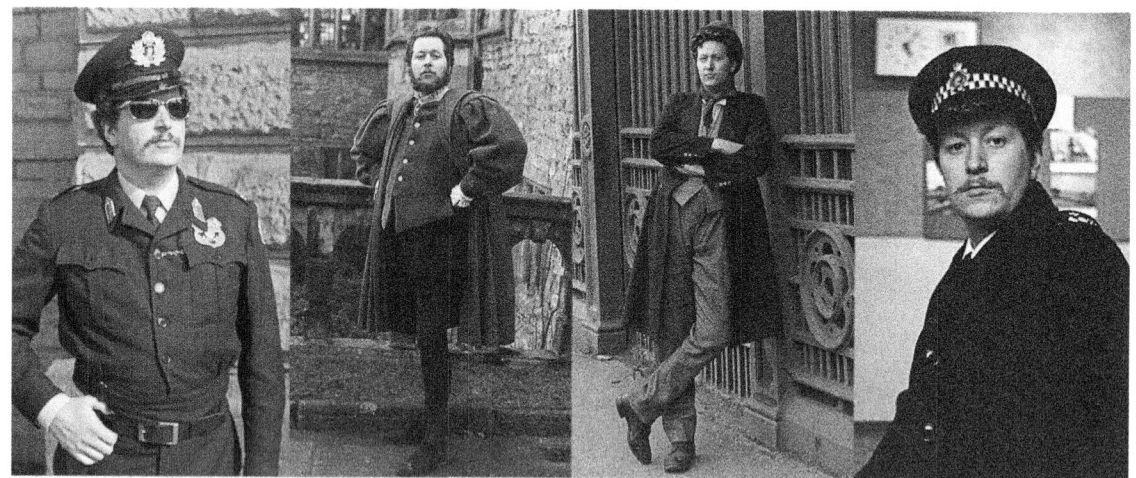

I have appeared in more television programmes than I can remember, but here are a few of the big ones, the appropriately named Hard Times, Brideshead Revisited, Spoils of War, Passage to India, Jewel in the Crown, Till We Meet Again, Sherlock Holmes, Poirot, Coronation Street, Brookside, Emmerdale farm, well pretty much all the British soap operas of the day, even my elbow was seen in Eastenders!

I was able to bring all my talents to bare, photography, horse riding, juggling and trumpet playing even my soldiering became invaluable. I was playing one nearly every week, British, German,

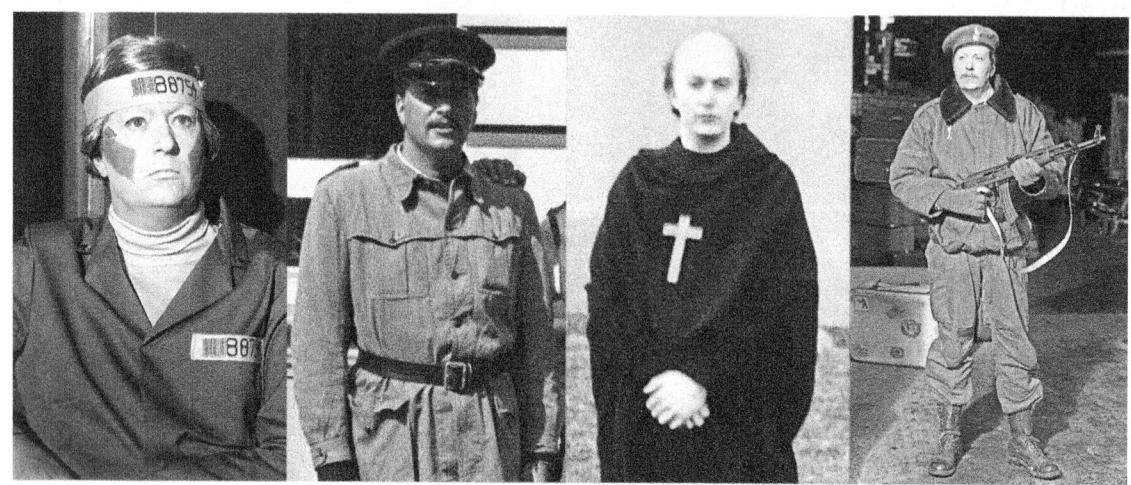

NEARLY FAMOUS

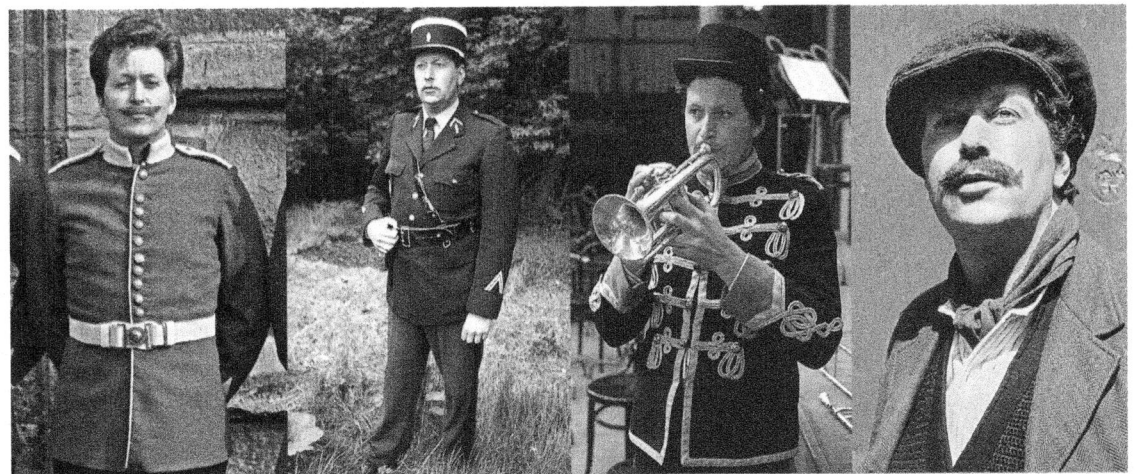

Polish and Russian, sometimes even fighting on both sides in the same episode, once I was even captured and guarded by myself!

I often hear people praise Granada TV for their period dramas, and it's no wonder. I worked as an extra, (oops sorry, they liked to be called supporting cast), on the series called Hard Times. I was up at literally the crack of dawn, an hours drive to the Manchester TV studio, into make up where I was covered in dirt and mud, not all make up! Then into wardrobe for costume, well I say costume actually it was more like a dirty ripped shirt with filthy trousers, a torn period jacket, and a bad fitting hat of the time, that was just the good news!

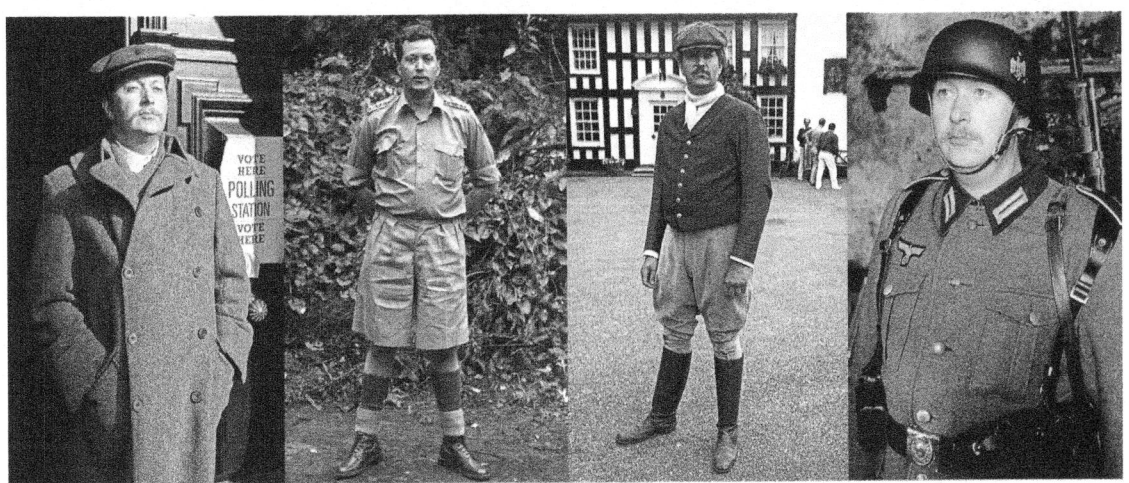

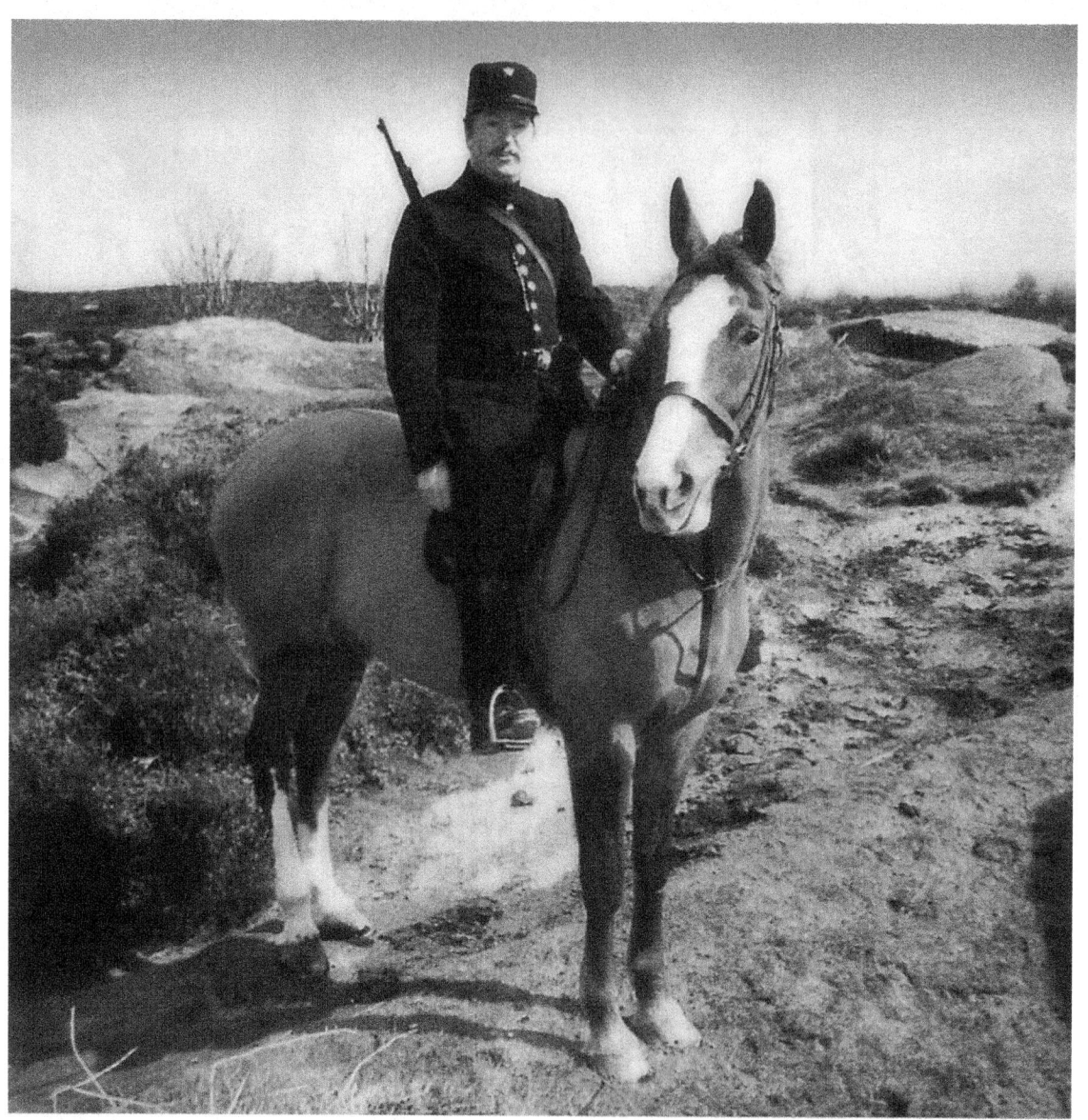

NEARLY FAMOUS

We were then sent down to the outside set in the freezing cold, it was the winter months and no thermal underwear was allowed, if seen it would have ruined the shoot. We spent all day, every day in these conditions for several weeks, come wind rain or snow, returning home every night about 10pm.

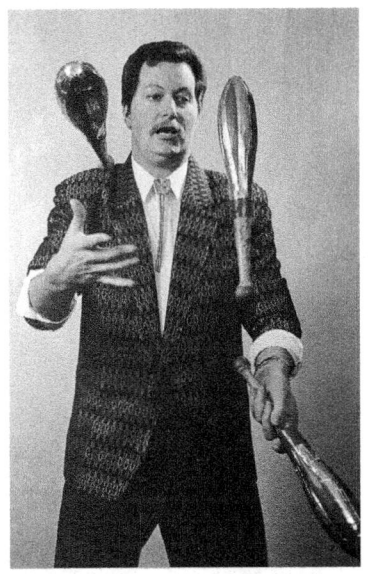

A picture from the series featuring me used to hang in the GTV studio hallway, a group of us were huddled around an old fashion fire brazier, people who saw it commented on how real it looked, well I've got news for them, it was real, we didn't act those scenes we lived them. It really was Hard Times!

Brideshead was another series I played many parts in, but as the Adjutant I was featured and even in the credits, you can also find me on Google as a listed member of the cast!

One of my favourite parts though was the solo policeman on horseback in 'Sherlock Holmes - The Hound of the Baskervilles'. They spent most of the day just shooting my scene, and for one very rare occasion I was treated like a member of the cast, well almost!

One thing is for sure, it did give me lots of opportunities to experiment on photography, another potential career I was developing, and no that's not meant to be a pun!

I thought I may have to change my career again when Granada Reports, a news channel, called up and asked me to do a three minute feature on juggling, a new craze sweeping the country. I spent the day acting the star juggler, trying to get people to try it out, even the famous Robin Cousins who was appearing at the Ice Show had a go!

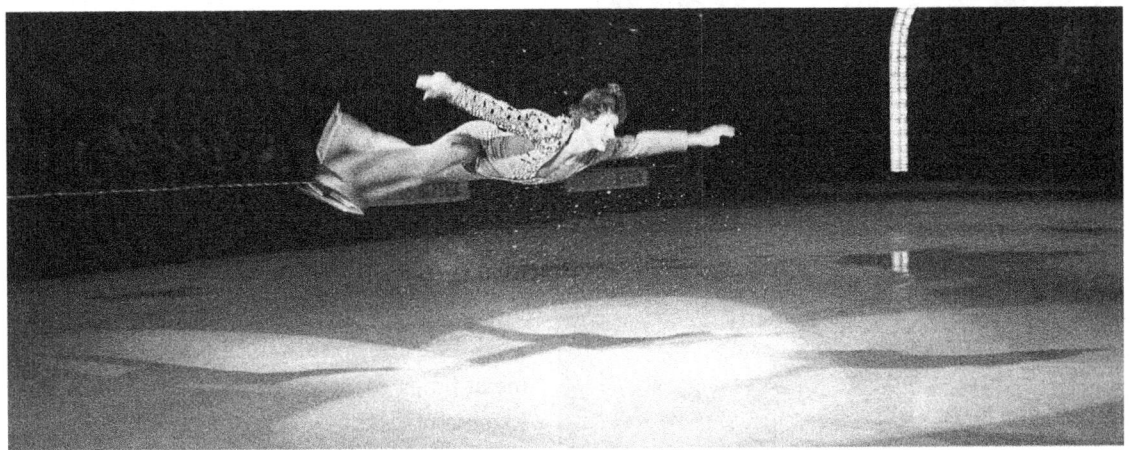

Back to photography. My mother had given me another camera, not a new one but one that was from the 'lost and found' department at the Chessington Zoo, my mother handed it in and after a year nobody collected it, so they gave it her back and she sent it to me. It coincided with a Rock 'n' Roll group I was recording in the studio and them needing some promotional pictures for their record, well I was already producing everything else, why not the photos? It became my first Portfolio, a professional shoot and a new Photographic career was born!

The band was called 'Ready Steady Go' and that's pretty much what I did. I jumped in with both feet, bought the whole shebang, darkroom enlarger, chemicals, drums and water tanks, I just started processing and printing my own Black & White prints within weeks!

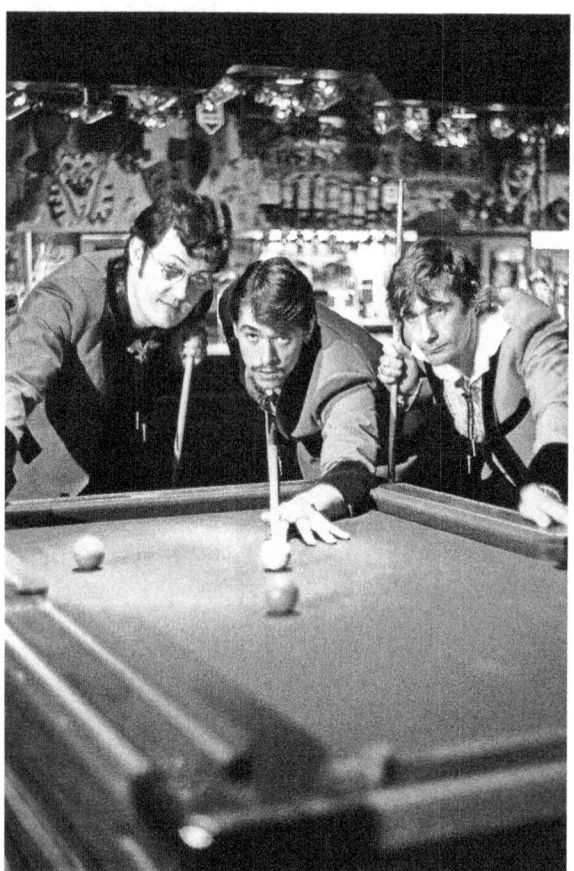

My makeshift darkroom was the bathroom, the 8 x 10 trays would sit in the bath, and a board on top would be the base for the enlarger. I would get down on my hands and knees in the dark to complete the work. If you think that sounds difficult you should have been there when I started processing colour prints and transparencies, it took three times longer and there was so many mistakes. I would spend more time in the bathroom than the rest of the house put together, just to learn more and faster.

I joined a local camera club, read books, photographed just about everything I could and experimented constantly.

Going to a college was out of the question as I had no academic qualifications to get in, plus it would have been a day course and by now I had a wife and child to support!

Having said that, it really depended on which week it was, because my wife was also supporting me at times, many, many times more than I care to remember!

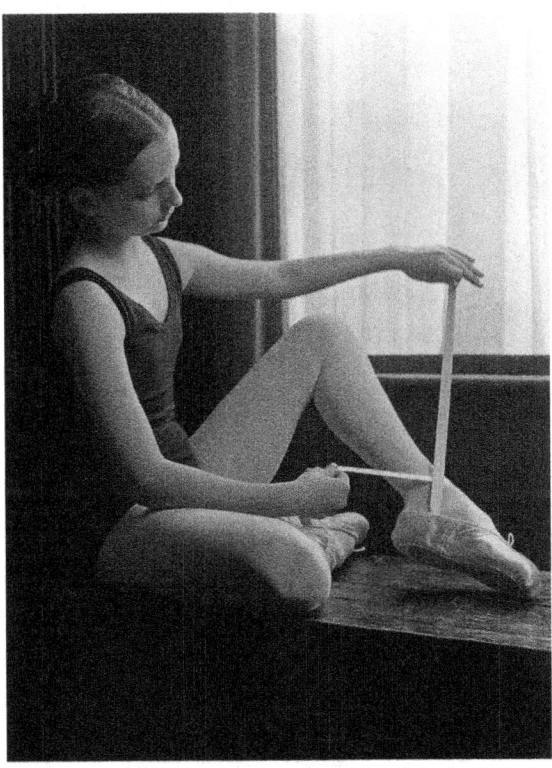
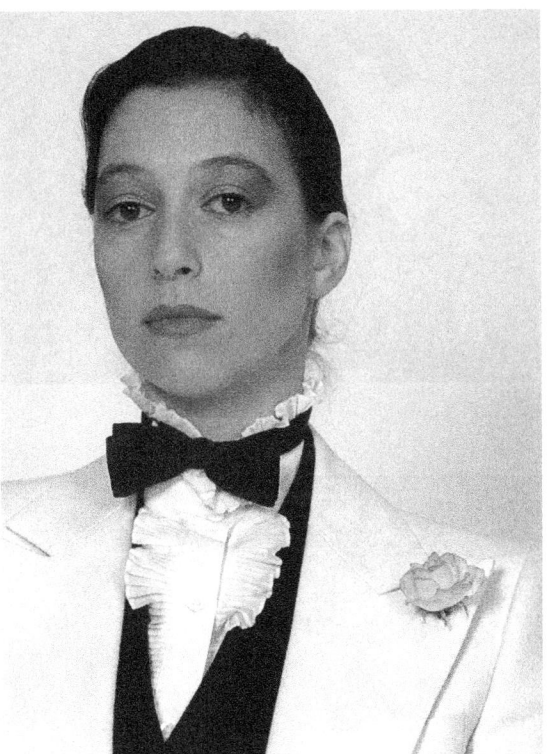

I strongly recommend camera clubs for all you enthusiasts out there, for a nominal membership fee you can learn from a wealth of talent and usually at the end of each season you get to display your photographs in an exhibition.

It encouraged me to practise my photography on a myriad of subjects, helping develop techniques I might have otherwise missed. If you have an eye for it this will usually shine through, though don't be surprised if some judges don't like your work. Over the few years I entered these competitions, I received mixed results, but did in fact win several and received many commendations. Basically it was a good learning opportunity and a confidence builder, helping me shape my (new) professional career.

I also learnt very early on that I could not pursue photography as just a hobby. It was far too expensive and if I was going to continue I would need to get paid a lot more, and often!

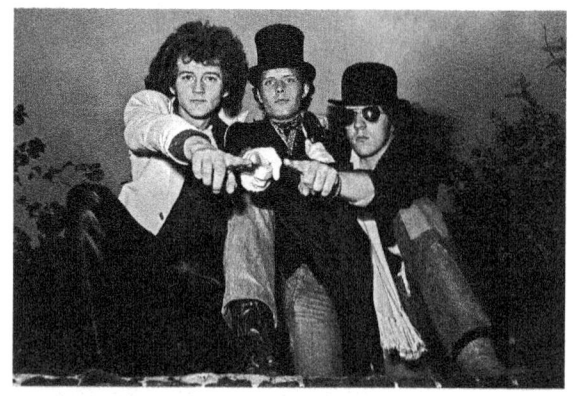

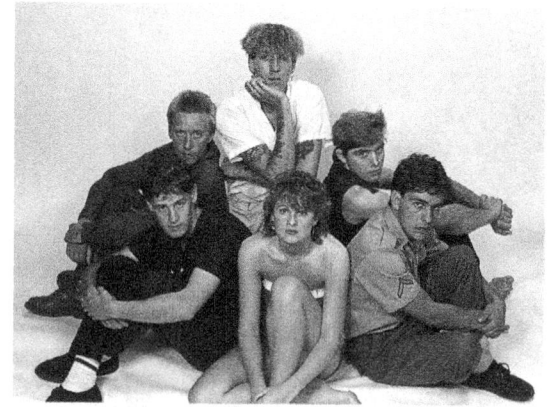

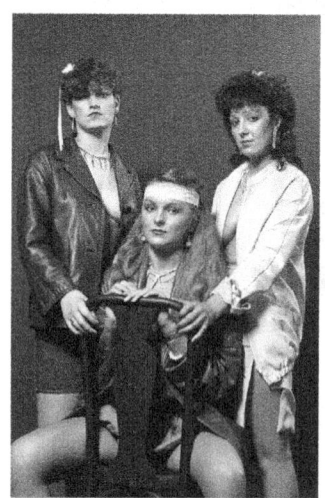

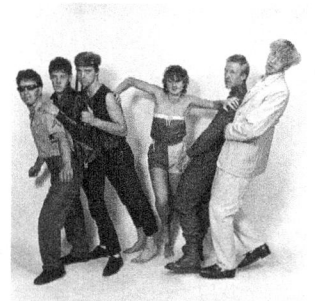

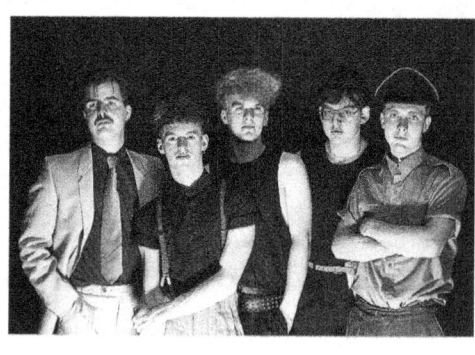

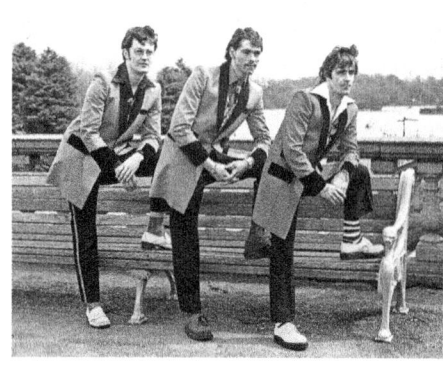

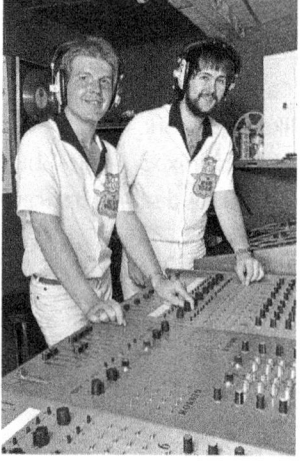

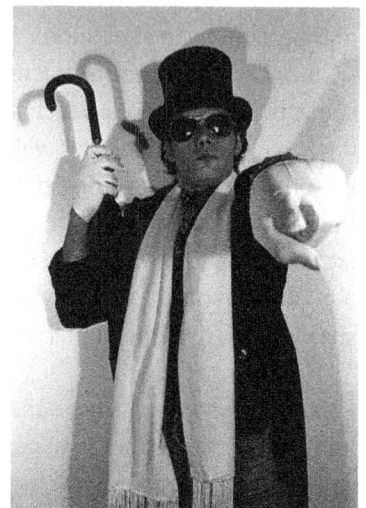

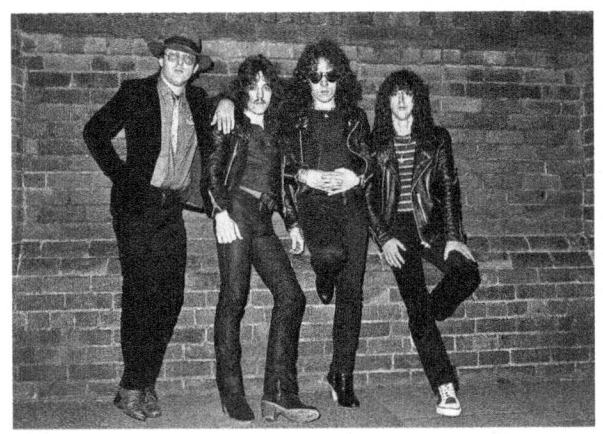
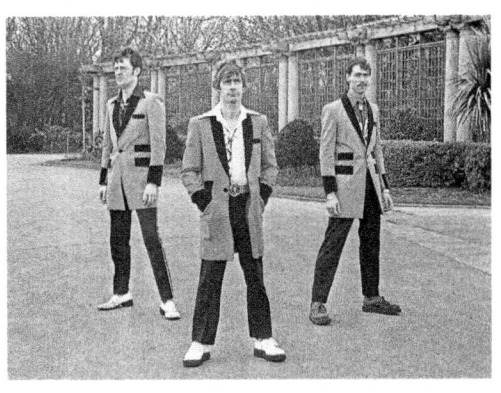
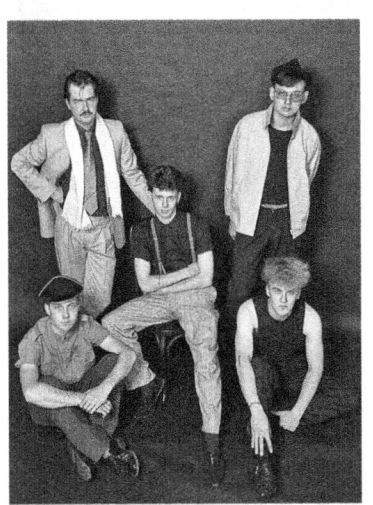
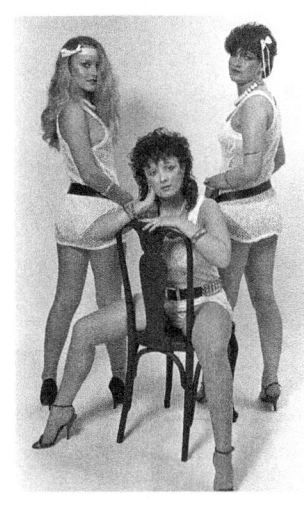
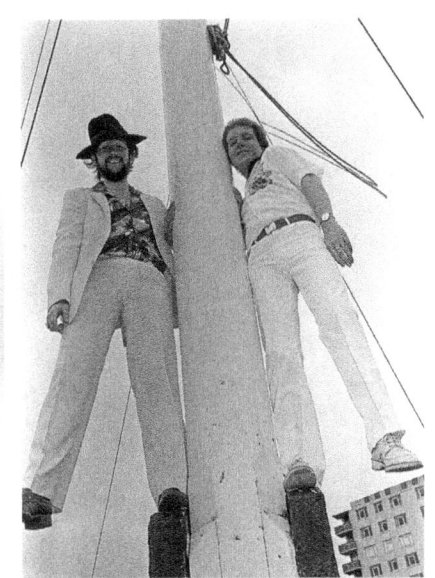
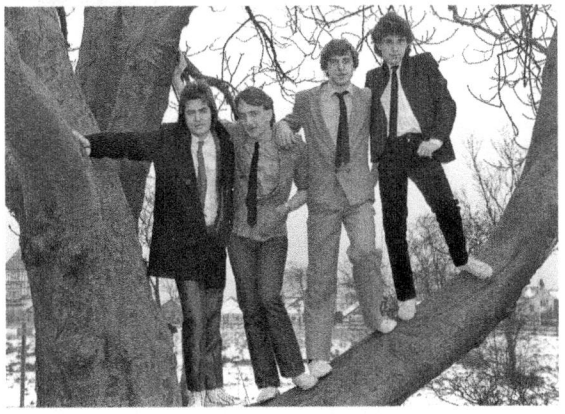
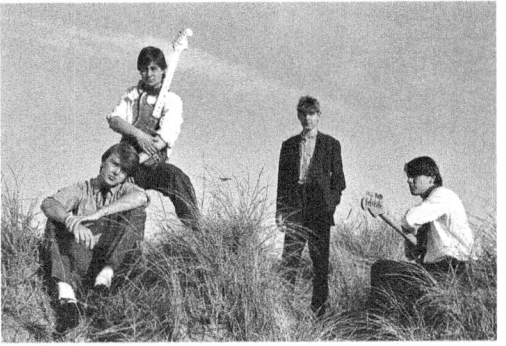

Photojournalism was obviously a key to my early success, getting a publication was an earner, most important, an endorsement and confidence builder, essential, but most of all a real buzz and it didn't matter where it was published. My first publication was two Orangutans taken at Chessington Zoo, how bizarre is that? Along with the story on how they were trying to get them to mate by showing them sex education movies, the loving couple below were published in the National Enquirer and Titbits and went on to be featured in a book called The Freelance Book, it didn't make my fortune but again it was that all important confidence booster.

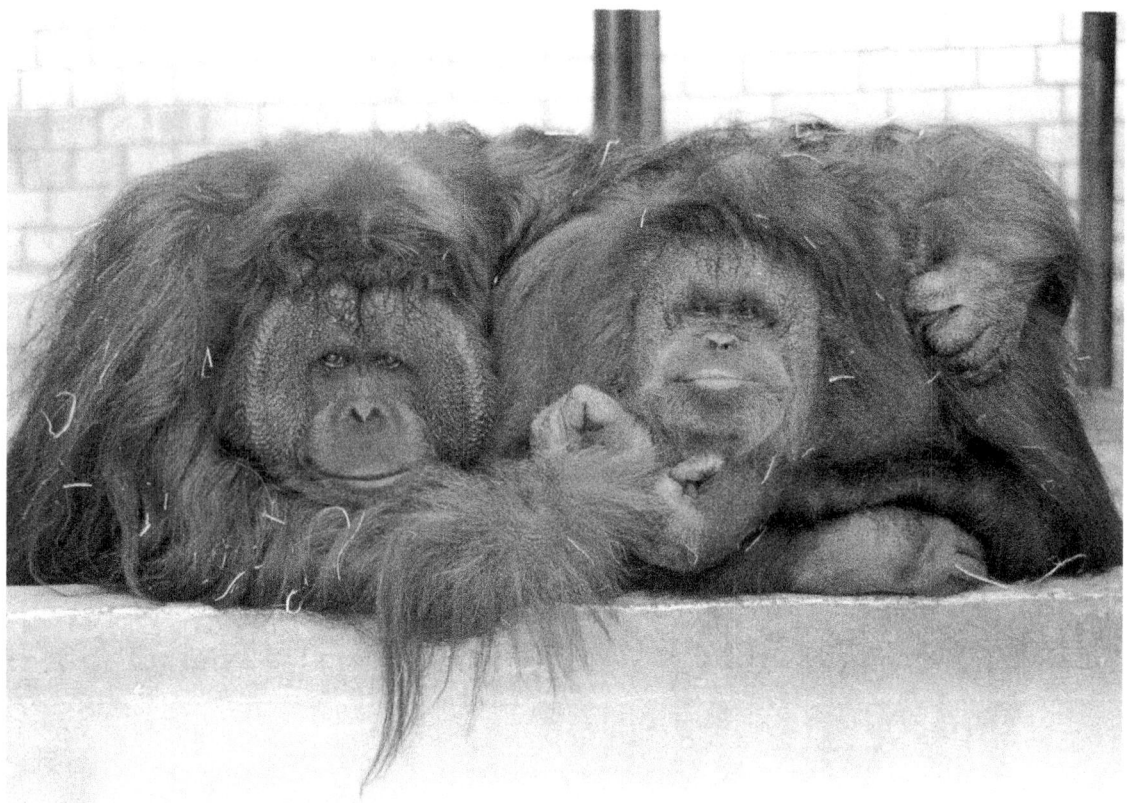

NEARLY FAMOUS

Confidence!

By now you're thinking he's mentioned confidence again and yes there it is again, but you can't understate it. Remember I had changed jobs and direction a few times by now, though I hadn't really failed at any, I was starting to wonder if I could cut it at anything. So I would count confidence as number one, along with perseverance as the key to most things in life and endurance would be a third!

I used to watch the early TV programmes on photography and it may have been there that I heard someone say, if you want to be a successful photographer you have to specialise in a subject. That was easy to say but not so easy to do, especially when all the subjects you liked already had a wealth of talented photographers doing them, or it wasn't a big enough market to earn money from your chosen subject. With a lot of photographers of the time marrying their models or perhaps having affairs with them, Glamour Photography would have been very short lived in my house and not an option, at the time it ran synonymous with a possible divorce!

"I didn't have the urge or the chutzpah to be a Paparazzi"

I didn't have the urge or the chutzpah to be a Paparazzi Photographer so I pursued various Sports instead, some of which you will see examples of later, Motor Cycle racing, Motocross, Stock Car and virtually any kind of racing except Formula 1, which, like all

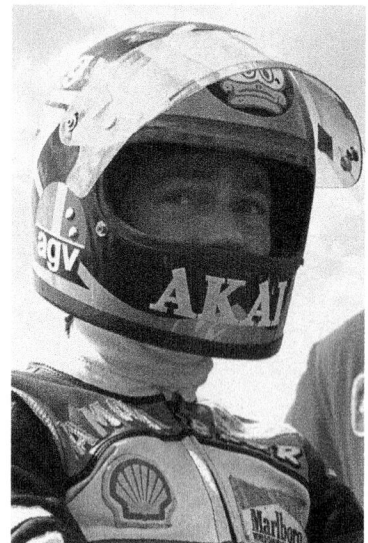

of the big events would be covered by all the top guys from sports agencies, it is pretty much a closed shop to anyone starting out, so I don't recommend them unless you are a spectator of course.

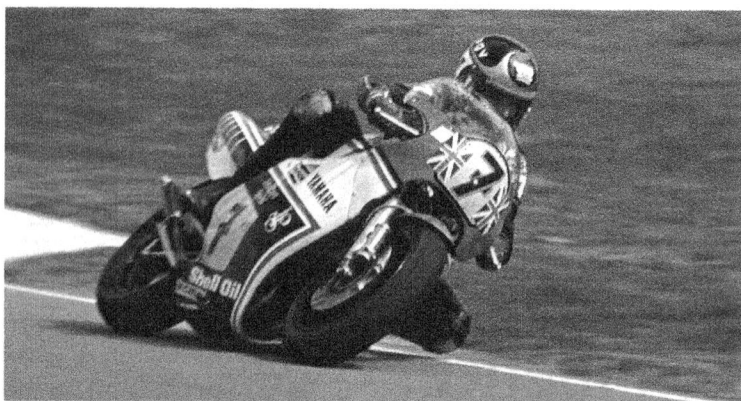

I would like to point out that I learnt very early on from experience, a lot of these sports are dangerous! One of my trips to photograph a stock car race ended in hospital, unlike the later day trips I have made to Stock car racing tracks where they put up cages to protect the spectators, the one I went to was in an open quarry. I guess we were tough in those days, obviously not tough enough. I was getting closer and closer to the track at the start of the race, I wanted an atmospheric picture of the dust created at the start, the sun would be glistening off the freshly painted car bodies as they set off for the first race of the day. The engines roared as a dozen cars lined up, the flag raised and they were off. Talk about fast, before I could press the trigger on the camera, I was hit by a flying quarry stone spun up from under a tyre. They had to stop the race to get the ambulance over, somebody shouted call the EMU, in a dazed state I thought no point in bringing animals over, I would never be able to photograph them in my state! It turned out to be the newly formed Emergency Medical Unit, as they stood over me a voice said, "I dunno, before we move him we better put some staples in", I thought STAPLES, No! Kerrchunk! Kerrchunk! and they put five staples in my head. Yes I said staples the latest thing in emergency medicine, I found out later, it was for closing wounds to prevent bleeding and scarring!

It was a good job I was only half conscious otherwise I would have passed out, You gotta laugh, well everybody else did. Now I know why they sat at the top of the quarry!

On the way to, and at, the hospital I would drift in and out of consciousness. The nurses would wake me up every hour and ask how do you feel, "Bloody awful," I replied, "you keep waking me up". It wasn't half as bad as when one of them crept up behind me and gave me a tetanus injection in my exposed parts, I assure you it wasn't just her cold hands, I nearly went through the roof!

The shocks didn't quite end there either. I know when my friends returned to my home with my hat covered in blood and said Wayne wasn't coming home, Estelle nearly collapsed, wicked sense of humour those guys!

A few weeks later I went to my local doctor's to have the staples removed. I had been given what looked like a pair of staple removers, exactly the same as you would use on paper except sterilised. I was in a room waiting and I could overhear the nurses talking, "I haven't done this before have you?", "no," came the reply, "you do it". The nurse came into my room with the staple remover in her hand and when I regained consciousness, they had been removed!

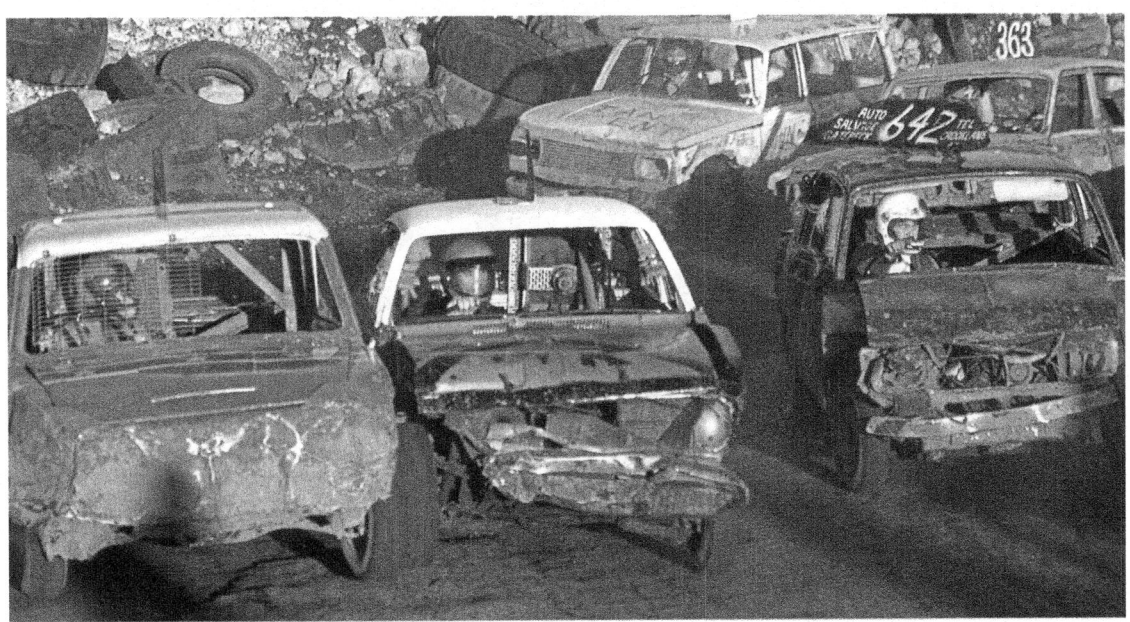

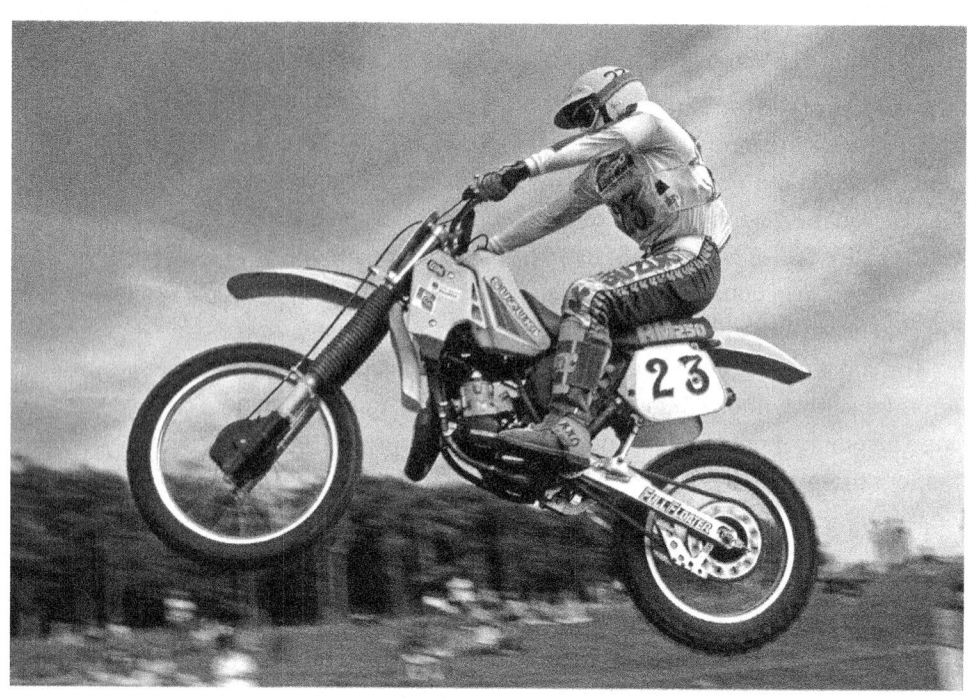

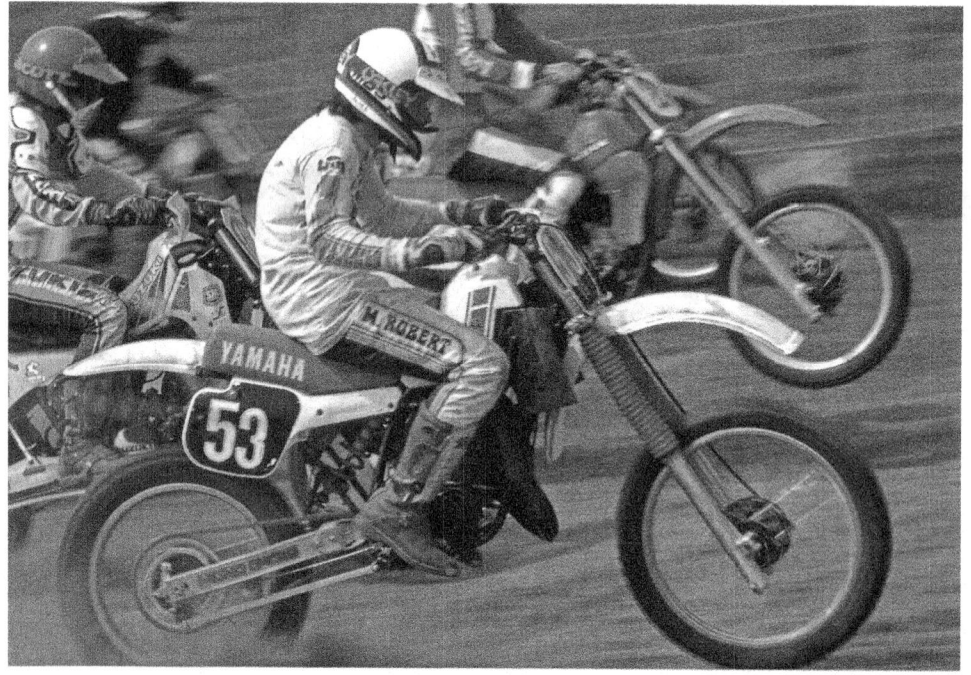

NEARLY FAMOUS

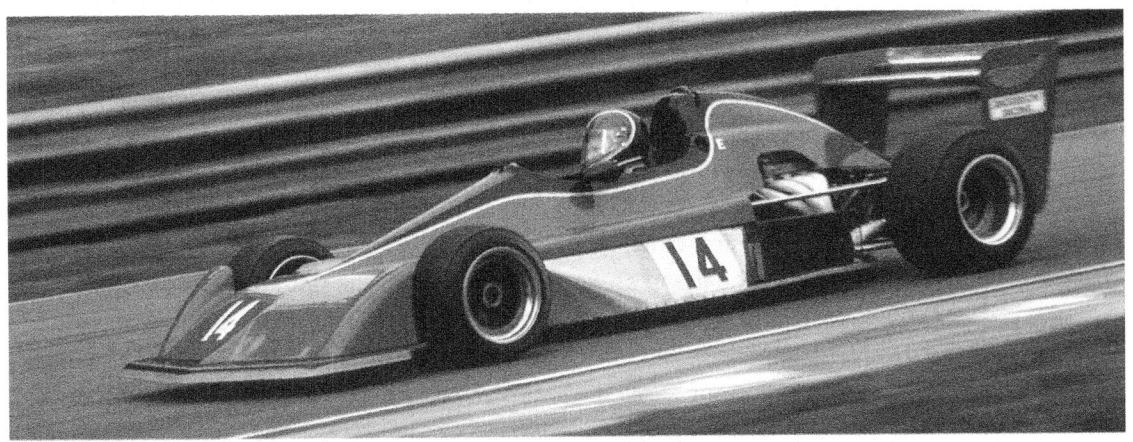

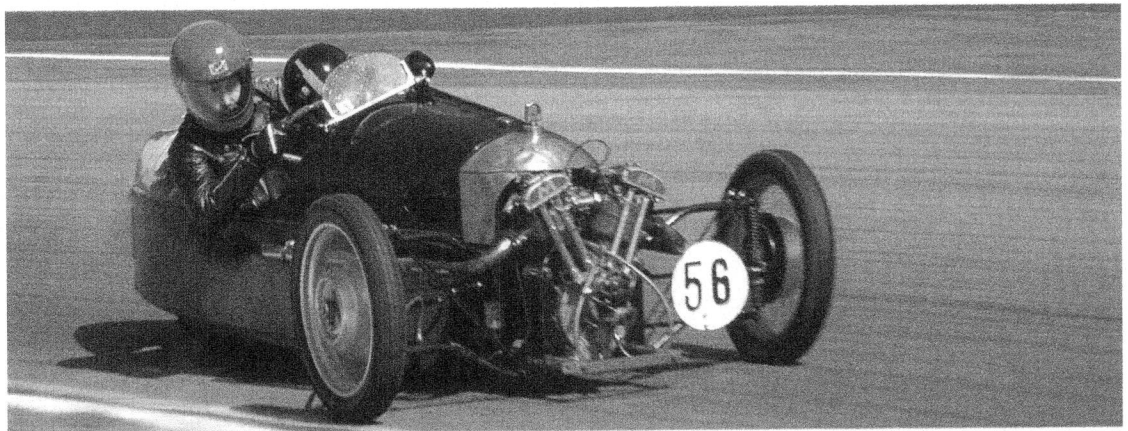

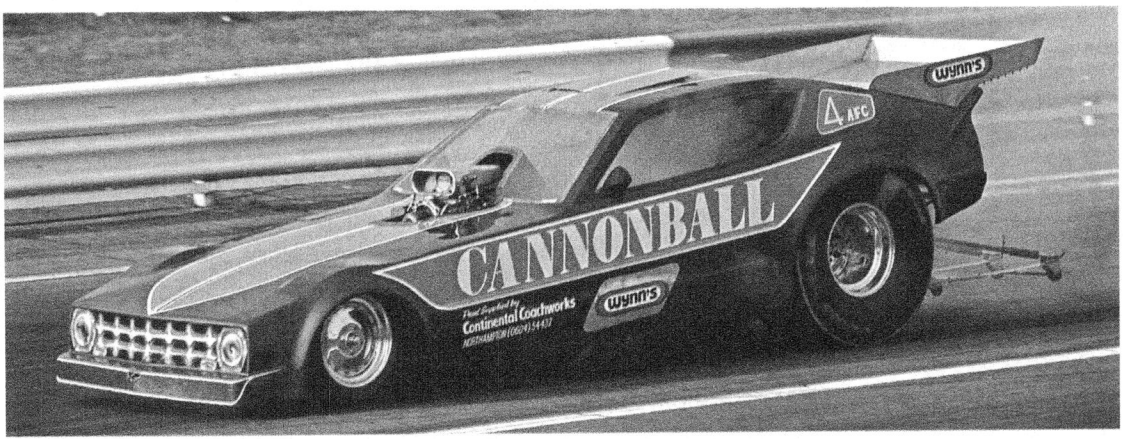

I even tried Speedboat Racing, photographing it that is. Now water sports are fine from the shore with a telephoto lens and I've done yachts and windsurfing, but without specialist equipment and in a boat following the race is something else I wouldn't recommend, not without a waterproof camera and a life jacket. I recall two hair raising occasions, the first was in a small speedboat following a race. When a race boat overturned our boat turned into the rescue boat and as we raced forward to the upturned boat I could see us being in the same condition, waves splashed over the bow and I was drenched from head to foot, including camera. Furthermore when I went to sell the exclusive picture scoop I had of the upturned boat, the owner pleaded with me not to, he wasn't insured for racing, come to think of it, I wasn't insured either!

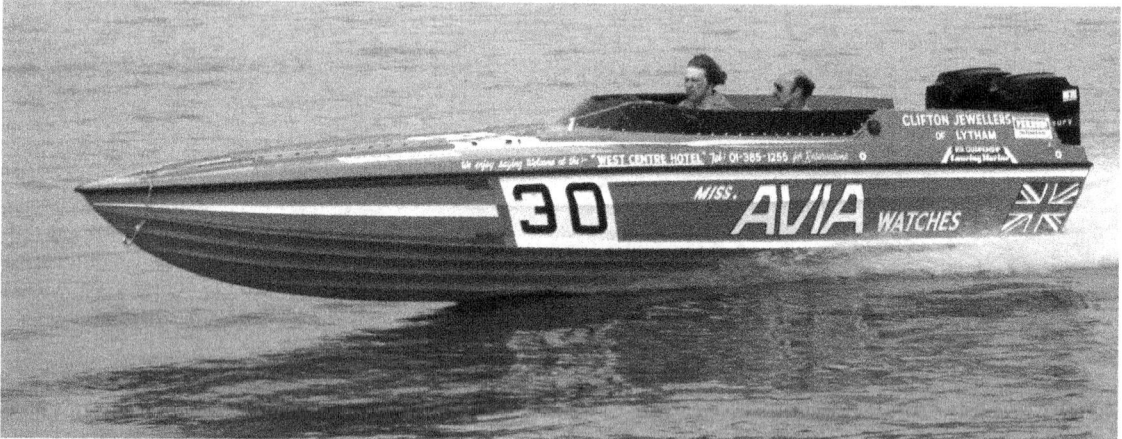

The second was the Round The World Yacht Race a few years later when they started from Cowes, England. I was working for the sponsors and invited on to their boat for the start of the race, it was all very calm and proper, Bucks Fizz, (the drink not the group), and things on a stick, I say, it was rather jolly!

Unfortunately, when the gun went off at the start, 600 motor vessels sped off too following the race. They left a rather large wake behind them, at our casual yacht like speed we were in that wake, in minutes they appeared miles away. Everyone wanted to watch from the Bow, the sharp end, so I took up a position at the blunt end of the

NEARLY FAMOUS

yacht, right on the edge, hanging on to the yardarm or something, and it was a good job too, one minute my feet were in the water and the next I was as high as the crows nest as 15 foot waves went by, at which point all my skills as a photographer went all to sea so to speak, as I hung on for dear life!

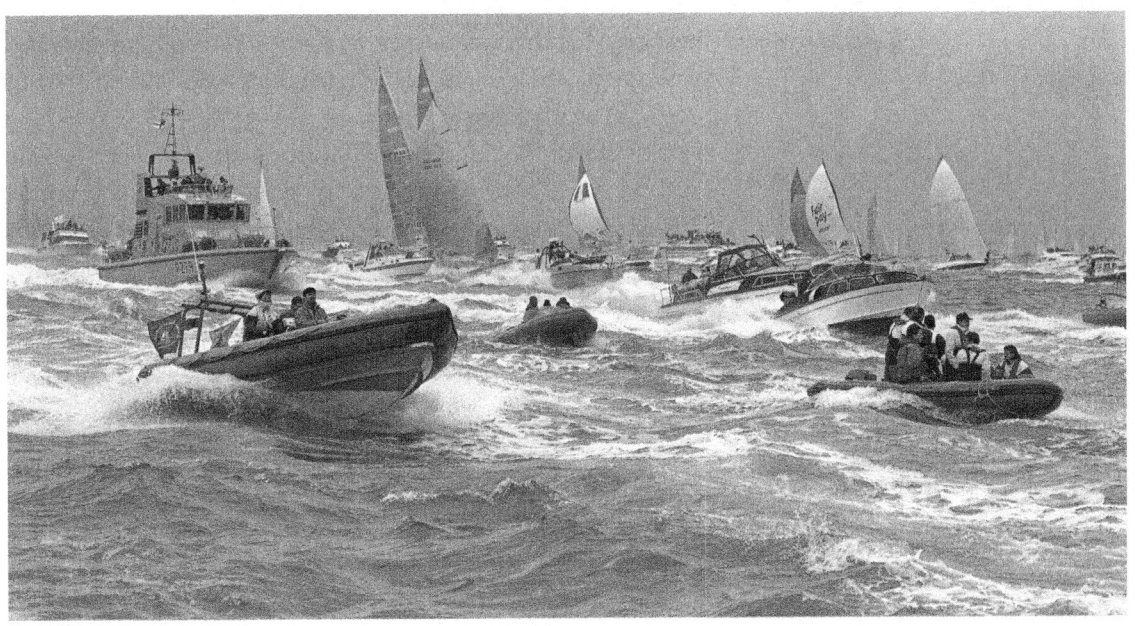

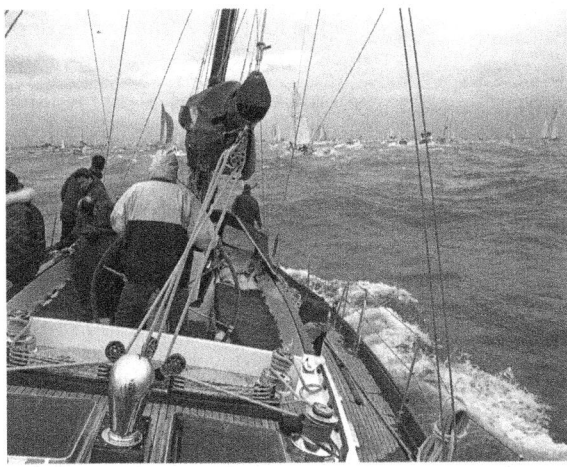

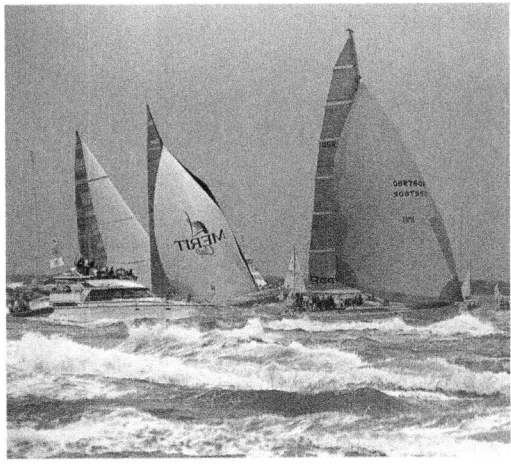

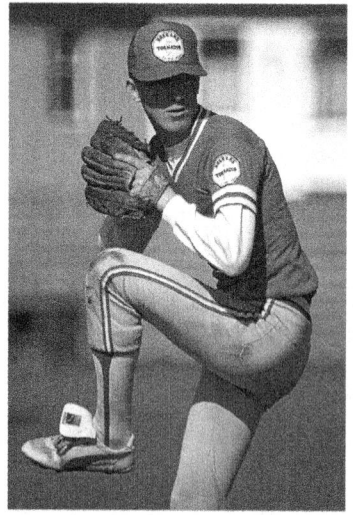

Another one of those other minor events in England I covered was Baseball, usually more people turned up to play it rather than watch it! So it was no surprise publications were going to be extremely limited and they were. A few years later on I would get to photograph some Major League Baseball games in the States, including some Baseball Hall Of Famers I think, but it didn't help me with those important early publications I needed!

Hey, I spot another theme here, Basketball, Baseball and American Football, aren't they all American sports? Not forgetting the Ice Hockey, yes I've tried them all!

I did try the British Sports, Rugby wasn't as colourful and lacking the razzmatazz, it always seemed to be played in miserable winter conditions and the smaller games were poorly supported, Rugby League back in those days was similar, though it has changed it's modern day image. Cricket, well I'm not a major fan, but to do it justice you needed long telephoto lenses, not only were my lenses out of range, the long and fast telephoto lenses were way out of my affordable price range!

That leaves me with Football British style, Soccer, yes I managed to get into a few Premier League games, but you might as well have worked on Mars, if you didn't work for a newspaper or news agency, it was all pretty well stitched up, pretty much a closed shop, though

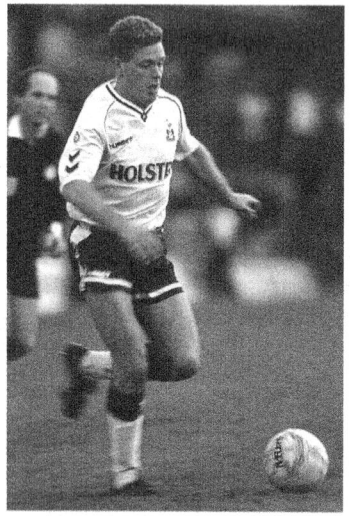
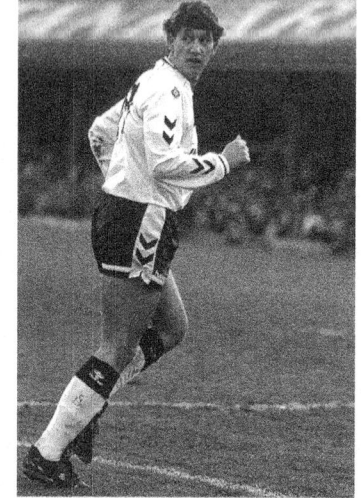

legally they would not admit to it. I turned up at my first Premier League football game, at the door they asked what I wanted, and when I said I was a professional freelance photographer wanting to cover the game, I was just about to get turned away, when I asked, is this a closed shop? It was at a time that the Unions were having problems creating closed shops. The guy said just a minute and went away, he came back a few minutes later and invited me into the photographers press room, and said have a cup of tea, where I spent an uncomfortable wait for the game to start, as the other photographers talked about me behind my back all wondering

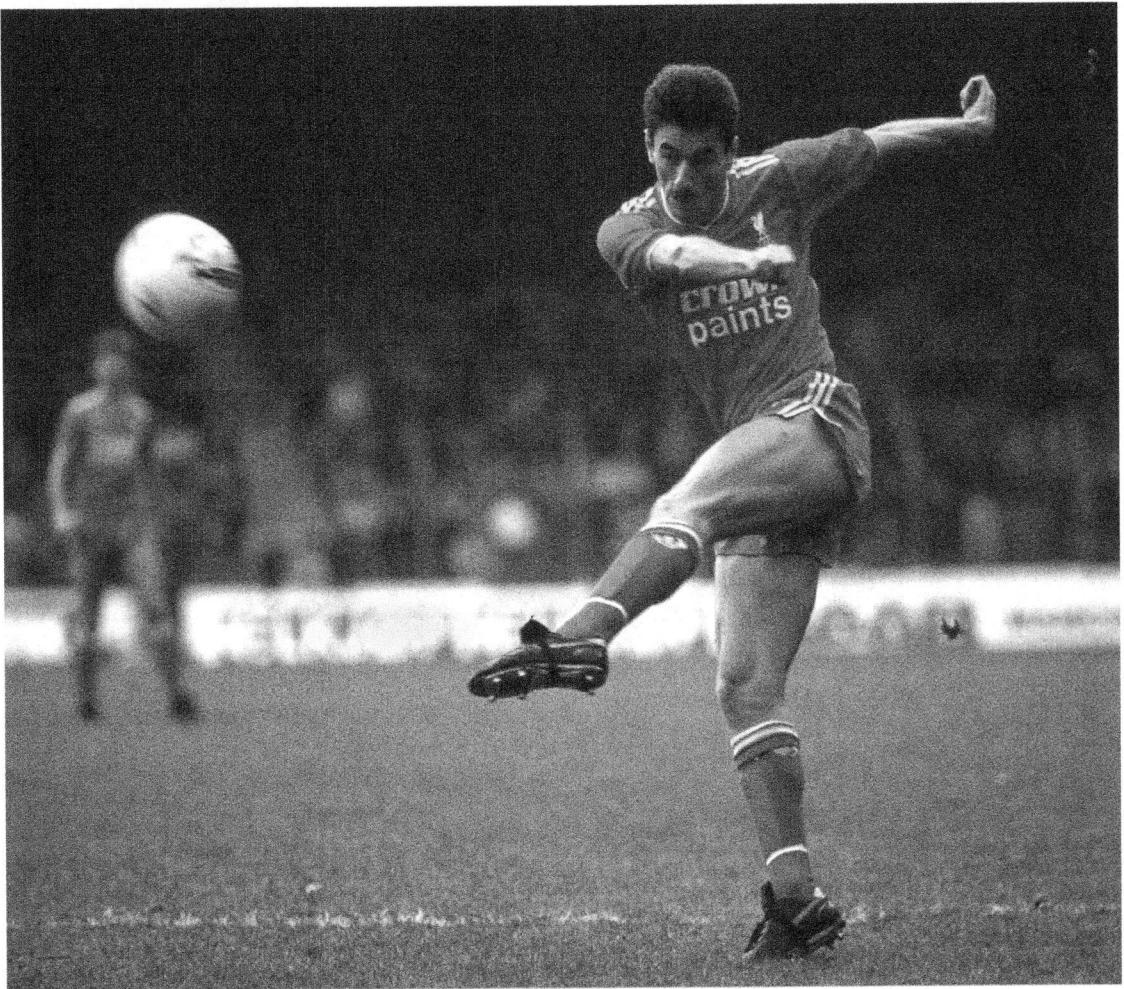

how I got in and who was I working for. I tried about a half dozen games but decided I just didn't like sitting behind the goal waiting for a 1-0 score, and if it was at the other end of the field you missed it, there was just something lacking, very little friendship, plus the overall atmosphere at the games, that and the worry my car might be trashed by hooligans by the time I returned to the car park.

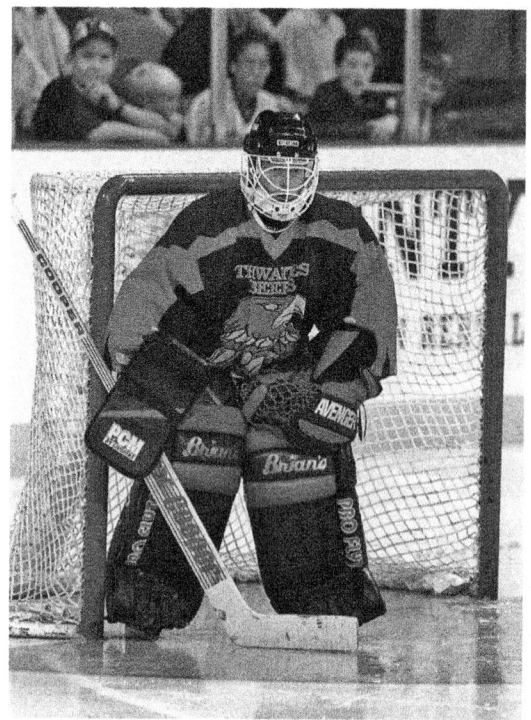

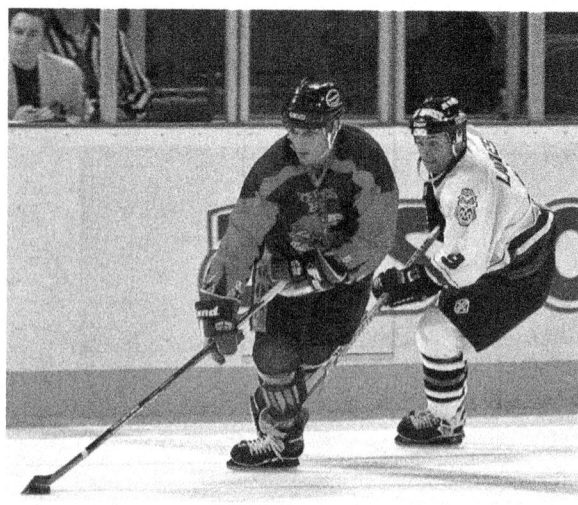

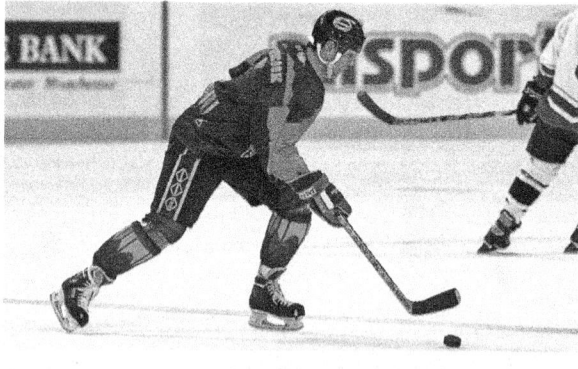

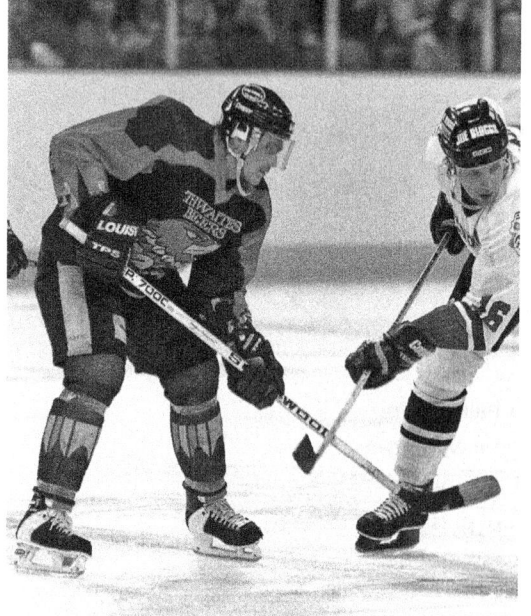

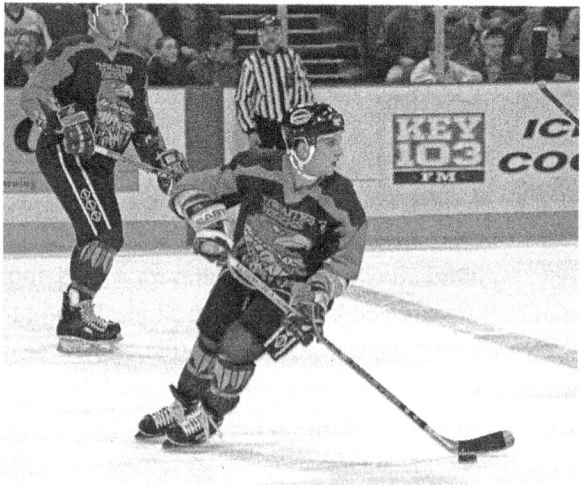

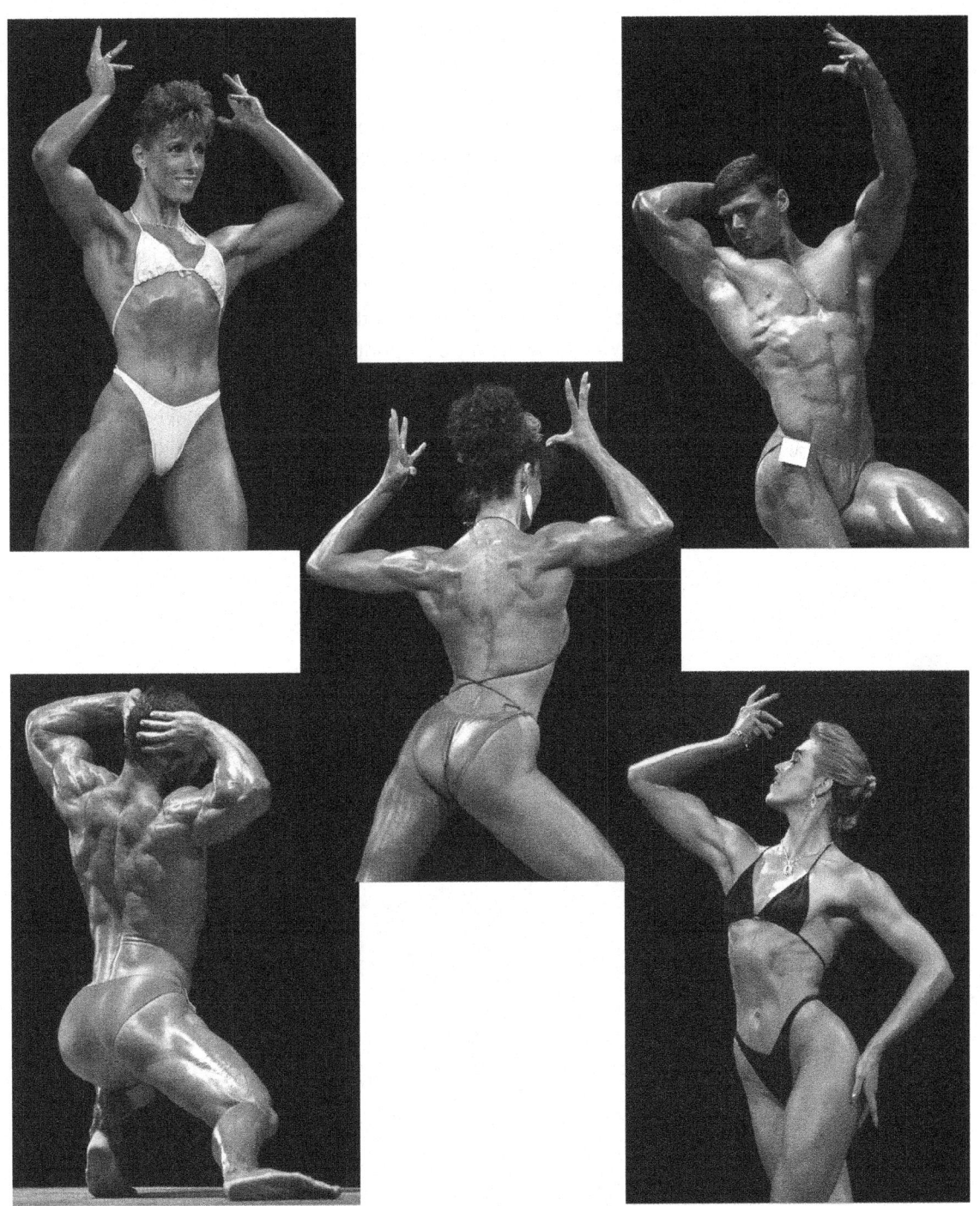

I was definitely born the wrong side of the pond when it comes to sports. In 1984 I went to an American Football game in Fleetwood England between the Northampton Stormbringers and a local team the Fylde Falcons, it didn't seem much at the time but I enjoyed the sport. I knew there was a dedicated magazine on American Football which had a section on the British Gridiron game, there didn't seem to be much press interest at the event, especially not by national papers and very little from the local photographers, so I decided to cover the Falcons games the following season. The publications were slow at first (about one a month), but I could shoot it cheaply on Black & White film, do my own prints in my bathroom and travel with the team on the bus to the away games, of course I had to pay my fare, about £3 ($5) but then so did all the team, it was an amateur league and that was the way it worked. You could say I paid my way for the first two years, but in return I learnt the sport and the technique to photograph it, gradually perseverance paid off and I started to get regular publications to pay for my travel.

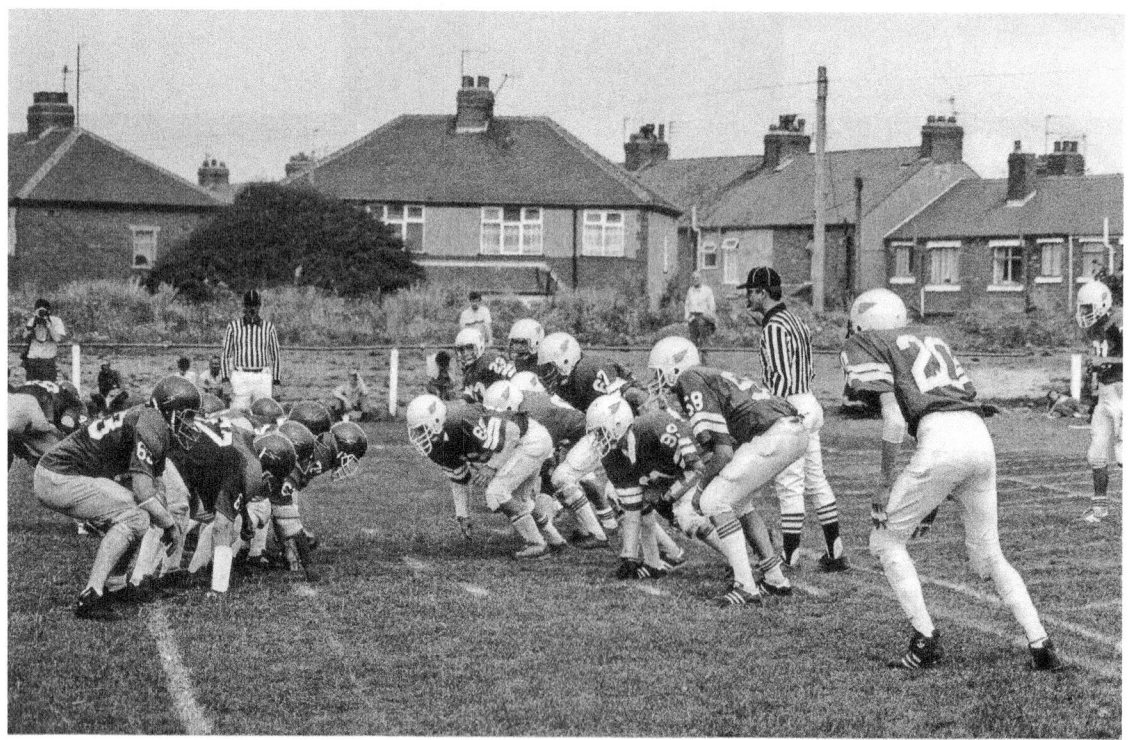

NEARLY FAMOUS

Actually, Basketball photography was one of my early successes. I was pretty good at it if I say so myself, not surprising I guess, it was the only sport I actually played seriously and was reasonably good at for a short period in my life, you get much better results from your photography, if you understand the sport you are taking pictures of. I thought it was going to be my number one sport. Looking back I was surprised to see I photographed the British game for over ten years. I guess it was because it was my favourite sport at the time and there were a half dozen teams near me in the North West of England.

I have only covered a couple of the professional American teams and one of those games was on British soil featuring the Orlando Magic v Atlanta Hawks, in the days when Shaquille O'Neal played for them, but as everyone will know, in England it is not a major event and there just wasn't enough outlets for publications, there certainly wasn't enough to earn a living off. So I had to keep trying other events.

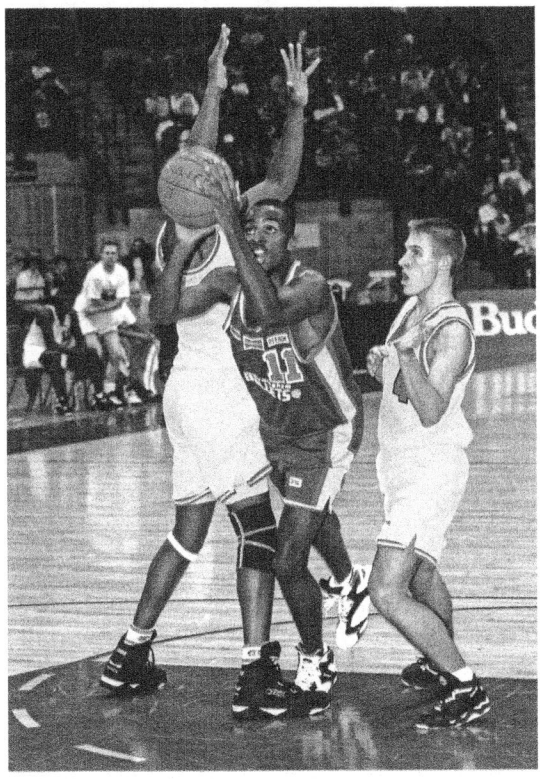
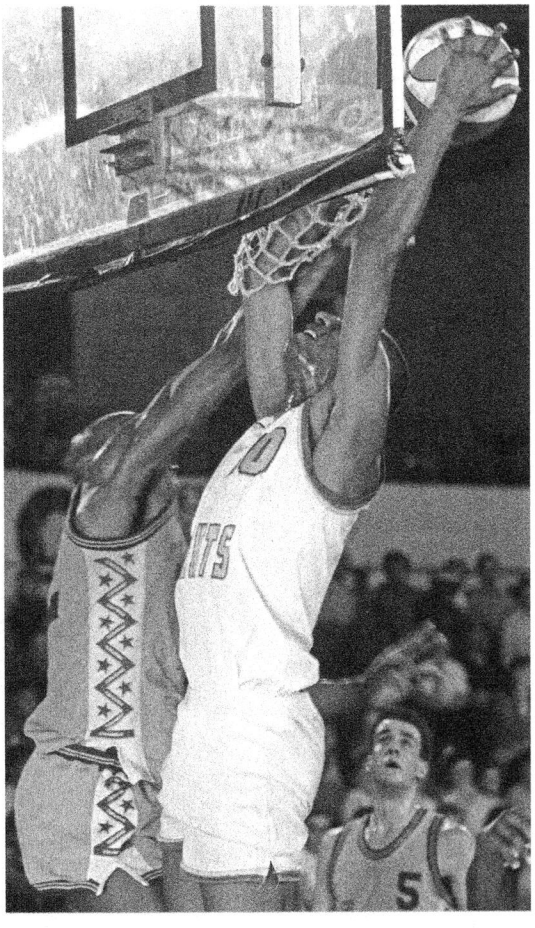

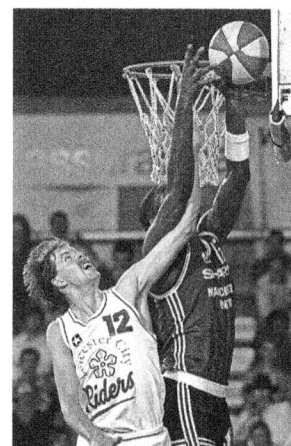

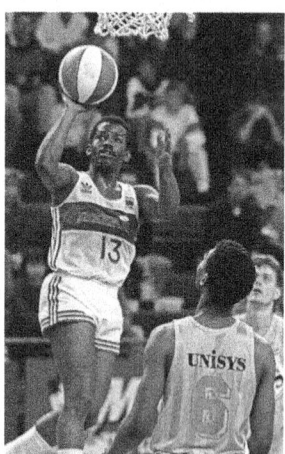

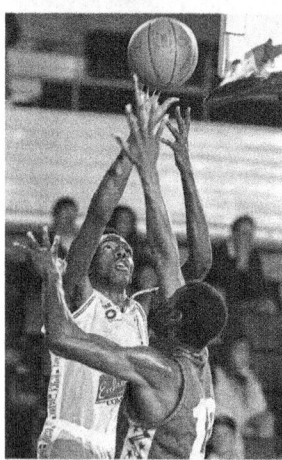

NEARLY FAMOUS

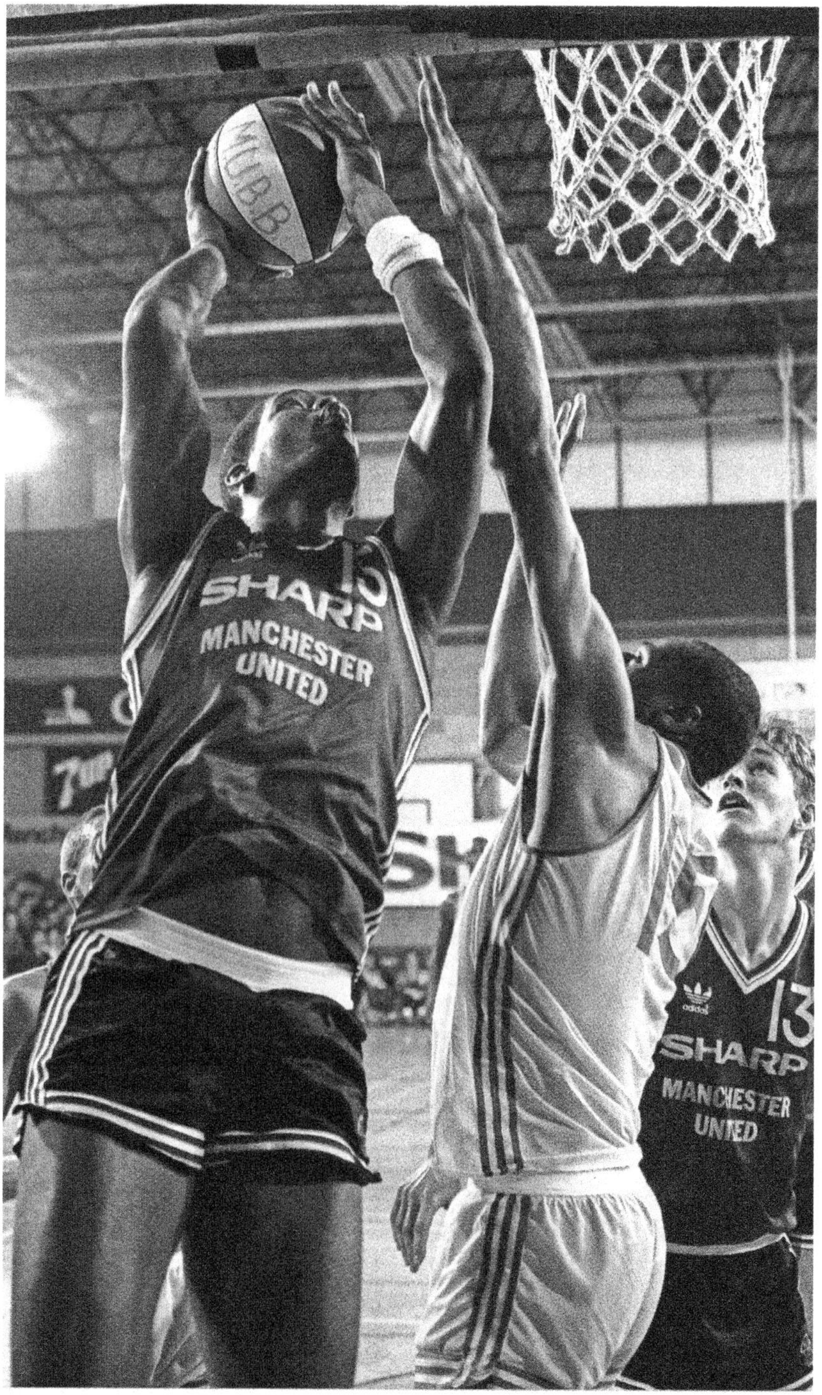

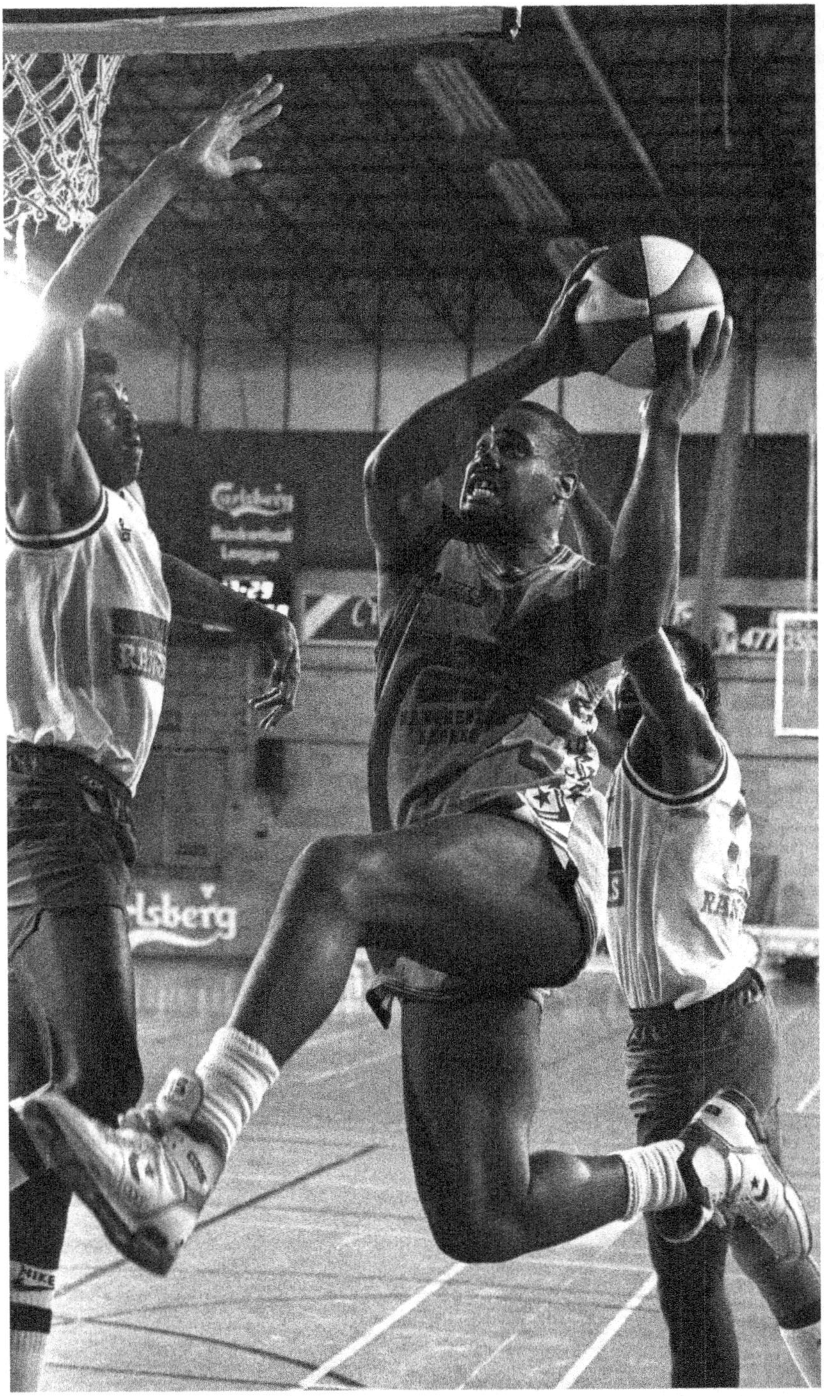

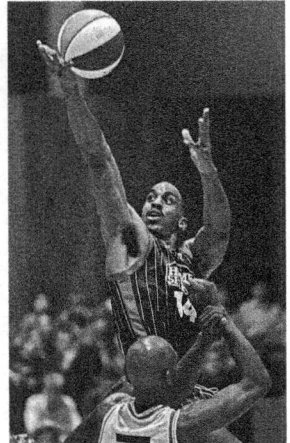

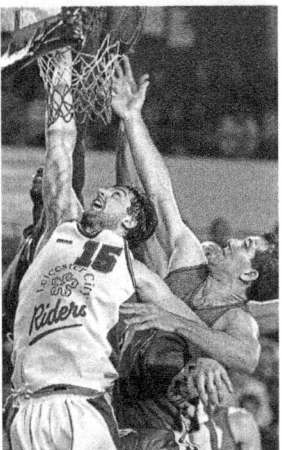

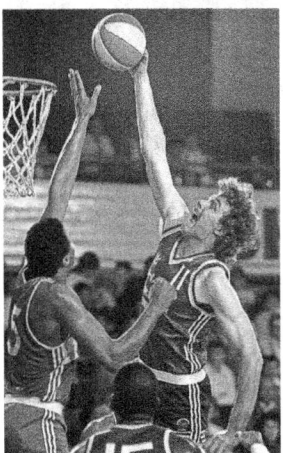

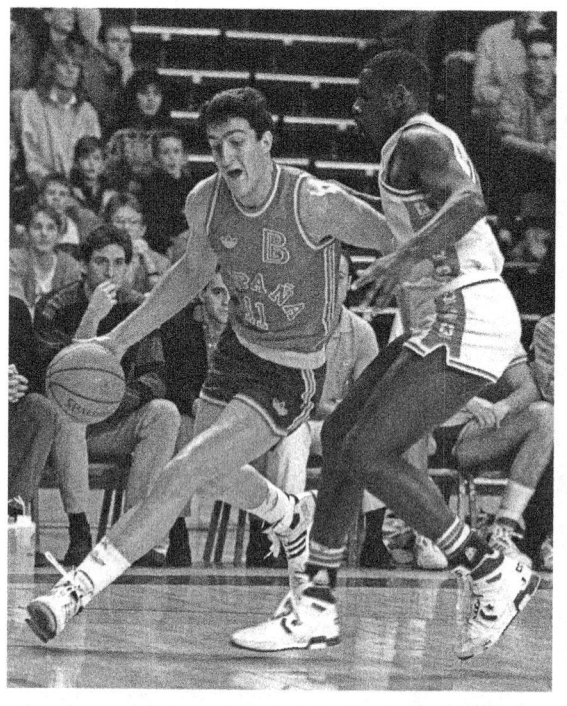 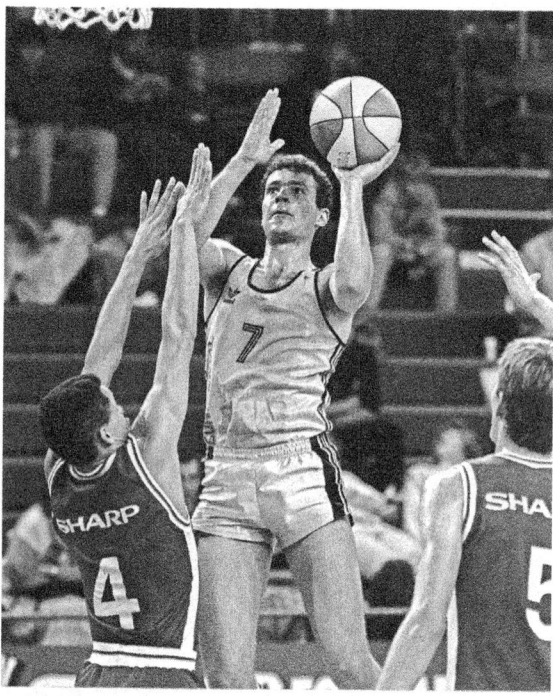

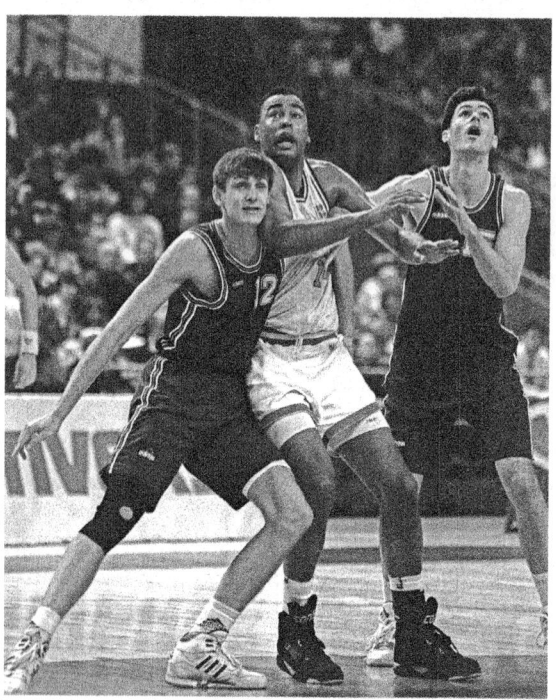 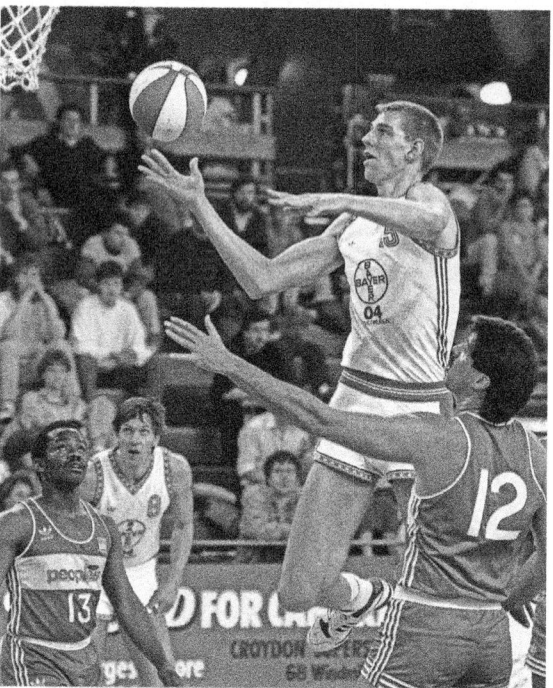

NEARLY FAMOUS

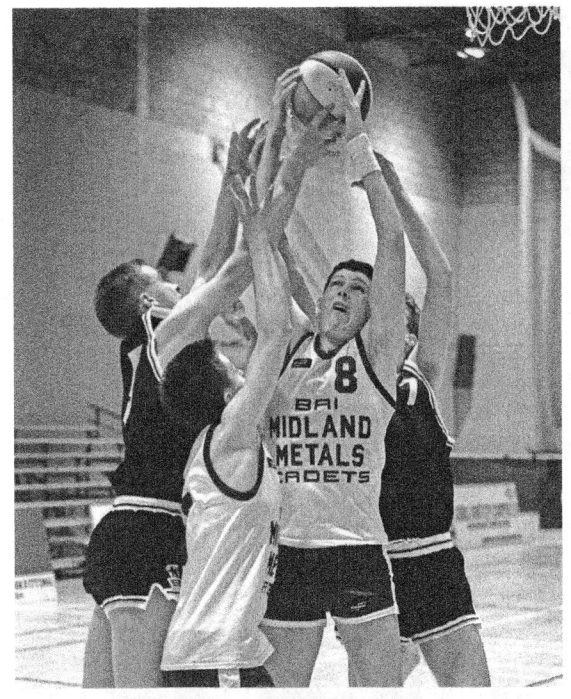
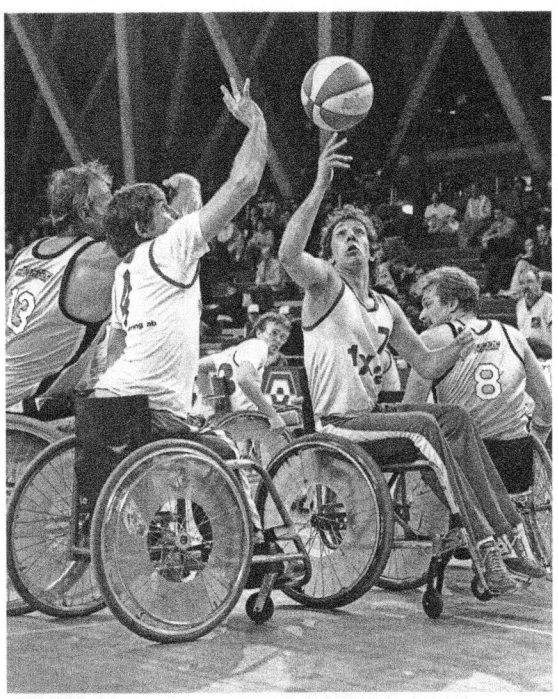
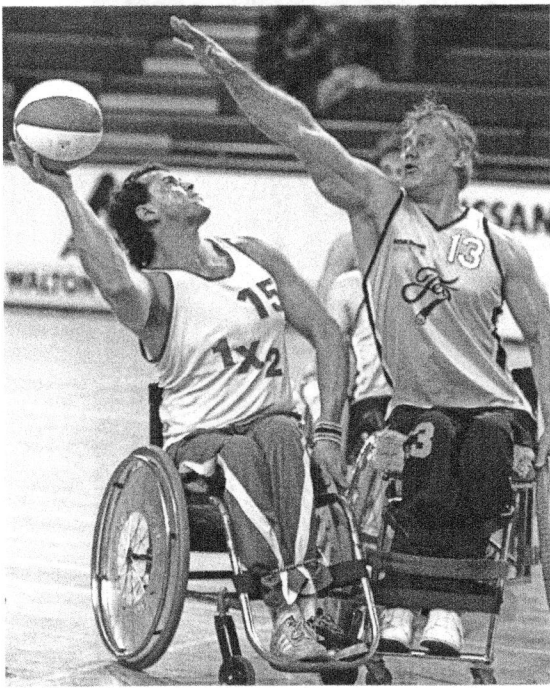
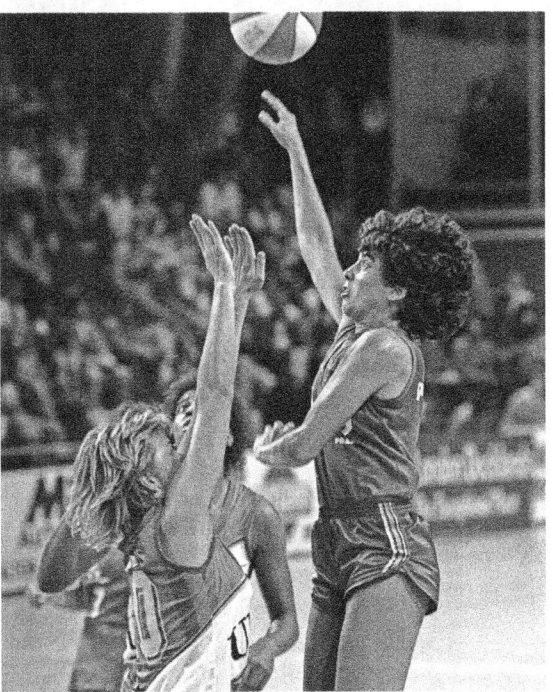

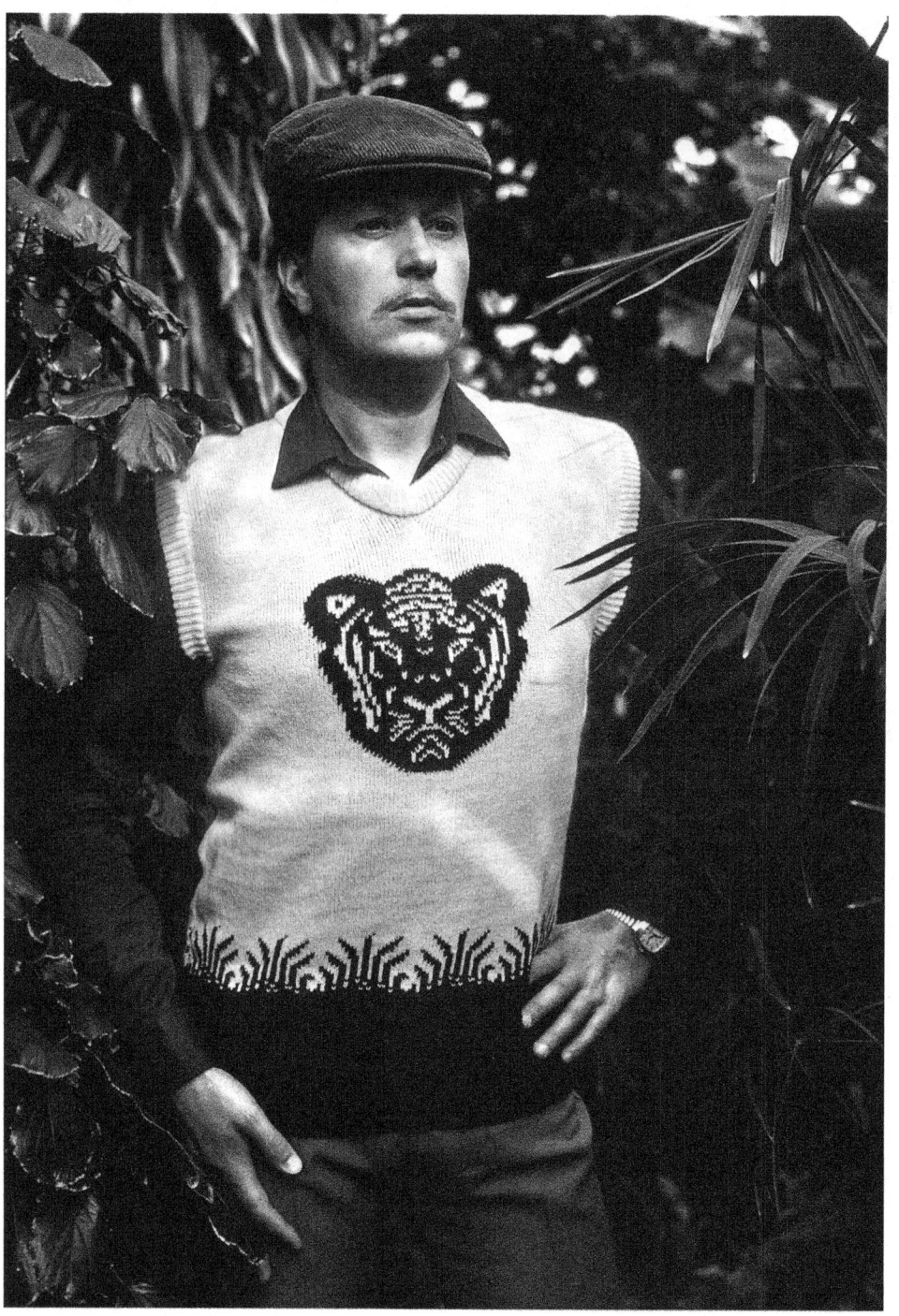

Fashion Guru

Early on, waiting for publications was a very slow progression. With all the bits of diversifying it was no more than a living for survival, we were still struggling and we had to try something more!

So we went into the Fashion business, one of the biggest mistakes I have ever made, I say 'I' because I'm pretty sure I talked Estelle into it, she should have had more sense, but then she did marry me!

So we jumped in with all four feet. Took out a bridging loan on the property we were in and a business loan on the combined shop and house, which was also going to be our home for the next couple of years.

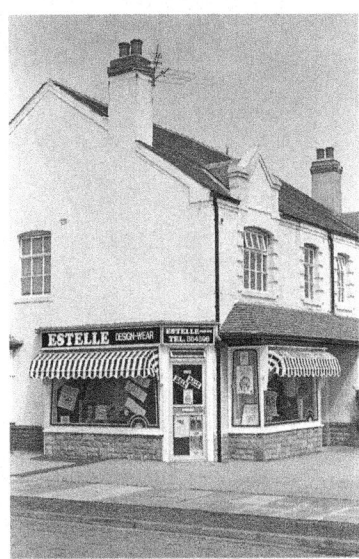

Now firstly in our defence, I would like to say without any modesty, we did a very good job on setting up the shop. We decorated it ourselves, we designed the signage to fit the existing frames and we found shop fittings that we could assemble, it was a very simple process and it was all our own work. Despite that, it looked good, in fact it looked very classy. We like to think we were mid priced on the ranges we stocked, but that can generally be based on what else is in the area and who your cliental were!

Here (see picture on left) I'm seen modelling the very unique Terrific Tiger Tank Top! An original design by Estelle with a little help from me on the pattern. To help build up our stock she had started to

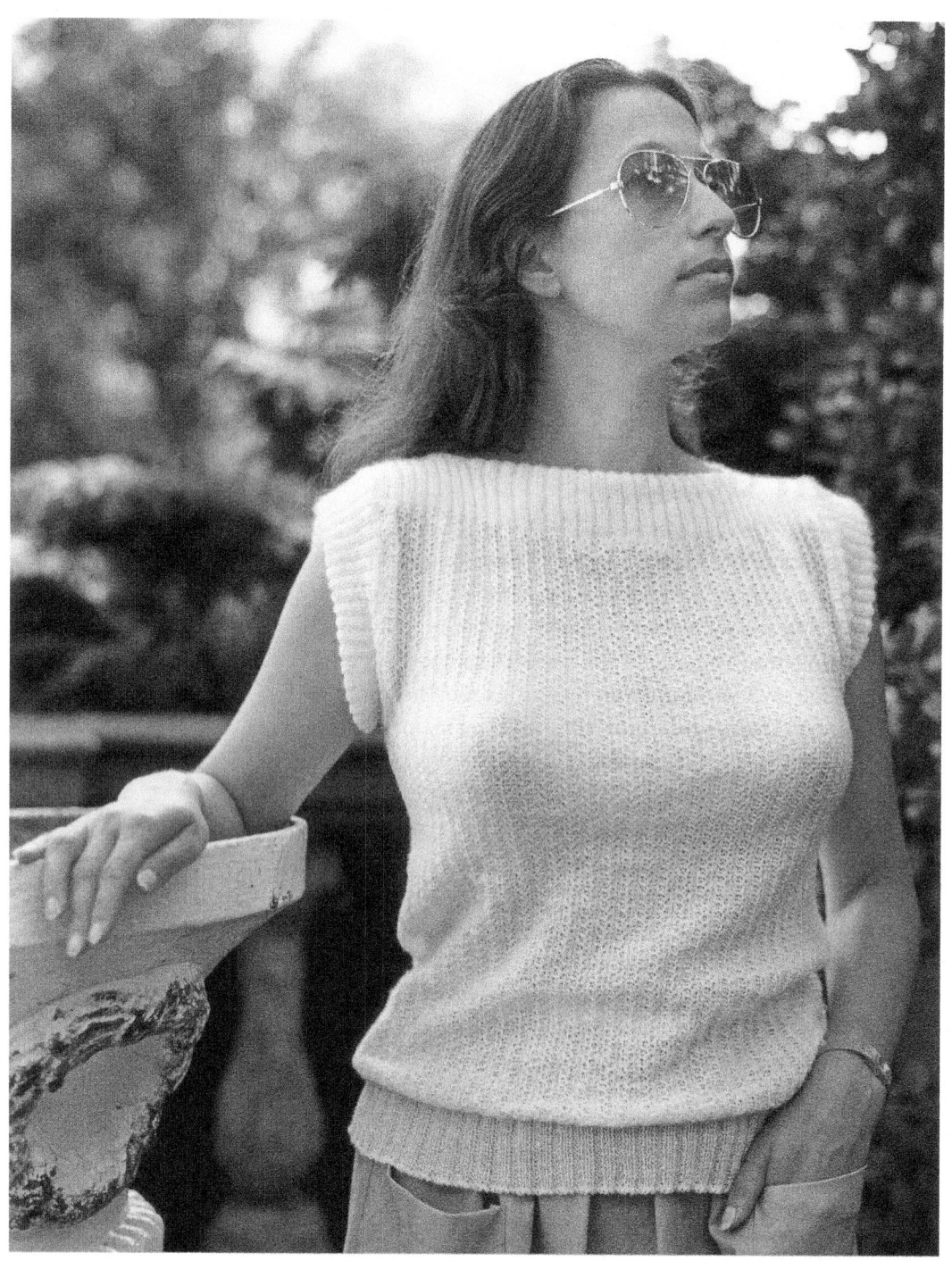

NEARLY FAMOUS

create her own knitting range and you can see that she made some nice, simple, but effective tops. The downside however is that you have to create an awful lot of knitwear to pay off a business loan!

We did try a few other ideas too, with some additional help from my mum when ever she visited, we managed to progress to shirt design and jump-suits (they were very big in the eighties), but neither of us had any schooling in fashion design or any knowledge of the industry, otherwise we probably could have marketed some of the designs into mass production, wait a minute let me think about that, we had no spare money, so we couldn't really, could we!

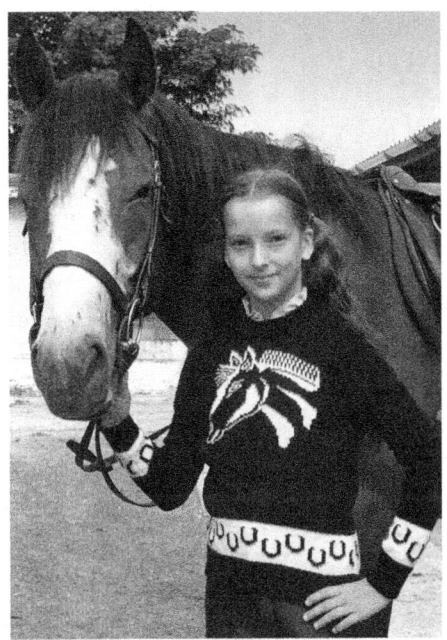

We went into it our fashion period during a time that turned out to be a retail recession, global warming allegedly upsetting the weather was also to blame, so we had the wrong clothes at the wrong time, winter, spring, summer, autumn, think about it, that's a lot of clothes just for one person to buy. The weather made the seasons overlap and the people didn't buy at the right time, least not for us, and eventually the bank that likes to say "yes" said "no" and foreclosed on us. That didn't sound bad enough, I'll explain, it meant in real terms, we ended up with two weeks to pay off the business loan or lose everything by declaring bankruptcy!

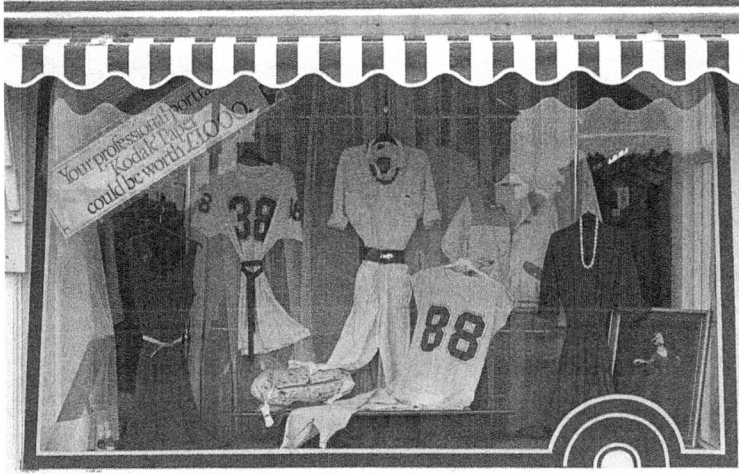

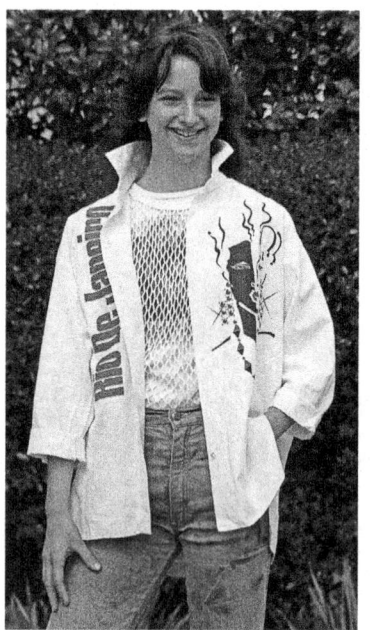

In fact we lost pretty much everything anyway but we didn't go bankrupt. I know that's just semantics but it meant something to us as an honest and proud family. If it hadn't been for Estelle getting a job and me running the shop on my own we would have.

I guess you could say we were lucky when we were made an offer on the property, it would be at a loss, it would just cover the bank loans, but that would bring us out even and without bankruptcy, so we took it, there was one small catch, the buyer gave us less than a week to get out or the deal was off. I guess he sensed the situation we were in, we had no choice.

Eventually we managed to accomplish one mistake after another! For the business minded people out there reading this contemplating some dramatic changes in their life, you'll see below, are my personal do's and don'ts list for fashion.

When I read this I see in a couple of paragraphs where we failed so easily, but I digress, where were we and what else happened along our way!

Do's and Donts

- Don't take out a bridging loan on the property you're going to sell unless you know you have a buyer for your original property! You lose more than your shirt if you can't pay back the interest and the value of the house drops on the eventual sale.

- Do attempt new ventures in life, but make sure you have a back up plan if it fails.

- Don't spend a fortune on a shop make over if you can do some of it yourself.

- Do spend money on the right fittings, but shop around and research, a lot!

- Don't buy loads and loads of clothing stock from large firms, just because you like it, your clients might not and in our experience we never received the full collection, which leaves you with a lot of bits and pieces to sell, if your lucky in the sales!

- Do take regular trips to the smaller wholesalers and be selective, buy within each weeks budget, that would certainly have kept us going a lot longer.

- And on a final note remember fashions change and very quickly, 'Watch and Learn' that could be the slogan for my very latest endeavour but more about that later, watch the Press and read the Fashion Magazines, then talk to your customers, and your wholesalers, you will learn automatically were the best bargain and regular sales can come from.

Here we go again!

We were going to be homeless at this point with absolutely no idea where we were going to live, and then it came to me, it wasn't actually a brain wave but I was determined not to be homeless. I bought a cheap secondhand 14 foot (4m) caravan (trailer) with my credit card, we arranged a removal firm and closed the shop.

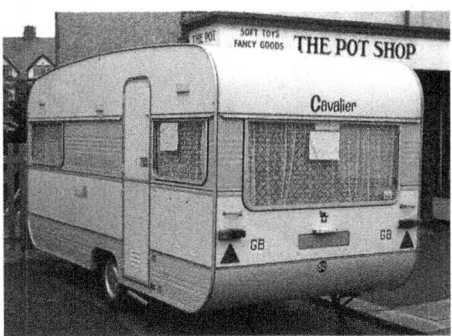

I forgot to tell you, when we moved to the shop it was lock stock and barrel from our previous home, which included our complete recording studio. We had to stack the whole recording studio into the small garage, intending to one day set it up somewhere else!

So we started packing, we filled two removal lorries, they were taking the tubs and boxes away as we filled them, in fact they were even filling the boxes for us (almost packing the dirty dishes out of the sink at one time). For 24 hours around the clock we did nothing but pack, pack, pack, even the shop clothes and fittings went with us!

We eventually ended up with what we thought were the bare necessities to take with us in our newly acquired home. It wasn't until later that night, after we had put Dani to bed in the caravan outside on the forecourt, that we sat on an empty shop floor together. It all seemed to happen so quick, we were so stressed out and exhausted from packing, we really hadn't had time to realise it was all over. We looked up and as our eyes met we both cried, it brings tears to my eyes again now just thinking about it. Okay I'm wiping my eyes now, so how did I get to where I'm at today from that situation, be patient!

I was back in a caravan but this time I had a wife, a daughter at school, and a trailer that was absolutely full to the brim of all our worldly goods, oh and by the way we now had a cat. A house cat at that, who on top of everything else was deaf and also needed looking after. The caravan was so low to the ground with weight that we had trouble getting it off the sidewalk parking spot onto the road. That next morning we moved the caravan at 5 mph about 3 miles down

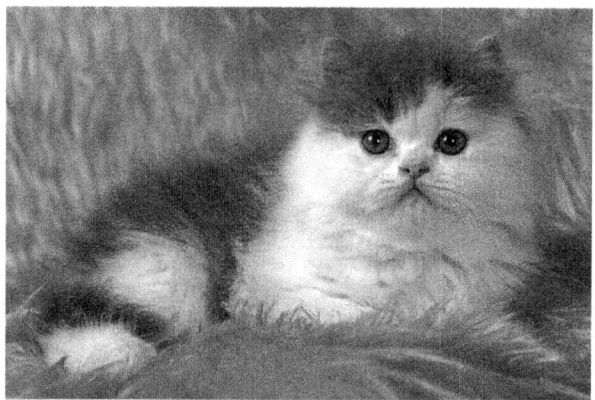

the road to a caravan park. Now when I say full, I mean FULL. For the next three months we went through a routine of emptying the caravan into the car, so that we could cook dinner and sleep, then each morning we would empty the car back into the caravan. I would take my daughter Dani to school and Estelle to work, the cat had to poop and pee in his litter tray inside, we did take him for walks with a cat harness. Once when asked what's he called? "Whatever you like," I said, "he's deaf!"

At this time I was still trying to get my photographic career moving along. One of the funniest things I remember was when I returned home from taking pictures, I would have to process my film. There were no digital cameras in those days so I would load the film canister into a special container. It had to be kept in the dark, so I had a special bag that you sealed up with your hands inside, I would sit on the caravan steps while I did this. You have to imagine seeing me fiddling with the bag between my legs to appreciate the look, I'm sure it amused the neighbours. Then, when I had finished the wet processing in the tiny trailer sink I would hang the film strips in the trees to dry. Sometimes there could be as many as eight rolls of film blowing in the wind. I'm sure they thought we had some kind of naughty thing going on!

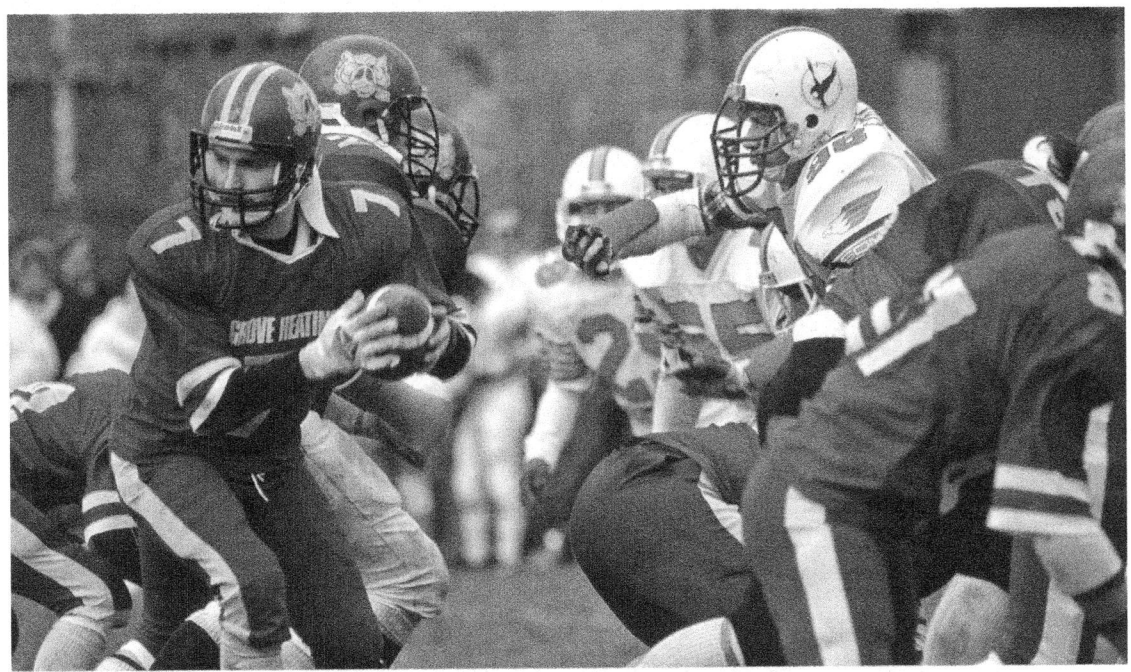

When winter came along we had to move out. A friend let us rent a small apartment above his junk shop and we could, at least, take a regular bath rather than a squirt down with a hose in the trees! We gained more room managing to improve living and working conditions with one exception, it was the coldest place we have ever stayed at and that includes a skiing trip we were to take later on, in northern Vermont, that was a bone chilling minus 10! I remember the icicles, on the inside, wearing ski suits, gloves, woolly hats and that was just in bed, though Estelle reckoned the mask was an improvement. It really was that cold. Christmas that year was spent with the three of us and the cat sitting in sleeping bags while we watched the TV specials, but then that was luxury for us, we even had hot and cold, cold, cold running water. We struggled through what turned out to be one of the coldest winters England had ever seen!

Having survived winter we headed into spring and summer. Eventually we knew it was time to look for somewhere else, especially when the house behind us went up in flames and exploded. We think they had gas cylinders and paint cans in their shed at the time!

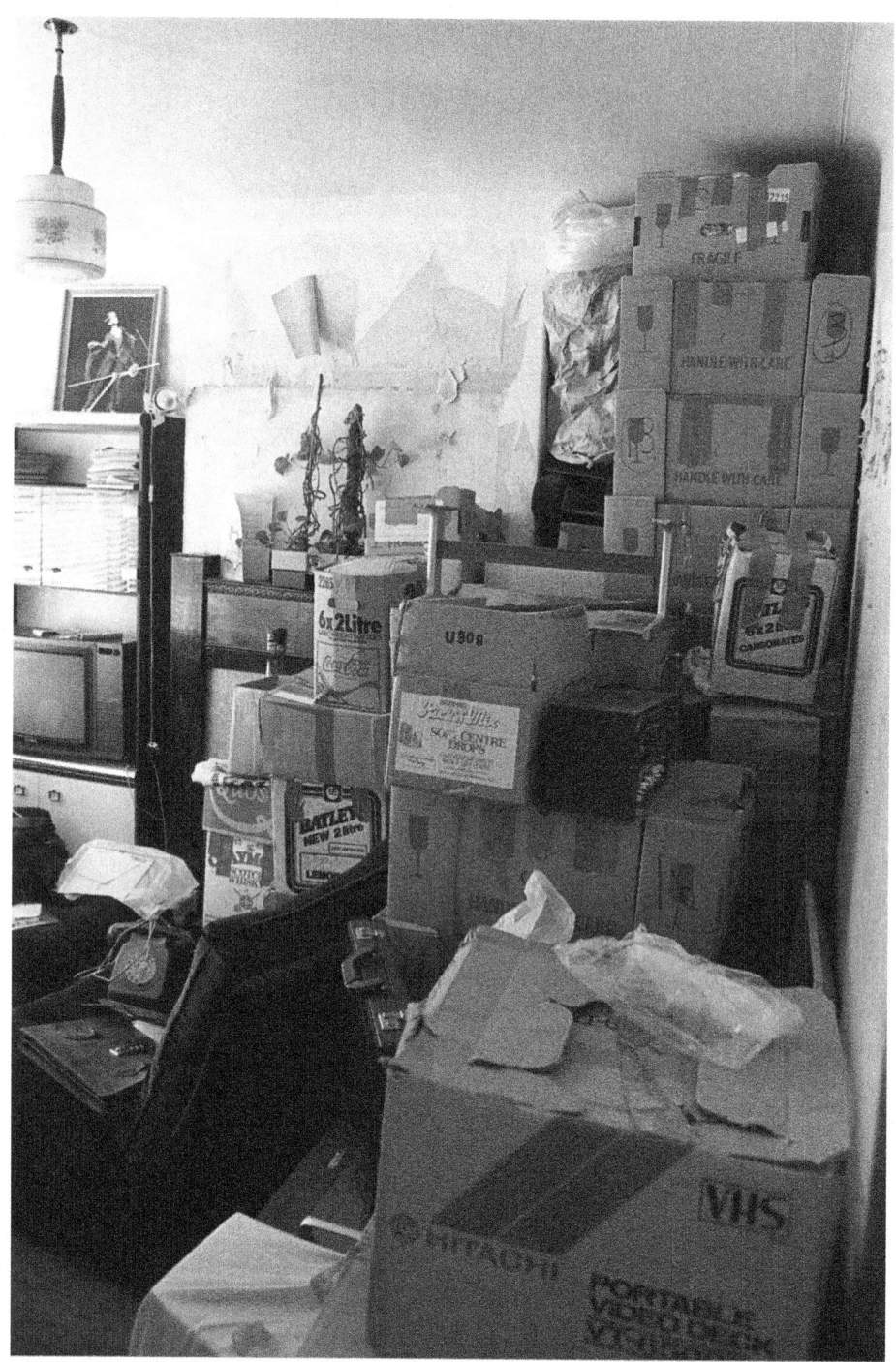

NEARLY FAMOUS

There's no place like home!

We went house hunting, hunting, and hunting. Just when we were about to give up on that because of the prices, I found a small semi detached house. It had been empty for some time so the price was reduced, Estelle hated it at first sight, but I convinced her we couldn't spend another winter in wonderland. We could raise a mortgage deposit by selling our trailer home plus using a few hundred pounds we had saved over the previous 6 months, the repayments were no more than we were already paying on the apartment and our furniture still in storage rental. She still had doubts, and was only prepared to make a silly offer on the house, we offered much less than they wanted but to my and her amazement they took it, so that is how we have our present very humble home, I guess It was meant to be.

"We awoke to the cat meowing, perched on 8 ft of boxes swaying precariously over us in bed!"

I was still only working occasionally, but, guess what? That one day we had arranged to move into our new house with all our worldly goods, work came in, well I had to go and work we needed the money. Apparently it's Murphy's law! The day arrived and I went off with a see you later kiss and the storage firm started to bring back all our goods, remember, we had a recording studio, a dress shop, a darkroom, camera equipment, musical amplifiers, not to mention our normal day to day stuff like beds, tables and chairs. I told you not to mention that! I returned from work late about 11pm and Estelle met me at the door. To be honest there wasn't anywhere else we could get together! She looked at me in despair and when I looked in the house I could see why. Now I know we packed a trailer from floor to ceiling and had to move everything into the car, but there was no way in the world we could empty the whole house into the car! We climbed over the boxes and boxes and boxes, until I figured we could stack them higher and higher and squeeze them up closer, eventually we made enough room to get around and make room for the beds. We went to sleep surrounded by a mountain of storage boxes, but hey, there is no place like home. We awoke to the cat meowing, perched on top of 8 ft of boxes swaying precariously over us in bed!

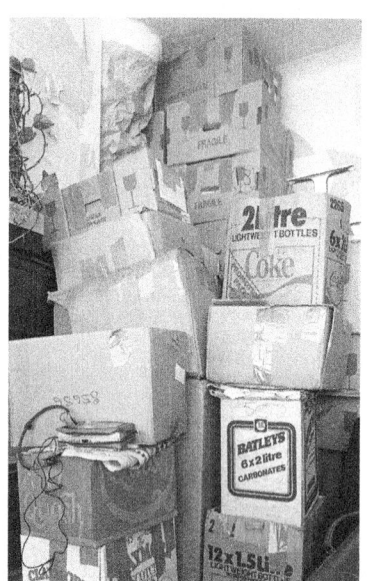

It took us months to get sorted plus a few years later before we could put carpets down and get every room painted. Estelle will tell you we haven't actually finished doing that either. We are still getting rid of some of those early possessions, remember I mentioned my hoarding! When you have to do all your own decorating and fitting it takes a while, you either don't have the money or don't have the time. Furthermore, when ever I did manage to earn some money I would spend it on equipment for work, well that's what I have always done. There I rest my case. Did I hit a soft spot? Good news though we are still using some of the shop fittings today in various places around the house!

Have I said how much I hate 'Do It Yourself', sometimes I think it's hard to separate the clown in me, I have stepped off a ladder into a pot of paint, once mixed some wall plaster at the bottom of the stairs, but by the time I got to the top of the stairs the mix in the bucket was solid as a rock. On another occasion I put rather nice ceramic tiles on the toilet wall, a couple of hours later when they should have dried and stuck on the wall nicely, I went to the use the toilet. I was just sitting there minding my own business so to speak and I just couldn't resist running my hands over this beautiful ceramic wall, as I did, they started to come loose and fall off. Now you will have to use your own imagination here, I am standing up now with my trousers around my feet trying to catch the remainder of the wall as the tiles are falling off. I'm laughing now! I have even fallen off the top of a ladder while

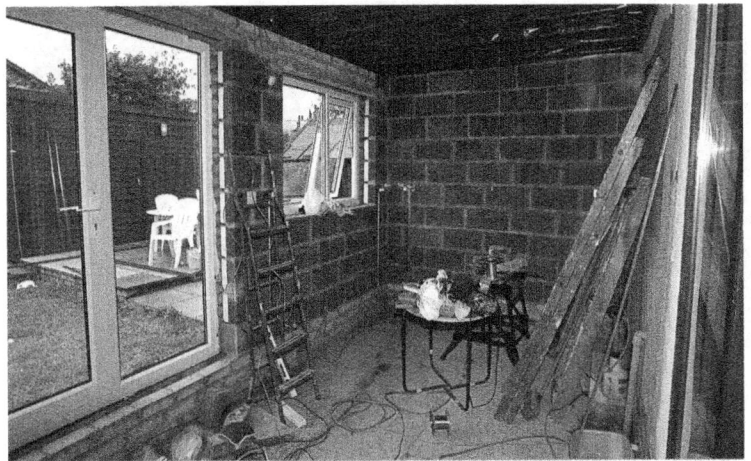
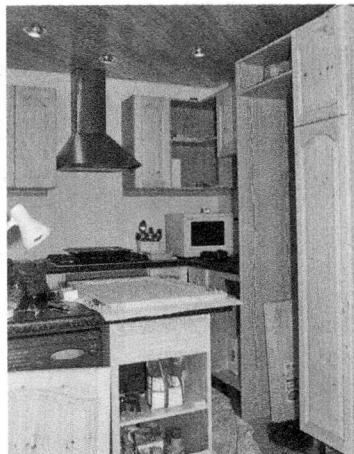

painting, fortunately I had a soft landing, Estelle, she was painting the wall at the bottom, she was okay by the way.

Regardless of that, I plumbed in the central heating, then built a wooden photographic studio 12 feet by 16 feet out in the back garden to move some of the equipment into. Back in the house I plumbed in two bathrooms (Estelle didn't like the first one, by the time it took me to finish it), I remodelled the chimney breast in our lounge and built a kitchen extension because I wanted to spend the money I had on a digital camera. OK that might need an explanation. Through a legal dispute over my photographs I had come into enough money for a new digital camera that had just come out, it was the same price as I had been quoted for someone to build us a kitchen extension, and we needed that badly. Our original kitchen was only 8 feet by 6 feet then you had the cabinets and cooker in it! Estelle insisted it was time for improvements in our life and she was right, but it took some convincing her that I could build the kitchen myself for an eighth of the price and still be able to buy my new camera, it was after all for work and without that we would go broke again, no point in a kitchen if you can't afford food! She agreed to it and I started reading books on DIY, then started digging the foundations to the kitchen we have today, it was double bricks and mortar, dry lined with an insulated roof, full spec and furnished, the full monty we like to say and stands proud today. Estelle was proud of it too and it was just as well, our marriage might have depended on it!

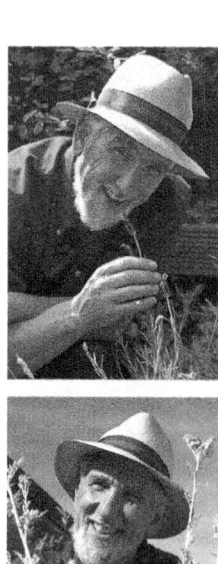
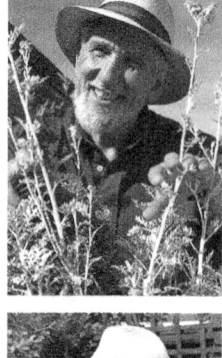
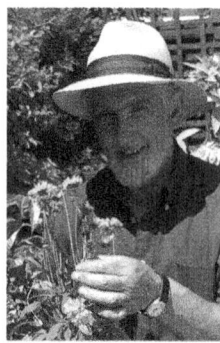
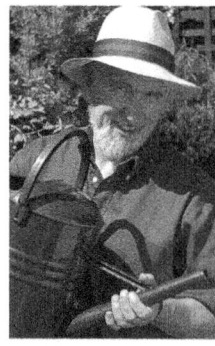

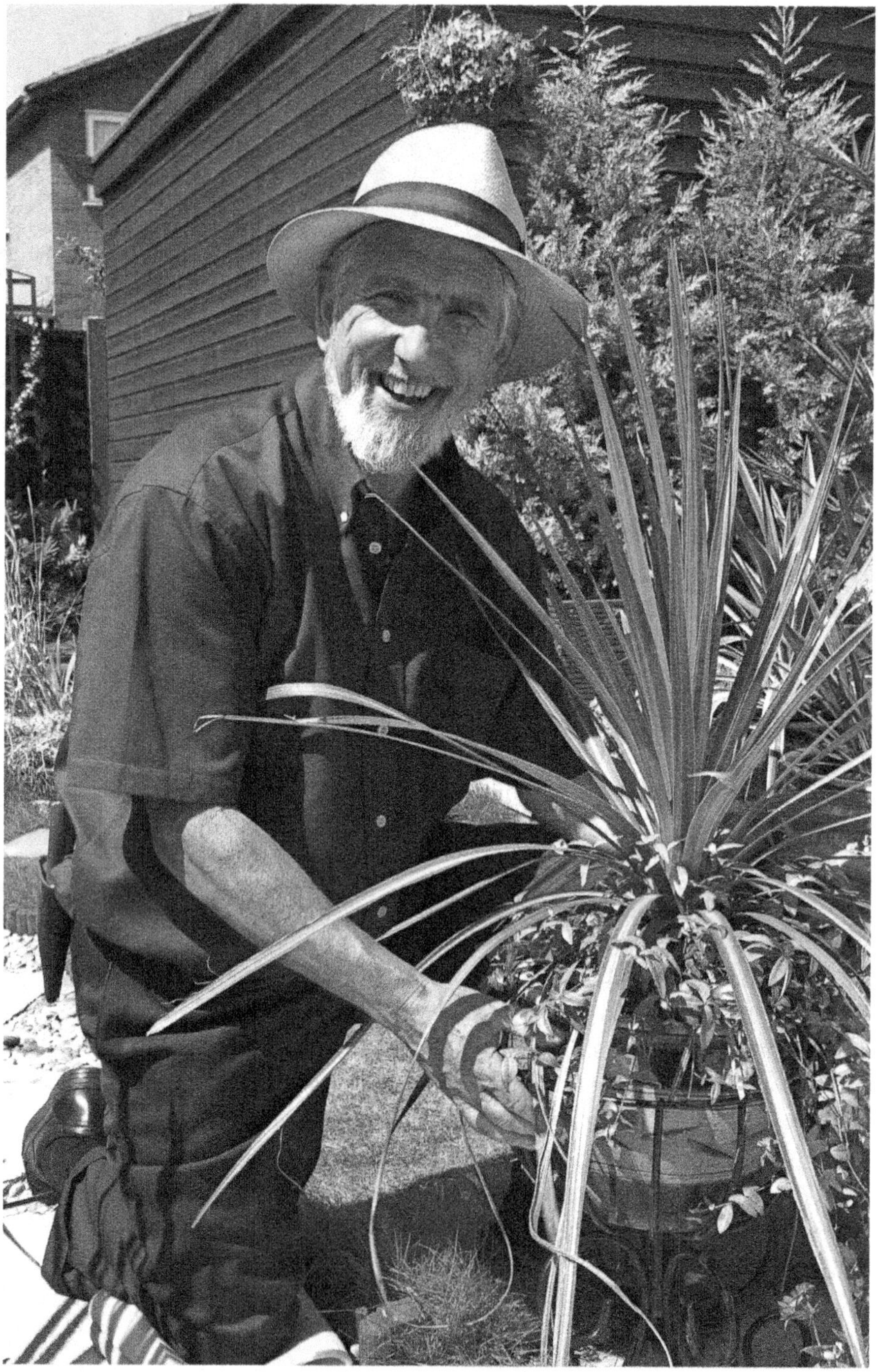

NEARLY FAMOUS

The Garden Detective

I went on to landscape the back yard with a fish pond and waterfall, but that was more because there was a video project that I wanted to do. Even that ended strangely!

I linked up with local gardener Robert Gault whom I'd met previously, to produce a garden video, I produced, directed and planted it you might say. For several weeks he came around and I would film him as he criticised constructively my planting and made suggestions for improvements.

He was going through some personal problems with his wife and we thought he was separated, he introduced us to a girl friend and we all got on very well. Then one day he just disappeared! His phone number was gone, his work place had changed and his girlfriend was calling us to ask where he was. His personal life was private and nothing at all to do with us,

"Or even worse, thought we'd buried him in the garden!"

so we didn't get involved, but it did start to worry us quite a bit. He literally just disappeared, leaving his hat, coat, pants and a shirt, (that was the costume he wore for his filming bits) all at our place. Well I had just dug a big hole in the ground for our pond and spent several weeks landscaping. We were expecting the police to turn up one day asking if we had seen him. Or even worse, thought we'd buried him in the garden!

About a year later he walked past me in a hospital, he was with another woman and he didn't stop to speak to me. I'd missed the chance to speak to him but at least I guess he is still around. I hope!

The video turned out really good so if you see it on release, it will be called 'The Garden Detectives', unless I rename it 'The Missing Garden Detective'. Suffice to say a lot of the things he said about my planting and choice of plants were true and the garden now really is overgrown to the extreme.

He was right with pretty much all he said, in my garden it either dies or has a metamorphosis. The beautiful grass I painstakingly laid was definitely wrong, it needed cutting every day, nurturing and feeding more than me, that wasn't on. It was definitely a wrong choice, you could eat your dinner off it, but I didn't have the time or for that matter the will to spend that much time on it. Eventually giving up on the struggle, I put down some green stones instead. Well I wasn't playing golf on it either, though I had considered a very small putting green. The potted Cordylines in the foreground, were re potted and

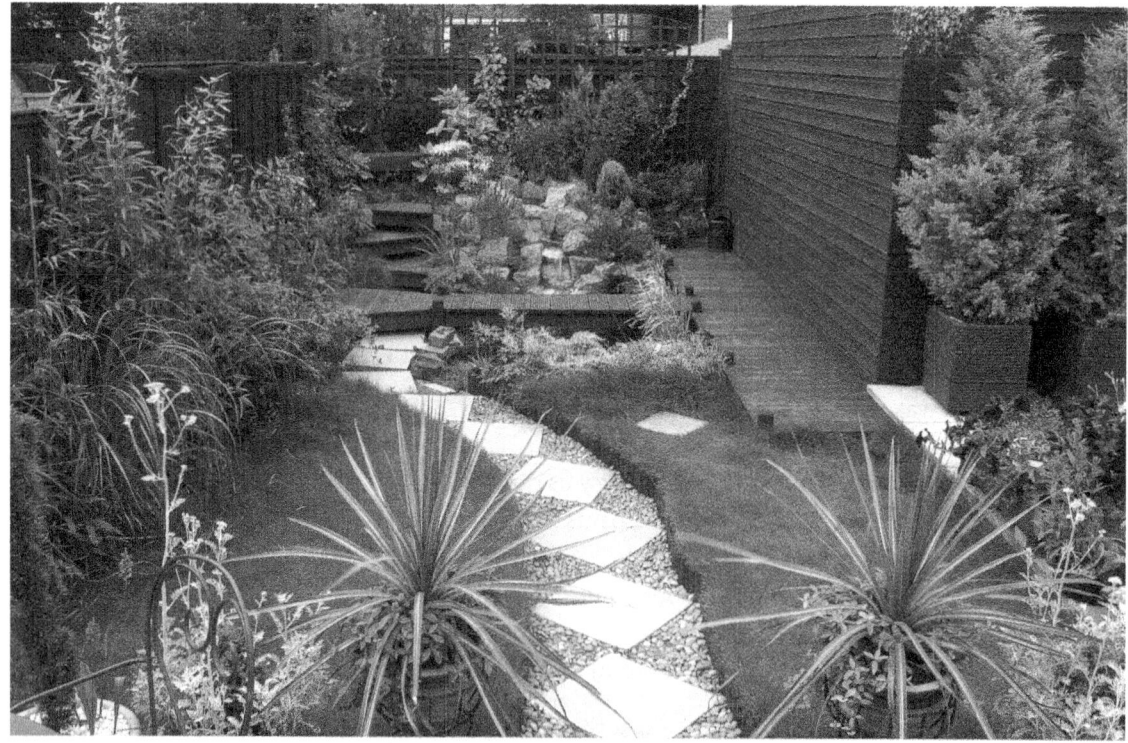

NEARLY FAMOUS

still kept growing. Eventually they were planted into the soil on the right side of the path. I left the rather large and tight woven root that had formed, so they would grow slowly, I hoped. I decided in my infinite wisdom to add another new one, it was a different colour and would look quaint between the other two. It was just a little sprig about 18 inches tall and cost just a few pennies, but I'm sure there is something weird in my garden soil because that little Cordyline flew past the others and is now about ten foot tall, it looks more like a Palm tree. The small Bamboo's on the left that I was assured would only grow to five or six feet max, are now reaching fifteen foot, they bend over and bang on the back door when the high winds are blowing and if you open the door the Virginia Creeper comes in. At the very back in the corner of the garden there was a small Fir tree, I know it was actually dying when I saw it in the Garden Centre shop and was practically given to me with another plant that was really healthy, of course the latter died and the dying Fir tree is now so big I may have to lop the top off

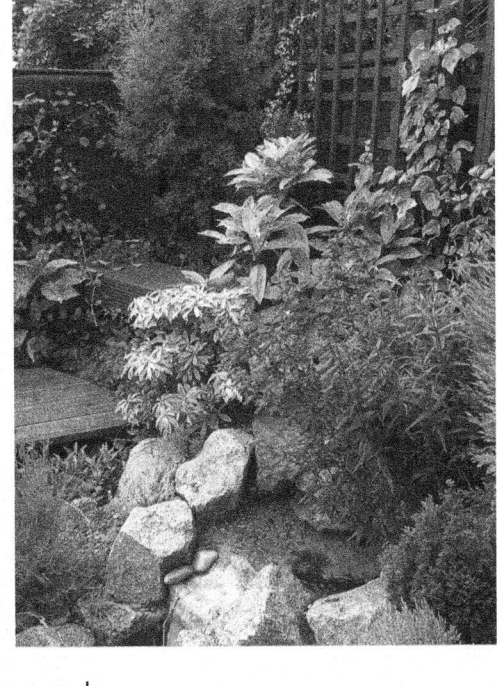

to contain it within twenty feet. I no longer refer to it as a garden but more of a natural history environment. We have had hedgehogs make their home in it, frogs galore slide down the waterfall and play with my goldfish in the pond, bees have created hives on a regular basis and all the normal dragonflies, butterflies and even birds nest there. I am considering running adventure training courses through it, though for a British garden it does look a bit exotic. Maybe I should fit in a zip line from the roof to the back of the garden and make it jungle training instead!

Back to the decorating which still goes on and on. I am still decorating this damn house years later, the photographic studio has now been rebuilt from the ground up as a log cabin and has a new lease of life. When we have decorated it on the inside, it will be the biggest open area we have ever had, if we can throw away the old recording studio. Yes we still have it, I told you I was a hoarder. So as a family, if we empty it, we are just going to sit in the middle of it, stare and admire the space. Did I say if!!!

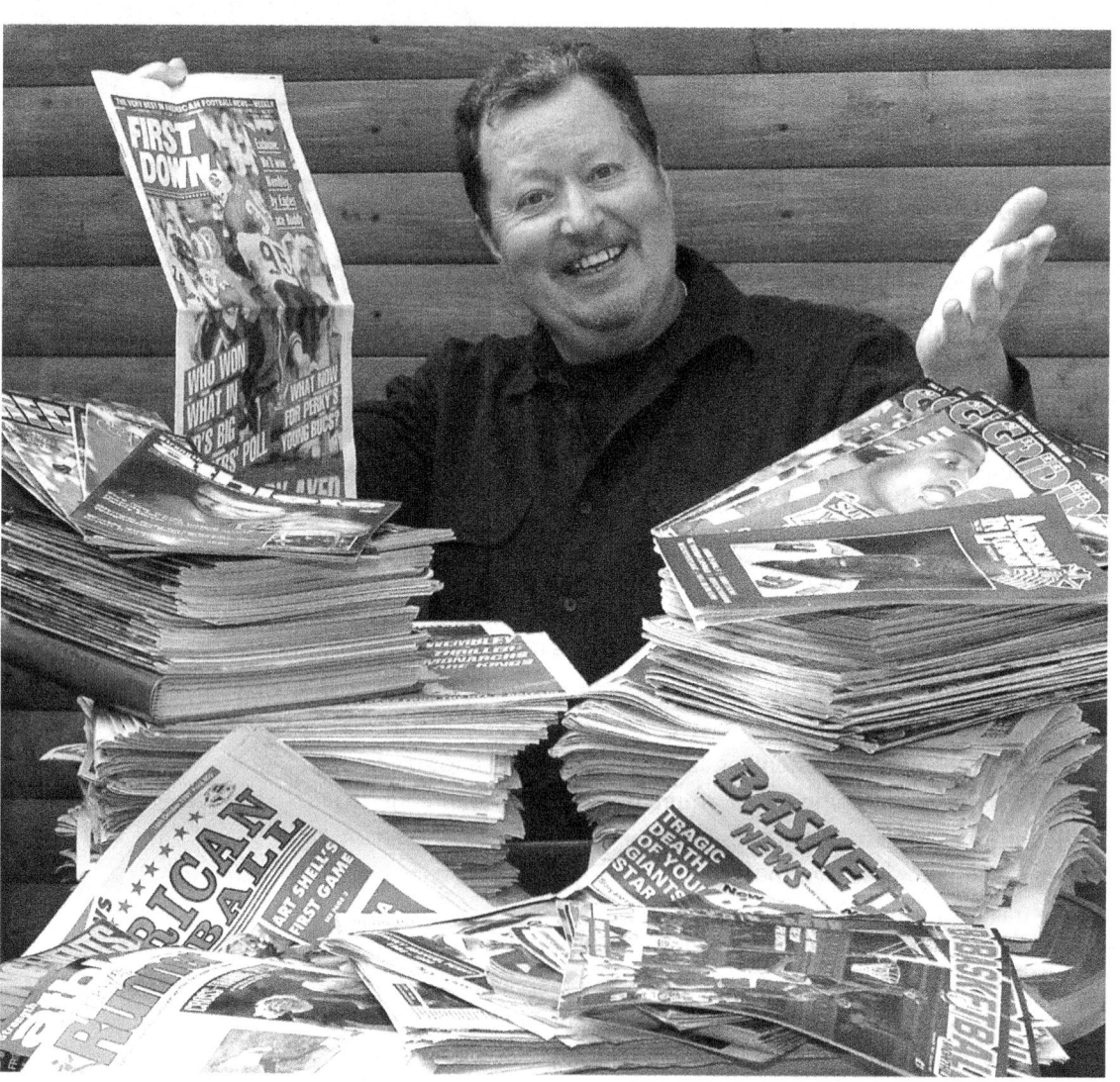

NEARLY FAMOUS

Back to the future

Somewhere along the way I mentioned American Football didn't I? American Football, or Gridiron as it's sometimes called, was starting to pick up. My files were building and I was getting regular publications, so much so that at one stage I was covering 58 domestic games a year in Great Britain. I took pictures at every level, from pee wees to flag and college to semi pro.

As a direct result of that coverage I became well known in the sport. Going to a game was like visiting your family, everyone would say hello and talk to you and players would tell you how and where they were going to score touchdowns, just so I could get their picture. They very rarely did of course that would have been way too easy, but the point was friendship. You might even say, to them, I became their personal photographer and maybe, just maybe, a little more fame had started creeping in!

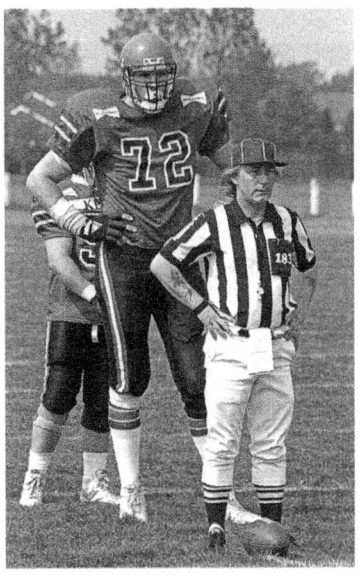

My career as a professional sports photographer was definitely starting to take shape. My portfolio had become the biggest in Britain on the domestic American Football scene, so much so I was able to start doing deals on a retainer to earn regular money. I was getting publications everywhere. Though It wasn't without it's ups and downs, and I don't mean the game!

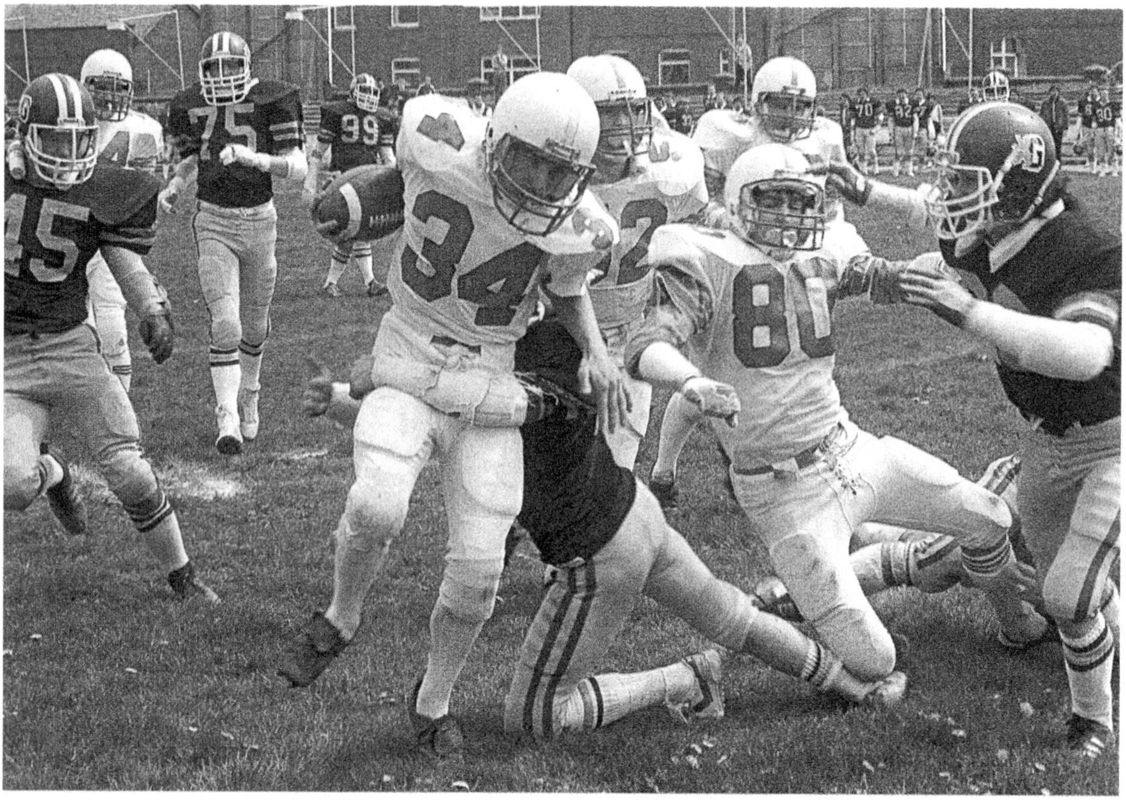

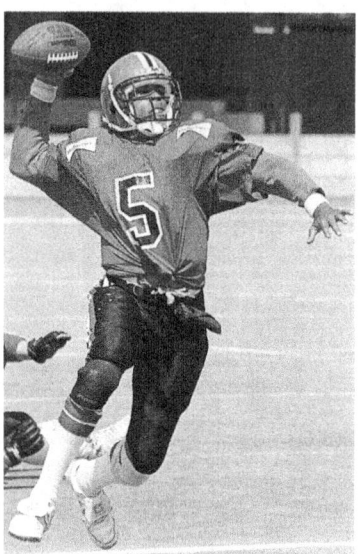

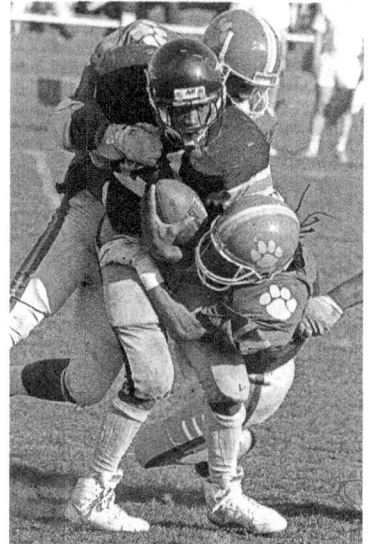

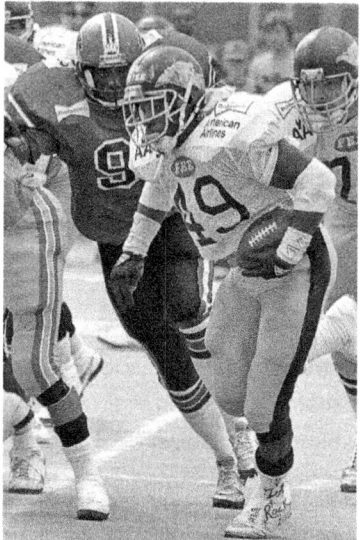

NEARLY FAMOUS

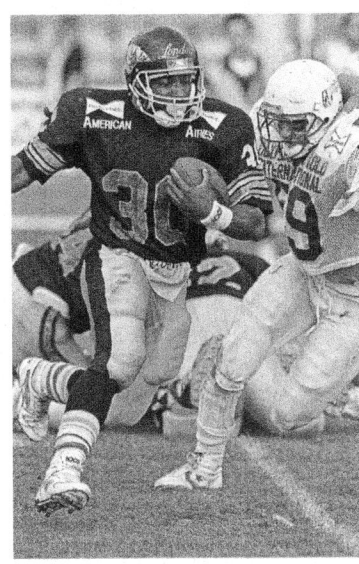

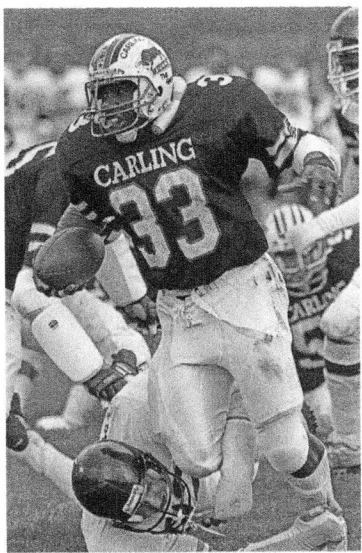

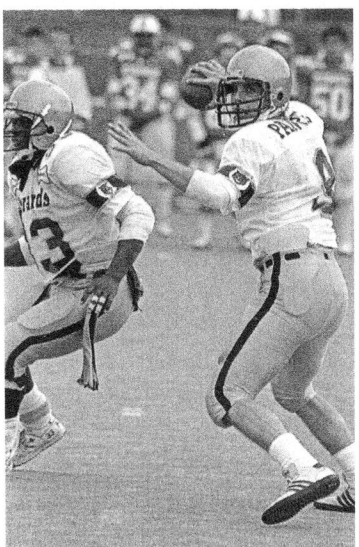

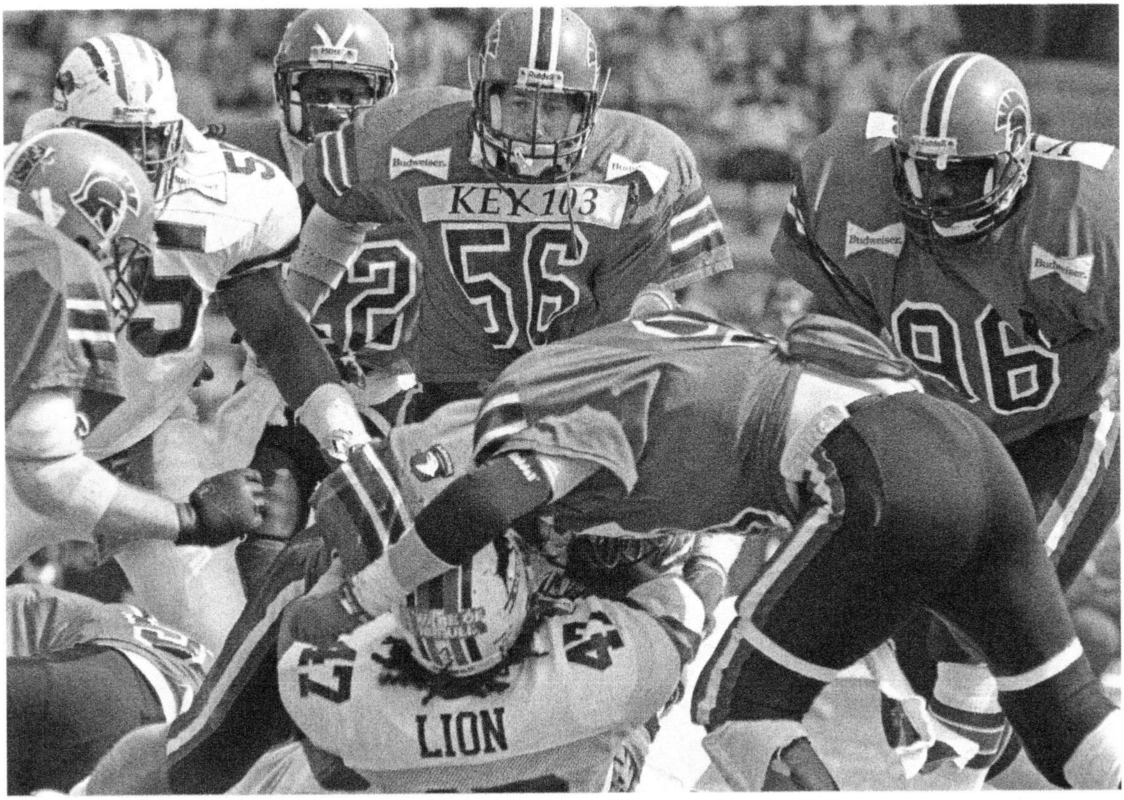

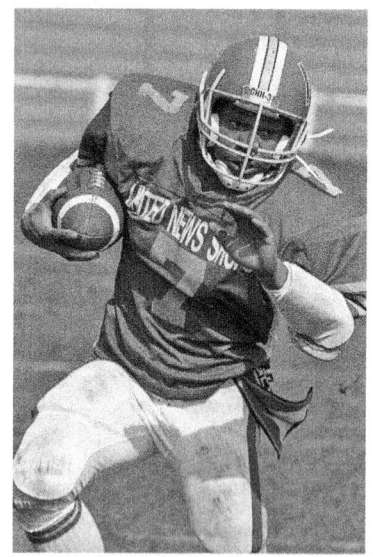
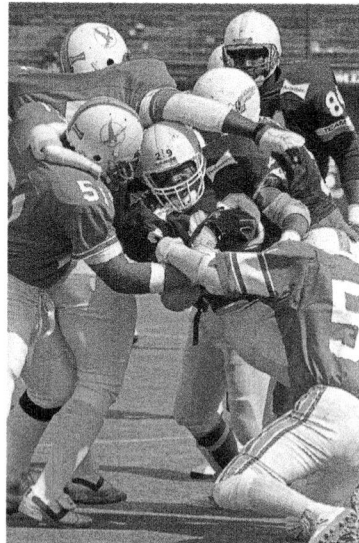
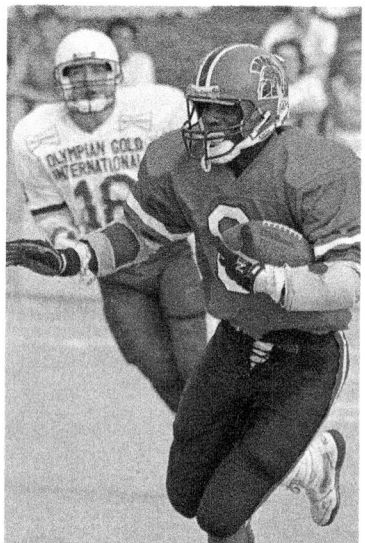

NEARLY FAMOUS

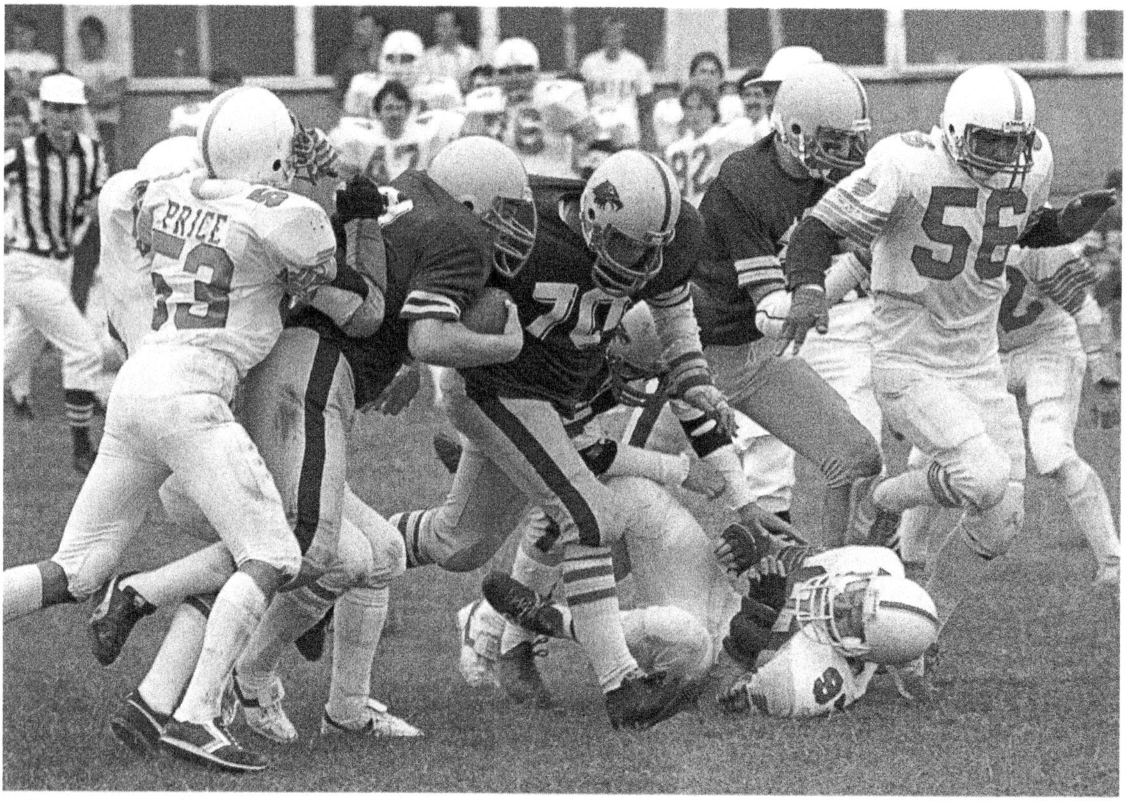

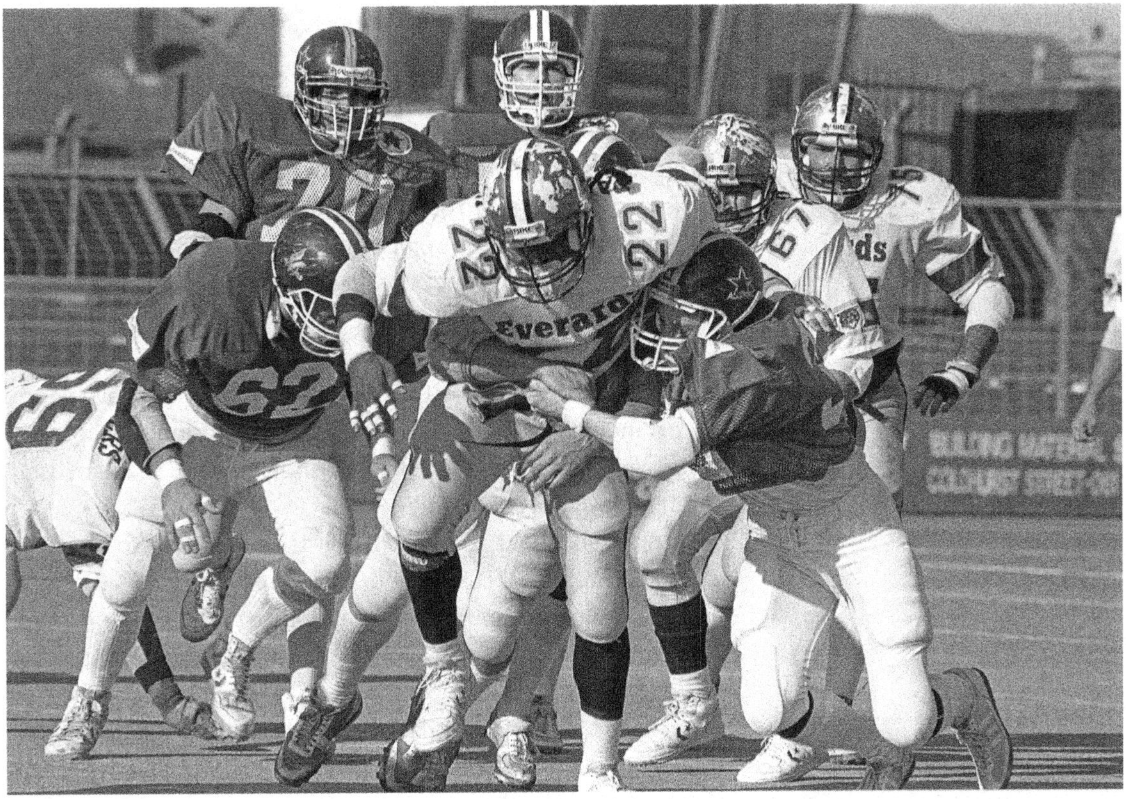

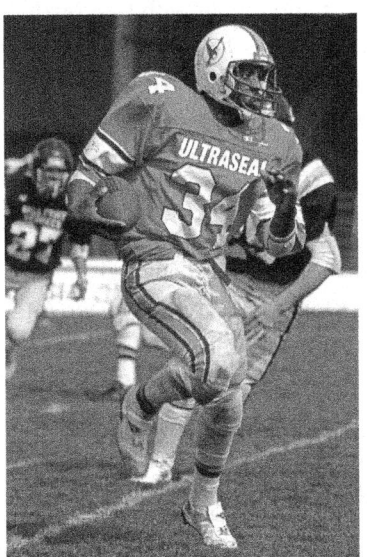

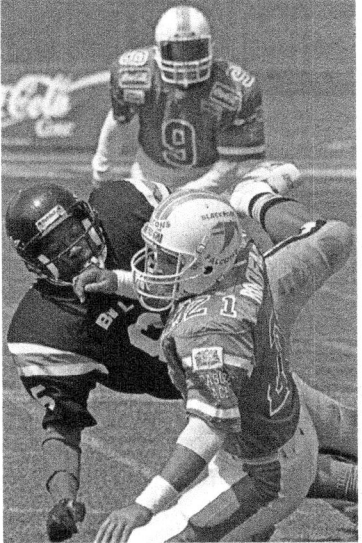

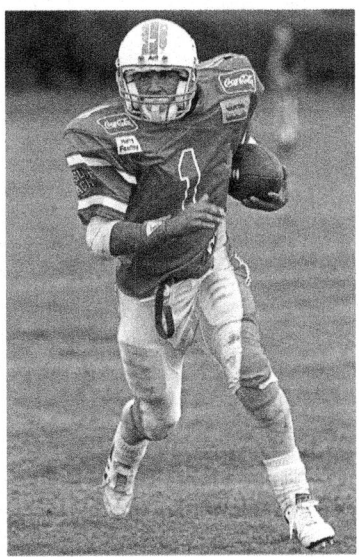

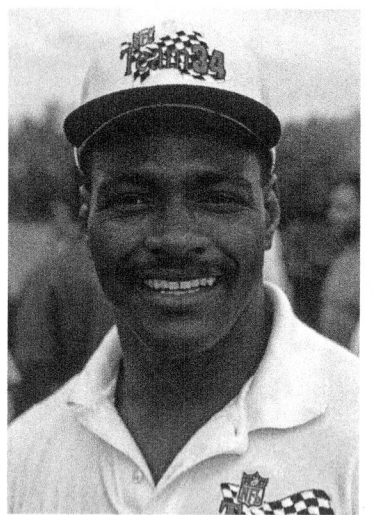

One magazine called the Receiver launched it's first three editions totally with hundreds of my photographs, unfortunately just as I was discussing money it went into receivership!

The publication side of the Gridiron scene in Britain was shaky to say the least. I managed to get pictures in all of them at different times and it was only by getting sufficient publications that I managed to hang on. They weren't the best payers and they were not always consistent in the use of my work, I even had to continually watch every magazine and ask for payments when my work was used, if you don't ask you don't get. I have to be honest I might have been a little paranoid at the time, I was sure they were using small parts of photographs and even reversing head shots to disguise them just to get out of payments, sorry guys!

Despite this I have to thank the likes of Ross Bidiscombe, Alan Lees, Keith Webster, Nick Halling, Mike Preston and all the other dedicated editors and journalists. They helped me along the way with publications and stories that allowed me to photograph the sport.

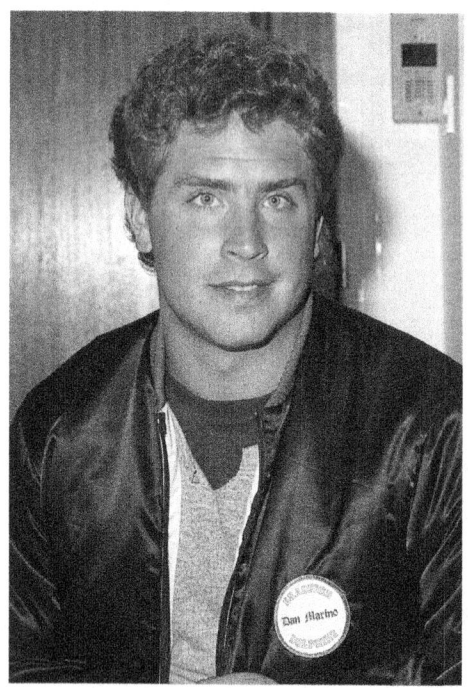

More importantly it gave me the opportunity to have a coffee with sport stars like Dan Fouts, Quarterback for the San Diego Chargers, lunch with John Riggins, Running Back for the Washington Redskins and dinner with Dan Marino, Quarterback for the Miami Dolphins. I even met sweetness himself Walter Payton, Running Back for the Chicago Bears.

They came over to host playing clinics on the sport for the Brits, and I was there to get their pictures. Dan Marino spent the day in Luton showing passing techniques, with a special talk and dinner in the evening hosted by Nicky Horne, as a member of the press I was also invited.

Dan Fouts, I met in the old Roman city of Chester. After taking a few traditional meet the people press pictures we went for a coffee break, during which I suggested rather than just meeting the locals, he should actually dress in the local Town Criers outfit, he was very accommodating as you can see from the results of this very exclusive Dan Fouts picture on the top right.

John Riggins was a gun enthusiast and I spent most of a day with him. Just me and a couple of his associates went around London to check out some guns in the morning and then on to a gun range to test them, we stopped to eat and chat, I was really pleased when he picked up the tab (hey I was still a struggling photographer). In the afternoon we went on to complete the football clinic. By the way, I saw him a few years later and asked him if he had bought the gun "no" was his reply "it was a load of crap" That's what he said, honest!

American 'Pro Football Hall Of Famers' all of them, yet down to earth straight forward guys like you and I, for me in particular such large sports personalities were an inspiration to an aspiring photographer.

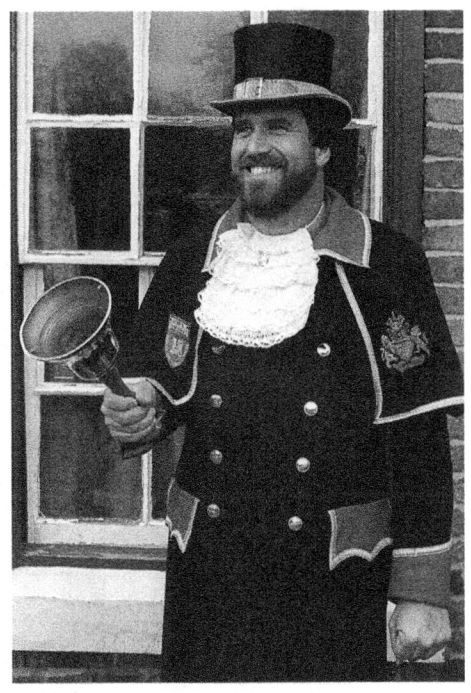

There were a lot of enthusiastic Brits in the British American Football scene of those days and for a time it started to prosper, carried along by the amateur players alone, they paid their subs on a regular basis and turned up to play, often travelling miles only to lose and have to drive themselves back home and get up for work the next day.

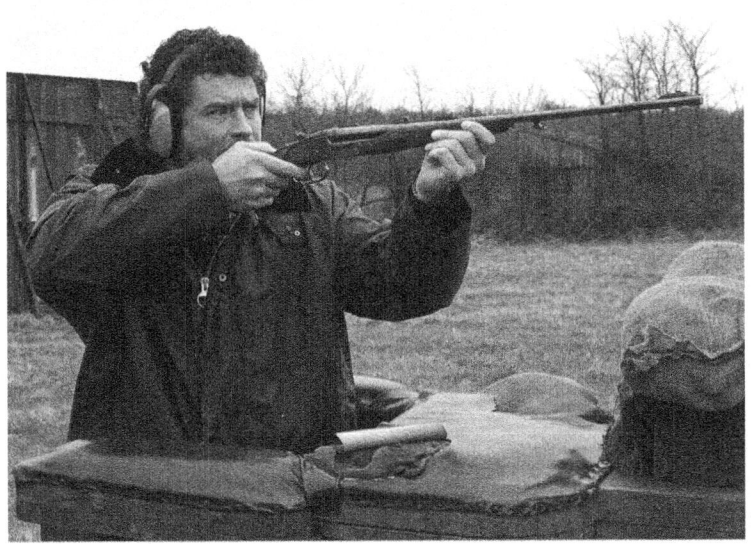

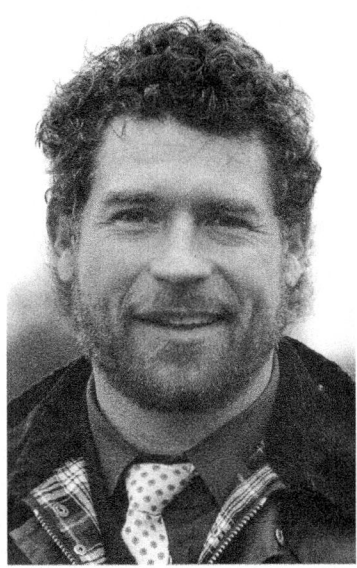

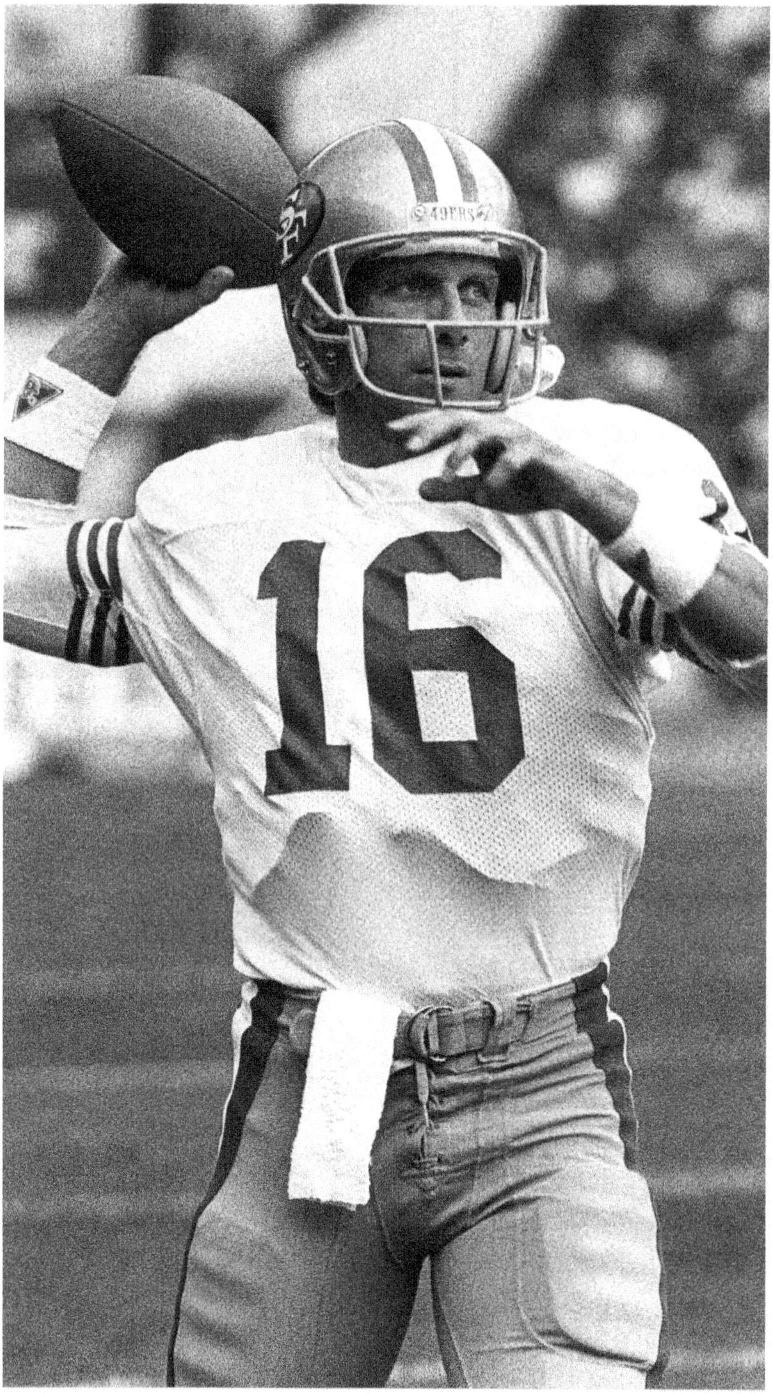

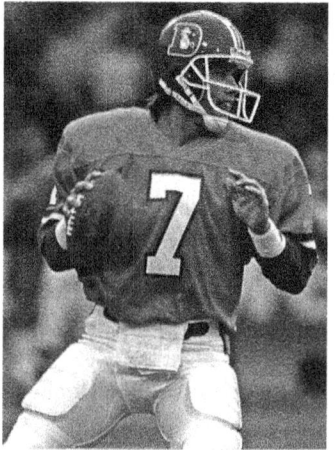

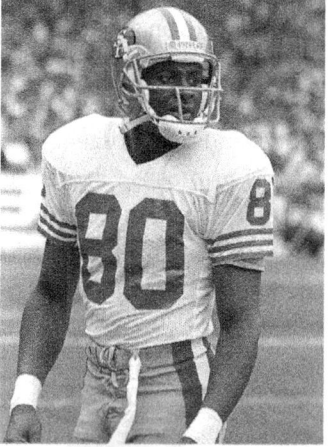

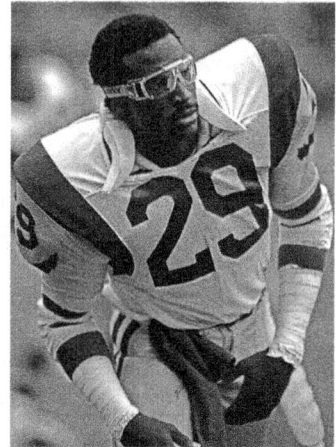

NEARLY FAMOUS

I know because in the early days I travelled with them, in their cars and their coaches, and as I said, paid my travel fees the same as the players. At it's peak British Gridiron was looking pretty good for a domestic league, I remember two thousand plus spectators at a few local games, the players reward, a little bit of fame and notoriety.

The NFL hooked on to the British success and started a series of pre season American Bowl games held at Wembley. I went to photograph all eight of them from 1986 to 1993 along with what appeared to be every other photographer in the world who turned up to do the same. Amazing how I didn't see them on the sideline at the Wirral Wolves and the Harrogate Hawks. Up to their necks in mud and rain at Leeds Cougars. Sorry that may have sounded a bit bitchy!

I struggled with the photography for a while at first, the professional game was a lot faster and was played at night. It needed fast and long telephoto lenses, the longer the better and as always in those days I just didn't have the budget for it. None the less I made adjustments and still managed publications from all the games I went to. Considering I didn't even get on the sideline for the first American Bowl game I thought it was quite an achievement. For the Chicago Bears v Dallas Cowboys game I travelled with and stood

alongside my friends the British players and fans, in the Soccer stands. For those that don't remember, in those days there weren't any seats behind the goal posts at Wembley, it was still an English football stadium with standing room only. Regardless of where I stood, behind the goal posts, I still managed to get a picture published in the weekly American Football magazine!

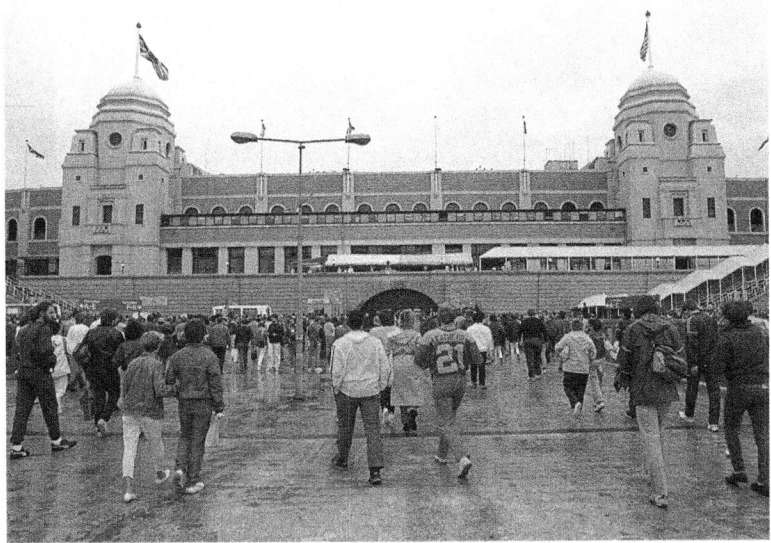

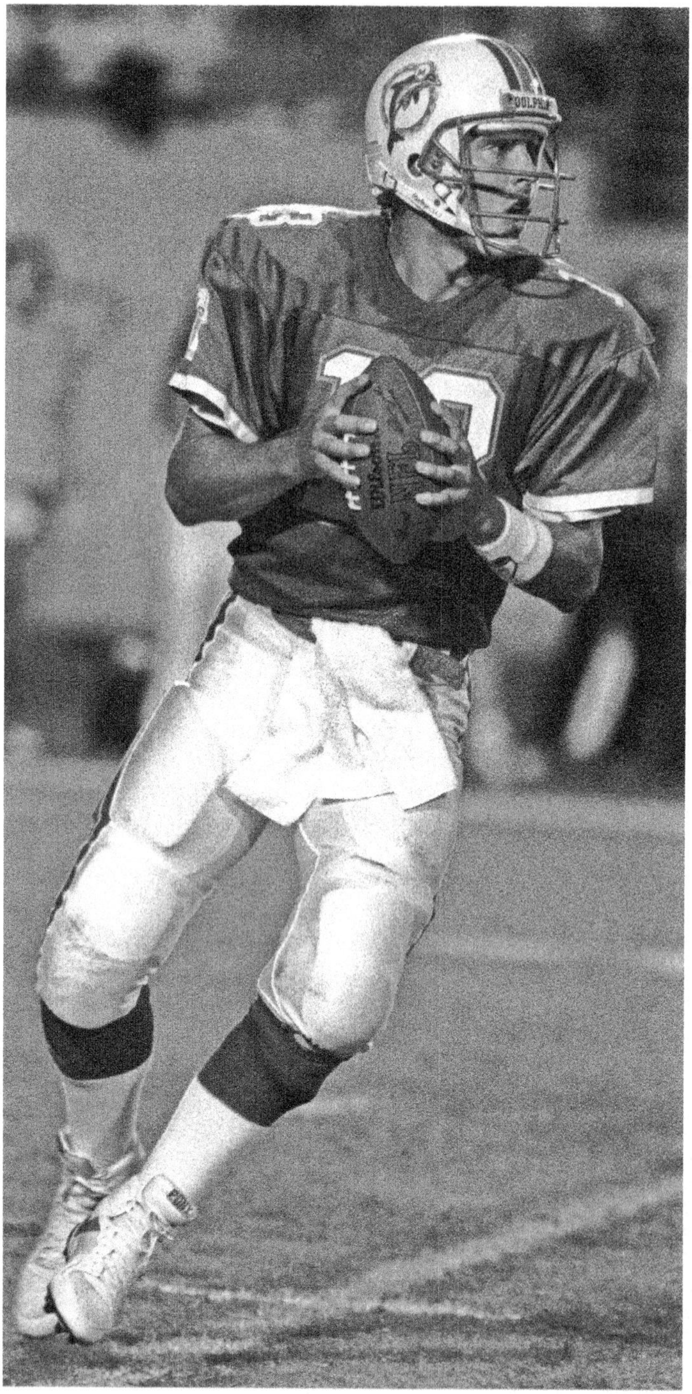

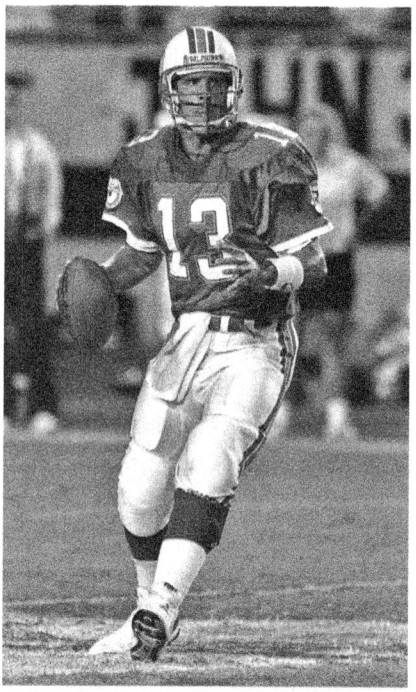

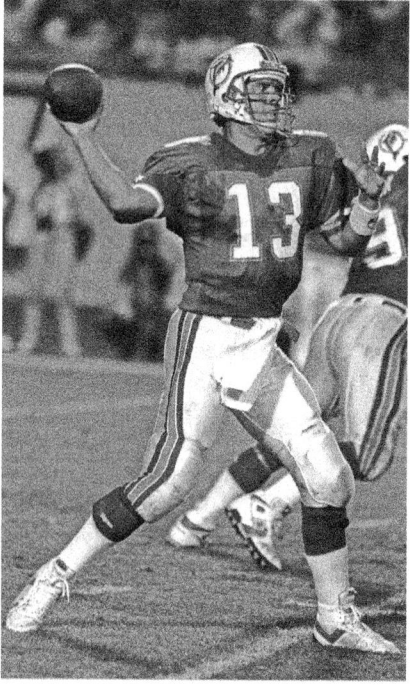

NEARLY FAMOUS

USA here we come

It would be 1988, four years after I started covering American Football in Britain, before I could afford a trip to the United States for my first game on American soil, but I picked a good one, several Hall Of Famers in one night, Miami Dolphins v Buffalo Bills, Dan Marino versus Jim Kelly. We arrived in Miami and went straight from the airport to the Monday night game. We were queuing on the expressway, when I rolled down the rental car window and asked some fans the way to the stadium, they said follow us and even gave us a spare car park pass. We were both jet lagged but adrenaline kept me going. For me a sports photographer this was it, the professional game where it was meant to be played, I had finally arrived. Though I'm sure Estelle had a harder time in the press box as she made notes and tried not to fall asleep through most of the game. This was my first ever trip to the USA and on the sideline, how could I sleep, the rest of that night was a daze. We did eventually find our motel after the game but I'm not exactly sure how we did it!

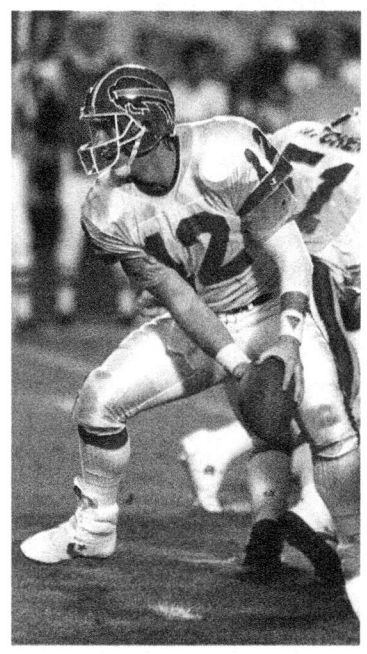

The next morning we went down to the Miami Hurricanes at Miami College, we had missed their game on the previous Saturday but had been told by photographers, that they always had a team press conference on Tuesdays. We arrived late and missed the traditional coaches conference, usually that meant you had missed the opportunity all together, so I explained to the Sports Director we had come thousands of miles, all the way from England just to see him. Within minutes we were whisked away and given an exclusive meeting with coach Jimmy Johnson, who was very amicable about the meeting, he gave us an interview and allowed us to take several pictures, all in his office at that!

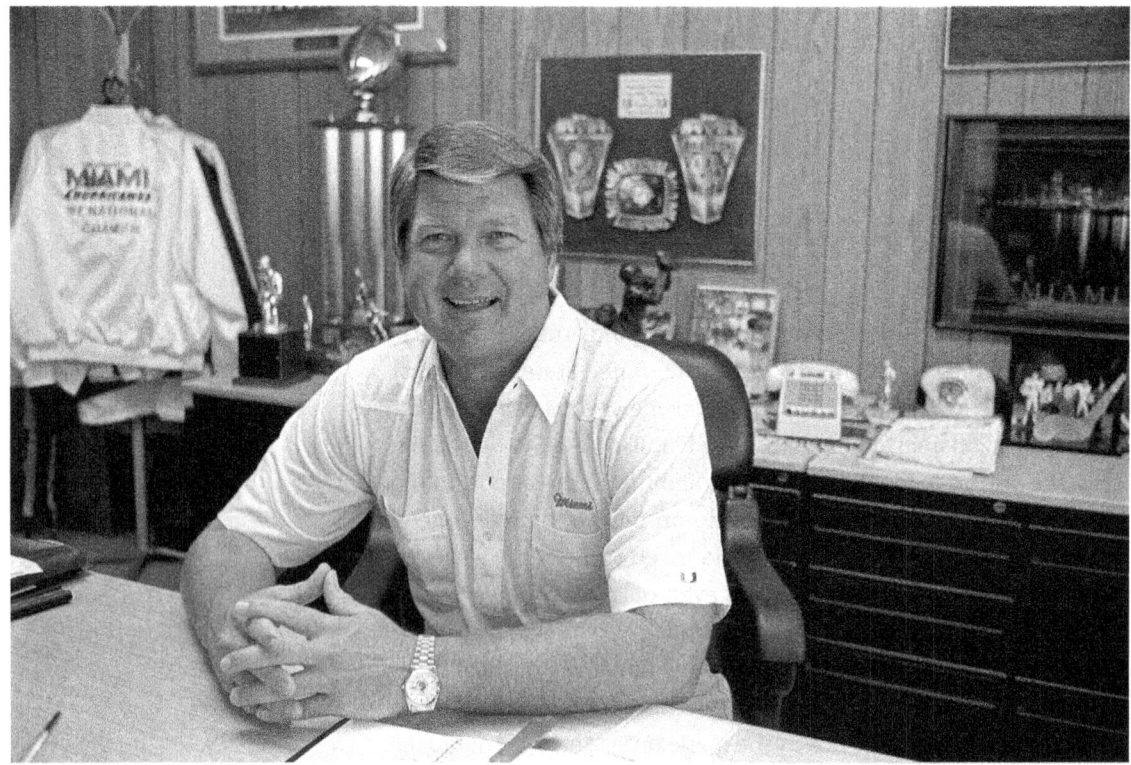

Fortunately for Estelle the next game wasn't until the Sunday, so we set off on what was supposed to be our vacation, at least that is what I told Estelle at the time. We managed a drive up the East coast and a trip over to Orlando. Even that was bizarre (my favourite word), we were invited along to view a timeshare in return for breakfast and tickets for Sea World, well it was a cloudy morning first thing, so we went along and had a nice breakfast, then the sun came out and we left to have a fabulous day at Sea World. At the time we had no

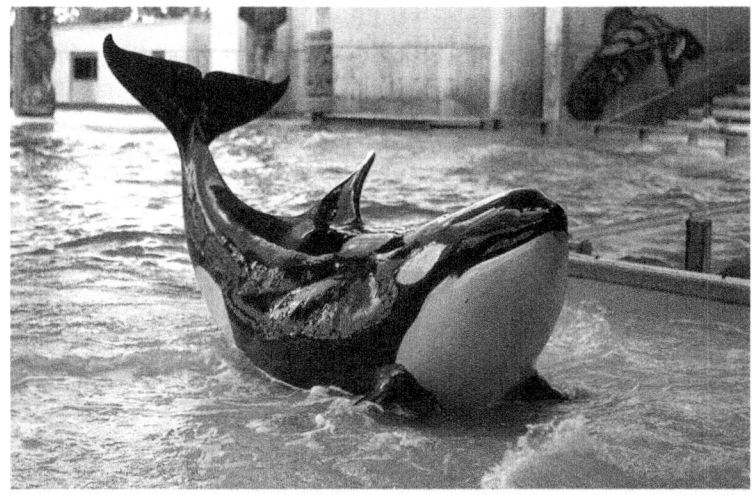

intention of buying a property in Florida, though I now regret not buying anything as it would be worth a bob or two today!

Sunday arrived quickly and we went over to the Tampa game, the Tampa Bay Buccaneers v Chicago Bears, The Bucs Quarterback was Vinny Testarverde versus the Bears Mike Tomczak, no contest at the time, although Vinny was a Heisman Trophy winner.

A few days later we were on our way home, we attempted a couple of beach days but the weather broke with rumours of a hurricane coming in, so we gave it a miss and headed across Alligator Alley. We didn't see one gator and when we did arrive at the airport in Miami our plane was delayed for 24 hours because of the weather, so we spent the day by a hotel pool courtesy of the airline. It was only a short break but enjoyable, enough to create a liking for America and most importantly it has become an historic event in my personal calendar.

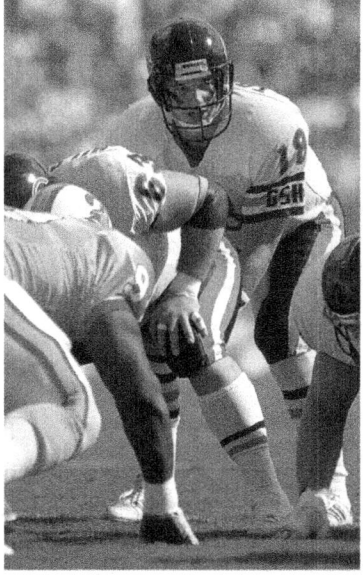

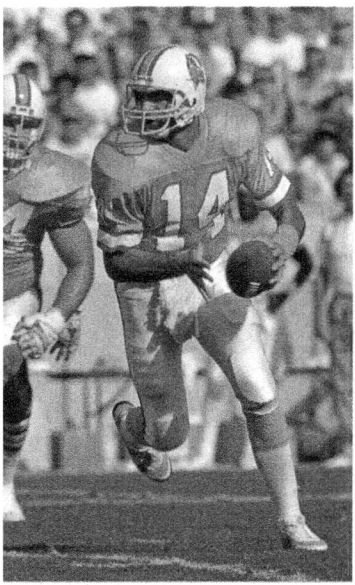

The next year 1989 we decided, well I did, to go to the USA again, I had to convince Estelle it was another vacation for her, while I would be building up the stock in my travel picture library, and we could of course go to the occasional American Football game!

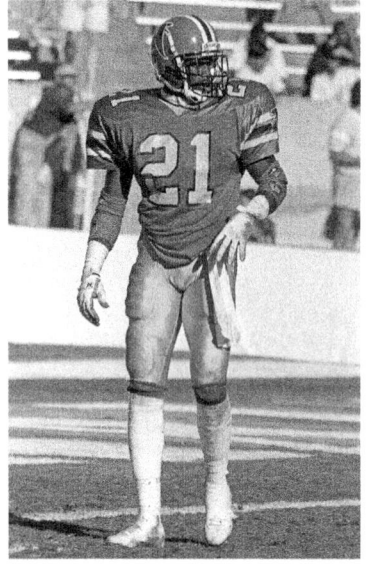
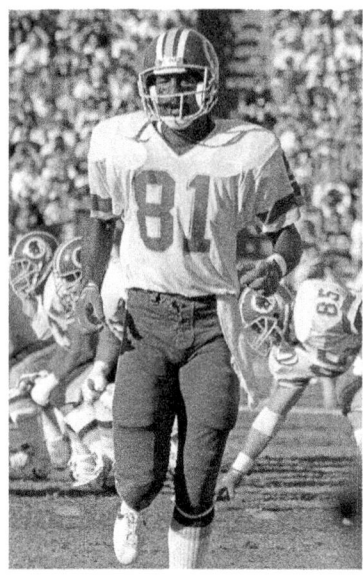
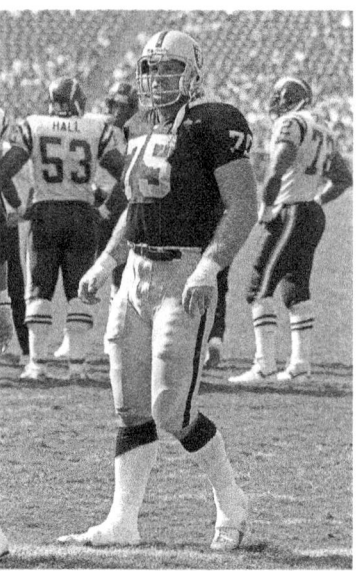

So I planned a trip with a couple of thousand miles driving, well you do don't you? San Diego, Los Angeles, Phoenix, the Grand Canyon and Las Vegas. With just a few games slipped in along the way. Well

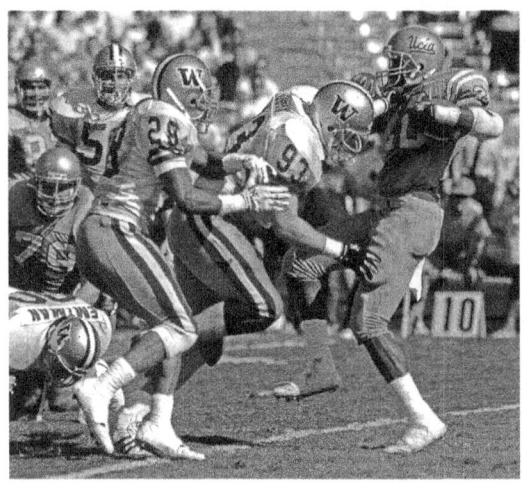

here are the 'few' games we saw, San Diego Chargers v Seattle Seahawks, Arizona Wildcats practice, Arizona Sundevils v Oregon Ducks. That game was wild they had to stop the game for an hour because of thunder and lightning, the heavens opened up and it poured with rain, well they were playing the Ducks, I guess they travel with their own weather. Fortunately for me the sun came back out the next day for the Phoenix Cardinals v Atlanta Falcons game. While we were there we checked out the old western town of Tombstone, to see the OK Coral, then we headed over to Vegas, via the Grand Canyon and the Hoover Dam, on the way to Los Angeles, well it is on the way sort of.

In LA we saw the UCLA Bruins v Washington Huskies and finally the LA Raiders v Washington Redskins.

I had a funny moment at the Raiders game and I don't mean my health. I was taking pictures from the sidelines of the Raiders Bo Jackson when a gentleman tapped me on the shoulder and said, "you'll have to take a knee," I turned around expecting to see an official security guard making this demand, but no, to my surprise I recognised the man as that well known television and movie actor James Garner, (now I know what he does on weekends) he went on to explain, "so the spectators can see over your shoulder" fair enough

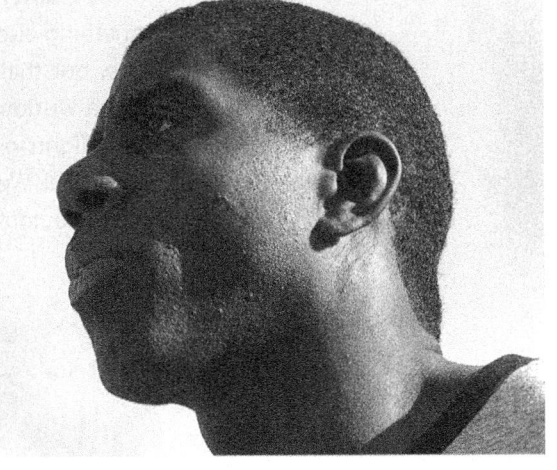

I thought, but here is the funny bit, as I took a knee I noticed another person standing along side me, I turned around and realised I was in line with his knee cap. As I looked up and up, I was thinking just who does this guy think he is with his head in the clouds, then I realised who it was, the NBA's all time leading scorer basketball player Kareem Abdul Jabbar all seven foot two of him. I guess the spectators didn't mind if he was standing in the way!

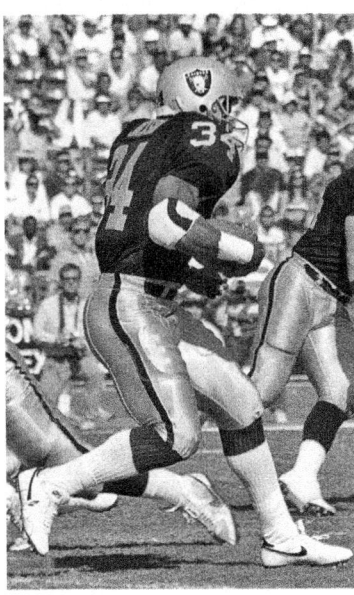

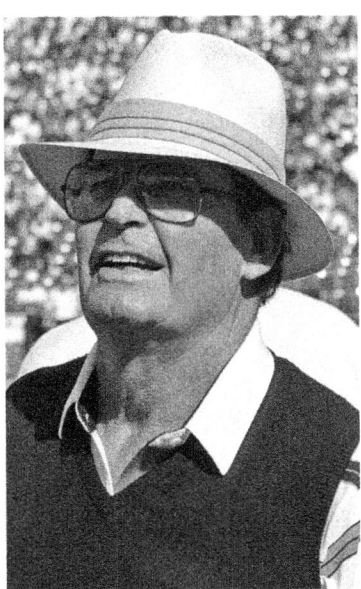

The Hoover Dam was big but our Grand Canyon experience was something else. We went to the usual tourist site along the canyon ridge, but that wasn't enough for me, was it. So I decided in my infinite wisdom, I could get some great pictures if we took one of those flights over the canyon. It was a beautiful sunny day and no wind, ideal. Well we boarded the little prop plane, I thought at the time it wouldn't need to go too high just to fly over the canyon, and

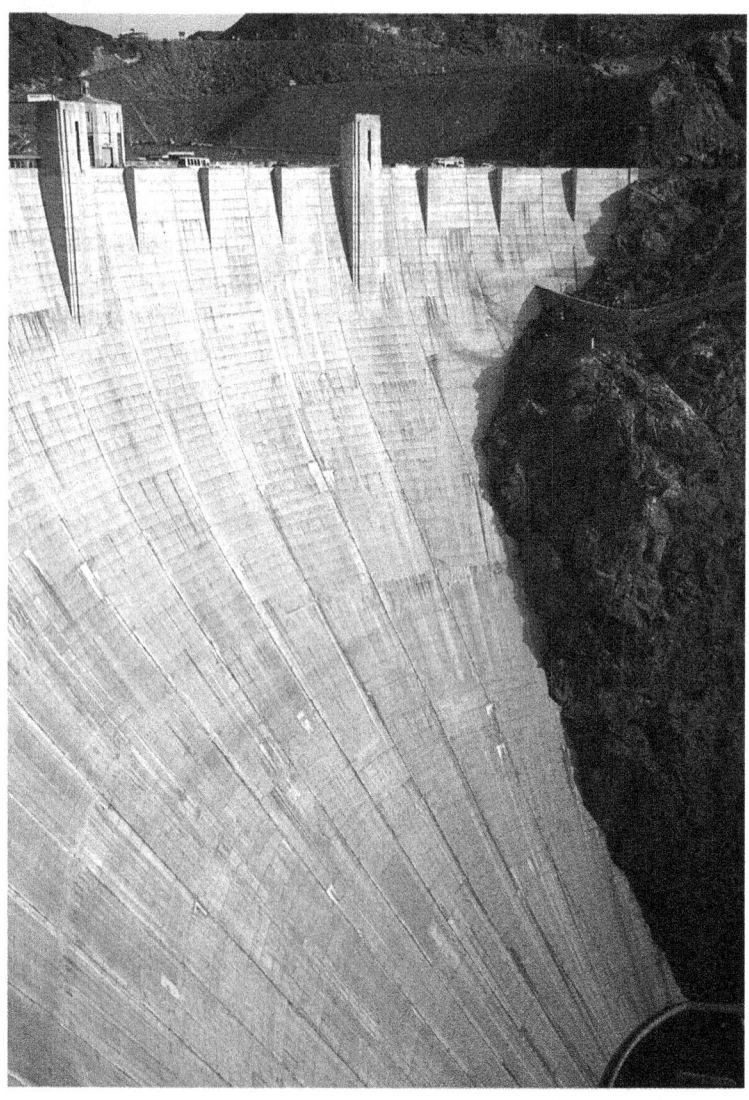

it didn't, but as it went out over the canyon it was obviously 1000's of feet from the bottom. I never thought of that. Duh! And what's more, as it entered over the canyon it hit the rising hot air pockets they forgot to tell us about. I have never photographed a subject as much as I did on that day, the camera never left the one eye I kept open, even when I was changing films. I got enough pictures for a book on it's own, and when we finally landed I was in need of a stiff drink!

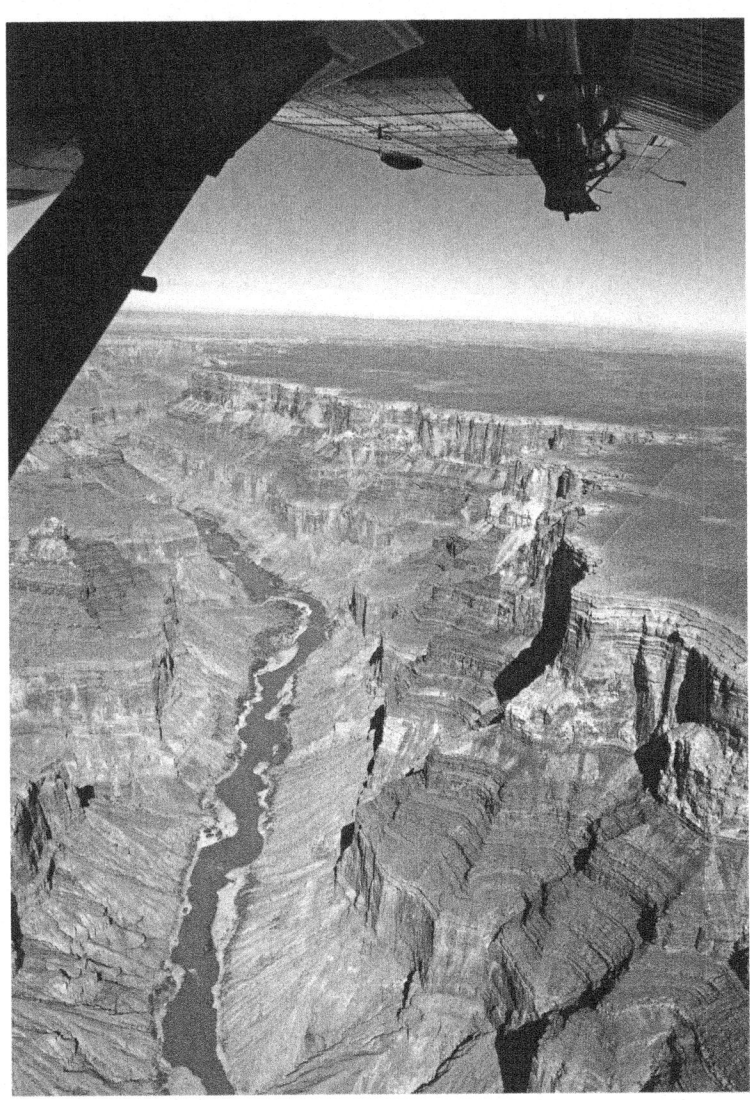

By the time the next NFL season came around in 1990 we were making it an annual pilgrimage. I figured I could work rest and play all in one trip. So we flew into Ohio for a weekend then on to New Orleans for the classic Monday Night Game and then the usual thousand or so miles driving while we went sight seeing to Vicksburg, Dallas, Fort Worth, Austin, Houston, Padre Island and even the Alamo in San Antonio, this book is starting to sound like a tourist guide. On the way of course we picked up the games at Cincinnati Bengals v New York Jets, New Orleans v San Francisco 49 ers, Dallas Cowboys v New York Giants, Texas Longhorns v Colorado Buffalos, Houston Oilers v Indianapolis Colts and as we were in Dallas even a Rodeo!

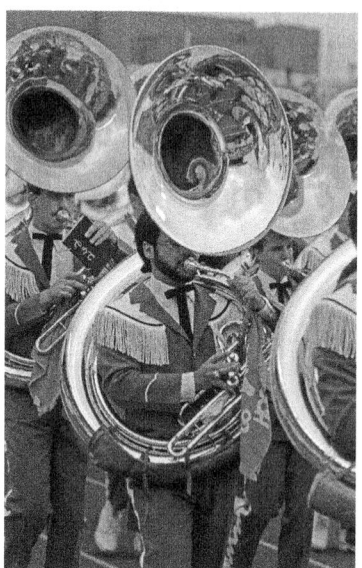 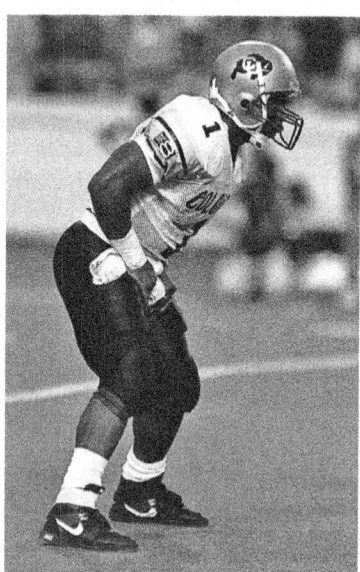 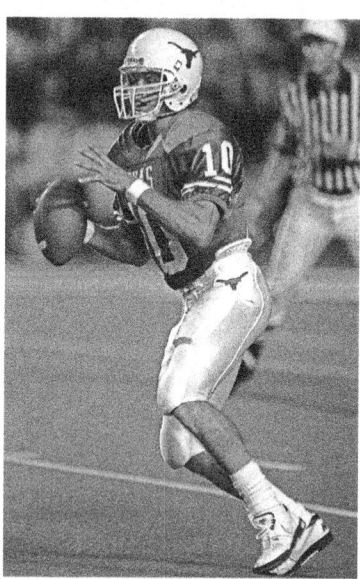

It does all look very glamorous, and as a member of the press we are often treated differently to the general public, I remember one occasion in particular at the Dallas game, we arrived at the press entrance to the stadium, showed our passes and got in the lift, or elevator if you prefer, we looked at the floor list and at the top it said press room, so we went straight to the top, came out the elevator and followed the signs for the press room, arrived at the open door and stepped inside. There was a lavish and an extravagantly laid out buffet, what looked like suckling pig with all the trimmings on it, we were just about to help ourselves to this pre game meal for the press, when we were approached and asked in a somewhat arrogant tone, what were we doing in here! Proudly I showed off my press pass. "Sorry," was the response, "you are not allowed in here you need to go downstairs." So we returned to the elevator and followed the directions for the next press room on the

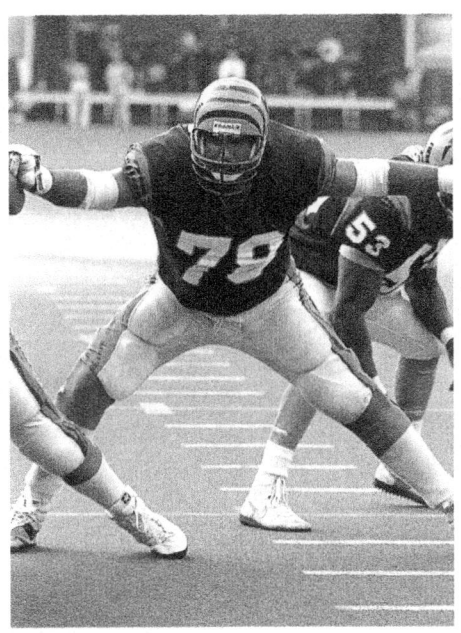

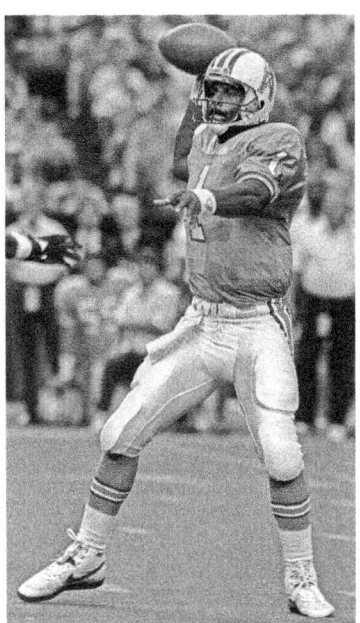

next level, we didn't make it into the door this time, as the doorman suggested we needed to follow the number on the press pass to find our room on a lower level, before we left he let us peep into the room, and sure enough there was another buffet laid out, only this time it just looked like chicken and chips. We climbed back into the elevator and asked someone where do we go with our passes? "Oh you need to go right down to the bottom", so we did and when the door opened we discovered what our pre game meal would be for the rest of the day, you can't wait can you? Guess what? A hotdog!

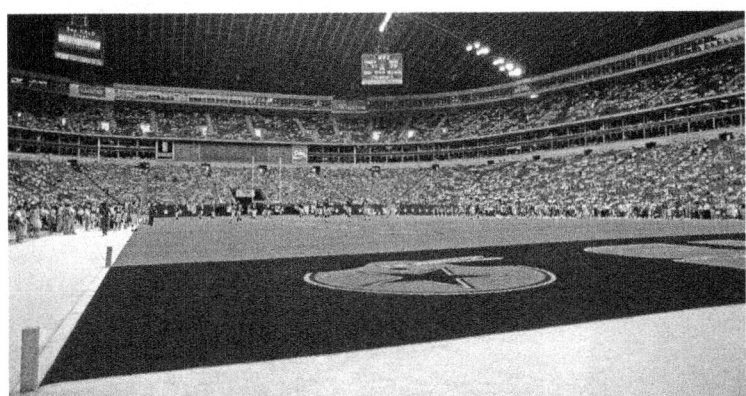

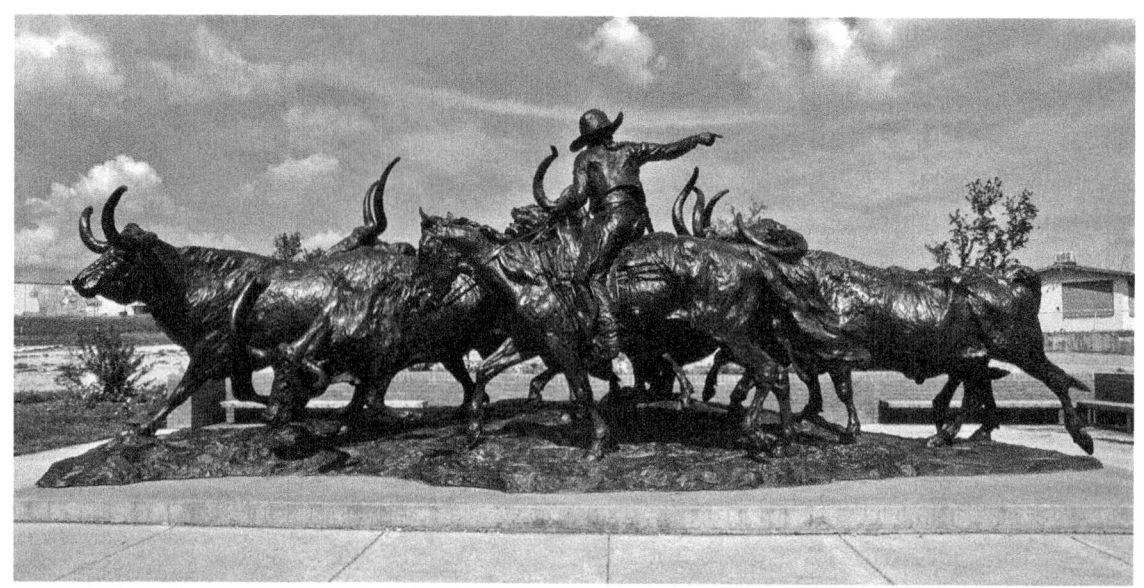

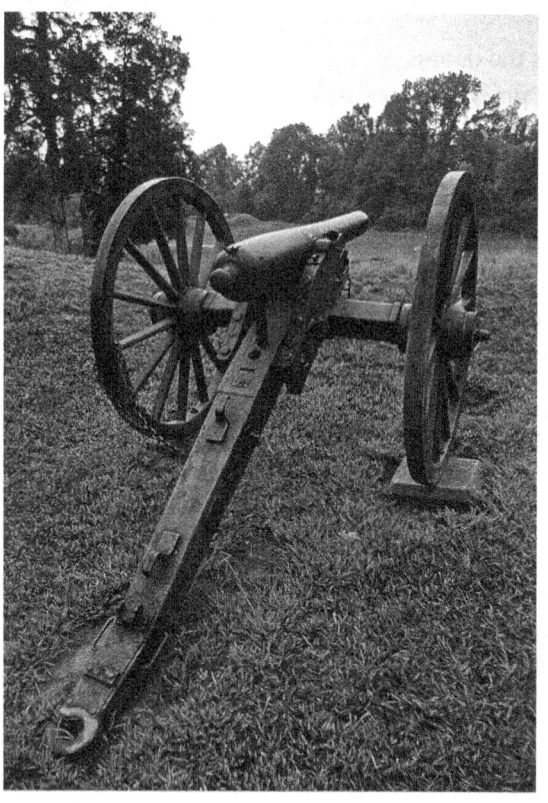

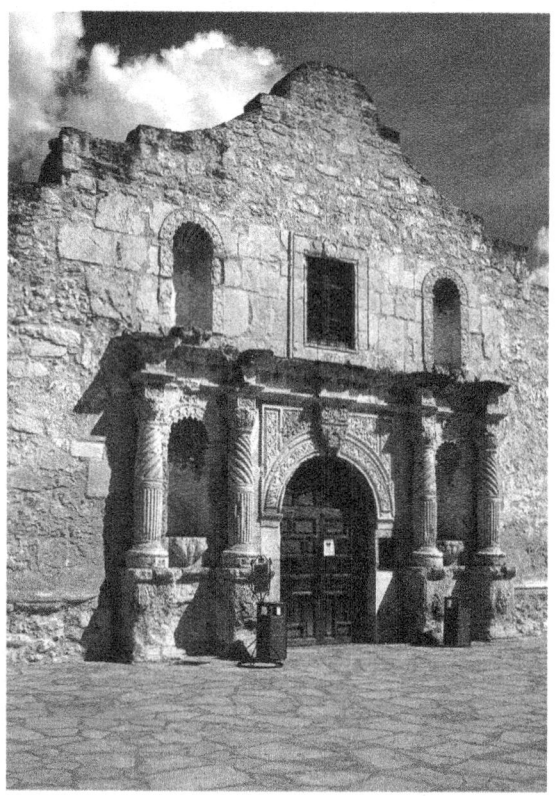

NEARLY FAMOUS

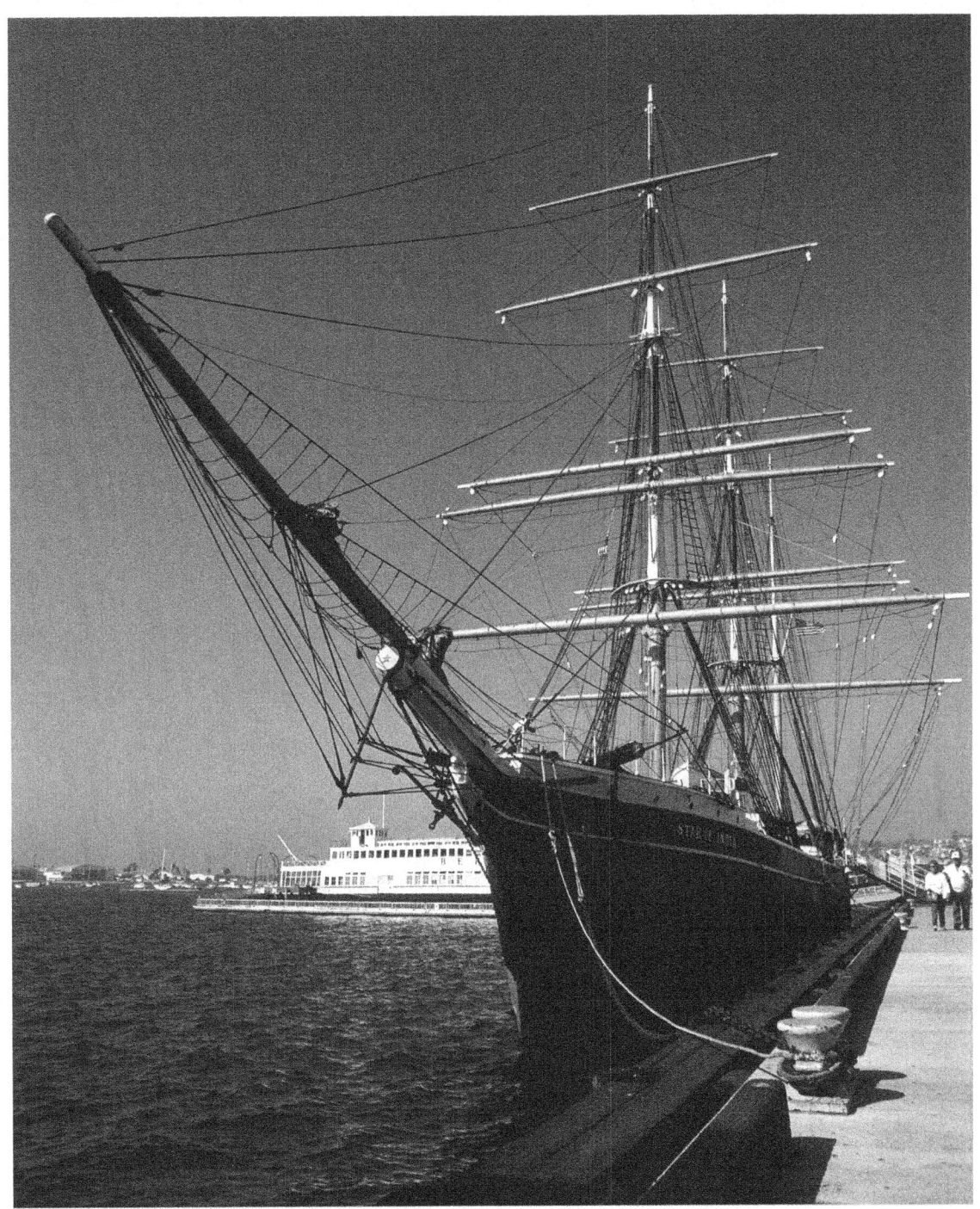

Oh, I nearly forgot, as well as all of the football and building up the travel stock photographs we also managed a couple of Baseball games too, Texas v Milwalkee and Houston Astros v LA Dodgers!

Texas was a great State but it's enormous and such a lot to see. We drove back to New Orleans for the flight home taking in Baton Rouge on the way, I was starting to think that my actual vacation was when we arrived back home and I went back to work covering the British amateur leagues.

By the time the NFL season came around again in 1991, we just couldn't stop, notice I say we, why should I take all the blame? We decided to go back to California again, this time we would do the Northern trip to San Francisco, Yosemite, Reno and back to Los Angeles, yeah only a small trip this time, we must have been getting tired, or we could have been running out of money. The usual mileage netted visits to the following games. San Francisco 49 ers v LA Rams, LA Rams v Green Bay Packers, UCLA Bruins v California Bears, LA Raiders v San Diego Chargers.

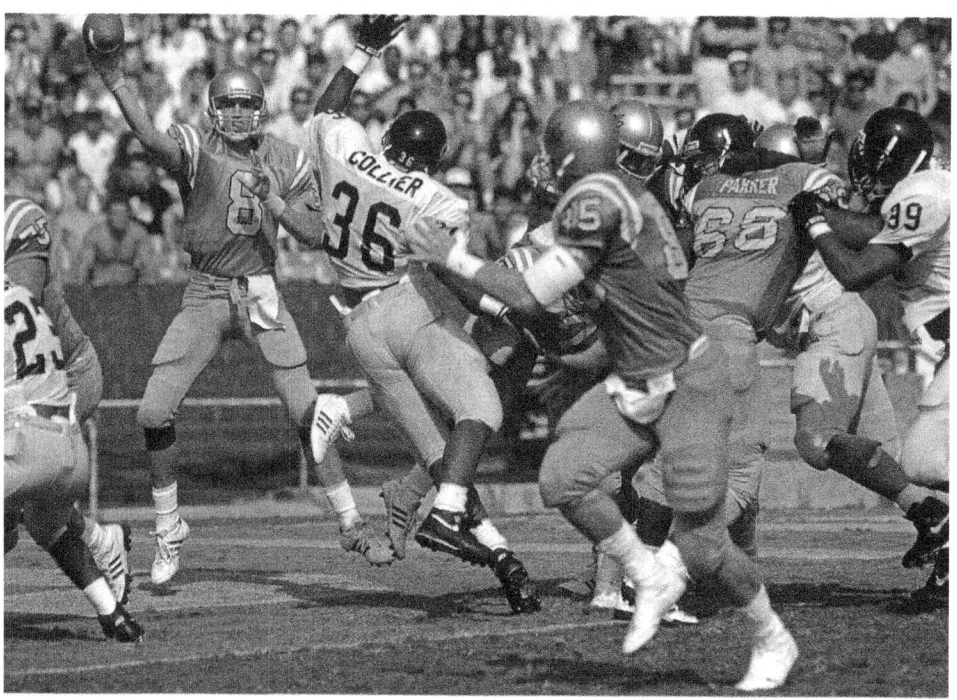

NEARLY FAMOUS

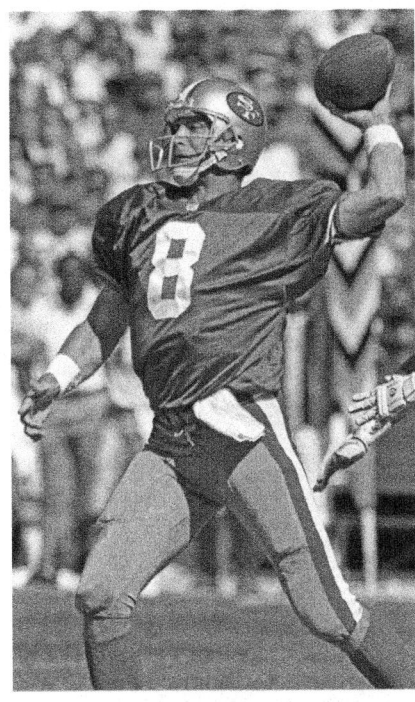

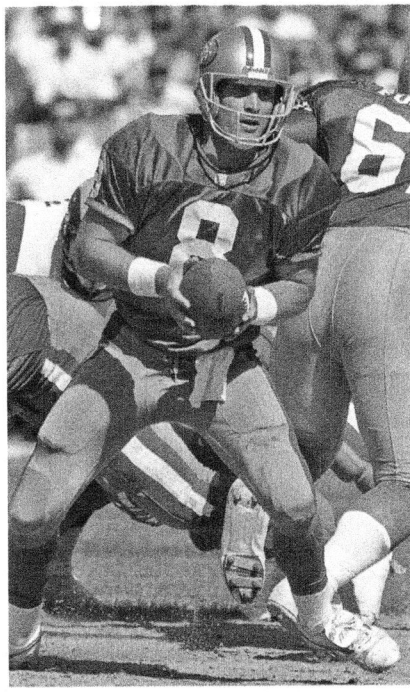

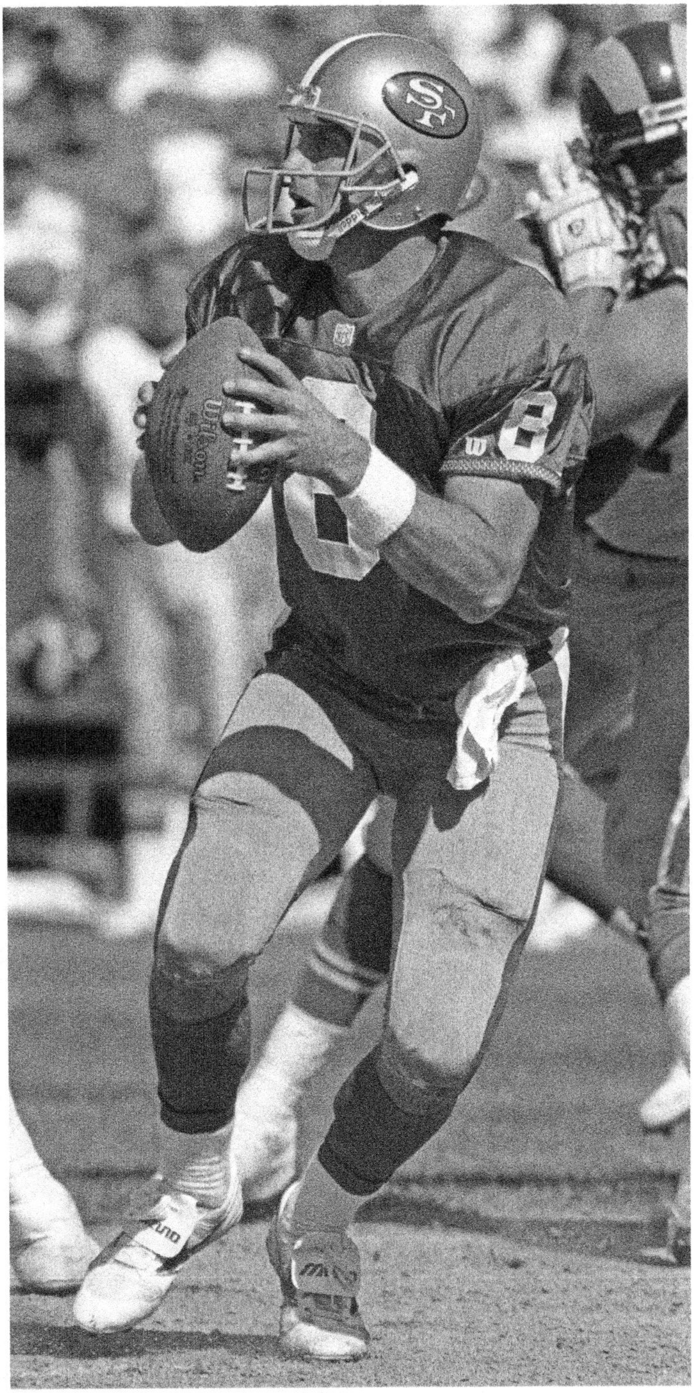

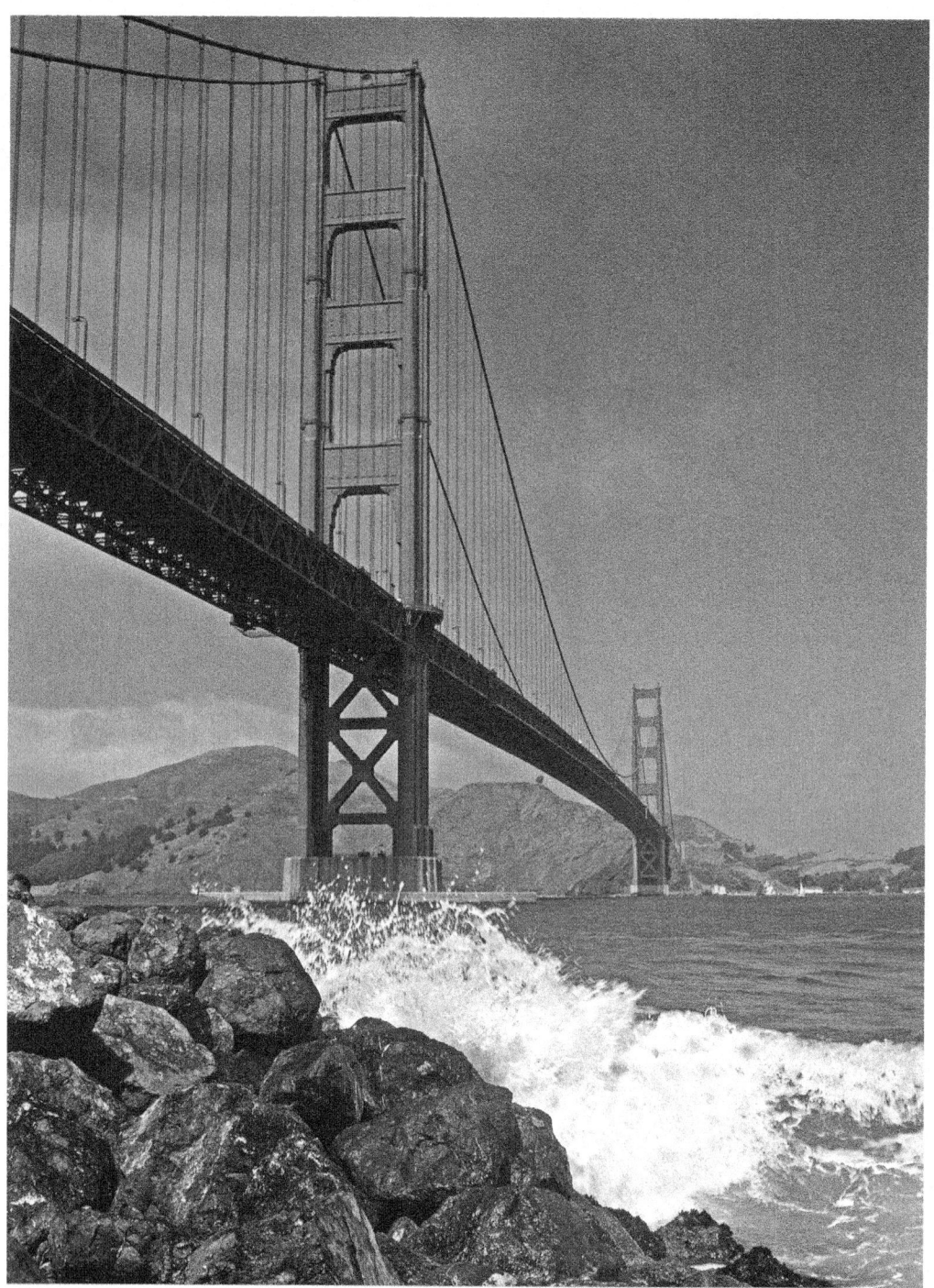

NEARLY FAMOUS

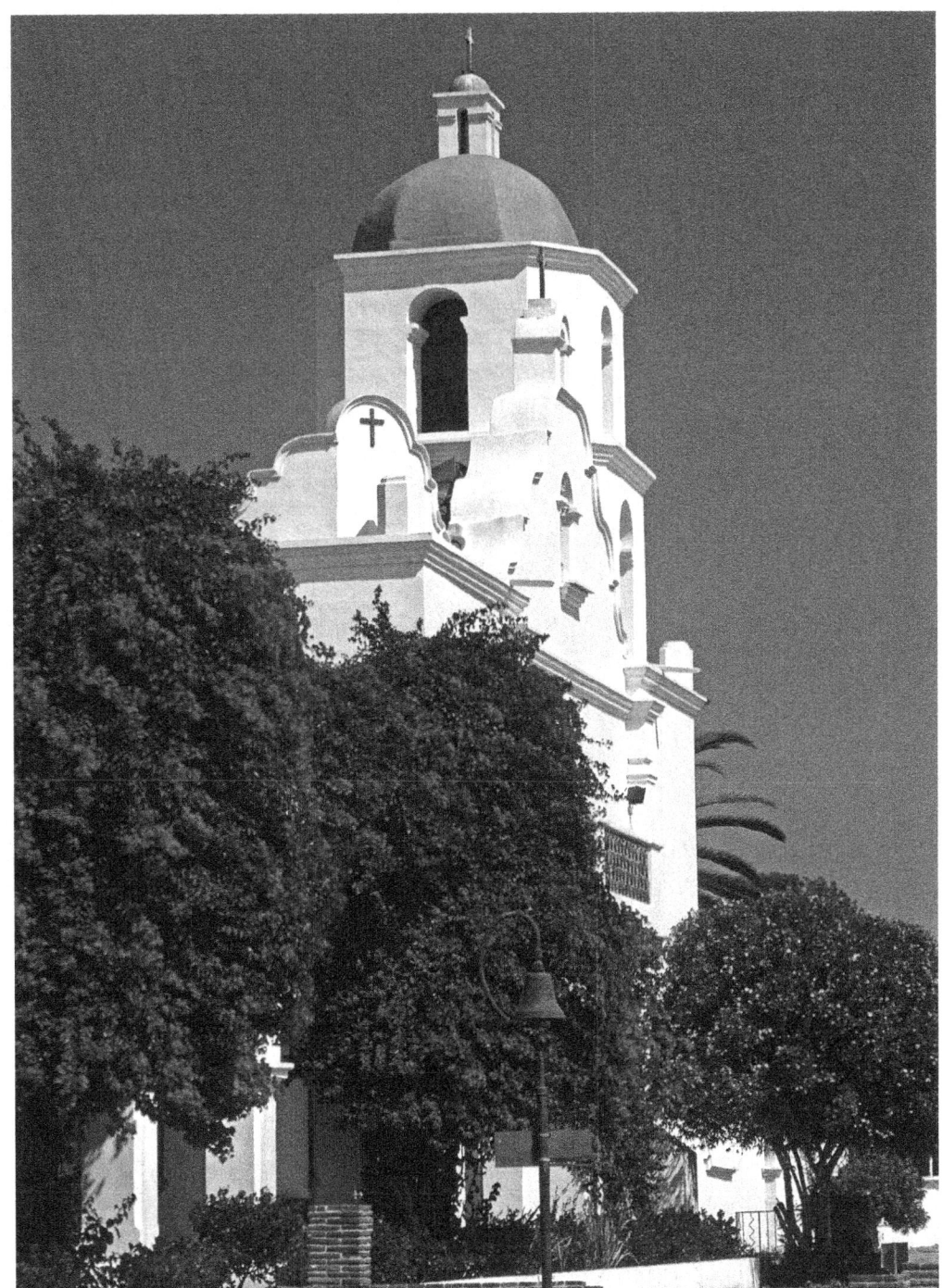

Back to the British game, which was great. There was a fantastic group of dedicated guys involved in the sport that kept it running, but the slow down was inevitable and sponsorship maybe had a lot to blame for it. Often the sponsors involvement had a psychological effect, lifting the teams out of the doldrums especially when they were struggling, but when they pulled out completely it demoralised the whole league.

Players were always complaining about the way they were treated, actually it was more the way they seemed to be ignored. I know a lot of players at the time thought the sponsors were only in it for themselves, in reality sponsors are in the business of promoting their product, I can't speak for the individuals involved!

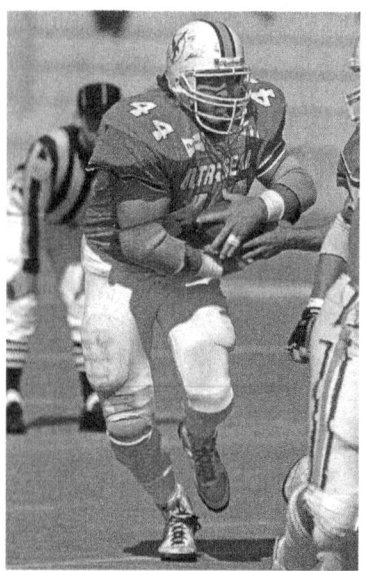 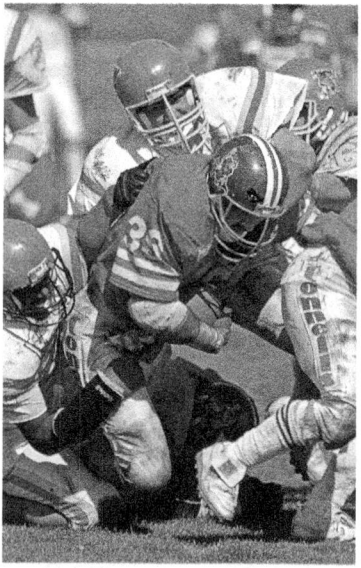 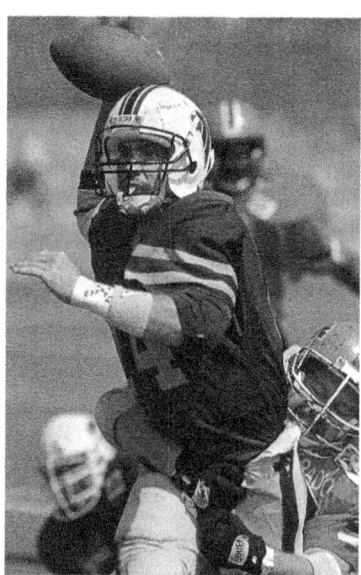

I know there were always lavish events put on for the VIP's, heck I was even asked to photograph a few, I also worked the sidelines and felt the heart of football, I just listened to what the players had to say.

Remember they were all amateurs, paying for the privilege to play in the leagues, sponsorship should have helped these teams, but somehow it never seemed enough or placed in the right place. Hey, what do I know? Economics was not my forte!

NEARLY FAMOUS

The World League 1991-1992

Just when the sport was starting to drop off the professional American football "World League" came along, and in 1991 the London Monarchs were born. Working as a freelance I always paid my own travel expenses, these costs were about to rise dramatically

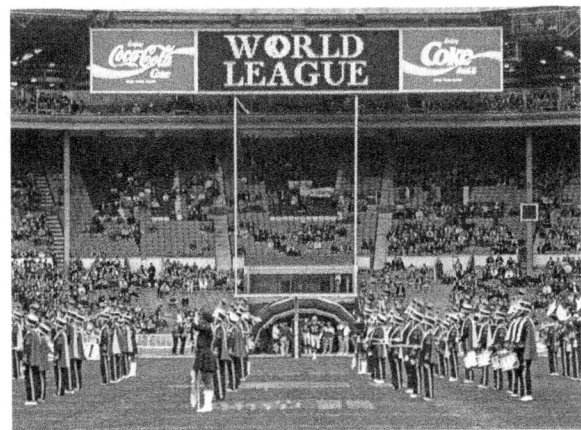

as I attempted to cover this new league. Despite this, I travelled out to Frankfurt to watch them play their first game in Europe, and I continued to travel even to the USA to get exclusive pictures, it kept me in the ball game so to speak. I was still supplying photographs to the main publications, only problem now, 'Uncle Tom Cobbly and all' were photographing this new intercontinental game and sending their pictures in, even the best photographers in the world can't be everywhere and capture everything, though I really did try. The main difference between most of them and me was that they all had regular nine to five jobs and football photography was only a paid hobby, where as it was my living. Basically it had the effect of reducing my income and the obvious effect of my travel budget going up explains why I don't have a pension today.

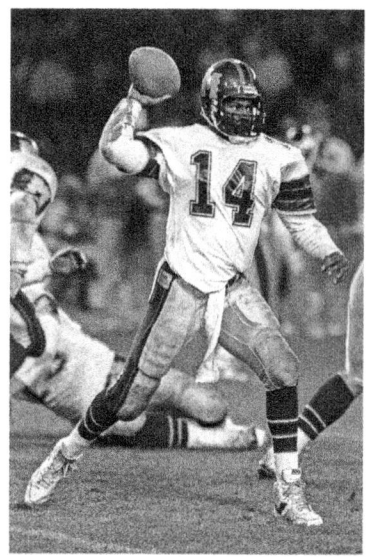
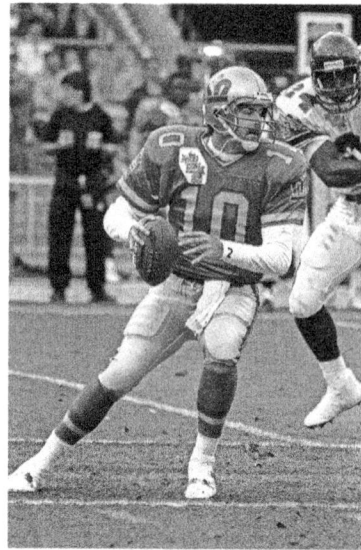
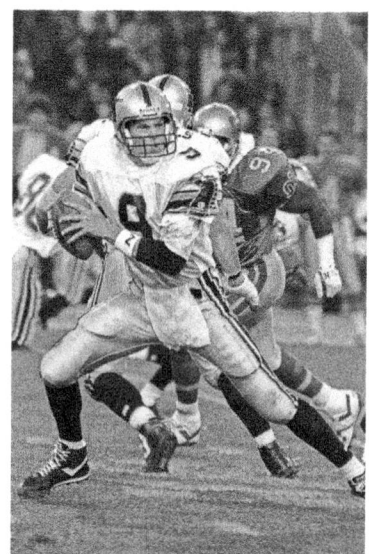

NEARLY FAMOUS

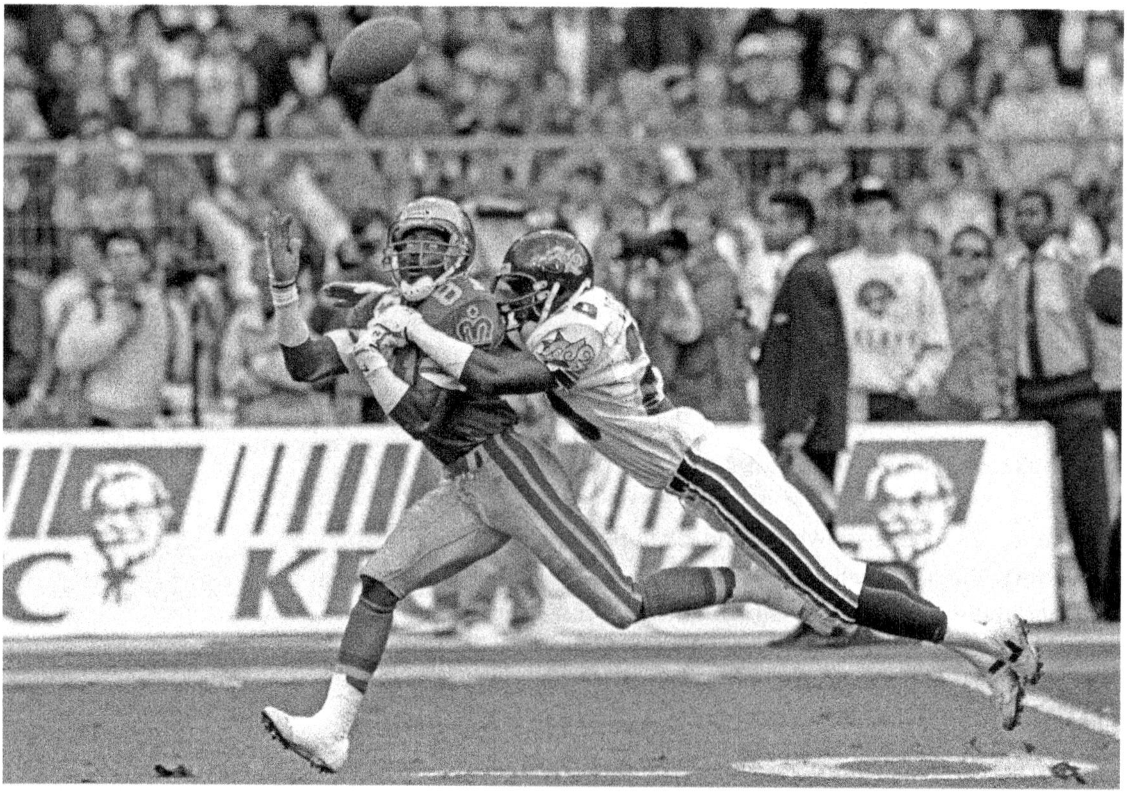

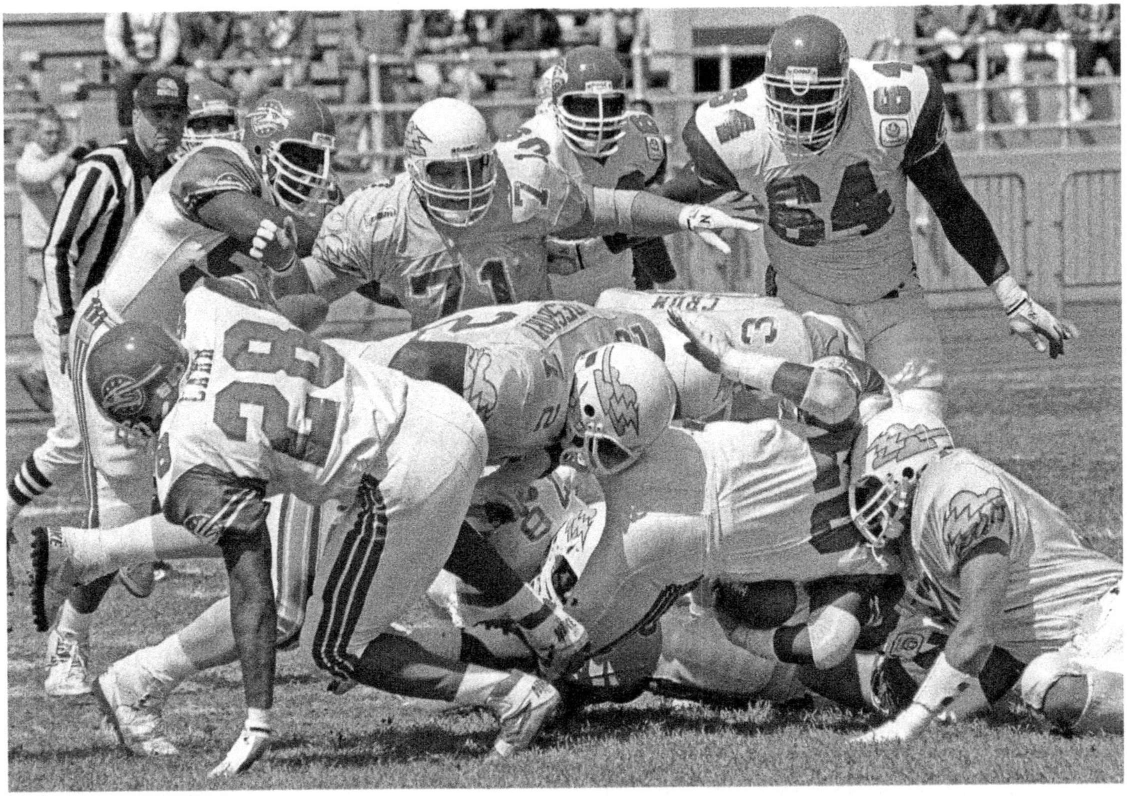

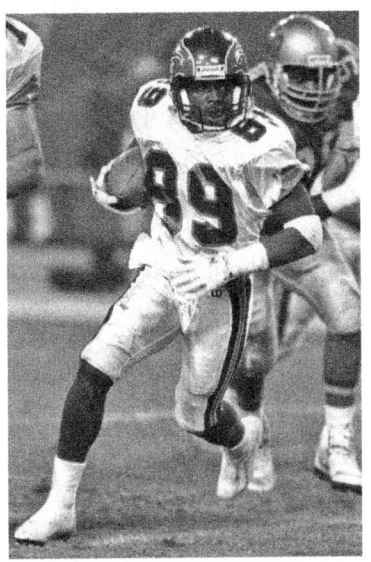

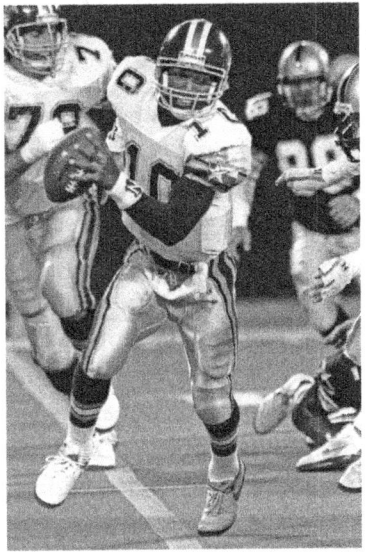

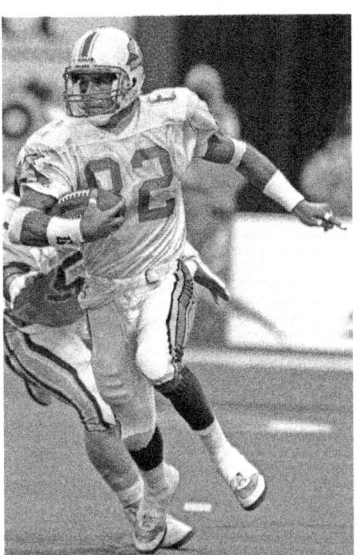

I decided to tough it out and hung in there. The Monarchs won the first World Bowl at Wembley beating the Barcelona Dragons and we all went happily into a second season!

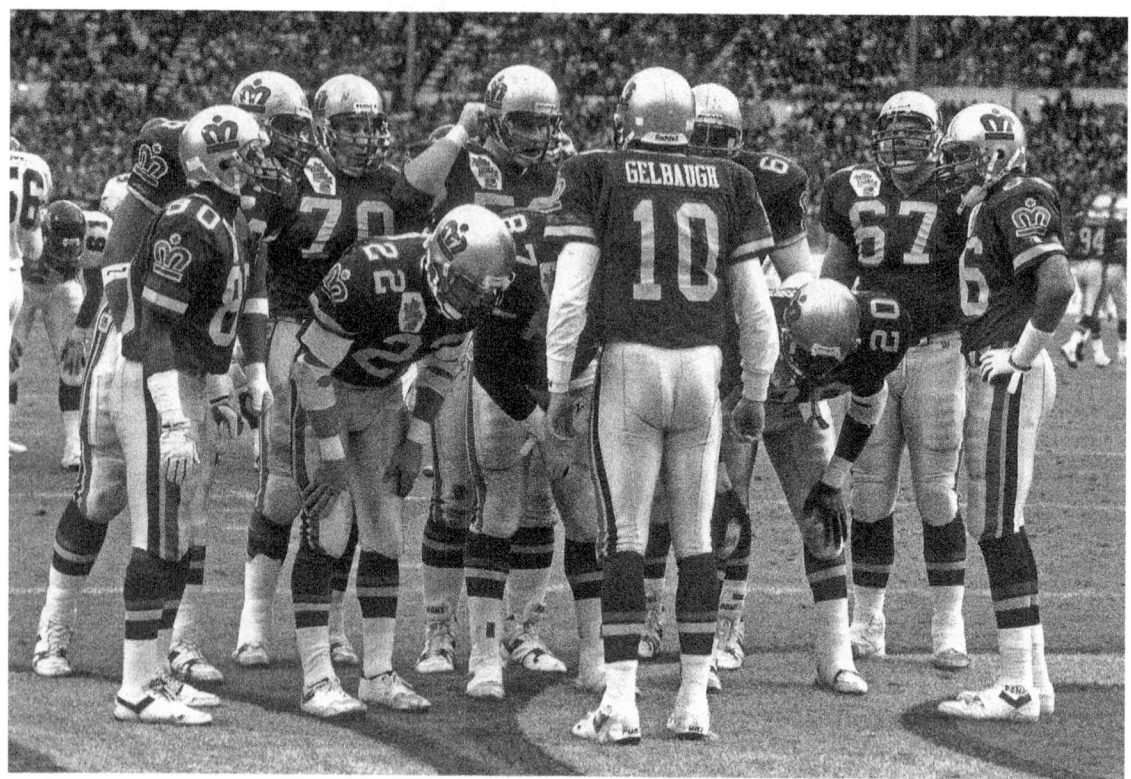

I carried on, knowing the more games I covered the better the chances of a publication and the bigger my stock library would get. I even flew off to Ohio to get pictures of the Glory at their home game against the Orlando Thunder, that was a colourful game, you needed sun glasses to watch it. Now flying is not my favourite form of travel, in fact I have stopped flying altogether now, this little story didn't help my concerns at all. I had to take an internal flight from Columbus to New Jersey for my connection home, it was a rather small plane I thought at the time, having just flown in a day earlier on a large transatlantic flight. Regardless, I boarded the plane with a half dozen passengers and because it was a small plane there was no first or business class, so I sat right at the front. After a long wait an announcement came over the internal system, there was going to be a short delay, so I waited, and waited. A guy came on late and sat down next to me, at that point I thought they had held the plane back just for this guy, but no we still didn't leave, now I was starting to panic as I needed to make my transatlantic connection in New Jersey. I called the stewardess over and asked her how long we would be, she said why don't you ask the captain your sitting right next to him. Yes the guy next to me who was now drinking his coffee and reading a newspaper, the one who had come on board late was the captain. He had been outside checking the engines. He explained "Oh, it's just like your car, when the alternator goes you have to replace it don't you? As soon as we get a new replacement part we will be off". Well he hasn't seen some of the beat up cars I have driven so you can imagine what was going through my mind at the time!

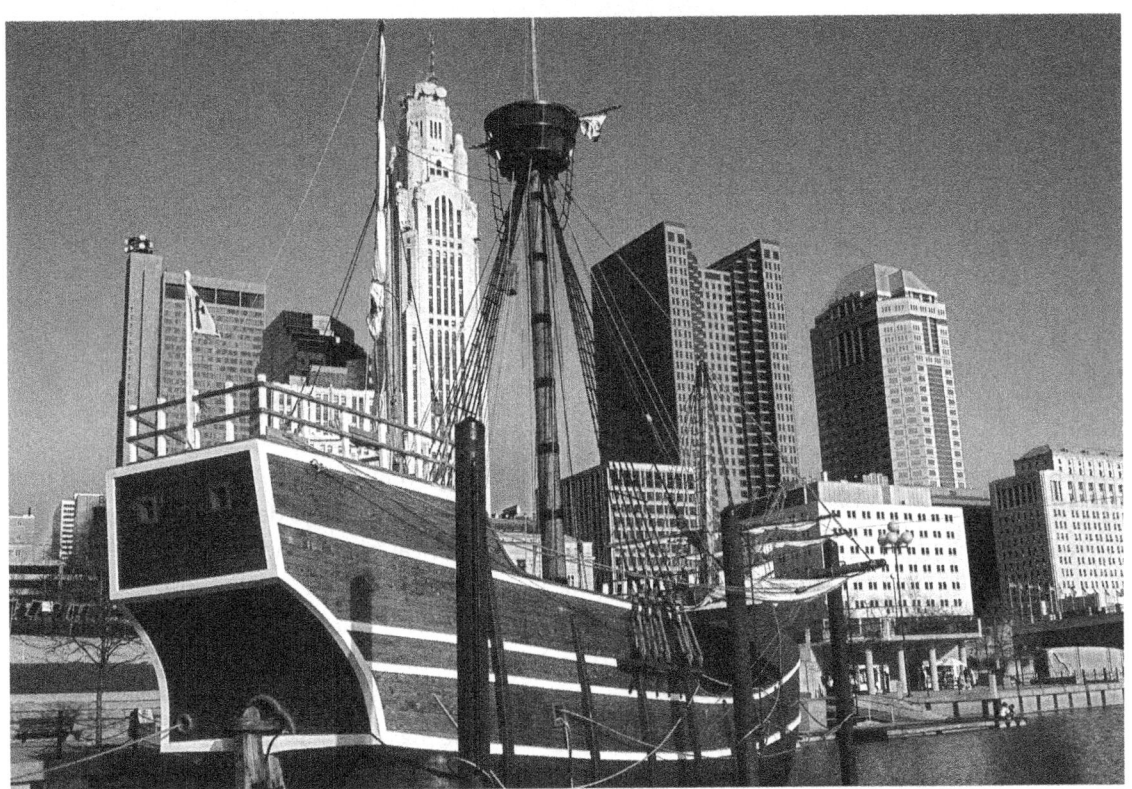

When the second World Bowl came along in 1992, I wasn't asked or commissioned to cover it, but you must know me by now, I went anyway. It was in Montreal and I called it a working vacation, sound familiar? Estelle and I flew into Toronto Canada, hired a car and, well first things first. We drove down to the Toronto Argonauts training camp to get pictures of Raghib Ismail the Argonauts wide receiver 'Rocket', we just had to, he was big news at the time. Then we started our traditional few thousand miles drive up through the country, taking in the capital Ottawa on the way, then all the way up to Quebec and finally back down to Montreal for the World Bowl.

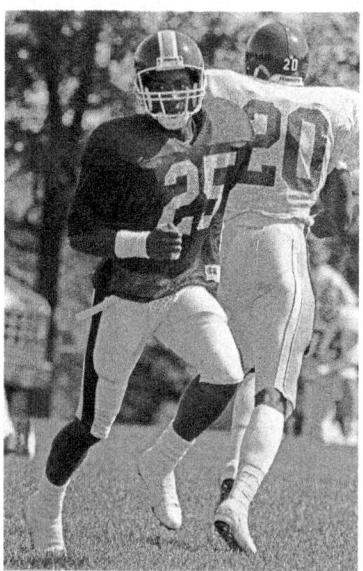 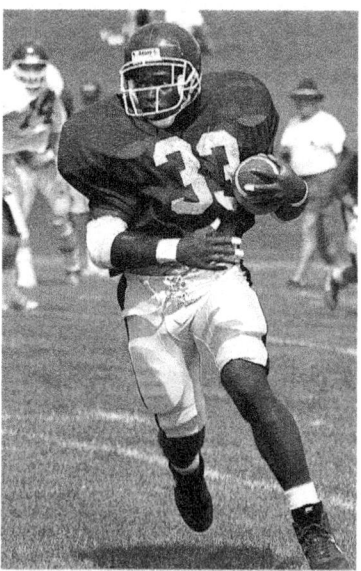

It was a good trip if somewhat strange. As you crossed the river at Ottawa, the roads, signs and countryside suddenly became like France, but I love the historical places and period style forts and events they held.

I'm pleased to say I was there when the Sacramento Surge beat the Orlando Thunder. I was at the press conference the next morning, when they announced all the great things they were going to do in this league, but, by the time my plane had landed on the return trip the 'World League' no longer existed!

NEARLY FAMOUS

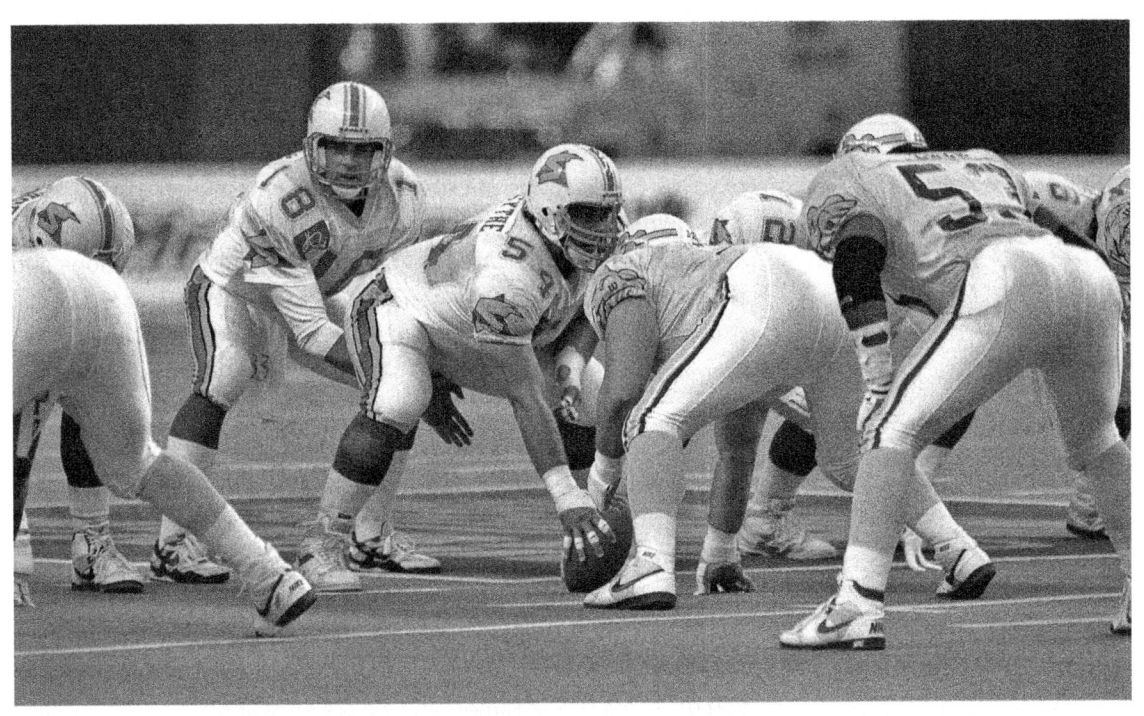

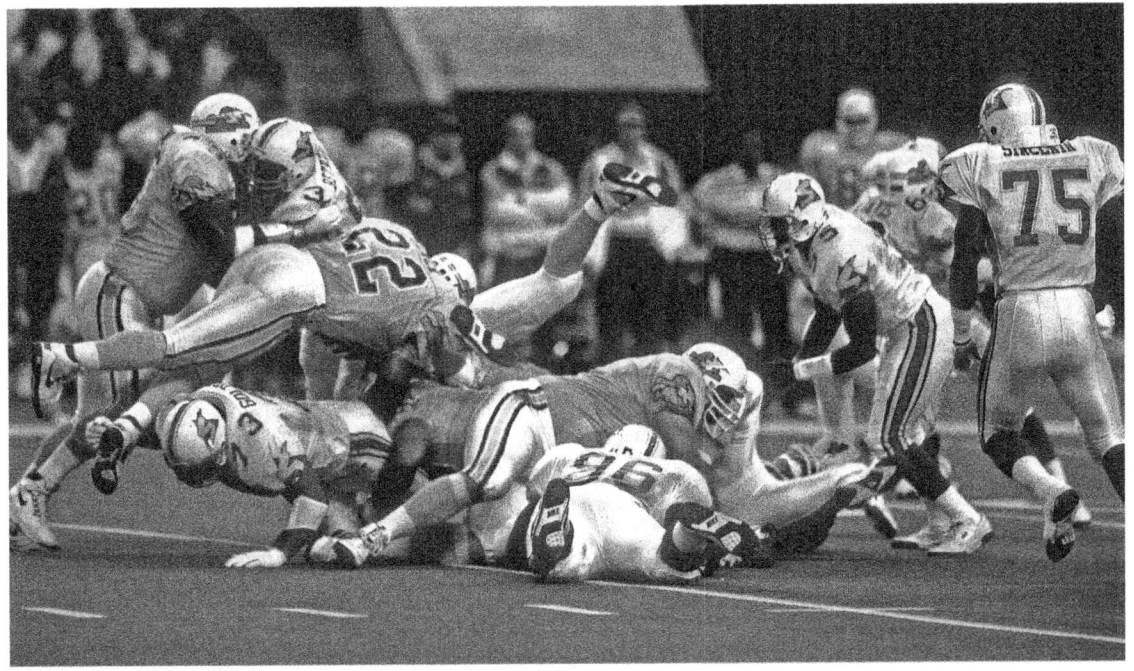

Now it was getting ridiculous, there was no way I could earn a living covering the British domestic league, and then suddenly, the bottom dropped out of my sports world completely. The main user of my American football photographs sold their magazine to a chain of soccer publications, not surprisingly the new owners started using their own photographers, the sport was diminishing and I just couldn't keep supporting my own coverage without regular publications, and that was that, the end of my serious coverage of American football at the domestic level. I would still go to local games, American bowls at Wembley and finals but it was all starting to fizzle out.

I still had the urge to travel to the States and sure enough in 1993 decided on the North East this time, and off we went, Boston, New York and Washington, inevitably we went to a few games for our vacation. Okay you're not surprised anymore, in fact your probably getting a little bored by now so I will keep this bit really short.

We saw the New England Patriots v Cincinnati Bengals, New York Jets v Dallas Cowboys, Washington Redskins v Atlanta Falcons, there you go, some Hall of Famers and we are off skiing!

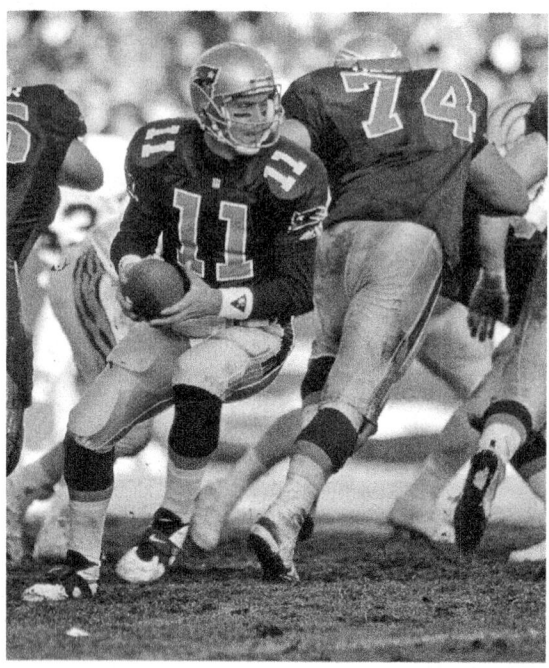
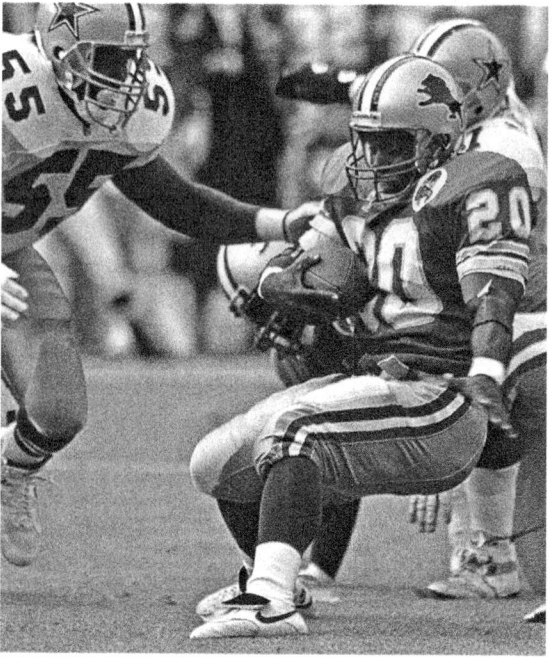

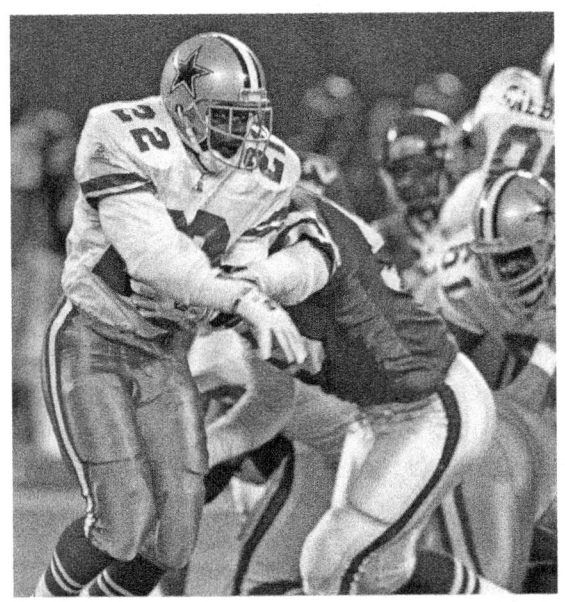
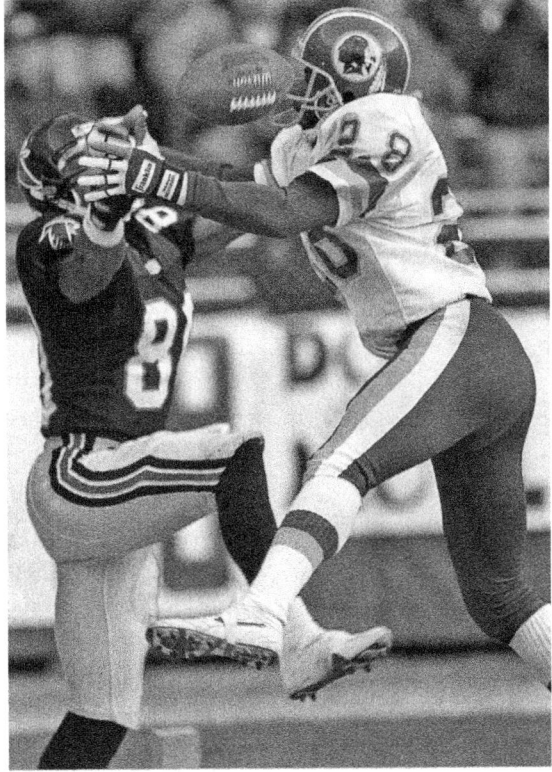
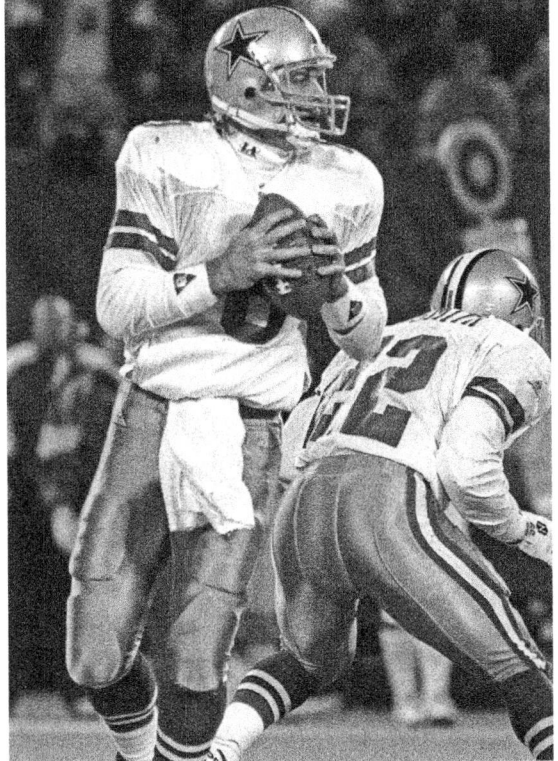
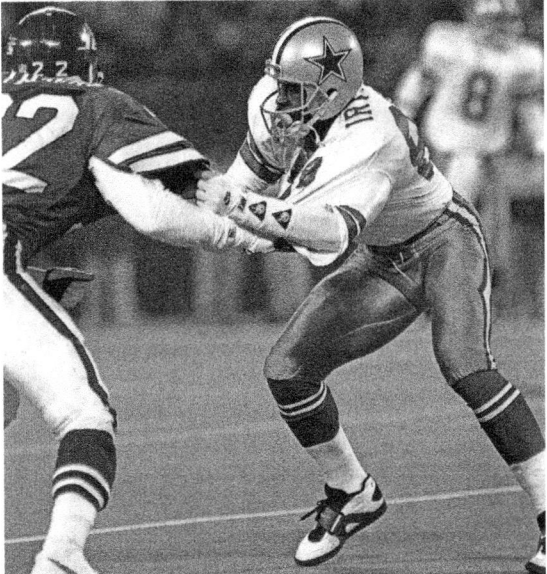

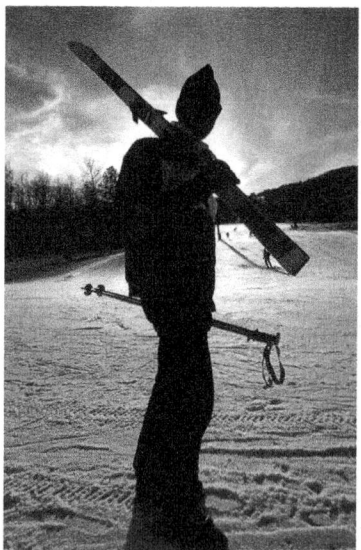

Yes I said skiing! Now that might sound like a precarious thing to do if you are frightened of heights, but it was on a whim and in a vain attempt to convince Estelle we could take a vacation, (honest) off we went. Well we were in New England, in the snow and needed something to do between the games, so we headed up to Killington for a five day break.

Have you been skiing in New England? Well it's certainly fun but it's also hard work, especially in the icy conditions of the North Eastern States, like our trips weren't tough enough to start with!

We spent the first few days taking lessons on the nursery slope, yes with all the other kids! Then we progressed to the beginners hill, which wasn't too high. As we got better I figured out that going straight downhill was fast and fun, until I got to the bottom one day heading in the direction of the lake and found I couldn't stop. Fortunately I just managed to squeeze my legs apart into the widest snow plough manoeuvre you could imagine, not a pretty sight. After a couple of days Estelle was convinced she was going to give it up altogether, it was only by talking to another group of skiers in the ski lodge that helped change her mind.

By the end of the week I thought we could at least try one of the Intermediate trails, well I did, Estelle wasn't sure, but I convinced her everything would be okay in my hands! So we set off, jumped on the chair lift and waited as it started to climb what seemed to be a rather slow ascent, three quarters of the way up I realised why, this slope

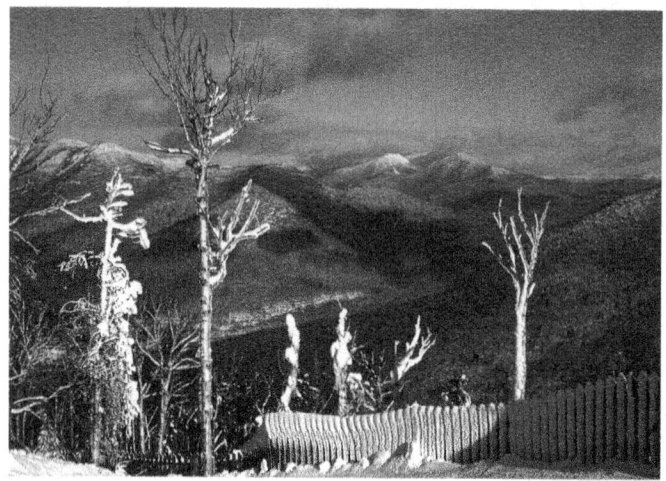

was twice as high and steep as we had been learning on. As we approached what seemed like nothing but fresh air, there wasn't another soul in sight, did they know something we didn't? Was the slope closed? Would we make it down before nightfall? I had a thousand questions I couldn't answer. I nervously suggested to Estelle to just hang on to me as we left the lift, as I had no idea what I was going to do in that terrified state! Fortunately as we came over the brow there was a wide stretch of soft snow before the drop off on either side. We gingerly made our way down the trail until it hit the tree level and then sped up when our confidence started to return. As it neared the bottom I was feeling quite confident, there was one final downhill run that went round a bend through a clearing, "Follow me" I shouted to Estelle and went tearing off, leaning into the bend like a professional downhill skier. Just then, as I came around the corner, a group of people appeared in the way. They had stopped on the narrow part of the slope to discuss something. I

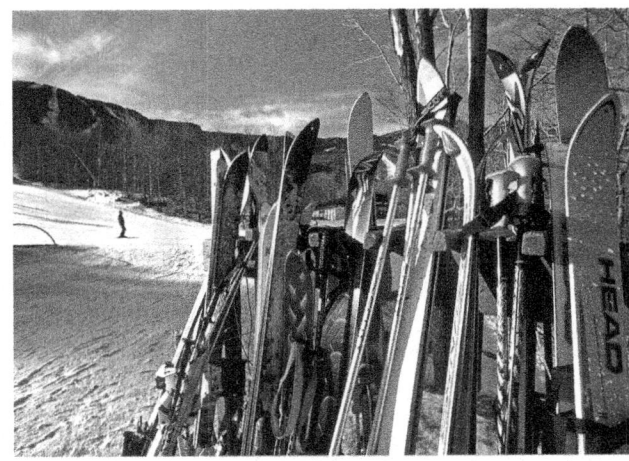

lifted my head and shouted, "Coming through," they parted and just as I thought my expertise as a downhill skier was coming to the fore, I hit a rut and landed in a heap right in the middle of this huddle of people. As the laughter died down Estelle casually glided down to me and asked, "Are you all right darling, are you hurt?" Of course I was hurt, my pride was shattered!

Unfortunately, rather than put me off, I started to think, maybe we could make a beginners guide to skiing and another vacation turned into a business venture. The next time, we all went skiing to Loon. Touring through the picturesque villages in New Hampshire along the way. I was carrying cameras and filmed the whole event for a DVD. With a year between each trip I was never going to be an accomplished skier, that and my fear of heights made it really difficult, fortunately for us we had a couple of good ski instructors and did start to improve, slightly. We tried to do some follow up filming at Aviemore in Scotland but the weather went against us on that occasion and we spent most of the time in the mist trying to find each other. It was an adventure but it was way too poor for filming.

So what did we do? Well we booked another trip to the USA. I had approached Smugglers Notch with the filming idea and they invited us up for a week to do a shoot. So slipping it in between the games as usual, Estelle, Dani and I trolled off up to Smugglers on the US Canadian border, a rather nice and exclusive Ski resort.

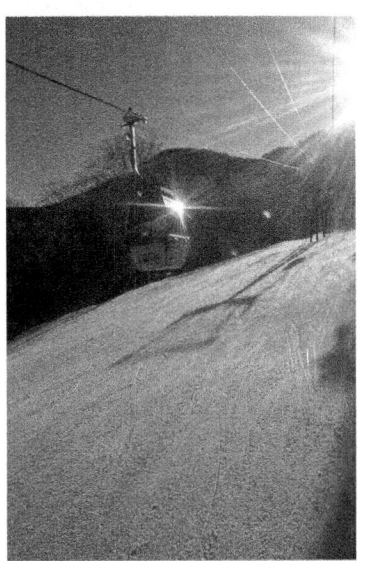

We were looked after really well and given access to the slopes and ski instructors. I was still struggling a bit with the skiing, but I was also having to photograph and film as I continued through the week, so my job wasn't easy. At least the camera work kept my mind off the heights! I never really made it to the very top it looked too extreme, even the intermediate trail looked really high and of course I had to look after my cameras, didn't I?

The day before we left the weather changed, it went wet and mild, so we decided to finish early and drive to the mall about twenty miles away. While we were inside it snowed heavily, returning to the car we discovered a complete white out, that's what you want right, when you are skiing? Well apparently not when the temperature is

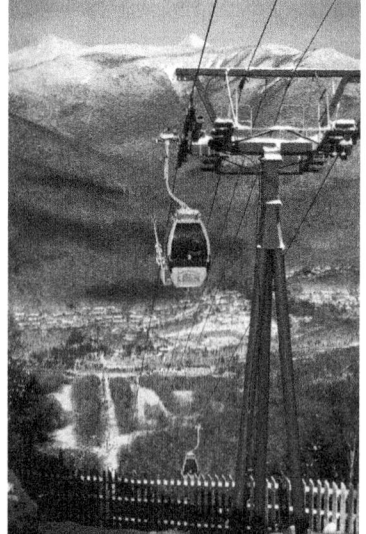

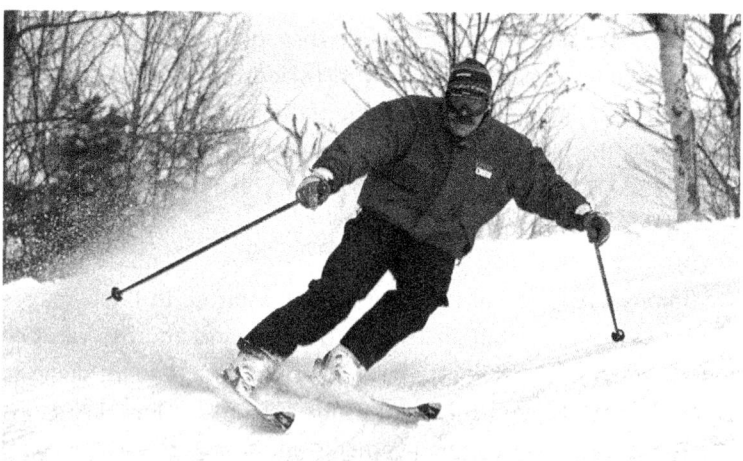

too high. It all melted very quickly and they started to close the roads because of flooding, and I mean excessive flooding, including our direct route back to Smugglers Notch. After being instructed to turn back by local police, we considered stopping in a motel, but we were due to leave in the morning and I needed my camera equipment. After checking the maps we saw there was another longer route through the back roads, it would take more time but should get us back, so we set off in the dark. After about an hour we were almost there, when suddenly we came to a spot in the road where the river had started to cross the road. I stopped just short of crossing, on the other side there was what looked like a snow plough truck with it's warning lights flashing. I flashed my lights at him and waved out of the window, but there was no response! I have to say at this point in the dark it was a bit like a scary movie, we waited but still nothing happened, now at this point there was no way I was going to get out of the car! I assumed it was there as a caution to make you slow down or the driver might have been asleep as it was really late, but as there were no signs saying don't cross and the water that was pouring over the road only looked shallow, I decided to go for it. On reflection it was probably a very silly thing to do given the circumstances, but I think I was more frightened of the unknown truck than the flooded road. Halfway across I could feel the car starting to slide slowly with the pressure from the river current. Though I was driving straight we

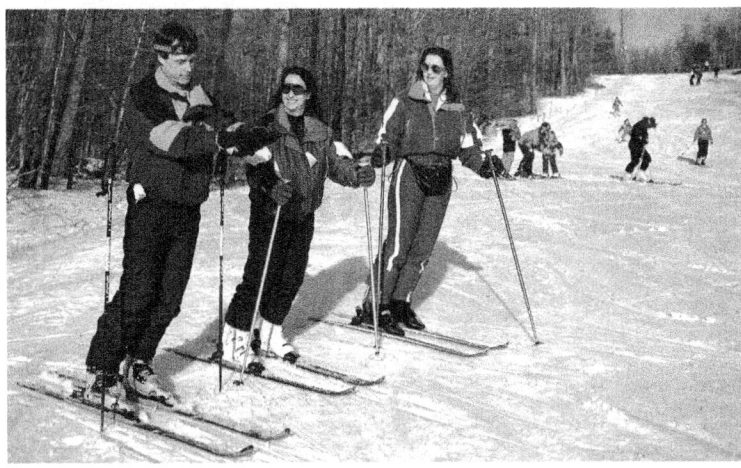

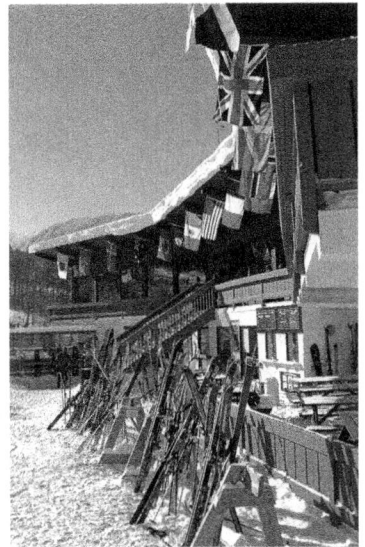

crossed the flooded road diagonally, but we did cross it and passing the truck we still didn't see anyone. It all stayed very quiet in the car until we got back to the resort safely, in our room I told the girls about the car slipping, Dani had felt it but kept quiet as she thought I was in control, if she'd only known, it really was a touch and go moment.

The next day we left via the same route and saw just how close and deep the river was to the road!

We did start working on the content for the DVD but completion has continually been kept on hold while so many of my ventures have changed and other priorities have taken over. We do intend to finish the DVD and when it's released it will be called Ski Fun!

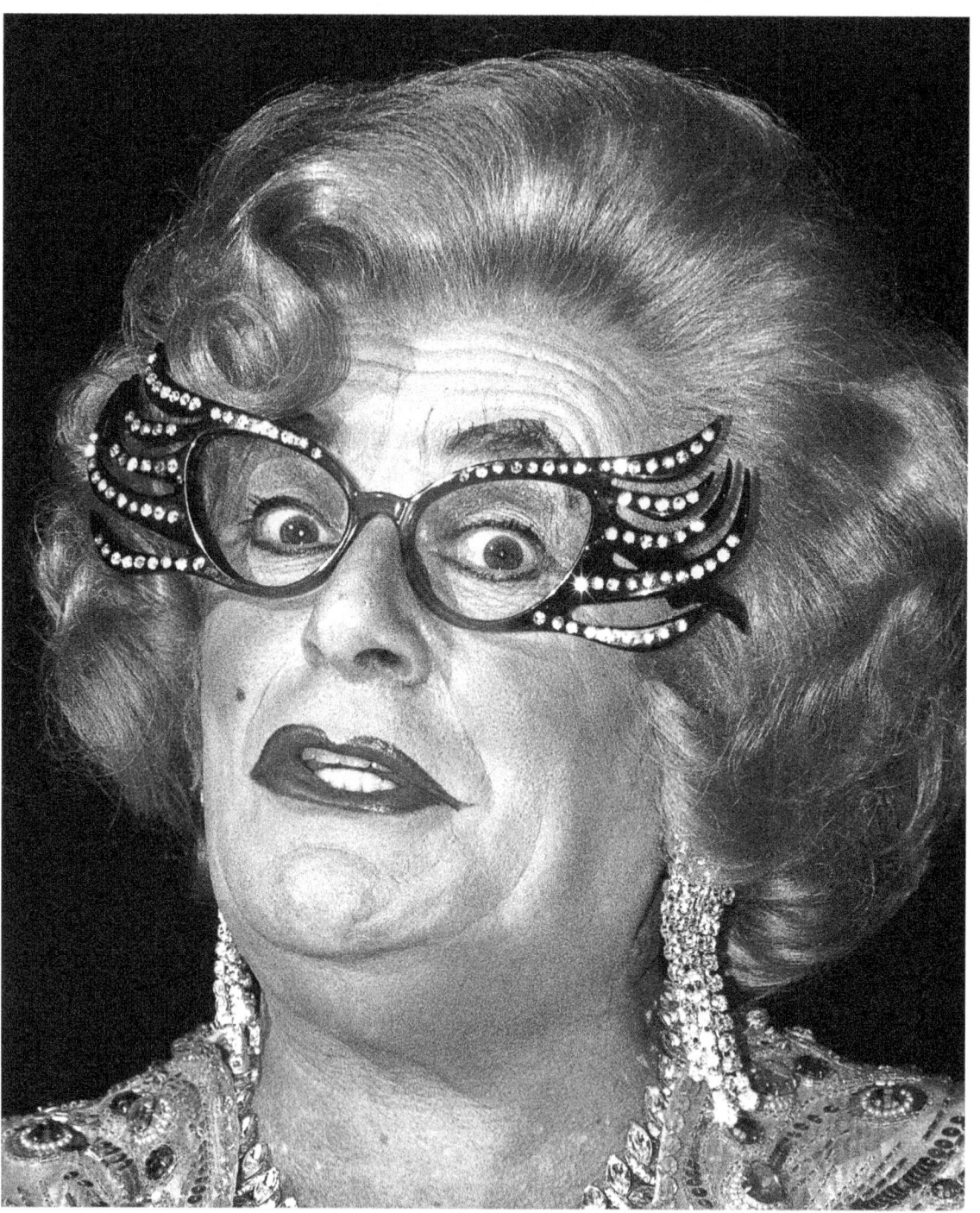

NEARLY FAMOUS

Everyone's a comedian or a Dame!

Fortunately for me I now had a proven record in publications and valuable experience, I had also started doing a few jobs for a locally based Public Relations company, so my main focus became PR photography for a couple of years.

My mixed bag of photographic knowledge now came to the fore, as I was called upon to photograph all kinds of events, from one of Northern Ireland's greatest footballers George Best, doing promotional cheque presentations in Lancashire pubs, to the Queens appearance in Blackpool for the Centenary year, and yes, I do mean Her Majesty the Queen of England!

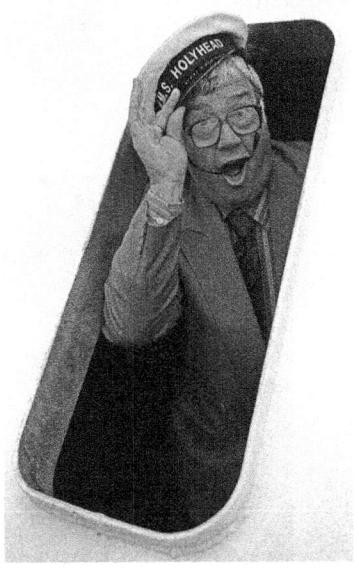

If you are British you will know Blackpool was known as the entertainment capital of the North, so no surprises that I would eventually photograph a lot of comedians en-route. One of the funniest was Frank Carson, 'it's the way I tell them' was his famous catchphrase. We picked him up for a Public Relations job once, it was 7am in Dublin Ireland when we met him and the jokes started. We were promoting the ferry crossing so we travelled by ferry to Holyhead in Wales, he talked and told jokes to all the passengers, I'm sure he told a gag to everyone, then we went onto the captains bridge and the jokes continued, even as he was trying to steer the ship out

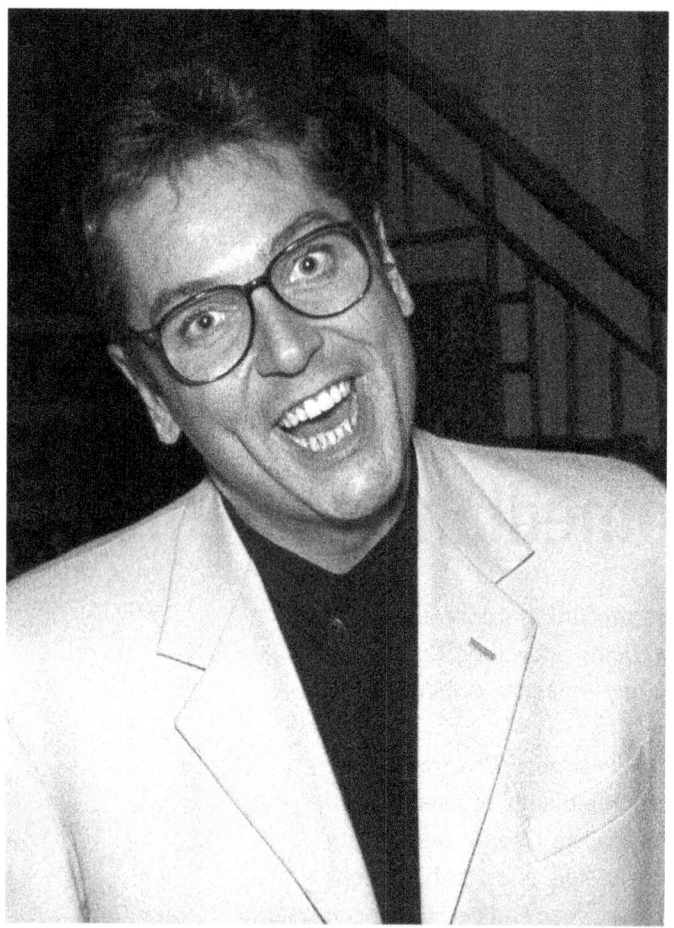
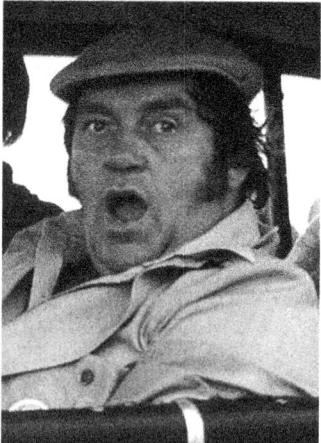
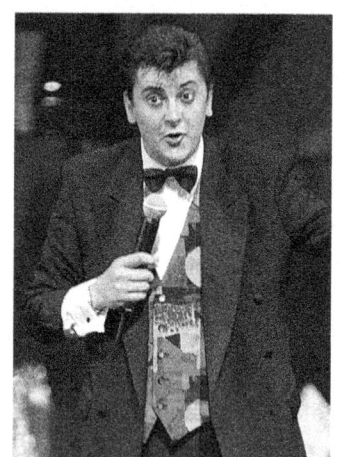
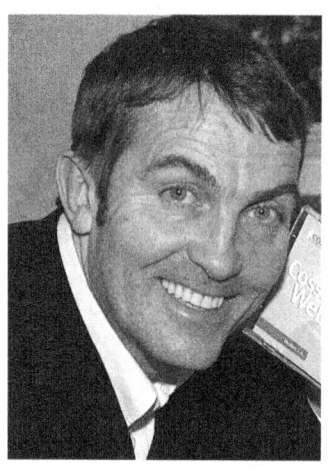
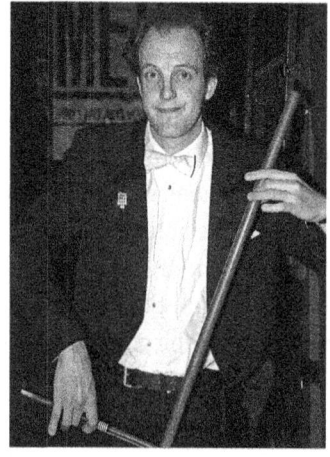
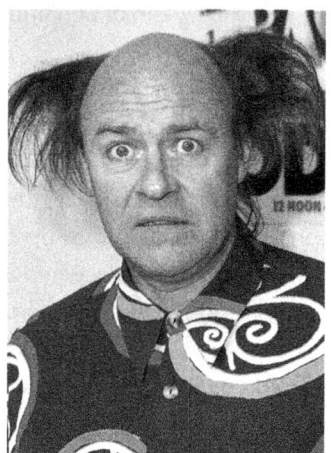

NEARLY FAMOUS

of the harbour. When we arrived Frank decided to walk through the streets meeting the local townsfolk, he was shouting jokes across the street at people when they shouted "Hello Frank". When we reached the end of the town we boarded a small bus and continued into the local countryside with the Mayor and a few dignitaries. The jokes continued too, then even more funnily, the bus was stopped by the police for a check on it's passenger license, as the organisers were trying to explain to the police the Mayor was on board for this special organised trip, Frank jumps up and starts cracking jokes to them, "did you hear the one about the policeman". Well we all thought that we might be arrested, but one thing is for sure the British Bobby has a sense of humour, we left Frank about 6pm and he was still telling jokes, it really is the way he tells them!

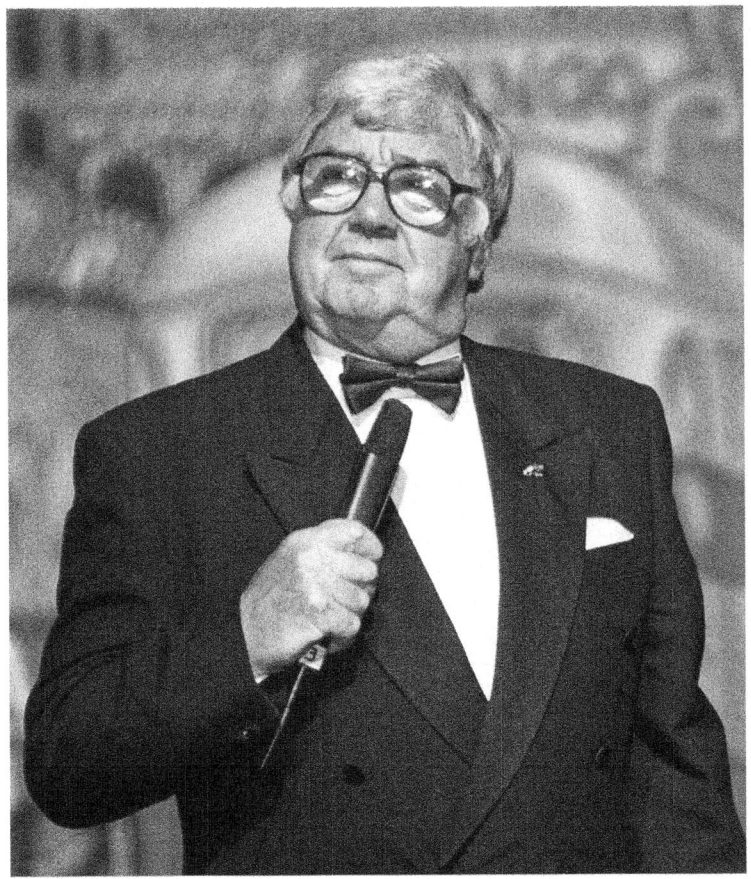

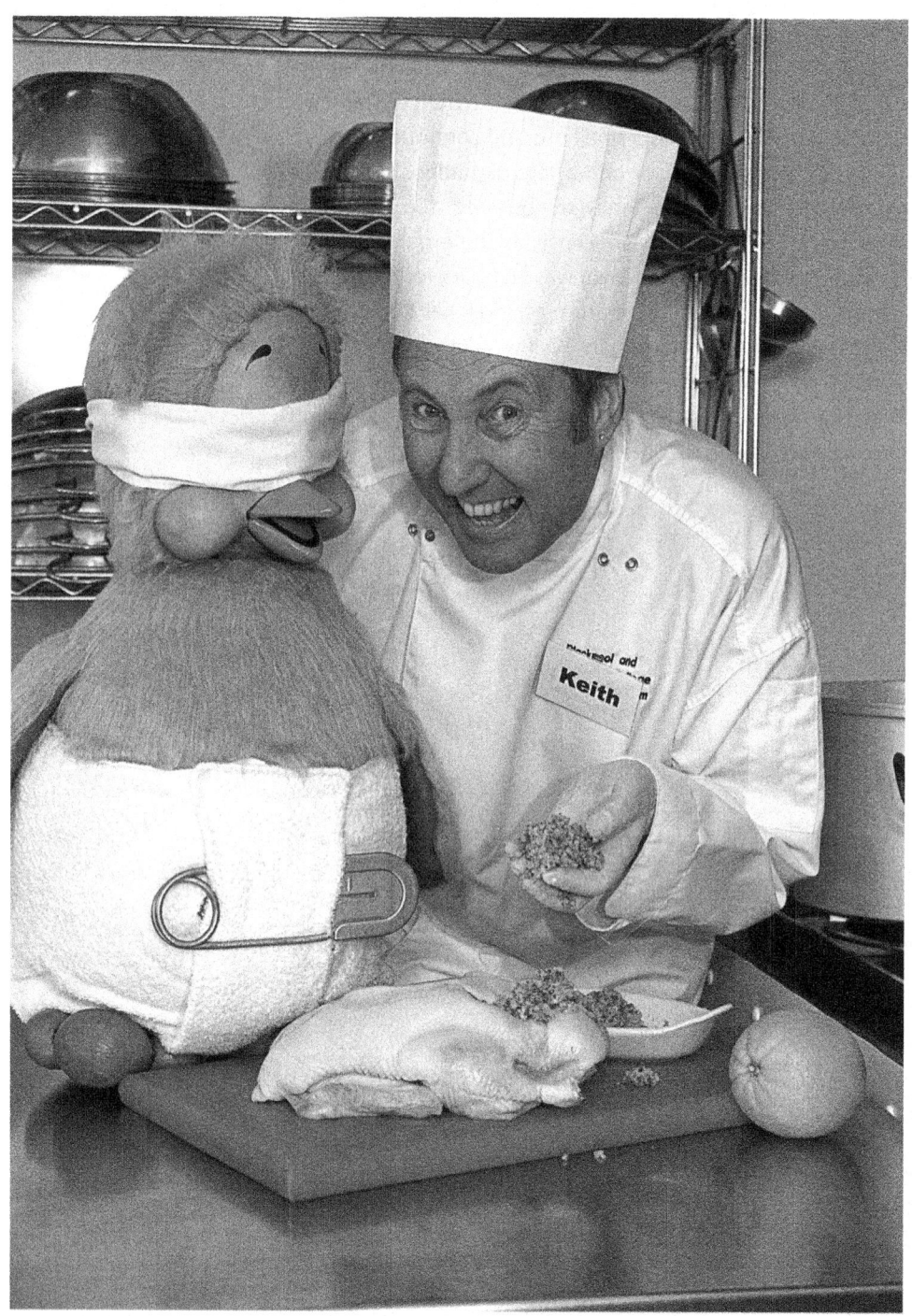

NEARLY FAMOUS

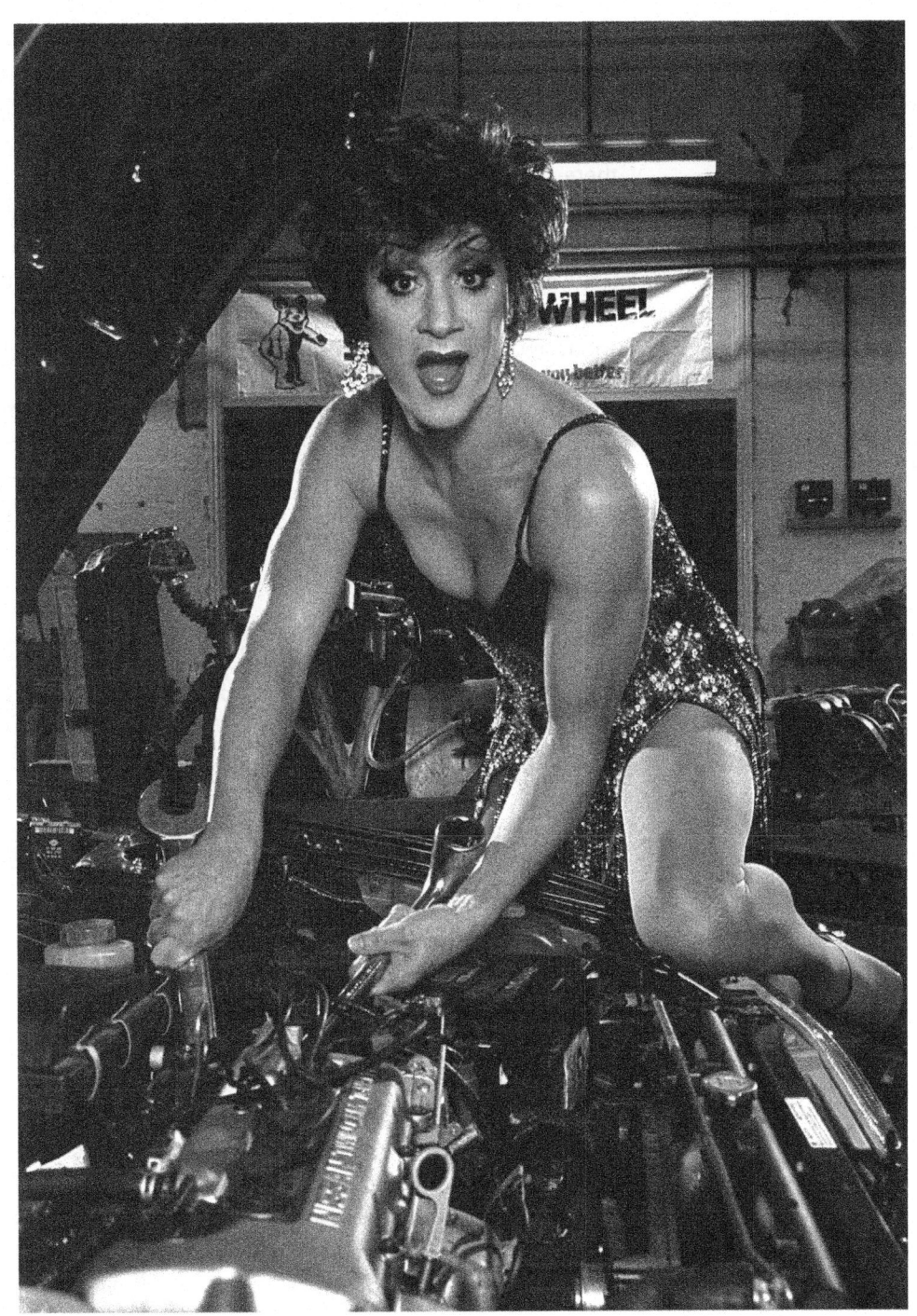

EVERYONE'S A COMEDIAN OR A DAME!

So I went on to do a lot of publicity shots for a lot of different companies, I may have started small locally but there are quite a few biggies on my CV. Thwaites a local brewery was one of the early ones, I was going to pubs three nights a week, nothing's changed there then, Slumberland a bed company was a bit more relaxed and laid back, Blackpool and Wyre Town councils were always a bit of a meeting. First Leisure, yes, that's where all the comedians came from, Regal cigarettes, well I got all choked up when they cut back, and Coca Cola, I did quite a lot of running about for them when they sponsored the marathons, the list goes on and on. One week It could

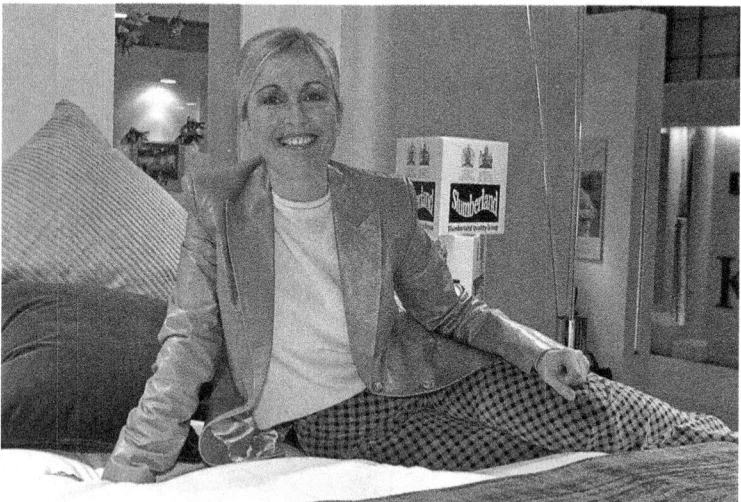

be a simple store opening with the local news broadcaster Gordon Burns cutting a ribbon, or it could be a major football star signing with Reebok like Ryan Giggs, or Sir Alex Ferguson showing off his trophies, there were a lot of fun events and all kinds of personalities.

It was an ideal medium for me and with my background I knew what it was like to be photographed, I had good communication skills, I knew how I would like to be photographed, so I was able to organise the celebrities reasonably well and get some great pictures. The secret to photographing people is rapport, if you don't develop that early on, the pictures get harder and harder, smiles look false and positioning gets awkward. Of course there were always some

NEARLY FAMOUS

who really didn't have the time of day for you, despite getting paid a lot of money to do the job, one a well behaved three year old could do, but they didn't faze me, I was born in the entertainment business, I may have only been a minor celebrity but I have never been in awe of anybody. Enough said about them, lets talk about the good ones, some were uncannily just like the parts they played, so were they really acting? A good question!

I have to mention two really nice morning TV presenters I did a few jobs with, Fiona Phillips was a really nice lady and she was happy to get her shoes off and down to work so to speak, well they were

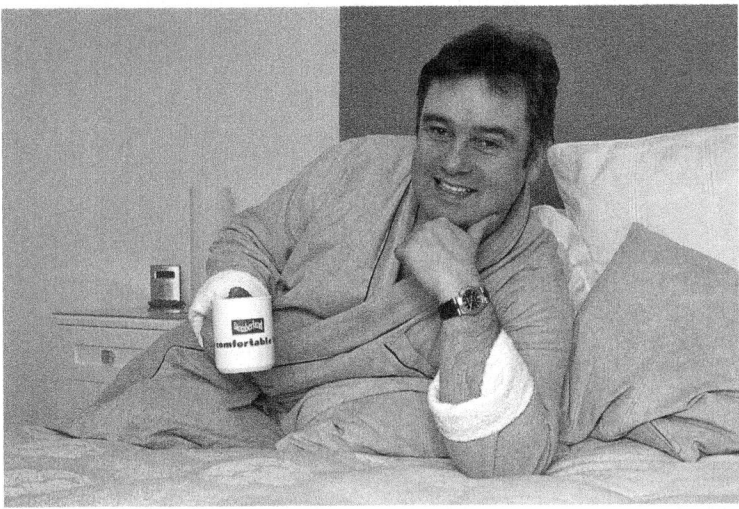

pictures for a bed company. The other one was Eamonn Holmes, I was quite proud of the picture I took, but felt I had missed the best picture of the day, it was taken in his bedroom at home, no it's not what you think. It was all about bed promotion, him casually lying on his bed with his dressing gown on after a really comfortable nights sleep, I should get a job as a bed seller. The shoot went fine, then as I started packing up my cameras, I heard Eamonn say to Darryl the PR Director "we better make the bed, my wife will kill me if it's a mess" I turned around and sure enough there they were, two men making the bed, if only I had not put my cameras away, what a picture that would have made in the press headlines the next day!

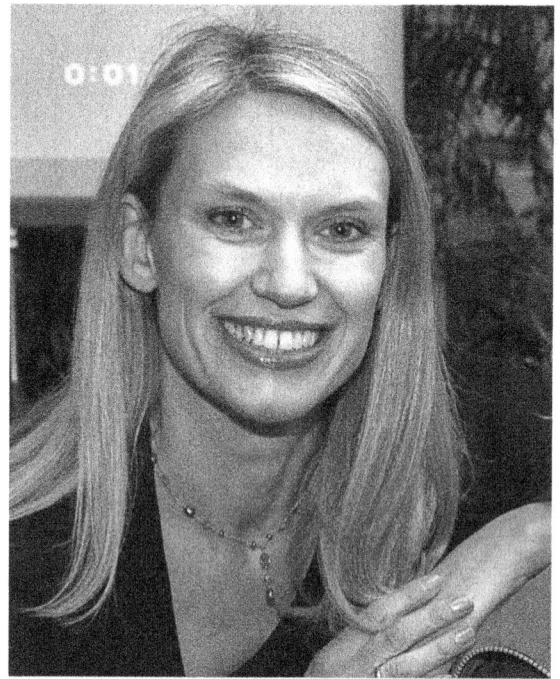
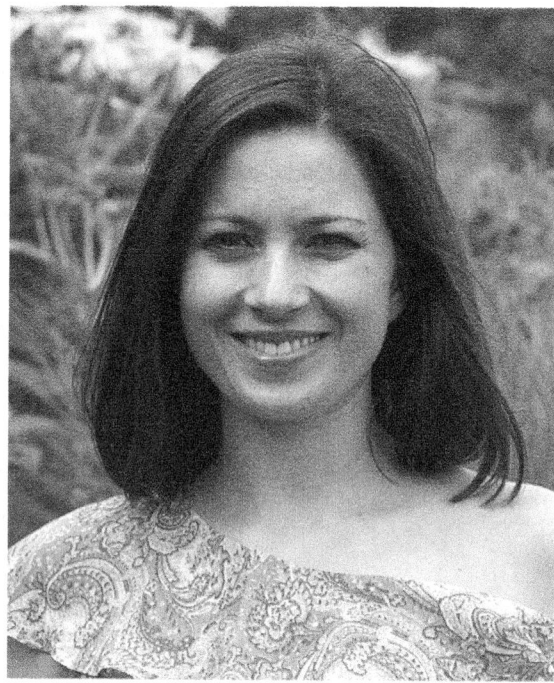
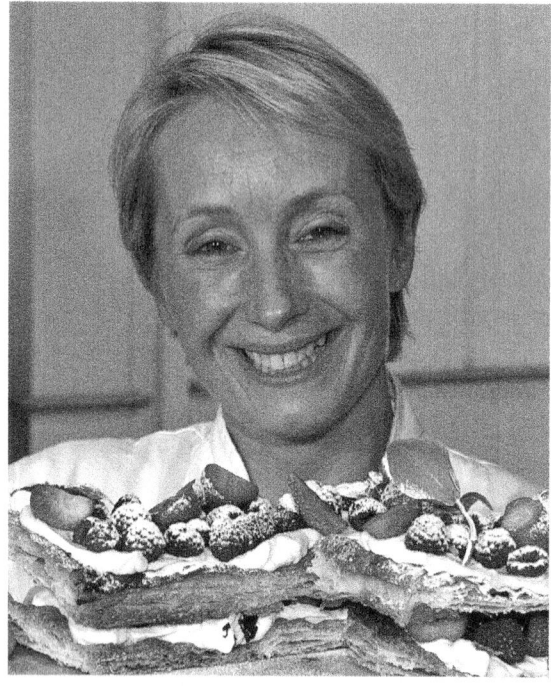
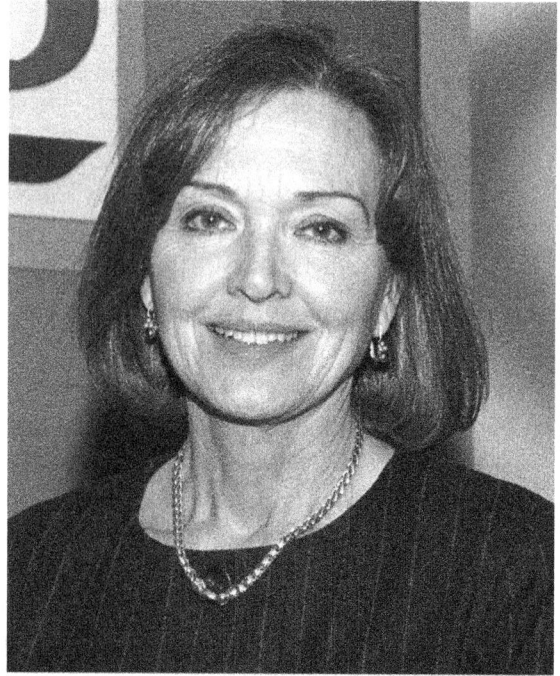

NEARLY FAMOUS

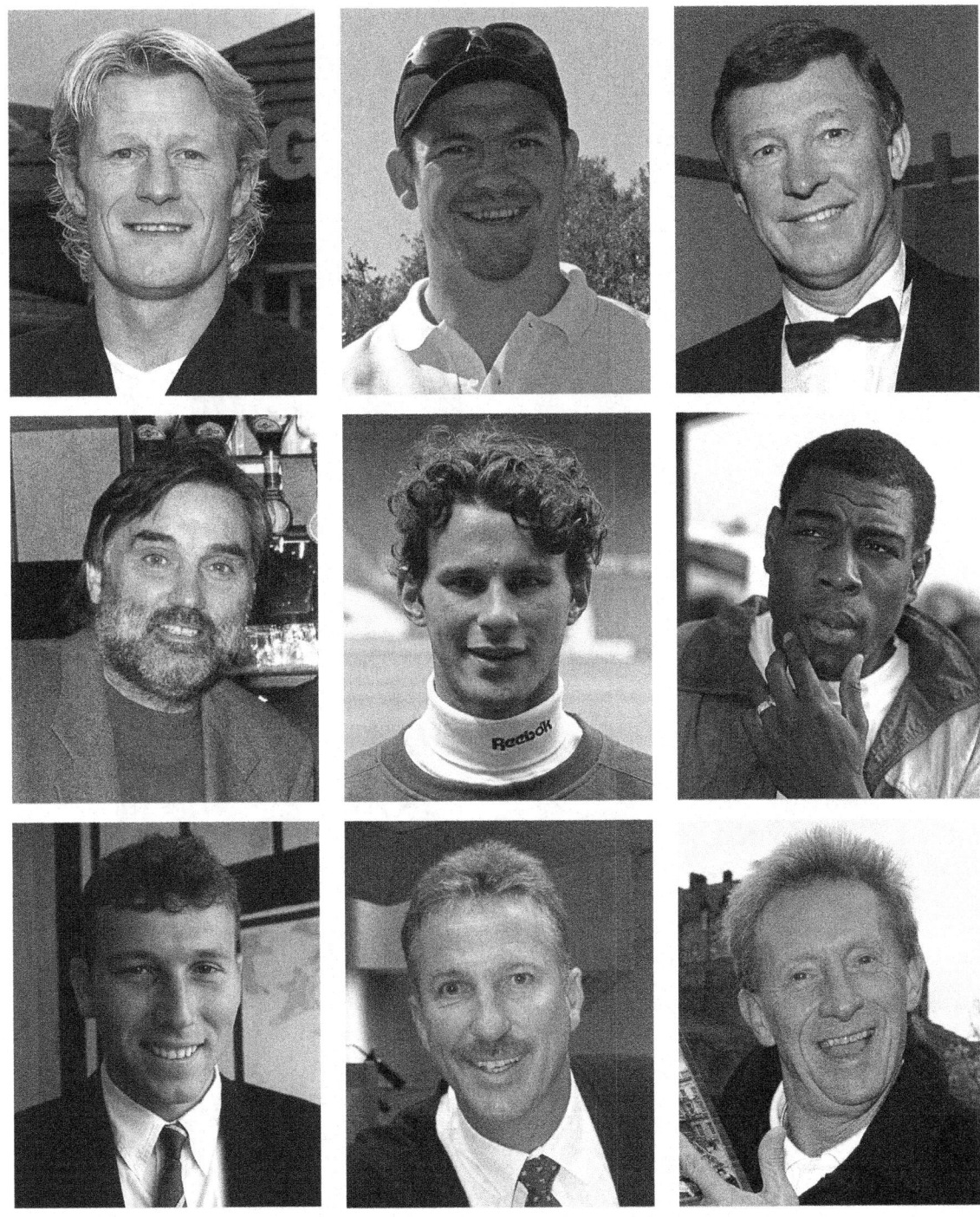

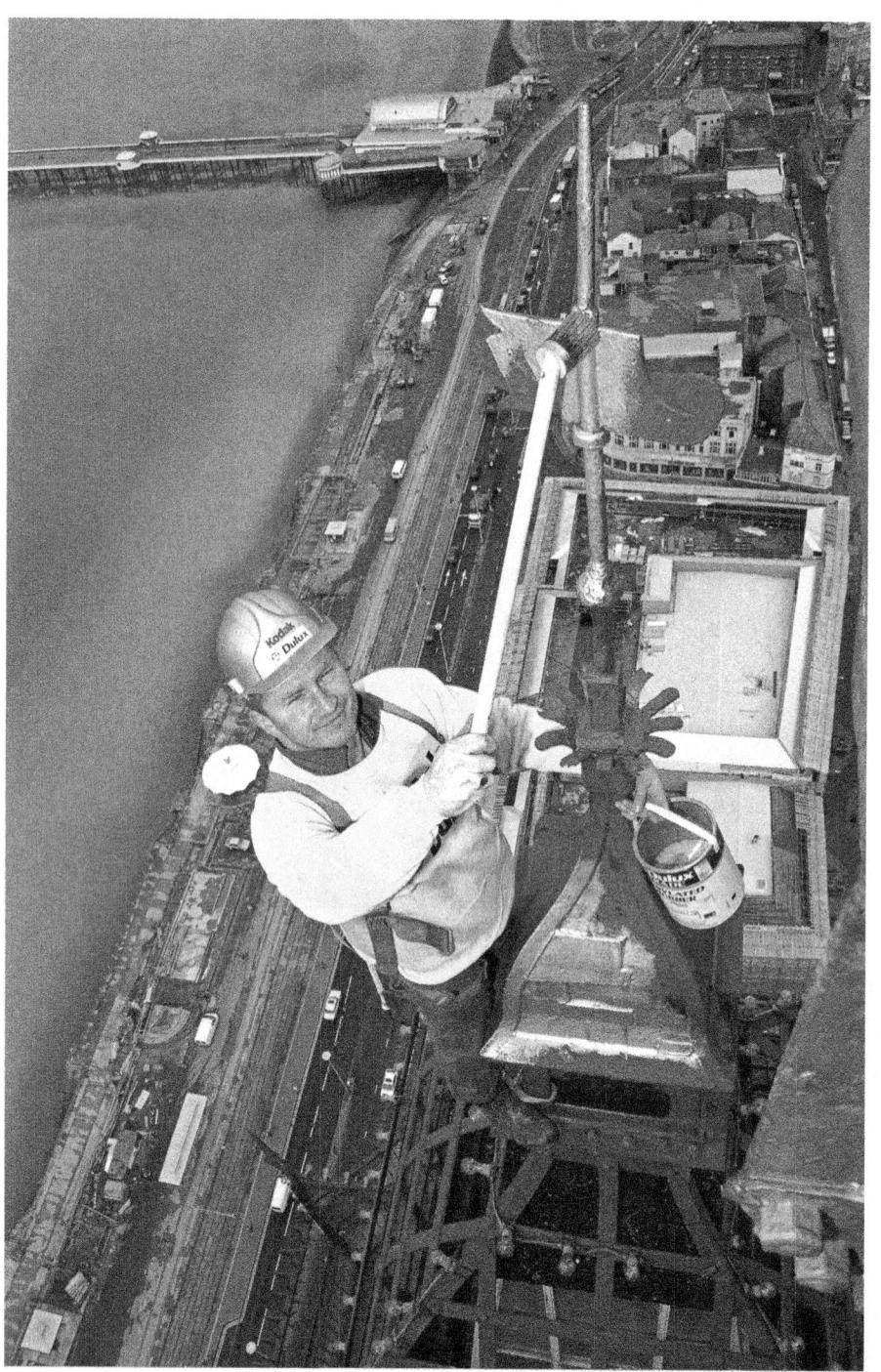

NEARLY FAMOUS

Her Majesty The Queen visits

When the Blackpool Tower Company decided to paint their 520 foot (158 metre) tower for its centenary, their PR company commissioned me to take some promotional pictures as it progressed. At first they started the job at the bottom, but it gradually got higher and higher. I've already mentioned that I have a fear of heights, right?

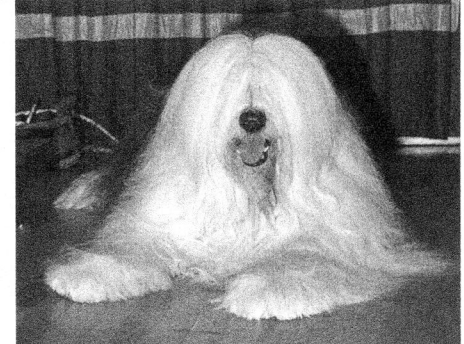

Well, first they decided to take the Dulux Paint mascot, an Old English Sheep Dog up the tower for some pictures with the painters. We managed to get one stage higher than the general public are allowed to access, and that was only by carrying the dog. Fortunately it was still slightly enclosed with only an open bit around the top so I wasn't too worried. The setting was okay but the press wanted a more dramatic picture of the painter. Some bright spark suggested that we could go up a little higher, WHAT, I thought we were at the top, but no, the very top was the area above where they hang the flag from!

The guy said there was a very small platform up there and if we were very careful we would be okay. Well I am nothing if not a true professional I said to myself, as I followed the other photographers up a tiny rusty ladder. I came up through the trapdoor into horror of horrors the fresh air. The other photographers were already standing at the edge looking over. They started giving directions to the painter below and if I didn't go now I would miss the shot, it was about 7 ft (2m) to the edge! Now this is no exaggeration, I crawled on all fours to the edge and grabbed hold of what looked like a corroded bar so I could hang on. Peeping through the camera viewfinder with one squinted

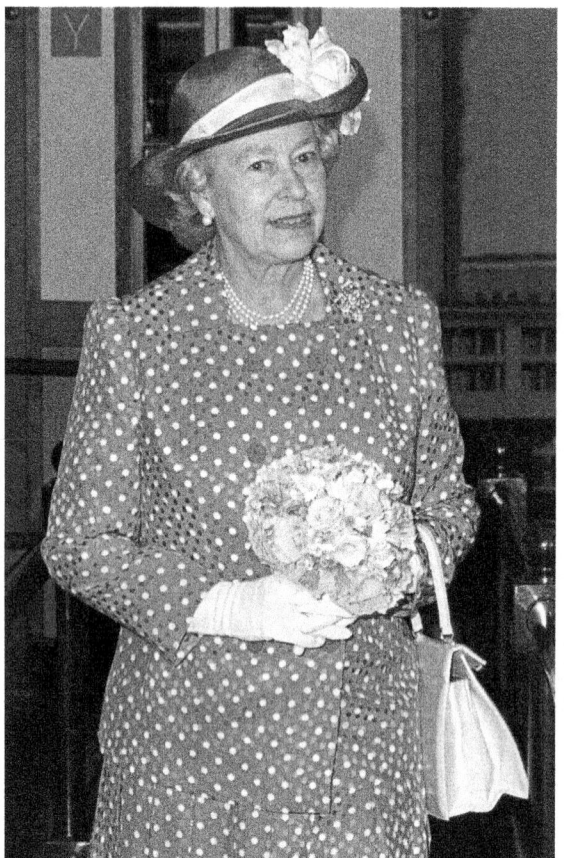

eye and with one hand I managed to point the camera at the painter. I heard a photographer say, "Up here Wayne, the views great." "No I'm okay here", came my reply, click, click, click, thank goodness for motor drives and I had crawled back down the ladder before anybody noticed, then I joined in on the bragging on what a great picture I had too. I did have to rush home and change my trousers though!

When the gold painting was completed, Her Majesty The Queen came to visit, and I was chosen as one of the three photographers allowed on the Royal roster to take pictures as she walked around. We were escorted everywhere by her personal bodyguard and kept a discreet distance away. At one point one of the other photographers wanted to get a little closer and was dragged back, he was given the option of leaving if he didn't like it. We carried on walking backwards and taking pictures, I'm not sure how it happened but somehow everyone went left and I went right, well that was the way Her Majesty looked to be heading. I backed up some more as she approached, suddenly, I came to a dead end, just me and the Queen. I think you can see here in the picture I took, as she was looking at the pictures on the wall, she was also looking at me out of the corner of her eye!

I also managed to photograph another couple of the Royal family members, the Princess Royal and Prince Andrew, another humorous event for me just look at the pictures. Prince Andrew went onto a yacht to congratulate a yachtsman on his proposed around the world adventure. I followed him onto the yacht, but stayed on the outside

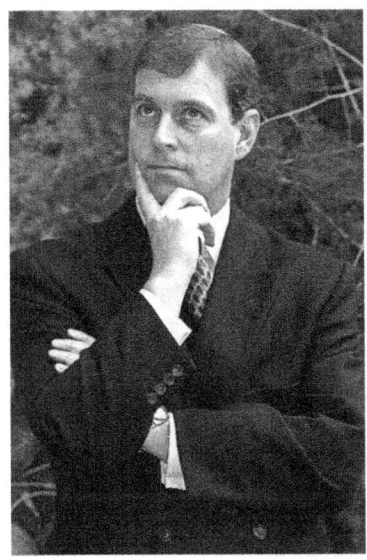 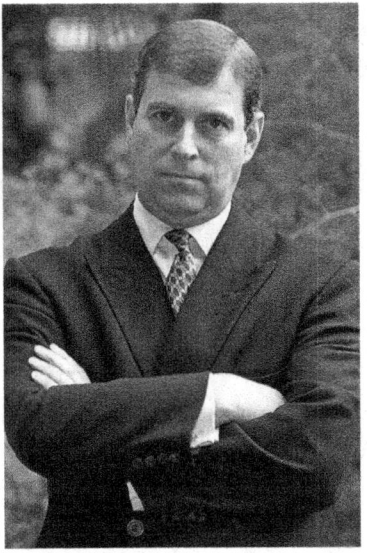 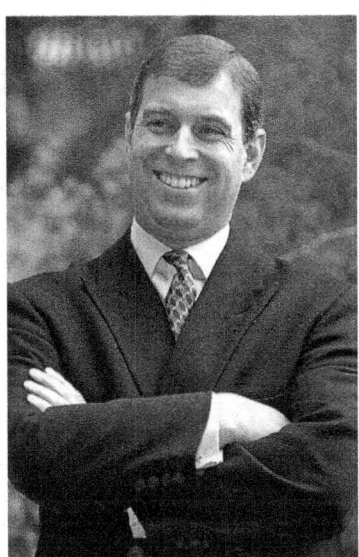

looking in, as I tried to get pictures through the portholes and windows, he noticed me, oops I thought, I'm in trouble with royalty, maybe I will be in the papers tomorrow. He looked directly at me and tapped on the window, now I knew I was in trouble, at least that was what I thought at the time, he beckoned me inside and when I arrived he asked if I would like to take his picture inside the yacht. Of course I would, but now I feel I am by Royal Appointment!

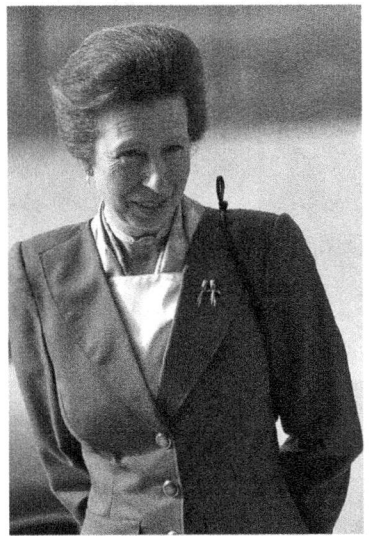 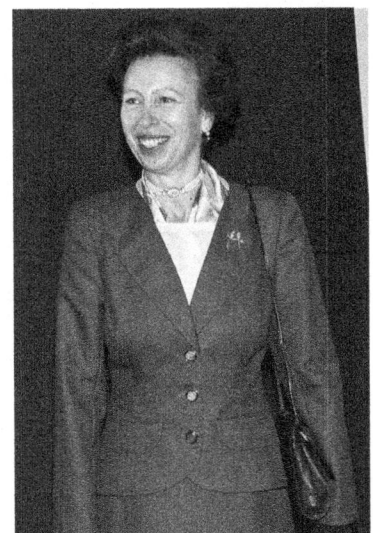

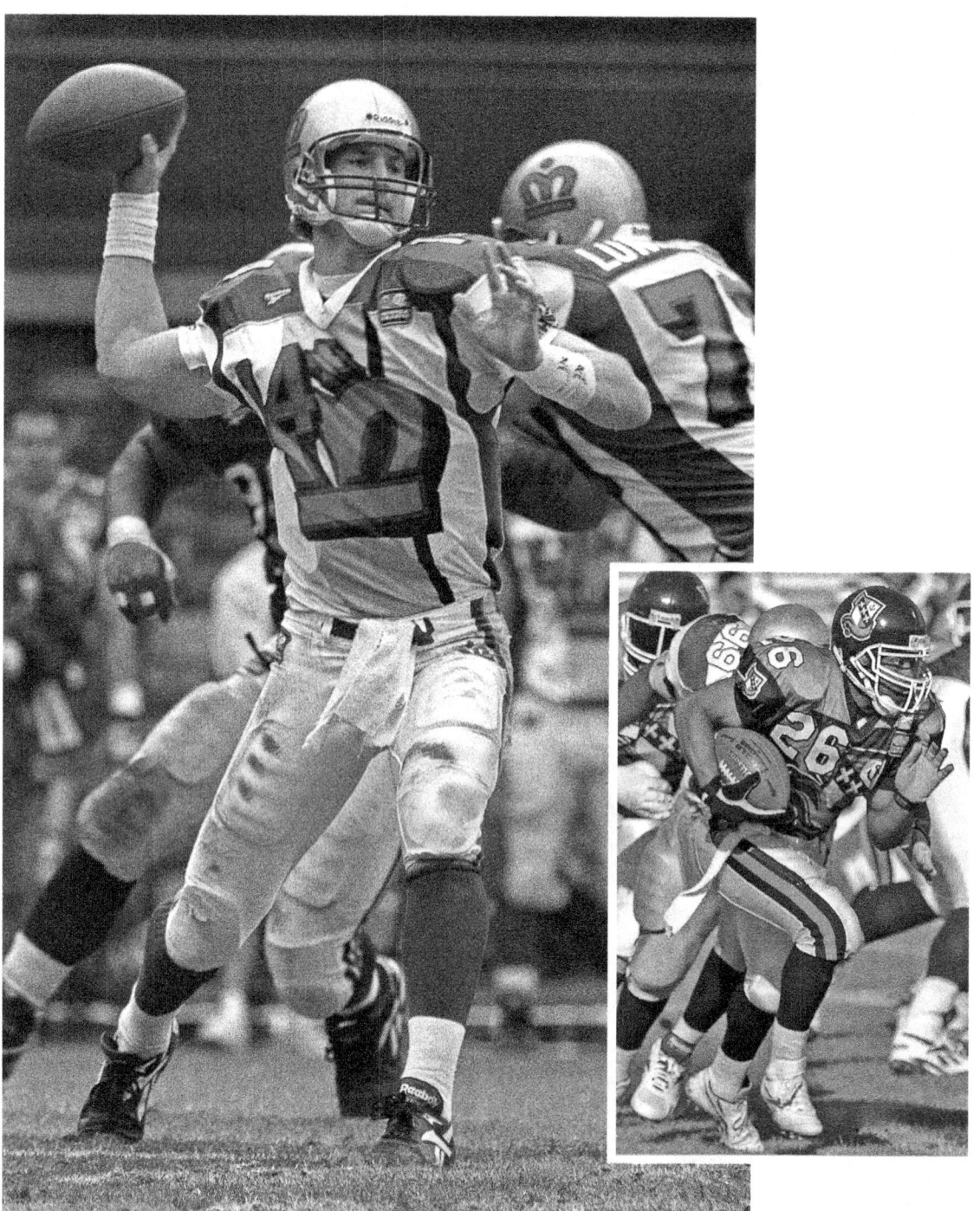

NEARLY FAMOUS

World League comeback

In 1995 the World League made a comeback, eventually being re-branded as the NFL Europe in 1998. They were back, and back with intent to stay. They were also going to have two British teams, the original London Monarchs who were now going to be joined by another team in Scotland, the Scottish Claymores.

I was born near London where the Monarchs played, so you would assume that they would have been the logical choice to follow, but I was living in Blackpool which is on the North West coast of England, and logistically it was much easier to get to the Claymores in Edinburgh, than drive down to London for the games.

I applied for a job as the team photographer with the Claymores and was instantly hired by the then PR Director Will Wilson. When I asked if it was the sample pictures I had sent that sealed the deal, he commented that my reputation preceded me and that I was "well known", well there you have it then. I told you in the foreword didn't I?

"He commented that my reputation preceded me!"

And that was the start of a great twelve year association with the NFL in Europe, albeit very small at first. I didn't have to move to Scotland or anything to cover the games, it was a pretty low budget job, I worked only for them on the weekends during the season with occasional trips to Scotland for the pre season and special events, we would drive 250 miles (450 km) up to the Edinburgh home game, then return straight home afterwards, a tough days work.

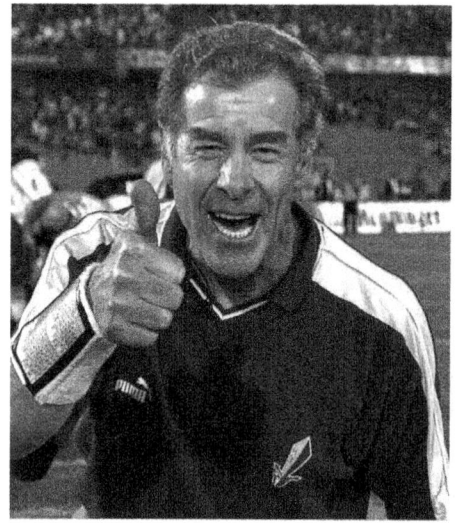

The Claymores had a turbulent start to their first season, sacking their head coach just a few days before the start of the season. Jim Criner who had picked up a World Bowl ring with the Sacromento Surge in 1992 was given the coaching job. Despite the Claymores having a bad first year going 2 and 8 in the win loss columns, he would turn their fortunes around within one season, and also become a close friend.

The first year I was only asked to cover the home games, but the second year they started to use me on the away games as well. I was too valuable to them supplying pictures to the press from the games, it meant more publicity.

I remember on one occasion I went to Barcelona, I packed a computer, negative scanner, development tanks and chemicals to process my films, as at that time I was using a 35 mm film camera with Black & White film loaded. I photographed the first half of the game, then at half time I went up the stairs to the press room, unpacked my back pack with all the oddments in it, suddenly, I realised I had forgotten my special film loading bag, so I proceeded to the gents toilet which would be the best place to find darkness. As I started to load my B/W film into a canister, somebody tried to get into the toilet, they couldn't because I had my foot against the door, "abra la puerta" came a shout from outside. "Sod off" was my reply! Hey I was under a bit of stress at the time and if I had opened the door it would have ruined the film. There was some violent knocking then "abra la puerta" again. I replied "si si uno momento", well that just about covered all my Spanish. When I came out there was a security guy standing there waiting for me, so I explained in broken English what I was doing, why do we always start talking like that when we can't speak the language? Anyway I asked him to hold the film for me while I dried it with a hair dryer, and I then spent the whole of the second half of the game just trying to

"abra la puerta, came a shout from outside!"

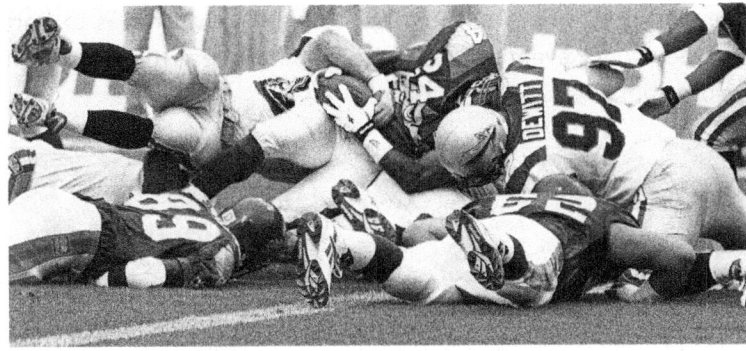

communicate with the papers to send the pictures out. It was a very slow process in those days, by modem, but it worked eventually, the more I sent out pictures to the press the more successful I became.

We eventually progressed to colour film developing using a heated rotary tank, and made sure we always had our special dark bag for loading films into a tank, but we did it mainly for the home games and only when I had help from Estelle and Dani, I needed them to watch the temperature, dry them and to send the pictures out to the press after they had been digitally scanned, I would never have managed to cover all those games otherwise.

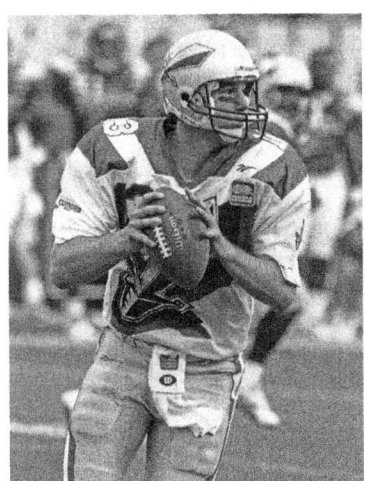
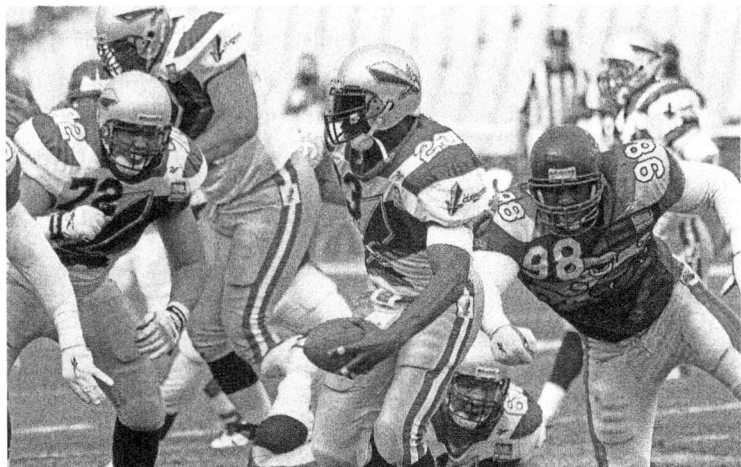

I was lucky that the league would fund the finals separately, so when the Claymores made the final in 1996 and hosted the game at Murrayfield stadium, I was commissioned to cover the game for them as the Official World Bowl photographer, which was to start another regular event between me and the league as the World Bowl photographer each year.

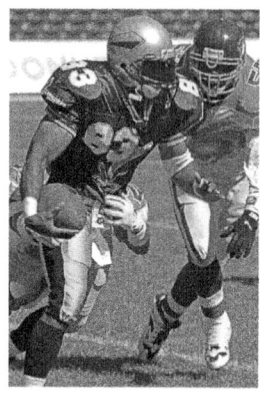 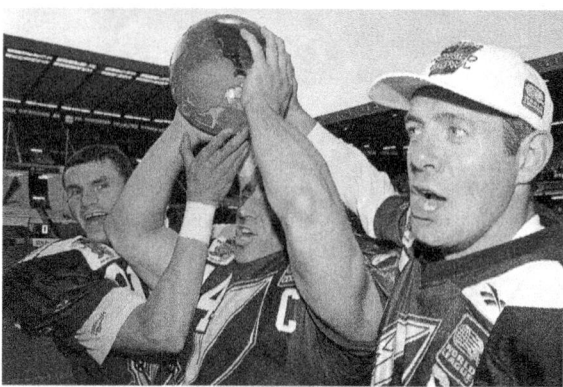 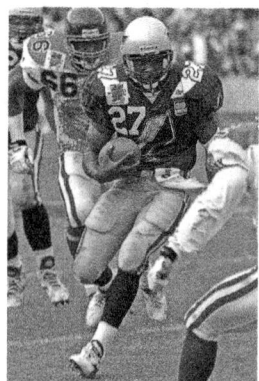

I was probably the only full time photographer covering the league at that time on a regular basis. It might have been that fact, plus I was already travelling to the Scottish Claymores training camp, which was way out in the boon docks at Carrollton, Georgia USA, that I was asked if I could also double up and be the photographer for the rest of the teams. I could do press and heads shots of the whole league whilst I was there, becoming the Training Camp photographer!

That meant taking pictures in the thousands and I do mean thousands, all the head shots and coverage of six teams for all the

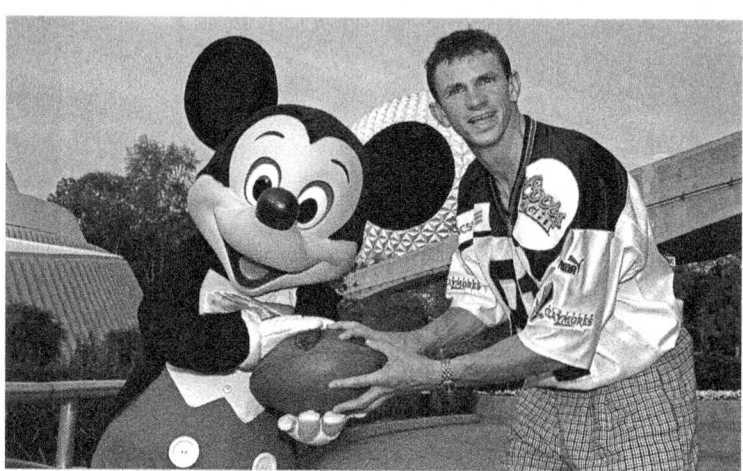

NEARLY FAMOUS

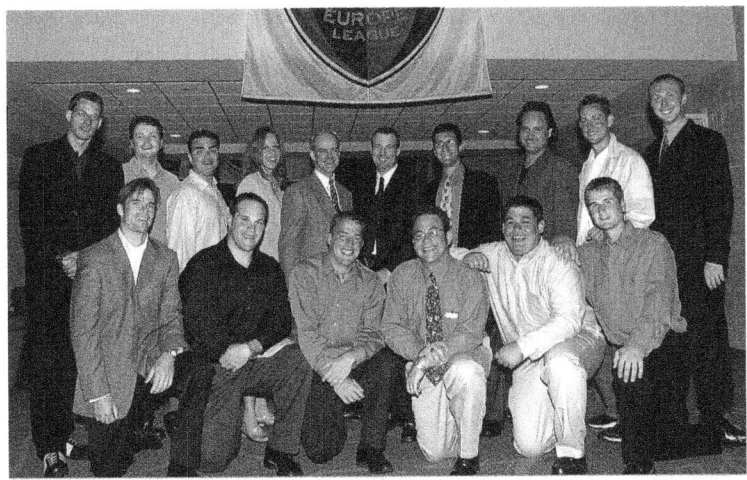

European press when ever needed, I was like a doctor on call with an emergency phone, and they used it. I was called all over the place for everything, one night a member of the PR staff even called me up and asked me to fetch a bottle opener! Of course I just told him politely what he could do, place one hand on the bottle and one hand on the bottle top and _ _ _ _ off! In case you are wondering the missing word was of course twist. It was all in good fun and helped with the camaraderie for the future, at least that was what I thought!

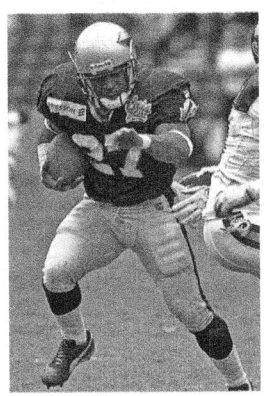 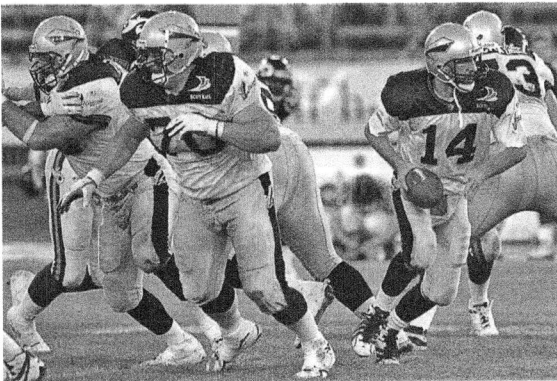 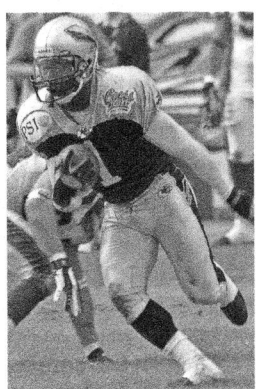

The Claymores had a few players make good in the NFL, Dante Hall became a prolific kick off return man with Kansas City, Aaron Stecker may still be playing for the Tampa Bay Buccaneers, Joe Andruzzi played in several Super Bowls with the New England Patriots, along with the first Brit to win a Super Bowl ring, Scot McCready, even though he never played a down in the game itself. I think he was on the reserve roster for the Patriots.

One player in particular, a Quarterback called Dameyune Craig, made it into the Pro Football Hall Of Fame, when he made the news by throwing five touchdowns for an historical 611 yards, all in a single game for the Scottish Claymores, it was against the Frankfurt Galaxy in 1999. They requested my picture of him to use in the display, so I guess I made it into the Hall Of Fame too. Does that count?

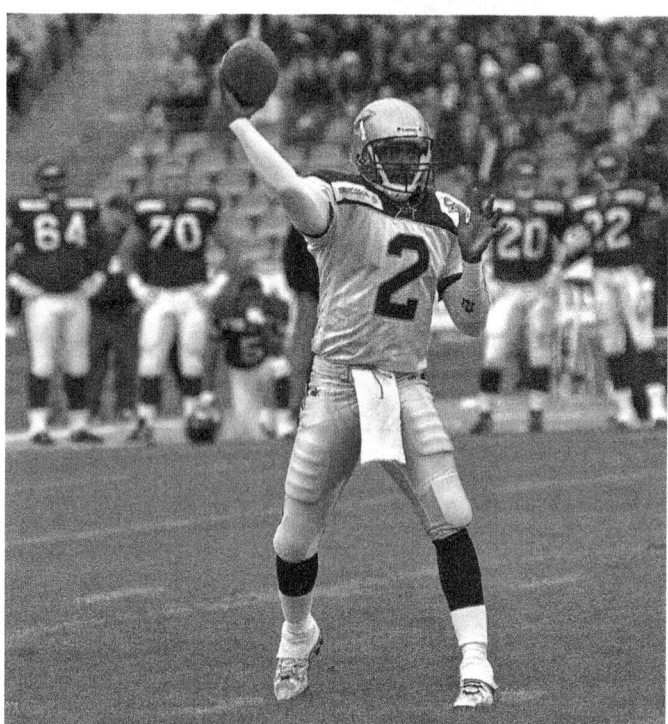 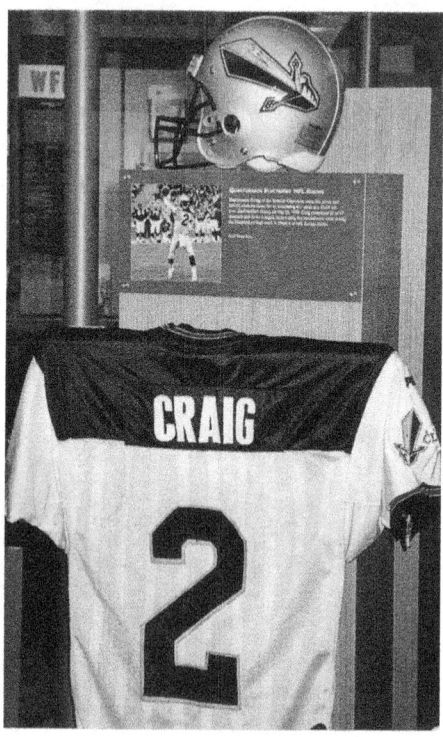

My time with the Claymores was enjoyable, I got on great with players, coaches and fans, but getting consistency with my photography was hard work and somewhat difficult at times when working to a very limited budget. At one point to keep the costs down I was asked to only shoot three rolls of film (that's 108 pictures).

That may sound a lot, unfortunately I had to get pictures of the back field pre game, the fans, the VIP's with the players and oh yes action shots from the game itself that runs for three hours, not forgetting a presentation if they won the game. At the end I would be lucky if I had about 40 action shots to select the best pictures from!

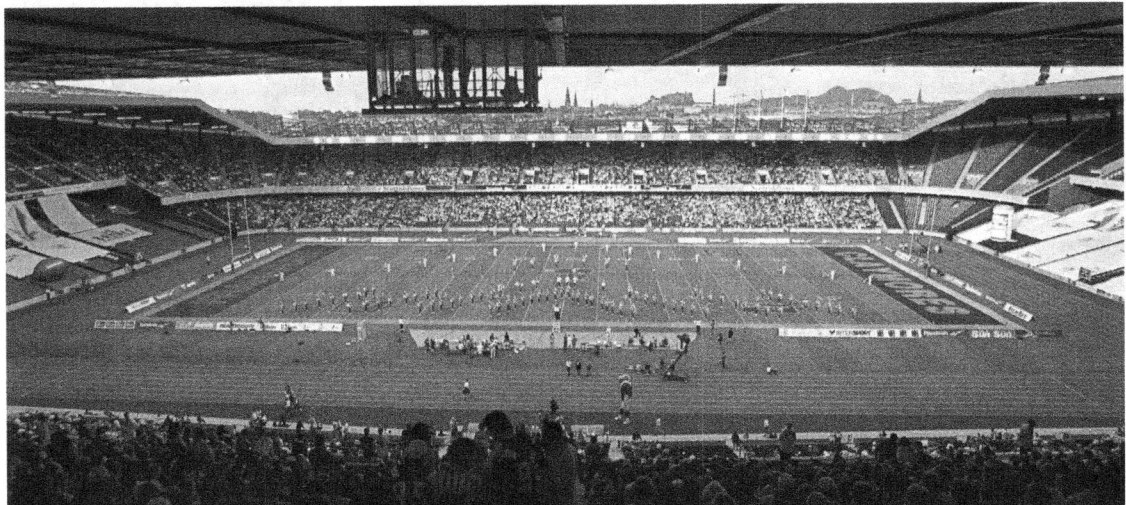

I hung in there for an amazing five years until the budget started to trickle away and it became obvious that it wouldn't last. Sure enough, pre season 2000 I was asked if I would work another season for the same money and could I do some extra midweek press coverage. I would have to travel up to Scotland again for the meetings. Were they extracting the urine? I just couldn't do it on their budget!

So I was in another dilemma. Do I retire early from American football sports photography? I no longer had a team to work for, the domestic league coverage in Britain had fizzled out as far as I was concerned. So there were two options left for me, retire or fund my own foray into continued coverage of the NFLE as a freelance.

I knew I had established my credentials with the press and the league themselves always needed pictures, so I decided to take the risk and fund all of the flying expenses myself. Well I was just addicted to the sport too much to stop. I was part of that family!

The players, coaches, back room staff, broadcasters and journalists, not forgetting all the fans were fantastic or fantastisch depending which side of the Channel you were on. They became another group of people I developed an affection for throughout that period, they were Cannie lads and lasses, meine schönen Freunde.

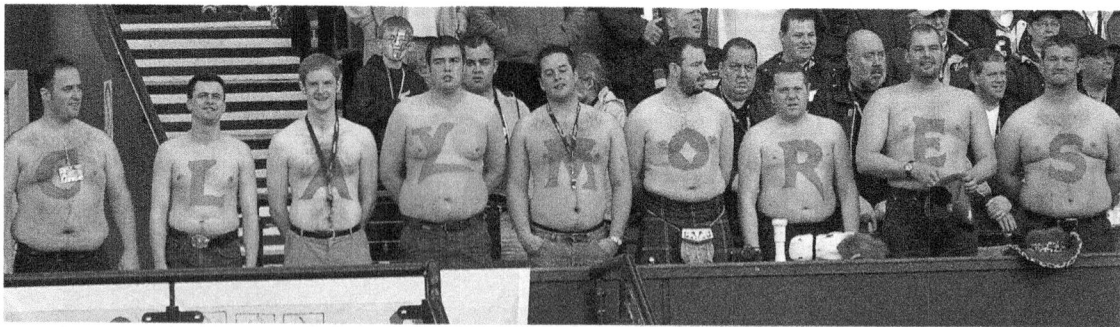

I may have been disappointed with the way I left the Claymores, but I never held a grudge against them, though I'm sure some people thought I had. I did have good reason in more ways than one. I know a lot of exclusive photo sessions with players were set up secretly, they kept them away from me so other photographers could get exclusive pictures to supply the press. Whether it was because I was a better photographer or had developed too good a relationship with the papers I don't know, but fortunately for me they were more loyal and continued to use the pictures I supplied on a regular basis.

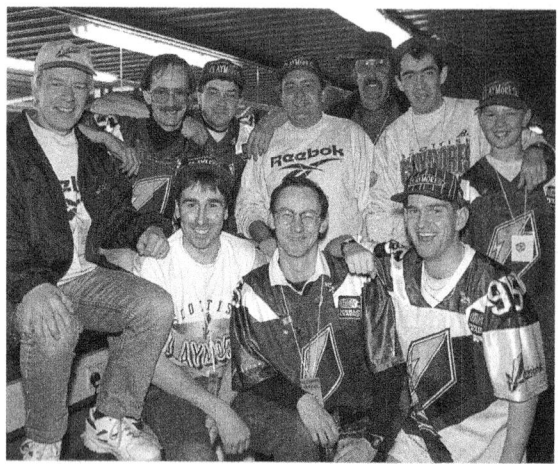

Anyway I took the risk of going solo again despite this, I would have to fund the travel on whatever I wanted to cover, but at least I was in charge of what, when and where, well it was a risk I'm glad I took. I managed to secure the training camp photograph requirements of press and head shots again, then the 2000 World Bowl week with the league in advance, and, by the end of the season I had made more money as a freelance than I ever thought I would do.

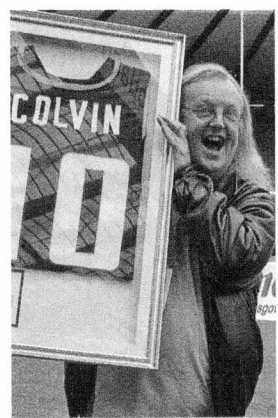
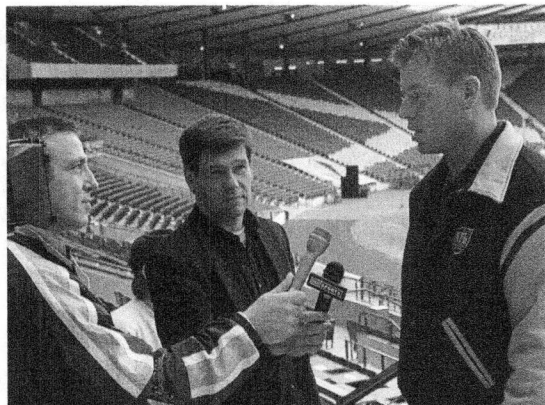
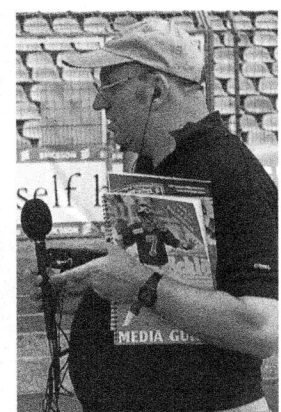
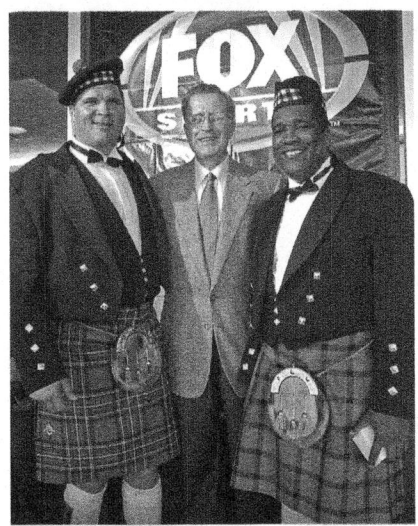
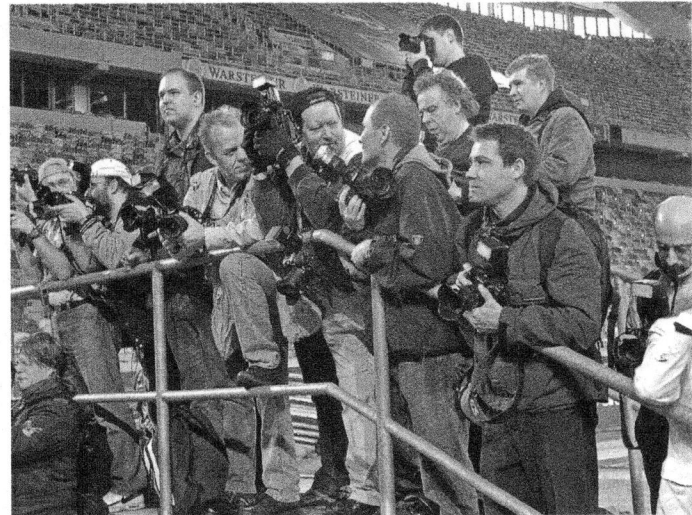
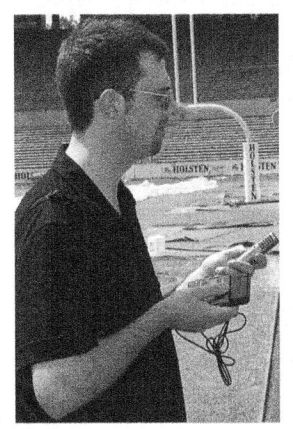
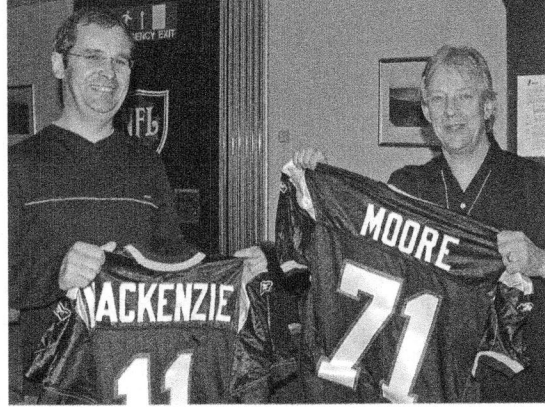
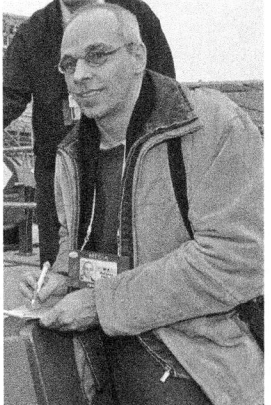

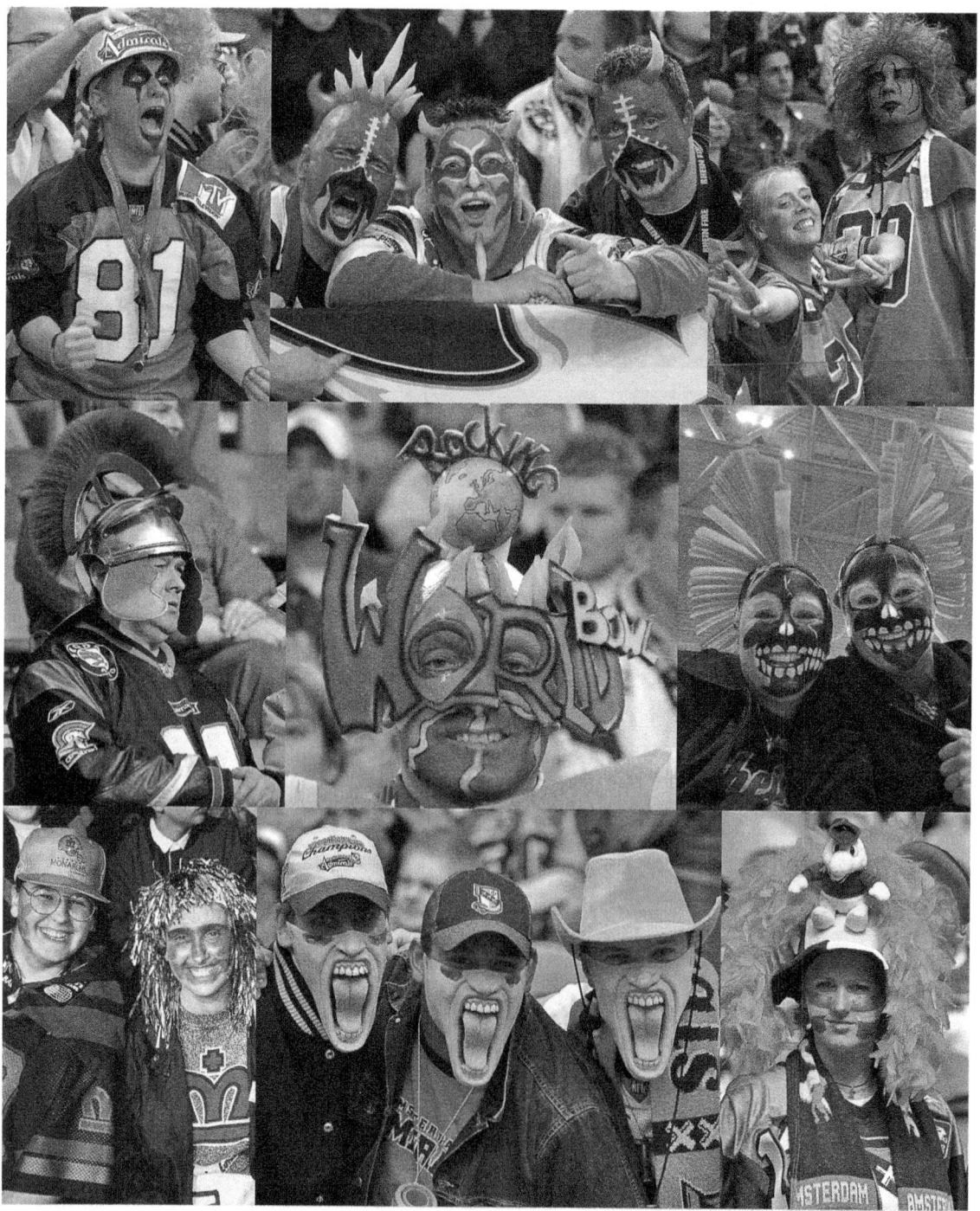

NEARLY FAMOUS

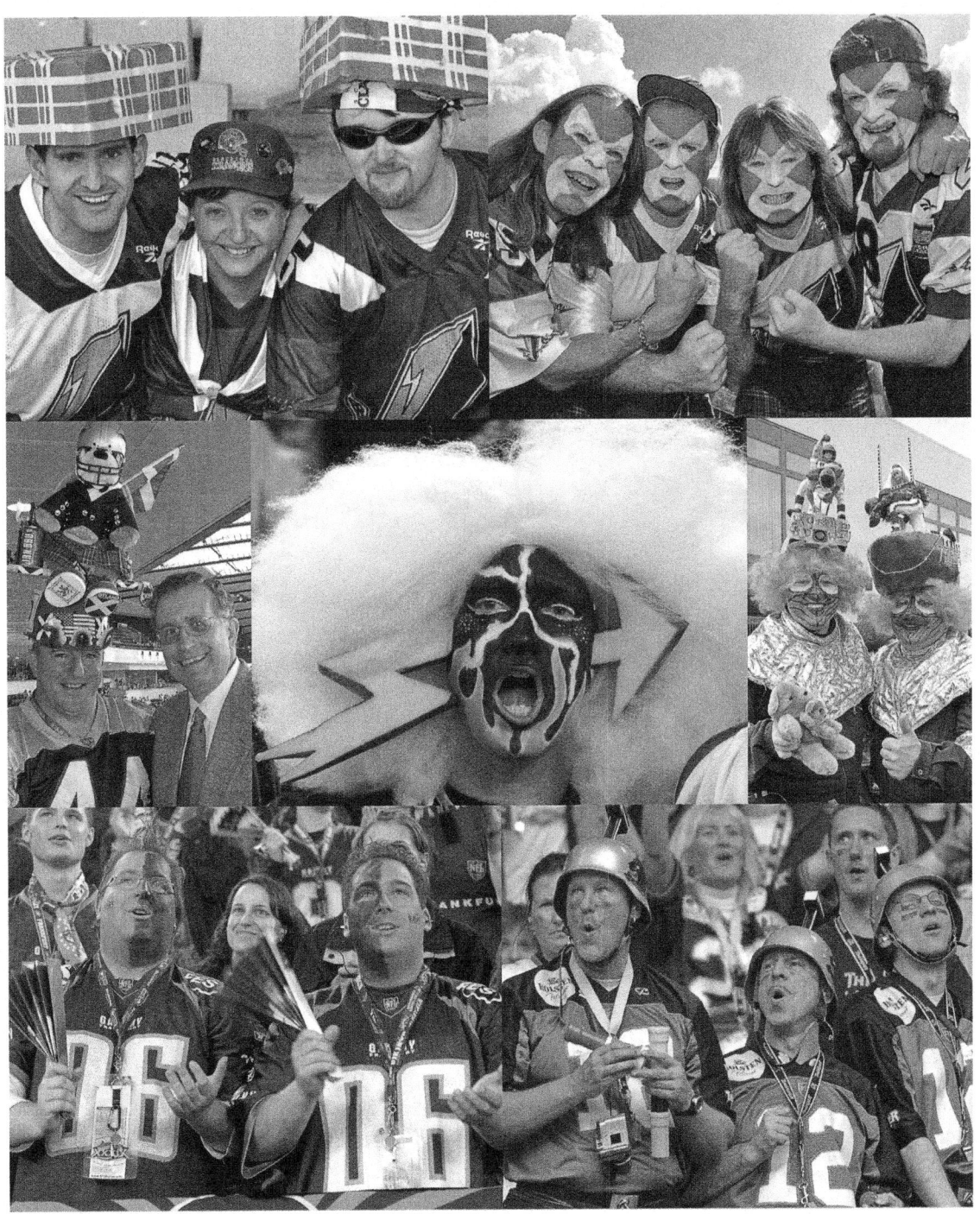

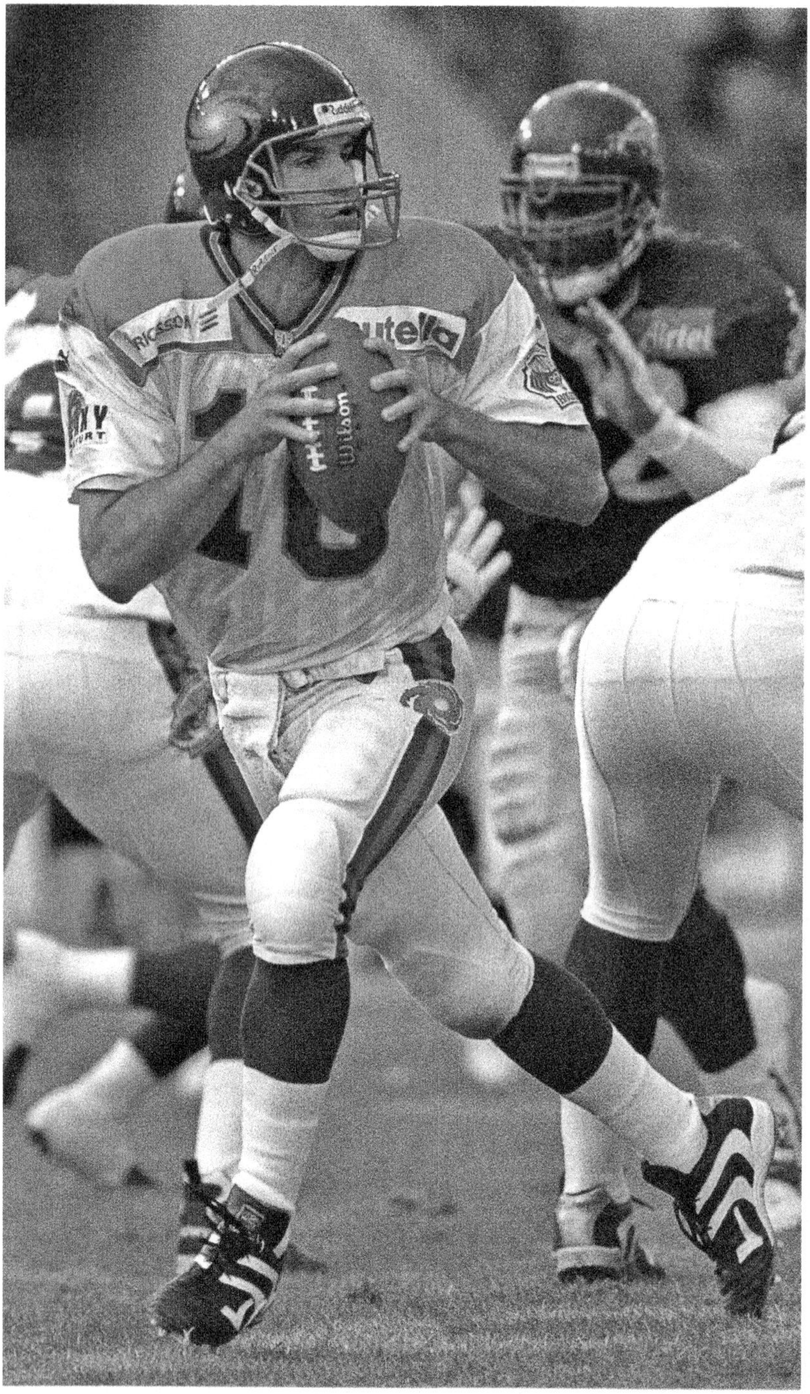

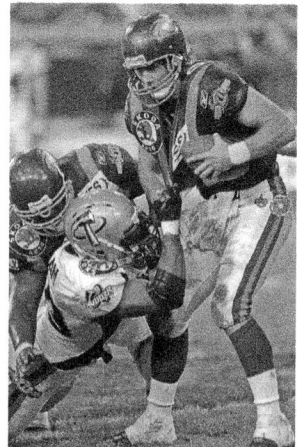

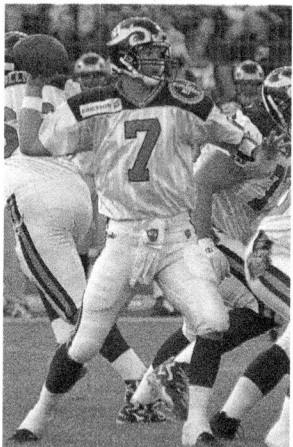

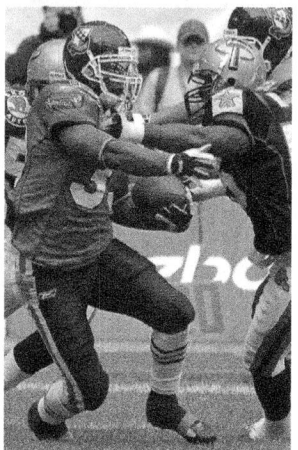

NFL Europe League Photographer

When the 2001 season came around, I suggested to the league they should contract me to cover all their requirements, and they did!

The PR Director for the league David Tossell came up to Blackpool to see me, we hammered out a deal to suit both parties and it was official. I became the first, one and only, Official League Photographer for the NFL Europe, a very exclusive position. That was it, I had finally made it to the top as a sports photographer!

If it breathed, walked or talked I photographed it, then again, come to think of it I photographed everything even if it didn't, well that was how I kept my contract going in the National Football League Europe for six years, going digital helped!

I was available around the clock and I mean around the clock. When they needed pictures for the worlds press they called, and it didn't matter what time zone you were on they called anyway and I supplied the pictures straight away. During those years I can only recall about two occasions when I was unable to supply a picture of a player, I was quite proud of that claim given how many changes were made during a season.

The job came with a few hazards though, apart from a lot of stress. To avoid players hitting you during their training sessions and games, ducking and weaving was definitely a requirement!

"I became the only Official League Photographer"

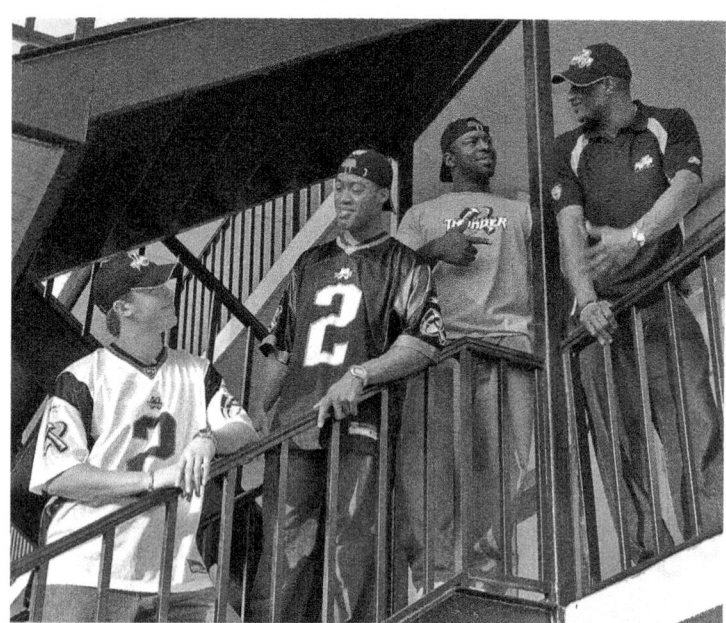

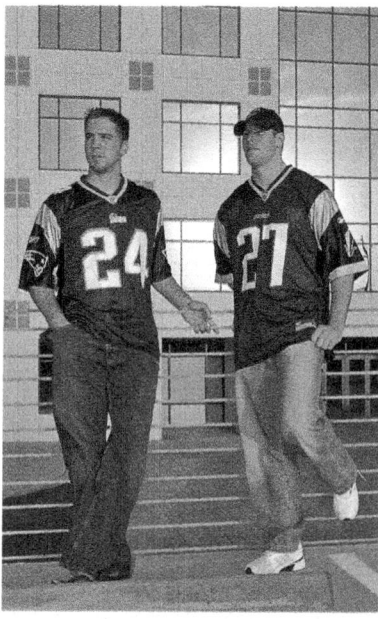

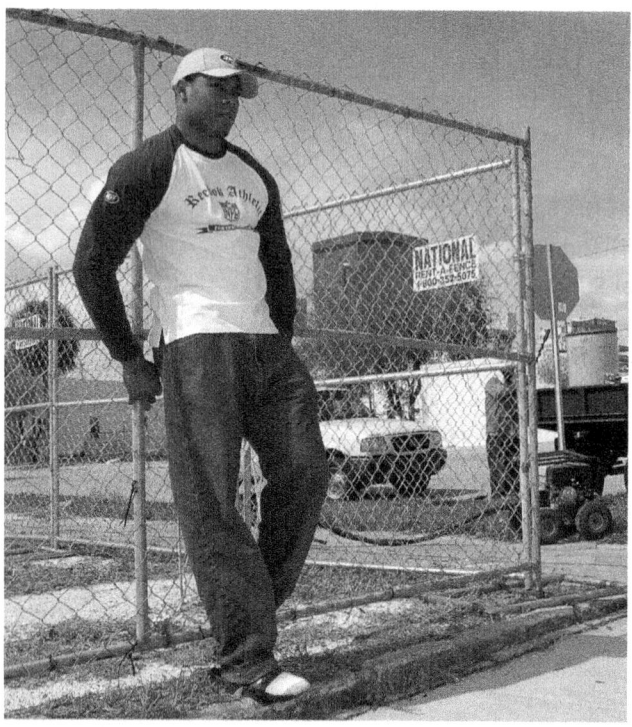

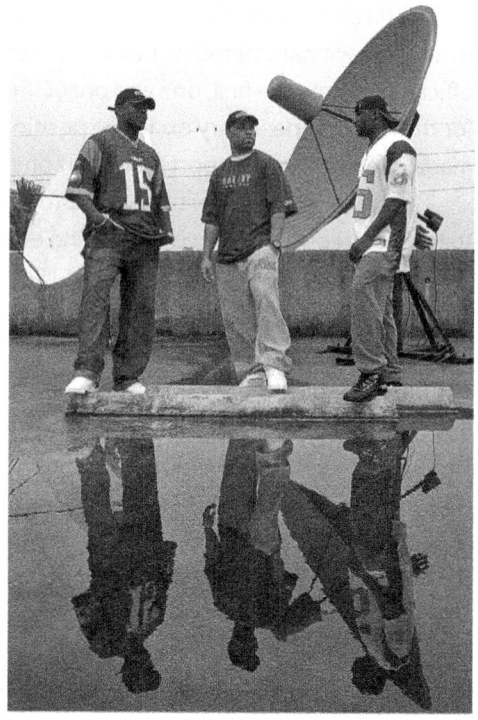

NEARLY FAMOUS

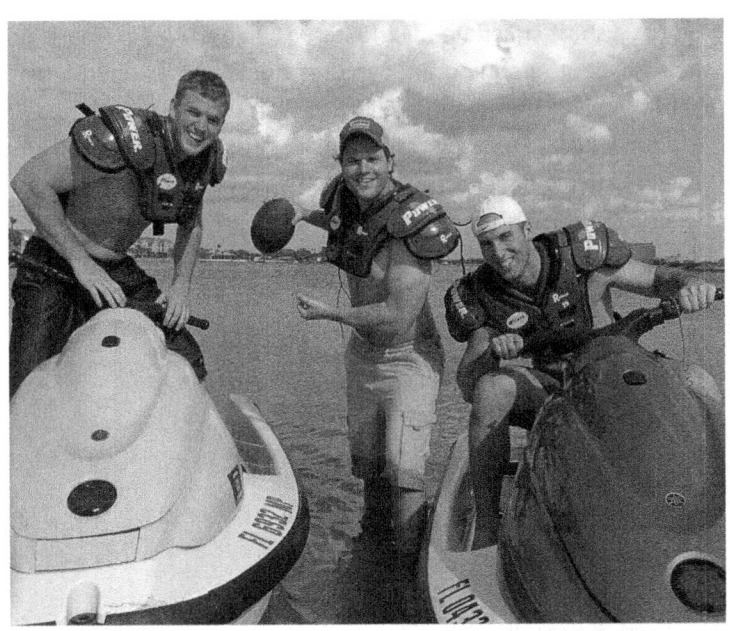
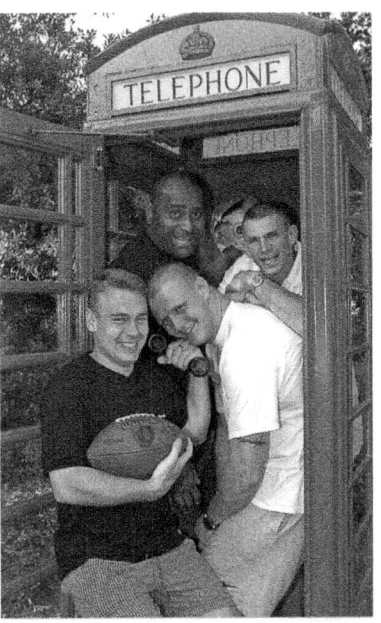
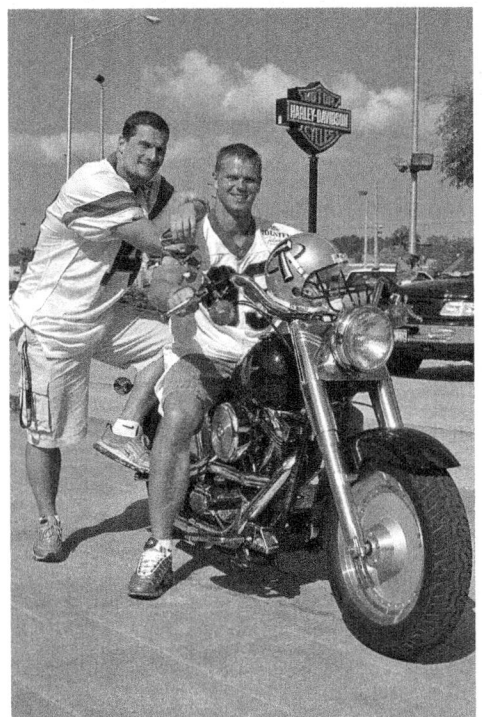
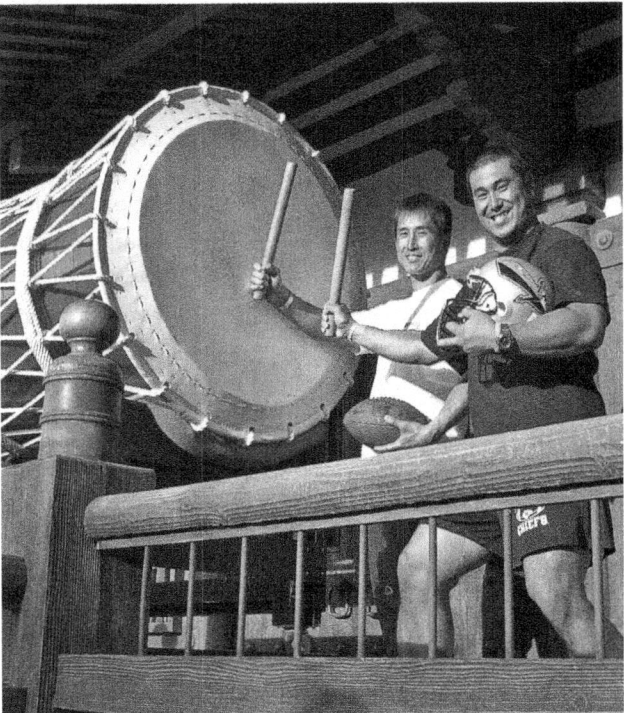

Here is a short anecdote my friends will enjoy. I was on the edge of the field photographing a Claymores home game, when a play came out towards me on the sideline. I saw it coming and turned to make a run for it, as I turned away the player was hit from behind and left the field in my direction, at double the normal speed, he hit me low taking my legs out from under me. I went up in the air and came

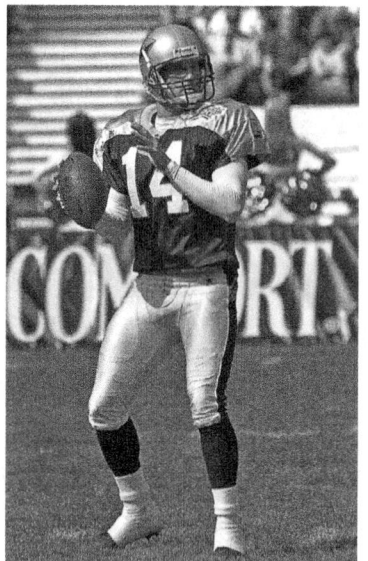 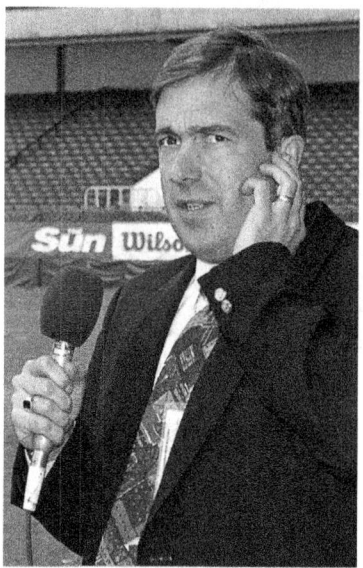 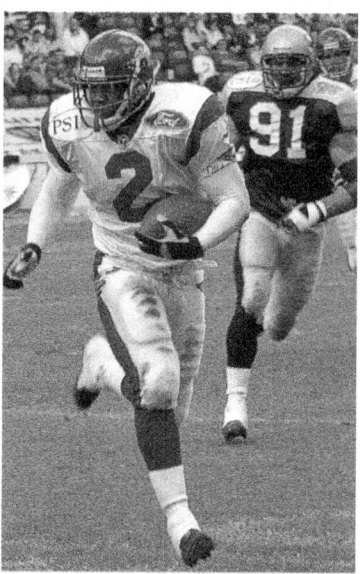

down flat on my back. I had a camera in each hand, miraculously I kept my hands outstretched as I came down but with the extra weight it knocked the wind out of me. For what seemed like an eternity I couldn't move or breath, I was prostrate, with two hands in the air like a statue that had fallen over, my life didn't flash before me only the cost in thousands of pounds to replace my cameras! Coaches and players rushed over as I finally started to breath, my daughter who was helping me with equipment rushed over and asked if I was all right, my answer, are my cameras okay? Look after them first. It nearly happened again minutes later when they sent another play the same way immediately after. The Claymores head coach told me after the game they did it on purpose to take advantage of everyone looking at me on the sideline, they wanted to catch the other team off guard and sneak a touchdown! In the TV booth, commentator

Nick Halling said it was the best hit he had seen all day, and definitely the highlight of the game!

Official League Photographer, sounds good and looks good in print too, but guess what, It was a bizarre period for me. From March to June, four months a year, I would work like a dog taking photographs, first at the Tampa training camp and then flying all over the place, Frankfurt, Barcelona, Glasgow, Dusseldorf, Amsterdam and Berlin, in an attempt to cover each team and as many games as I could on a weekend throughout the NFLE season.

On one occasion I had to get to Spain, I left home in Blackpool about 10 am, heading for Barcelona, at the airport they told me the pre booked flight was full. They offered me an alternative flight for the next day, it took a lot of explaining that I needed to get there today for a football game, but eventually they bumped somebody else and I got on the plane. When I arrived I got in a taxi and went straight to the stadium for the game. I was zipping off my trouser legs in the taxi and getting my cameras out as we approached, who knows what the driver thought at the time, he didn't know what I was taking off. I paid the fare, got out and walked up to and through the main gates to the field, the whistle went to start the game and I was taking pictures, still carrying all my equipment in a backpack. At half time I climbed to the top of the stadium where the press box was

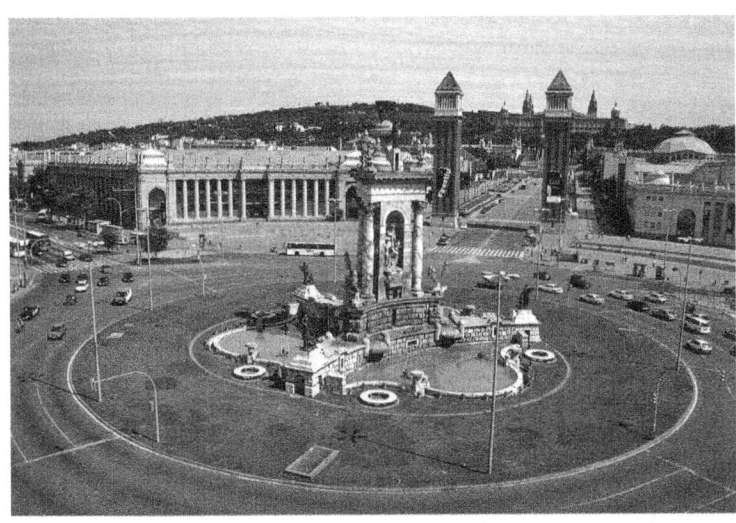
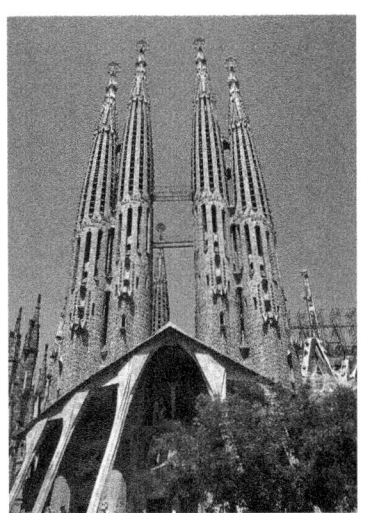

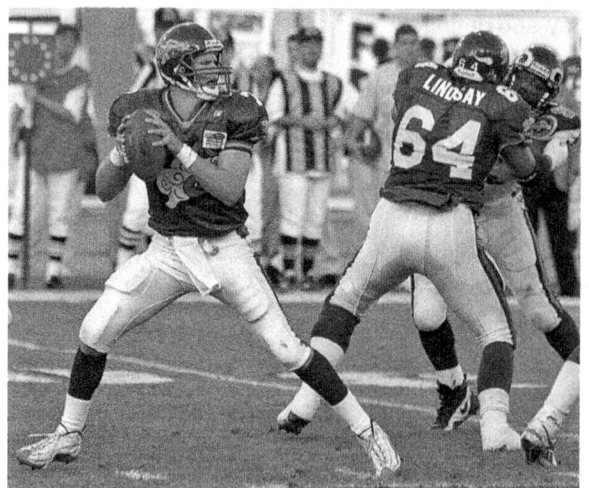

situated, then I started working on my computer to send the first half pictures off to the press and web sites, after, I headed back down to the field again to photograph the second half of the game. At the end of the game there were some presentations, I got pictures of that too, then started the long climb to the top of the stadium again to send more pictures out from the game, after that, back down again to field level for the after game press conference, a few more pictures then I was done, literally! Well not quite. I needed to check into the hotel and all the taxis had gone, so I joined a few of the Journalists who had flown in the day before with the team, they decided to walk, wanting to enjoy the fresh night air! I was fortunate the game was at the Olympic stadium and is situated on a hill, so it was downhill all the way. I finally arrived at the hotel about 11pm, what a day and what a glamorous sport!

You will appreciate now I hope what kind of stress was involved, I hope you won't laugh when on another occasion, a trip to Berlin, I had gone through the same type of game event. The morning after the game I was scheduled on the first flight back to England, so when my watch alarm went off and it looked like I was late, I flew out of bed, grabbed my equipment and dashed down to the hotel foyer,

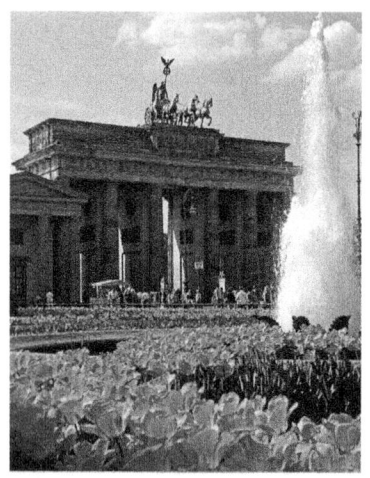

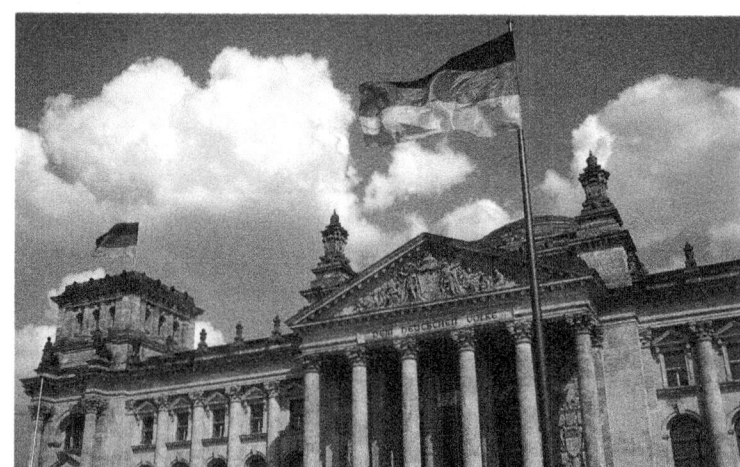

NEARLY FAMOUS

the taxi I had booked the night before wasn't there. I went into a rage at the reception desk, as they explained, at that time in the morning a taxi would take twenty minutes at least, I went a lovely shade of pink and started to break out in a sweat, then I started to blurt out all the German profanities I could, surprising how many you pick up over the years, I was furious. The taxi arrived, I dived in and rudely shouted schnell! Schnell! I just knew I would miss the plane. We pulled up at the airport and would you believe, it was shut. Worse than that, it wasn't due to open for another hour. At that point the penny dropped, my watch alarm was set on the wrong time zone and I had jumped out of bed two hours earlier then I needed too. Oops!

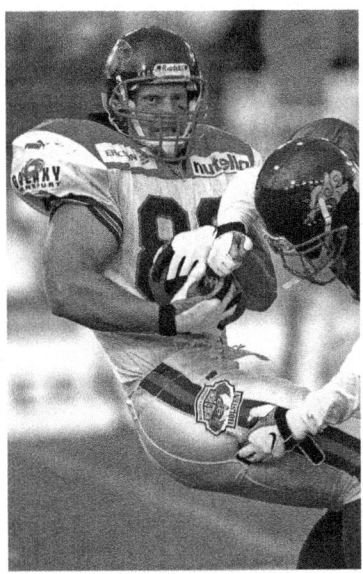
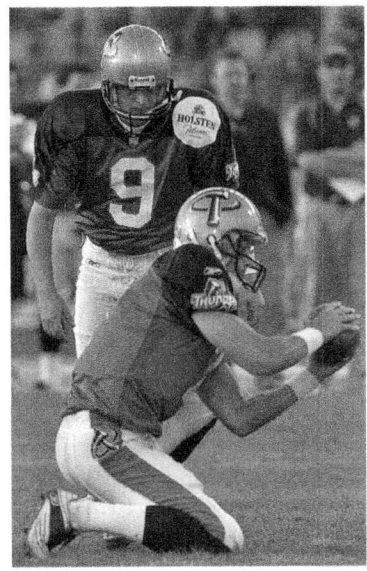
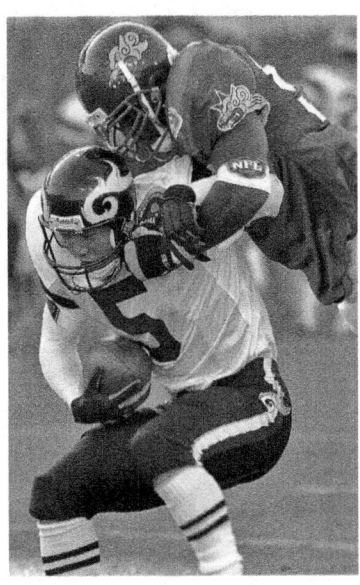

    You would think I could rest Monday to Friday, but no, I was still a freelance PR photographer during those days, yes, still taking pictures at those store openings, special events and promotions, for a variety of other clients, and the clients got bigger too. Warner Brothers cinema openings were great, but I had to travel some more! Tesco had stores all over the country but were a little bit more budget conscious, that meant no overnight stays and I had to travel even further. Although, some jobs were really fun, with the opportunity to meet and photograph some really big celebrities.

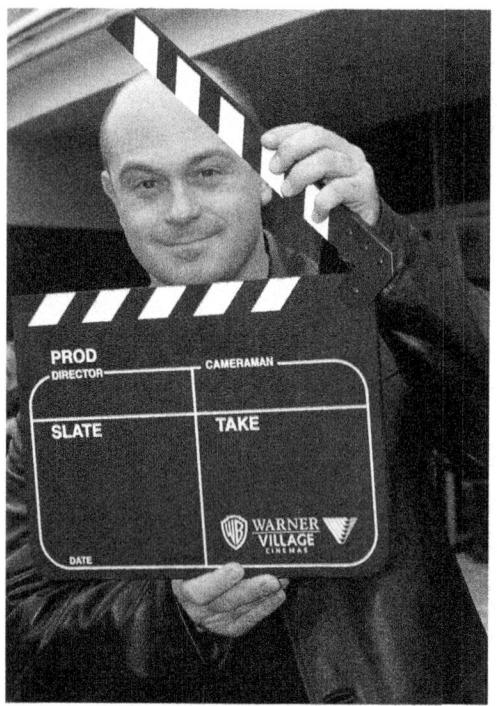

Ross Kemp has to have a mention here, he was the hard man of British TV soaps, Eastenders, most recently has continued his 'hard man image' by winning a BAFTA for the acclaimed TV documentary series 'Ross Kemp on Gangs', then more recently has spent time on the front lines with the British troops in Afghanistan.

I spent an evening with him prior to a cinema launch, we were having dinner and I called my wife to check everything was okay at home, joking, I asked him if he wanted to say hi to her and passed him the phone, he proceeded to have a ten minute social chat with her, "Hello it's Ross" he said "how are you? What are you doing? You're making dinner, so what's for dinner, oh, could we come round for dinner? The hotel food here is fine but I prefer home cooking," the conversation went on, "talk to your daughter, sure, hello Dani, what you up to?". What a great man, I found him quiet and humble, extremely amicable and one of the nicest people I have had the pleasure of working with. Here are a few others.

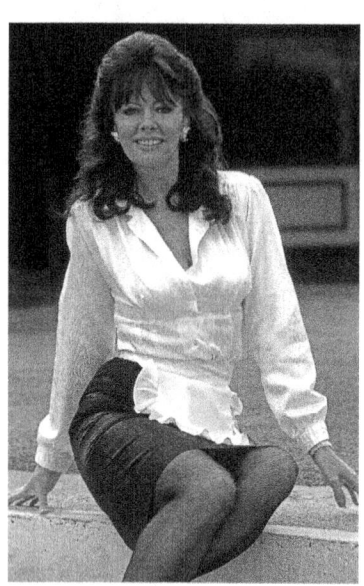
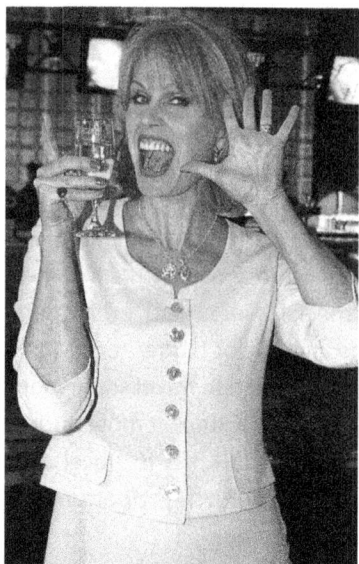
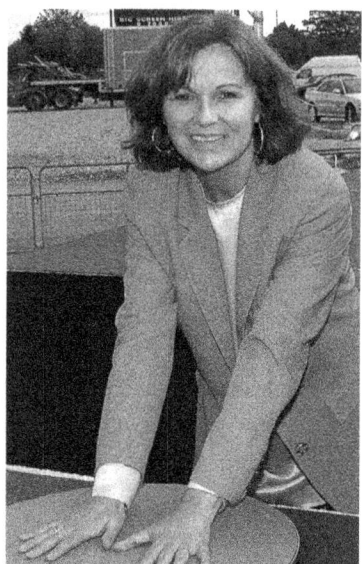

NEARLY FAMOUS

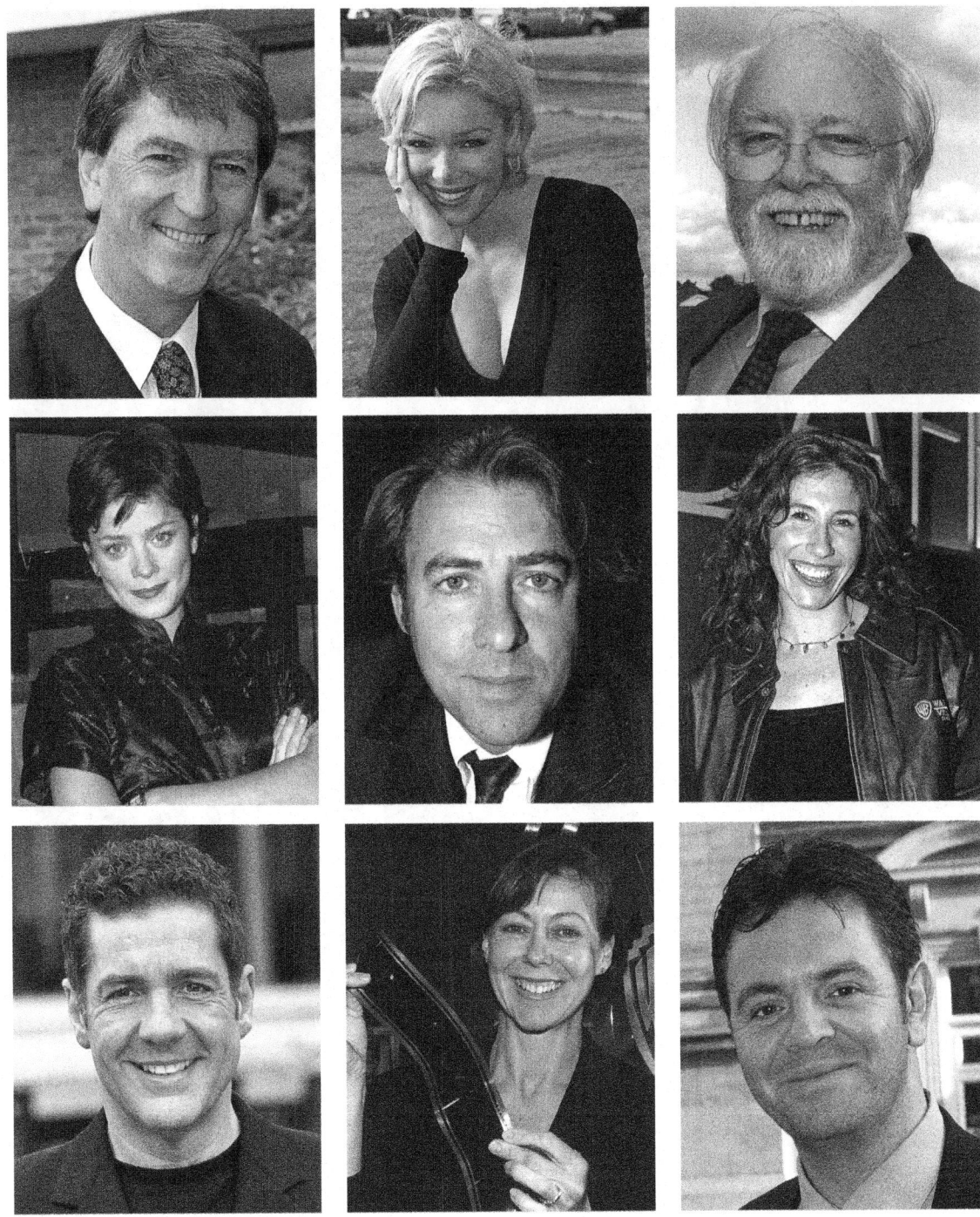

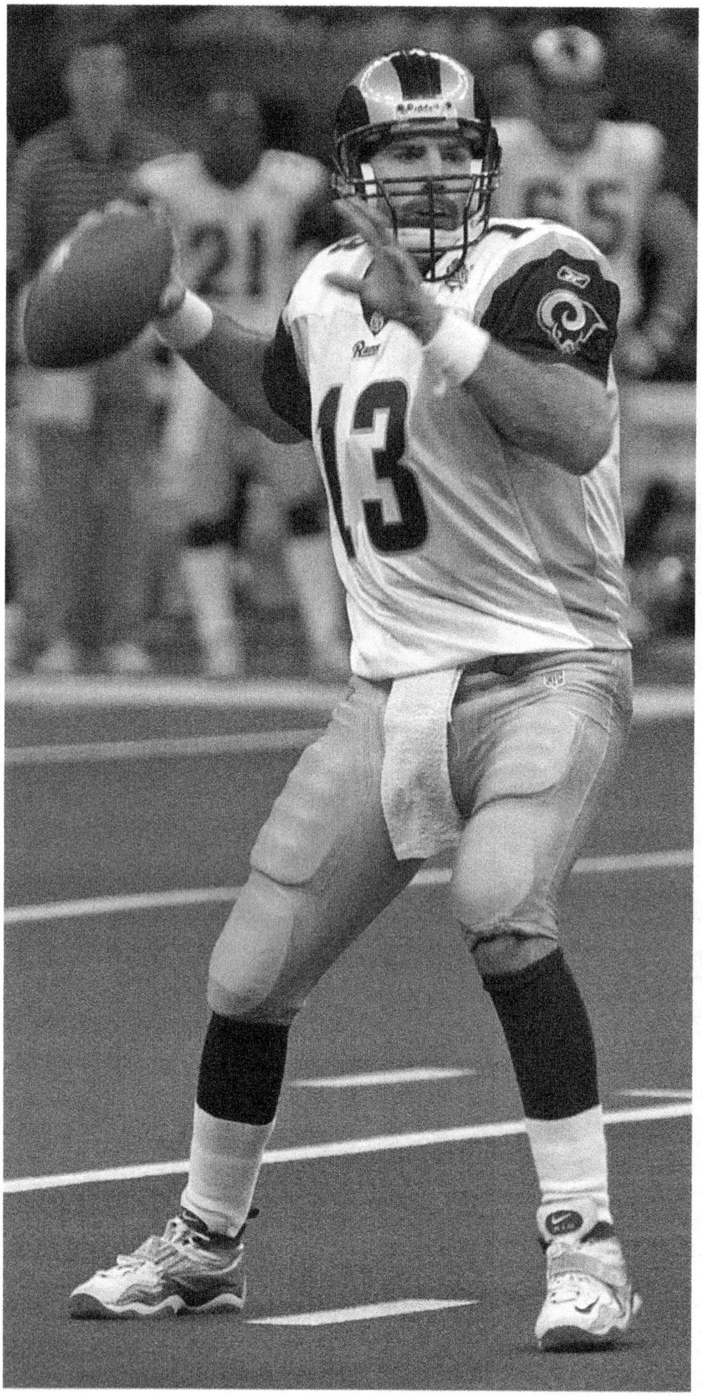

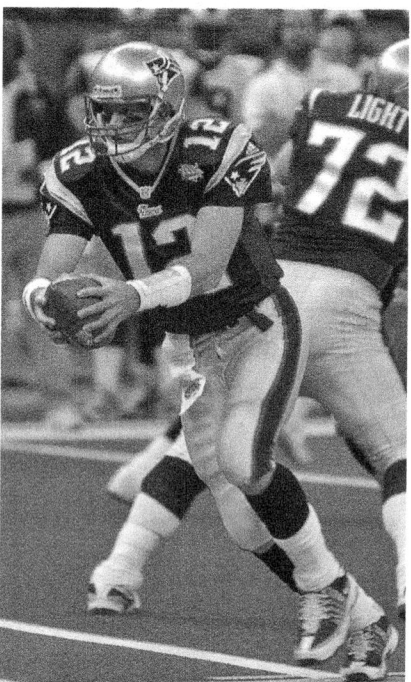

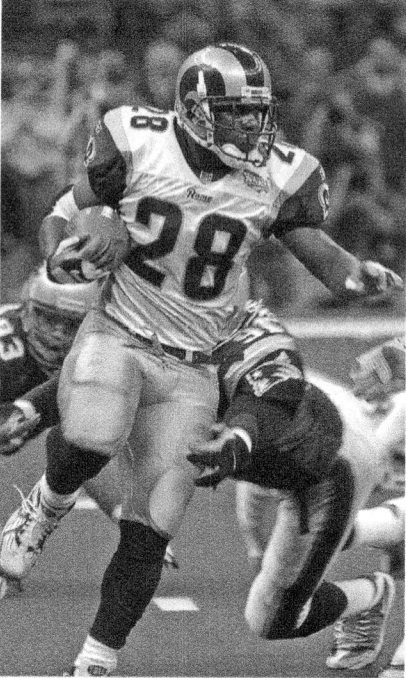

NEARLY FAMOUS

Super Bowl - at last!

When I started covering American football way back in 1984, it was a pipe dream to cover a Super Bowl, despite knowing other photographers that would pay their own way out to Super Bowls, just to say they were there and for the atmosphere. I always insisted I would not go until I was in an official capacity, not until somebody hired me to go!

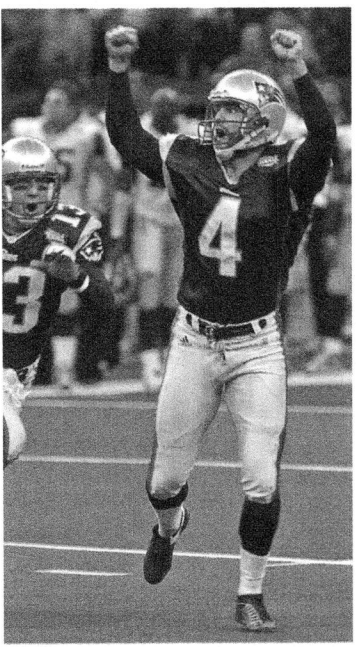

Well as the NFLE league photographer in 2001 I was finally asked to go to a Super Bowl, yes the NFL final in the USA. There was a pregnant pause, I hesitated, while I tried to make up my mind, it was a big decision, did I really want to go to one of the biggest sporting events in the world in an official capacity, mmm let me see, I had only waited seventeen years for this opportunity. It must have taken me quite a while to reply, I would have to go all the way to New Orleans, right? I asked, "Yes" came the reply, and photograph the game between the contenders St Louis Rams and the New England Patriots, right? "Yes! " From the sideline of course, right? "Yes!" mmm I'll do it!

Did I know what I was in for? No, It may have been the hardest week of photographic work I have ever done but this was it, I had finally arrived. My credentials as a top Sports Photographer were there for the whole world to see.

I arrived in New Orleans on the Monday for the week's build up to the game, my job over the next few days would be to get individual pictures of the NFLE players that had made it into the Super Bowl,

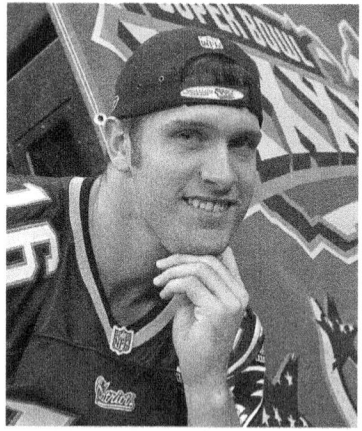 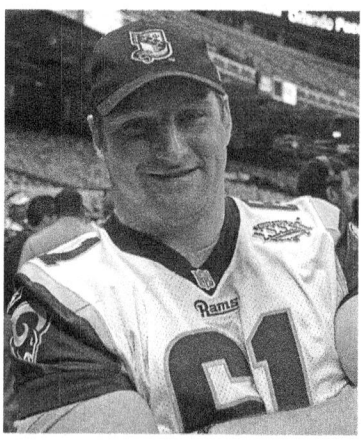 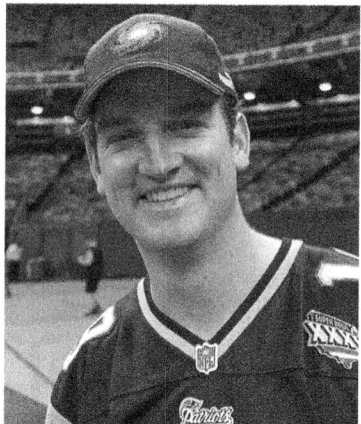

each with their respective NFL teams at Tuesday's Media Day, amongst 3,500 other photographers and journalists. Then to my surprise I would spend all day Wednesday about twenty miles away getting the Global Juniors tournament games, then on the Thursday would be the junior and NFL International press conferences, Saturday was the juniors play off games and the final itself, not forgetting Sunday, how could I, finally a trip to the Superdome and the Super Bowl itself.

All sounds easy enough, doesn't it? Well add to that little mix I also had to sort through thousands of pictures, then select and send pictures to Europe from each event via my laptop from my hotel room, and because they were six hours ahead, I had to start doing it immediately each event finished, well as soon as I could get back

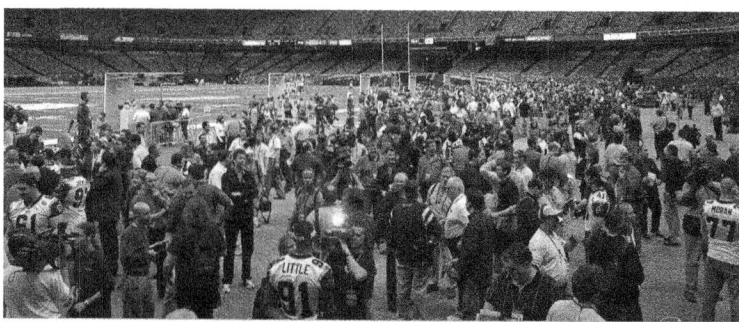

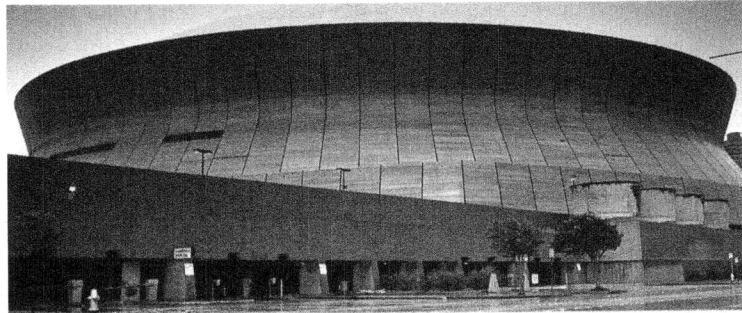

on the bus. That meant working at night and into the early hours to complete the work on time for the press deadlines!

OK I hear you say, what did I do on Friday? Well actually I photographed the fans and all the atmosphere of the NFL Experience and attempted to get my first sit down meal in a restaurant since arriving, I say very importantly, attempted!

I was invited to join a group of German journalists for dinner, strangely the only colleagues to actually invite me to join them during that week, despite half the office of the NFLE being there. Enough said. Anyway I digress, we all met up in the hotel foyer and walked, I needed the walk like I needed a hole in my head, up to a restaurant

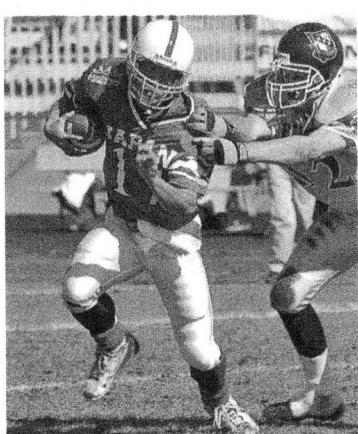
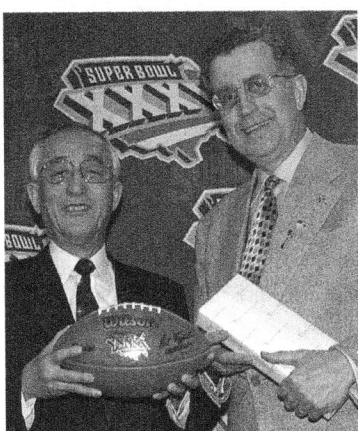
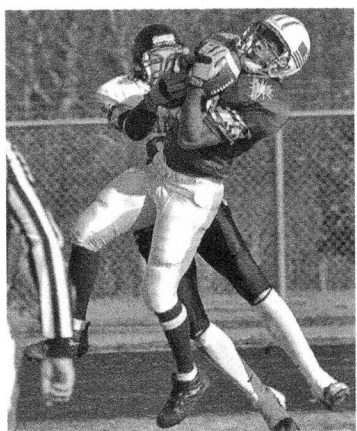

chain endorsed by a well known American football personality, arriving just after 9pm. Despite it being really busy we were shown to a table for eight. We talked and laughed for about an hour but no dinner turned up. I enquired with the waiter how long would it be? Well, remember I am still waiting for my first full meal of the week! "Any minute now sir", came the reply, about 10 minutes later there was an enormous crashing sound that came from the kitchen. As our table laughed and joked, "die war vermutlich unsere Mahlzeit" I heard in German. Yes It dawned on me it probably was our meal, but nobody came over to confirm this or suggest there might be a further delay. Another twenty minutes went by and so did my patience. I asked for the manager, he came over with all the usual apologies suggesting they were over booked and under staffed, which did little more than wind me up even more, if you can't stand the heat get

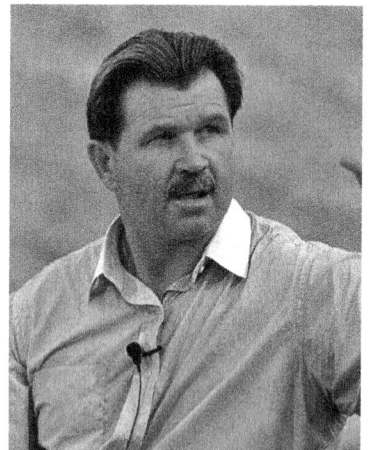

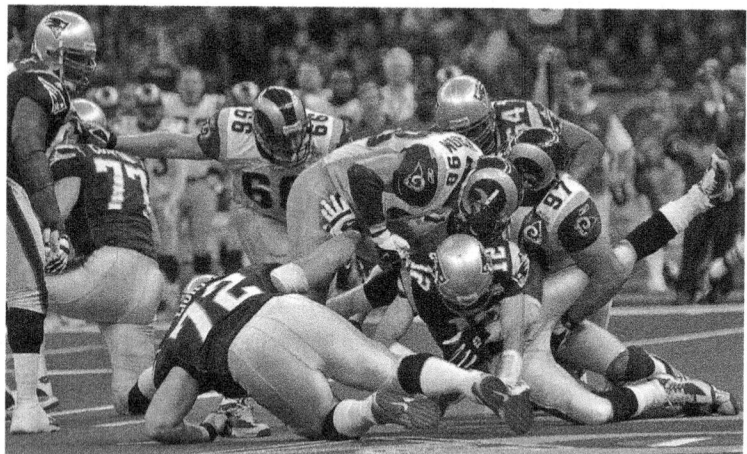

out of the kitchen, was a suggestion. Didn't really help the situation but seemed appropriate at the time. I went on to suggest that unless he wanted the restaurants name all over the European press as the worst service in the USA he might like to take charge of the situation, well he did, returning to advise dinner would only be a few minutes, a free round of drinks, like we hadn't had enough by then, and here is a free copy of Mike Dikta's book for everyone. We still laugh about it today and no I haven't read the book yet, I'm saving it for the next time I find myself half an inch away from starvation!

I spent another evening with those guys walking around the French Quarter, the place was absolutely packed, every Tom, Dikta and Madden were there, well the Super Bowl was on and it was full of fans. We were trying to get a table for about ten of us, everywhere was full, we walked through one end and out the other, then around the outside, we were just about to give up when one guy spotted a bar where we could get in and sit down, it turned out to be an Irish bar, where they were singing anti British IRA songs, well, I walked up to the bar, lifted myself to my full height, proudly raised my chest and said, "guten tages einer beer bitte", I knew my German would come in handy one day. My friend Wolfgang just laughed out loud.

I'm a quick learner and I realised, if you were in the right clique, you could get invited to some of the parties that were going on at the time and actually get food and drink throughout the week, I would

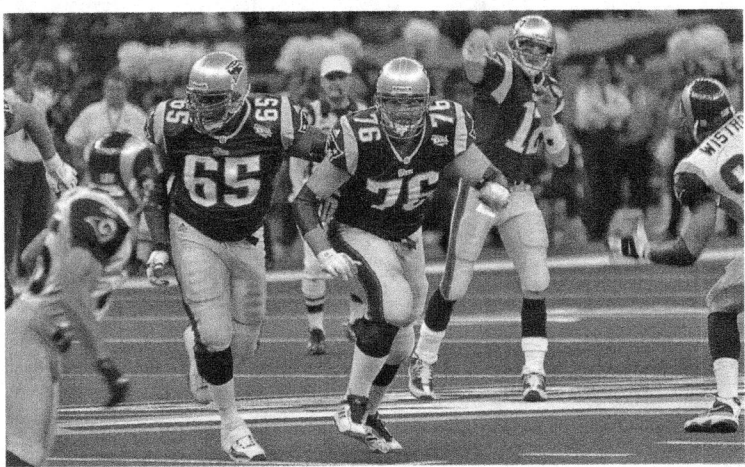 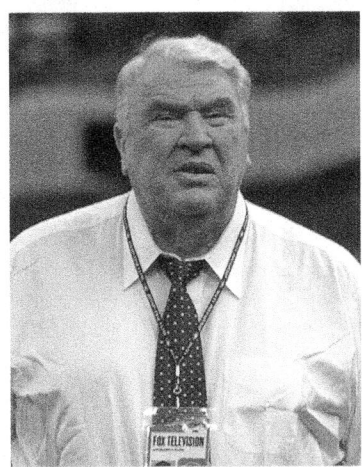

never starve again. If you could offer extra publicity and photographs at some of the side events put on by various sponsors, you could get invited to their parties too, so I worked on some of them over the next four years that the NFLE sent me to the Super Bowls.

I also learnt another valuable lesson, there was way too much work for a one man crew, so I brought Estelle in to help me out with the picture sorting and computer work. Well they were flying me out for the big game, then home, then out again for training camp within a month, Estelle was already helping me at training camp, so I had her join me for the Super Bowls, then instead of flying home we would stay out in USA for a vacation, then make our own way over to Florida for the training camp which started in March each year.

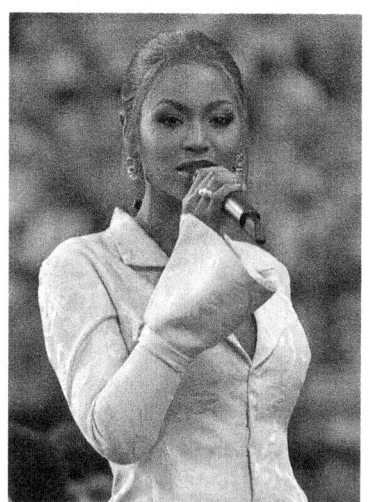

Another bonus, with the extra help I was able to attend more of the individual press conferences laid on by various different sponsors during Super Bowl week, including the pre and half time entertainment that featured some really big stars.

You might think that the work sharing should have made the whole event easier, in reality it just created more opportunities to photograph more people. Well how could you miss the opportunity to see your American football heroes and the singing stars you had grown up with? Just to be there, it's amazing.

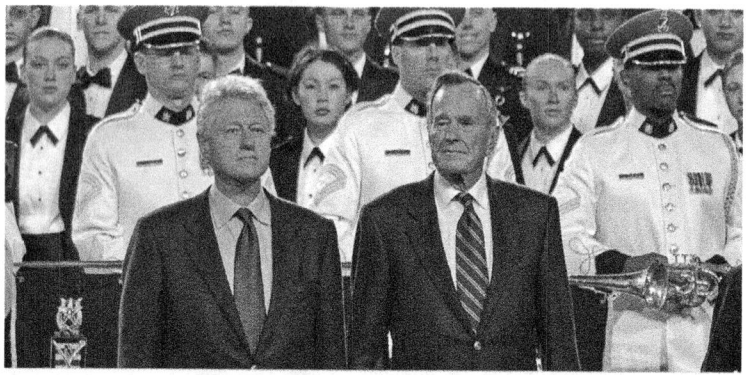

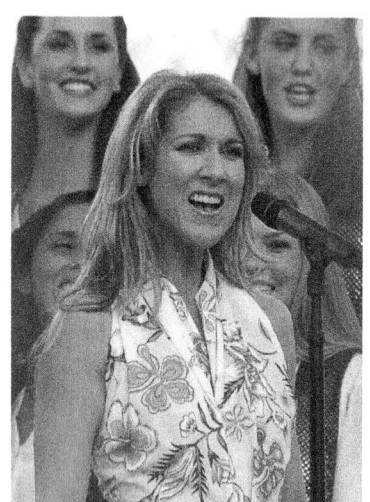

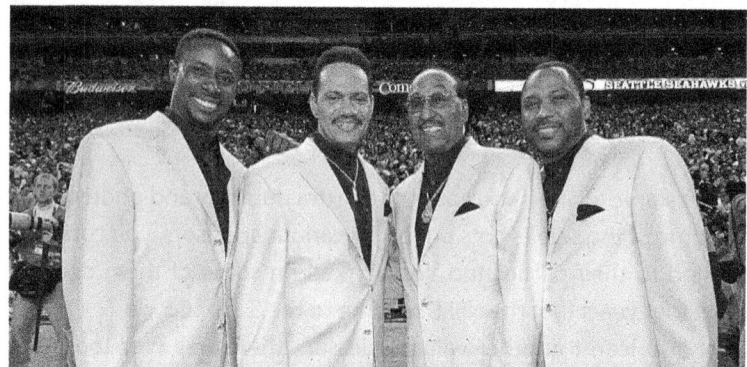

Super Bowl gamedays were marathons for me. Estelle wasn't given passes so I had to work them alone. By the time I had carried my equipment to the games through the miles of security, and there was a lot more after 9/11, then walked around the field for more hours than I can remember, photographing the team warm ups, pre game entertainment, the national anthem, first half of the game, the

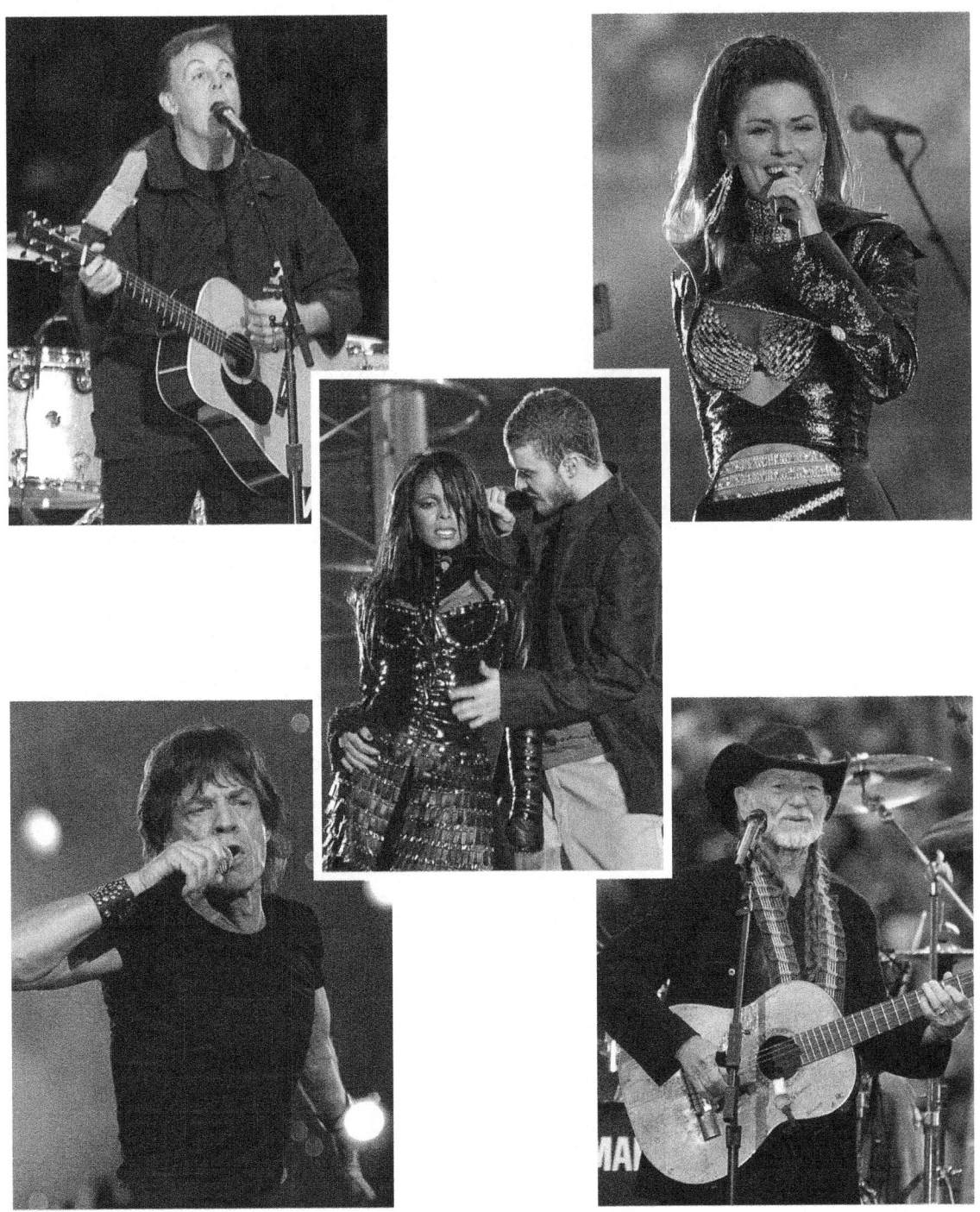

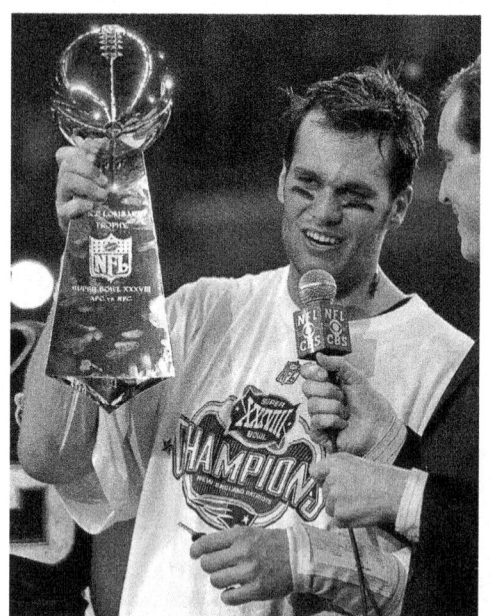

half time entertainment, second half of the game and finally the presentation followed by press interviews, then the walk back to the bus and eventually the hotel. It was usually about twelve hours from the morning start to the finish, I was always wiped out yet I still had to sort and send pictures off to Europe, that was my Super Bowl!

After the games it led to some very interesting but fun journeys across America, especially after the game in San Diego. We toured Palm Springs where the rich and famous all go to rehab, I needed it, but we couldn't afford to stay there. So of course we went over to Vegas, we didn't win any money but we were invited to stay with coach Jim Criner, we called him up from Circus Circus, he said check out immediately, your staying with us for the week, he was a great host. So I guess that was our lucky break in Vegas.

Los Angeles to Orlando by Amtrack was the next part of the journey. The train was slow by day as it gave way to all the commercial traffic, then trying to make up the lost time at night going so fast you couldn't sleep, every time we went round a bend the carriage door would open, strange, because I know it was locked! Add to that, the visual image I had of the passengers, It was like being in an old film, they included a doctor and his young nurse, a cowboy, a German in a trench coat and a rather tall waiter who had a funny walk, I guess he didn't want to spill the soup! See what I mean?

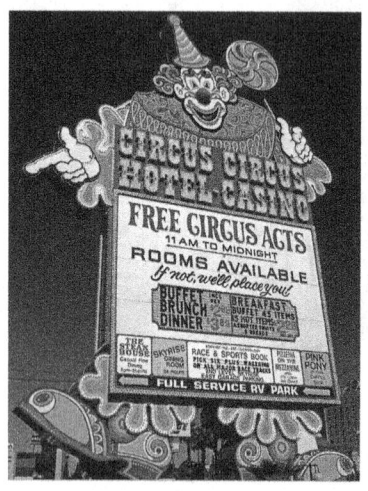

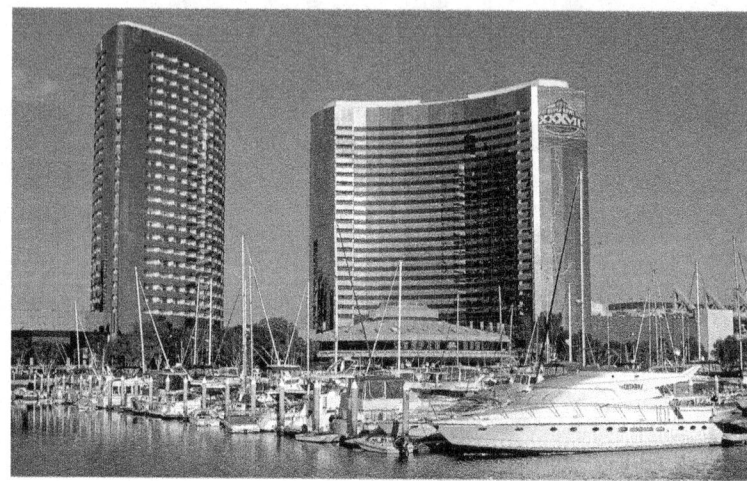

The last big trip was by road with our new found Super Bowl friends, Kathy and Jack. They offered us a lift to Florida going over the Smokey Mountains from Detroit to Tampa. Three days driving in a pickup truck, one overnight, but more or less none stop driving for Jack, who is an ex truck driver, then I drove for the last couple of hours just to make me feel good, and give me the right to say WE drove all the way. They did get some good laughs from me though, I must be the only person that has managed to throw himself into, not off, the

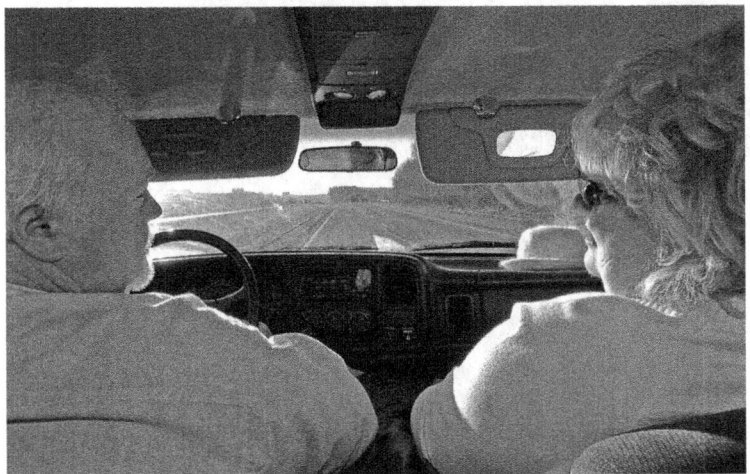 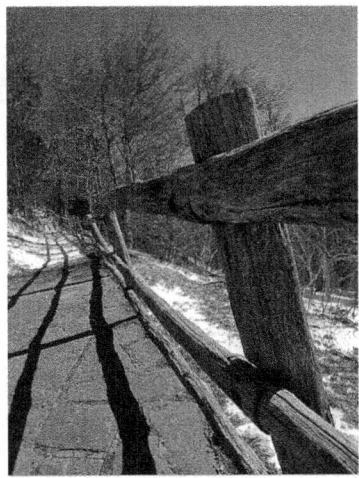

Smokey Mountains, complete with camera, just when we did a pit stop for some photographs, the laughter is still echoing across the Tennessee mountains. You know who you are!

Another funny thing happened in Detroit, I was walking through thousands of fans when I got a tap on the shoulder, "Hey Wayne, didn't you photograph my wedding in the Bahamas a couple of years ago?" said the man. Well, yes I had, I was walking along the beach when I spotted Matt and Paula's grandmother struggling to take their wedding pictures, so I asked if they would mind if I helped by taking some pictures, sure was the reply. It only took about ten minutes of my time but the happy couple were very grateful. How fame carries!

I have documented a lot of that first trip and some of the Super Bowls since on video, so look out for 'An Englishman's Road to the Super Bowl' documentary, that is, if you really want to see me stressed out in my jammies at three in the morning!

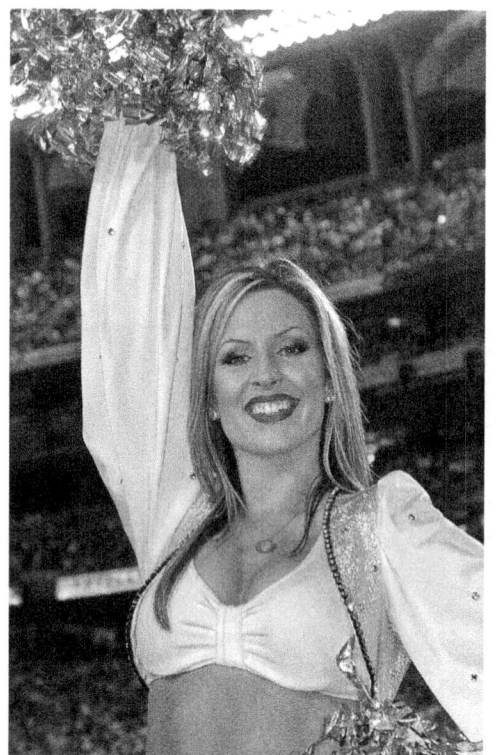

It would be remiss of me to forget the Cheerleaders, and not just the professional ones who dedicated themselves to dancing in the wind rain and snow from the United States to NFL in Europe, but the amateurs who placed all their hopes of a future cheerleading in the NFL. So here is a very small collection of the pictures I have taken over the years dedicated to them and their efforts.

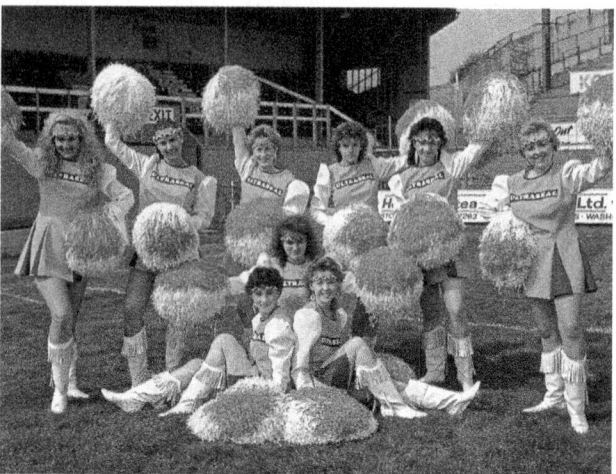

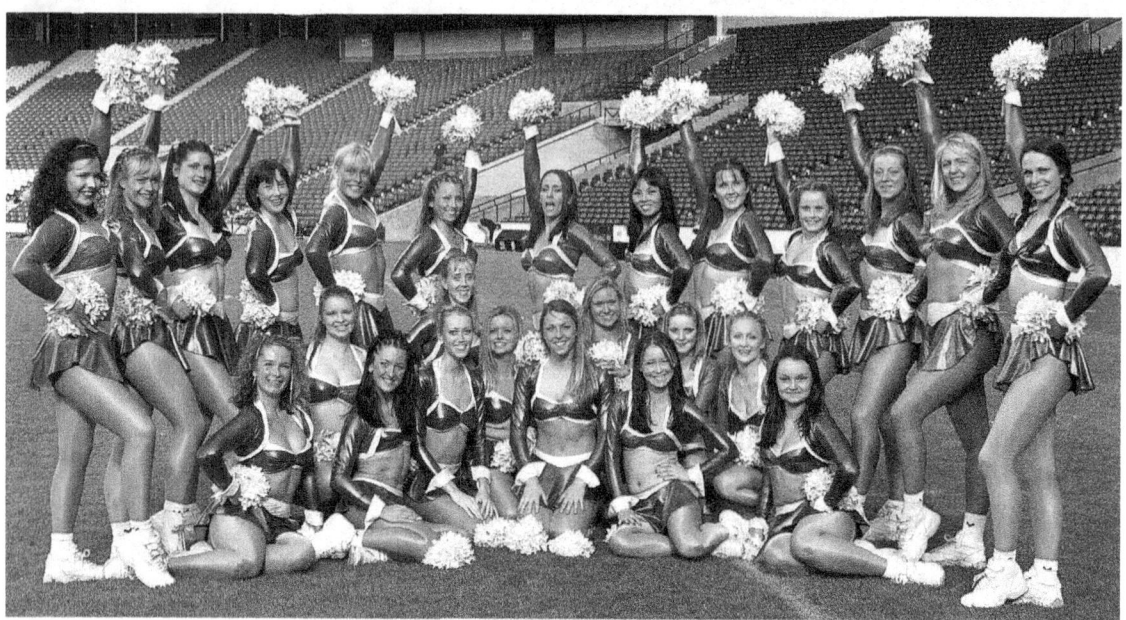

NEARLY FAMOUS

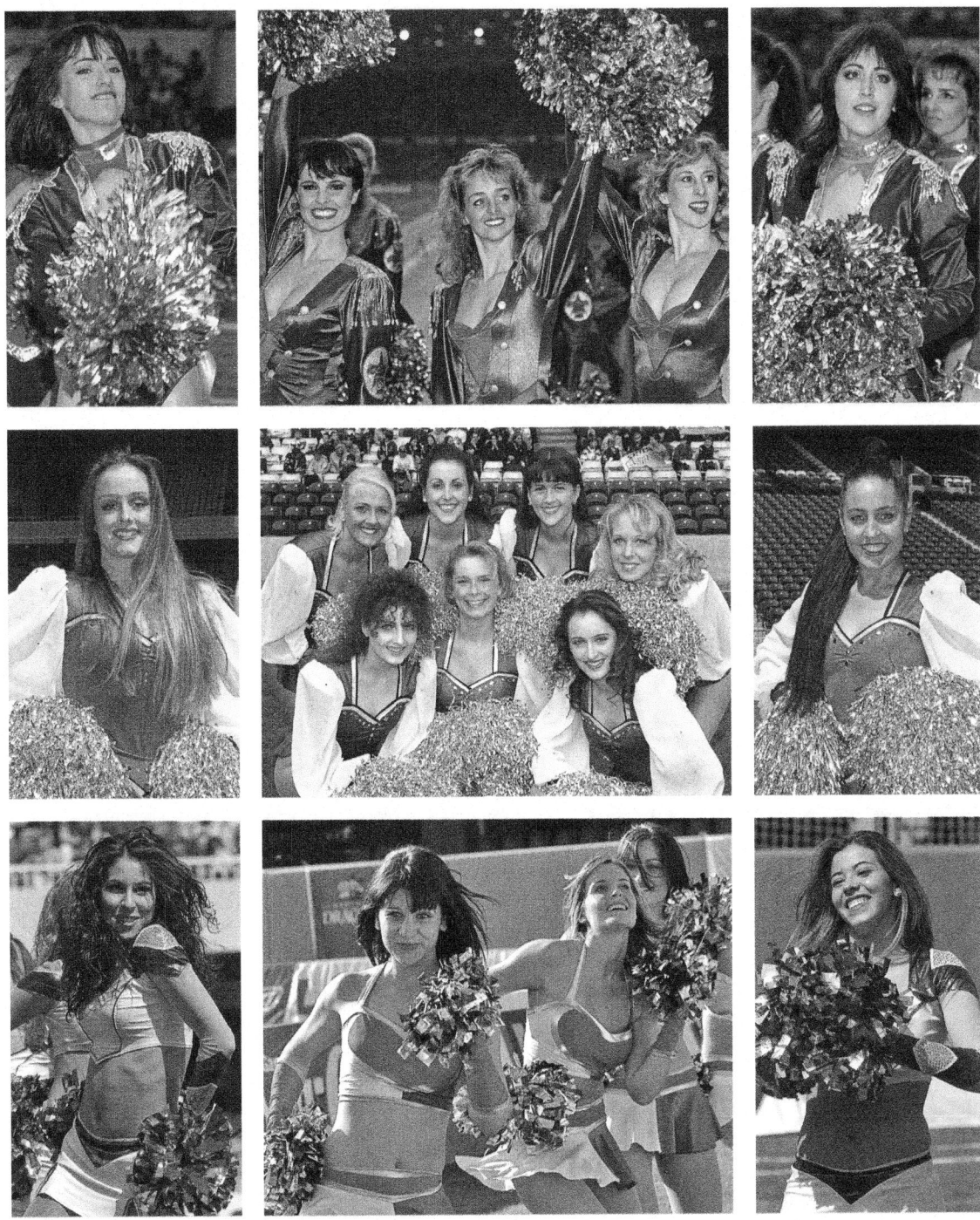

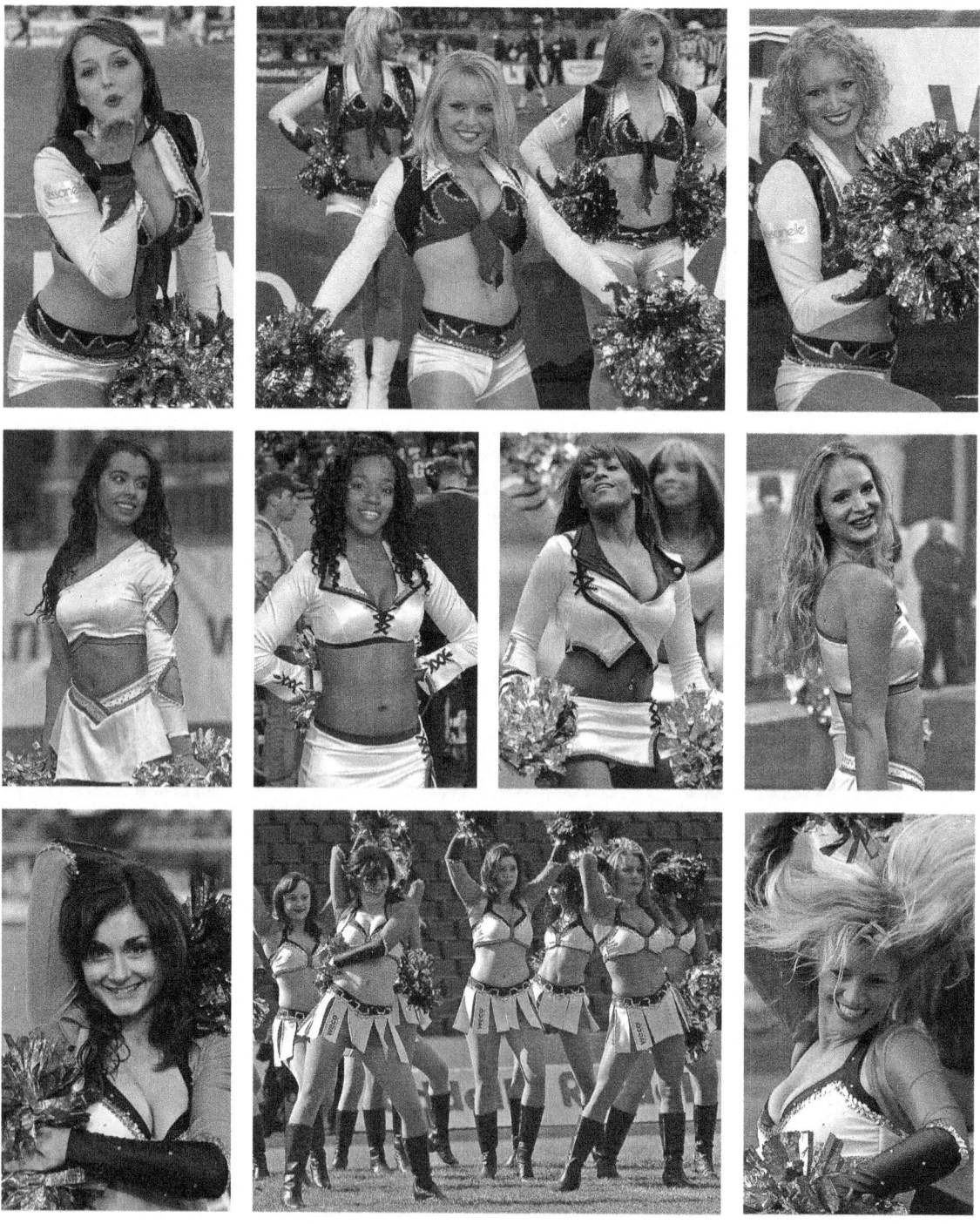

NEARLY FAMOUS

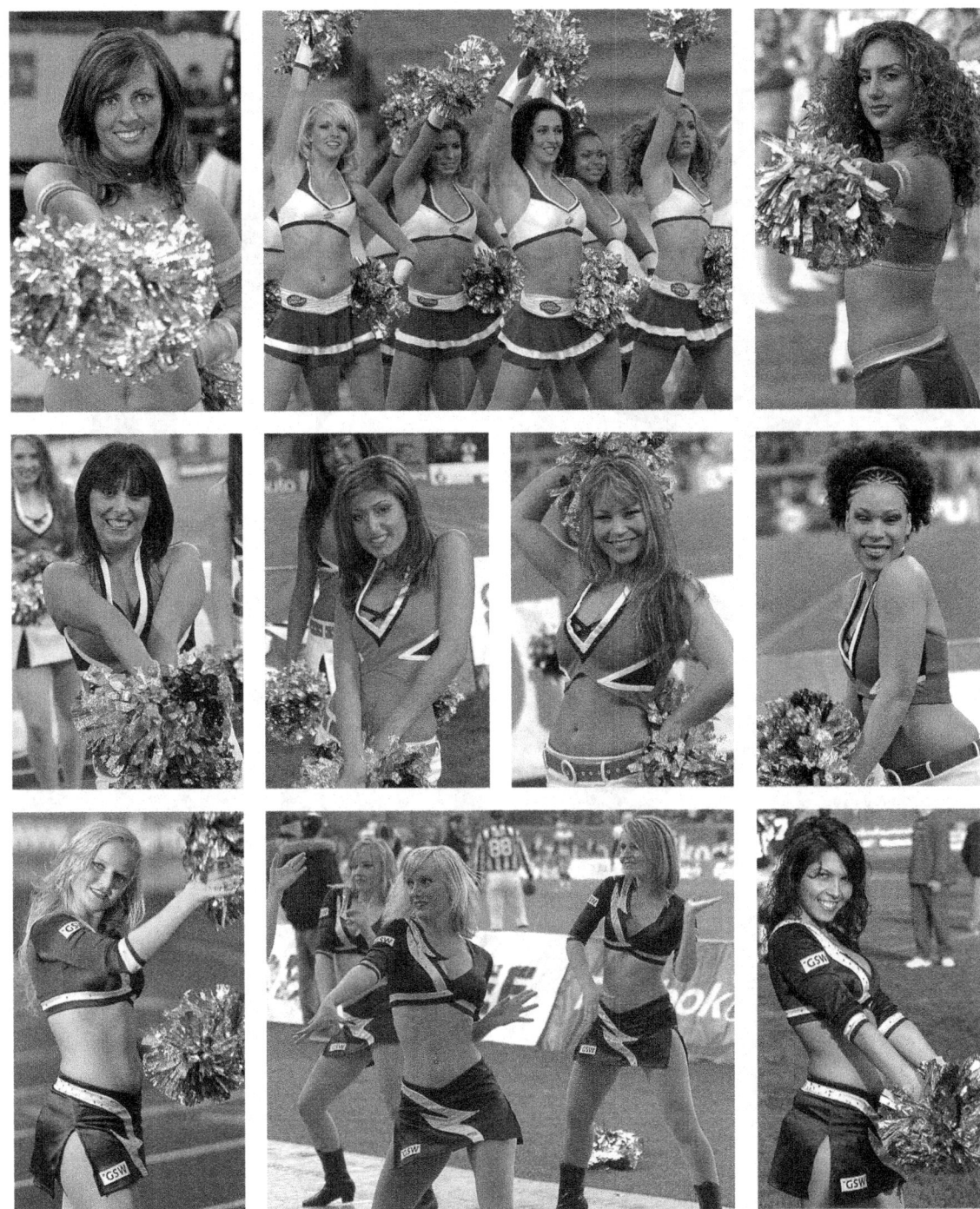

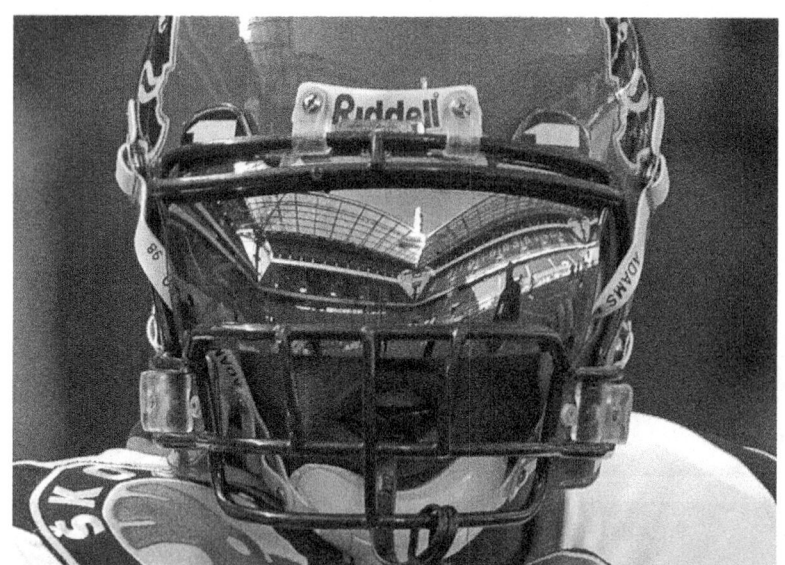
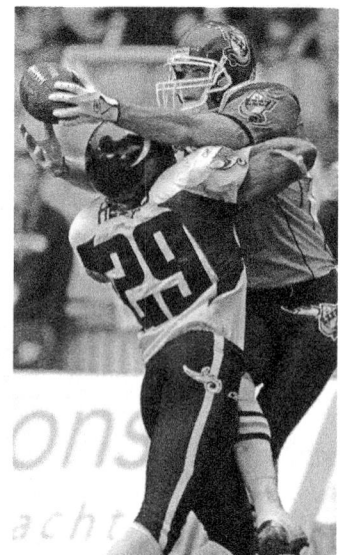
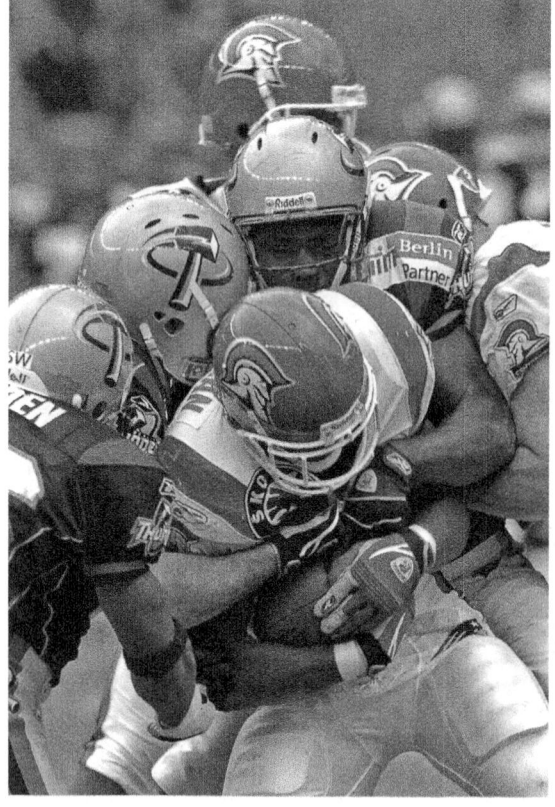
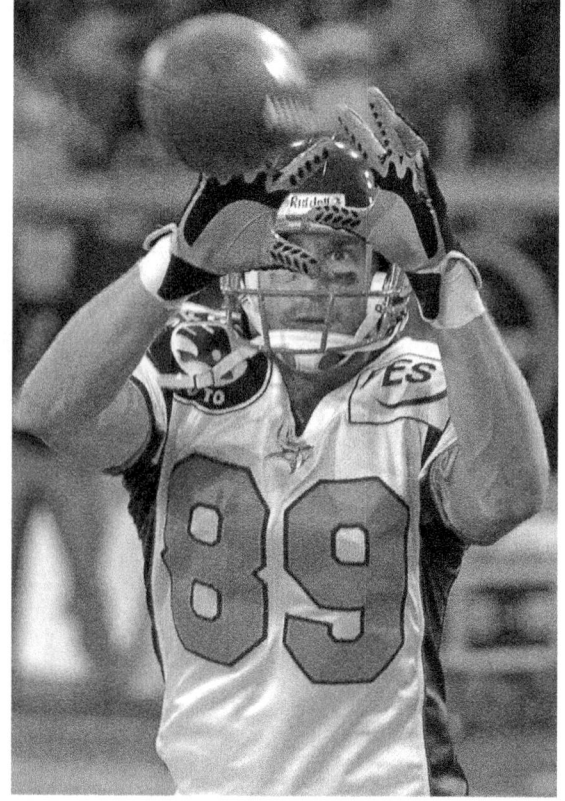

NEARLY FAMOUS

European changes

As each season went by more and more changes were made. Every year the organisation tried to make economies, they wanted the league to pay for itself rather than sponsor it, despite it being the ideal training ground for the new NFL rookies and second stringers.

The London Monarchs got cut from the league because of a 'drop off in fans', they said. I'm not surprised as they moved from place to place for games. They transferred their franchise to Berlin which also struggled in the early years. When the Barcelona Dragons went, nobody was surprised, only that it hadn't gone sooner, having the worst attendance. From that a new team in Cologne was formed and had a marginally better attendance, but never managed to compete with the big Frankfurt franchise. Then when the Scottish Claymores got the push and became Hamburg Sea Devils, allegedly for all the same reasons, mentioned above, most people blamed the logistics of travelling a whole team back and forth across Europe. The league was now five German teams and one Dutch!

"Why was an Englishman the League Photographer?"

When they cut the Claymores it had a roll on effect on me. The powers that be asked the question why was an Englishman the league photographer, when most of it was in Germany? It's funny I saw that coming too!

So another meeting to discuss contracts, (I had to renew them every year), ended with me offering to cover my own expenses during the season games and thereby levelling the playing field so to

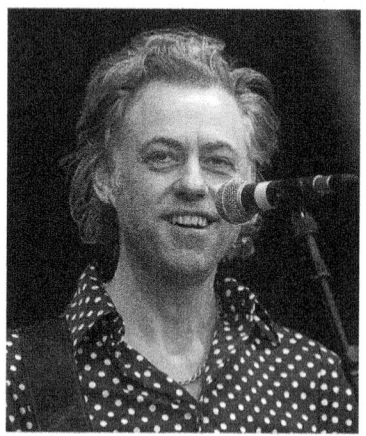

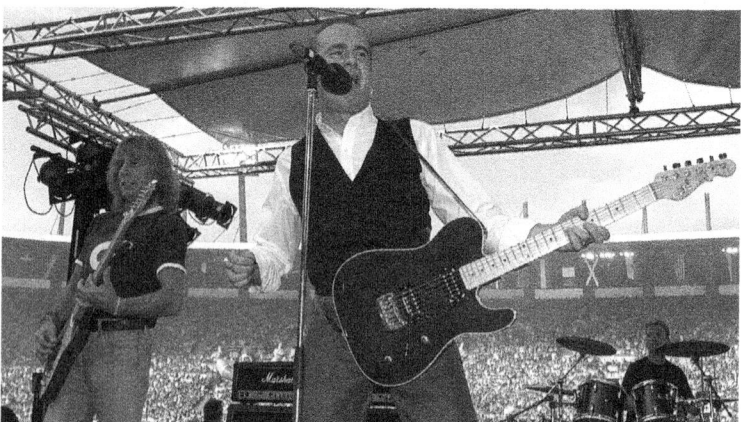

speak, they could make their own decision who would give them the best service. Based on my track record so far, I had already covered more NFLE games and World Bowls than any other photographer in the world, I think I still hold that record!

You can see by the variety of pictures here, I was shooting everything that happened in the league, not just the game but the back field shows, then the pre and half time entertainment as well!

Not surprisingly my contract carried on, but it made a dramatic change to the way I would get to games and the way I would cover them, fortunately it was in my favour!

I worked out, I could get a ferry crossing with my car for the price of the flights and take Estelle with me into the bargain. Given

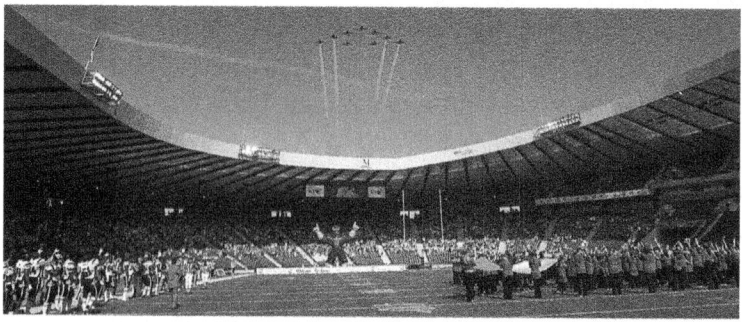

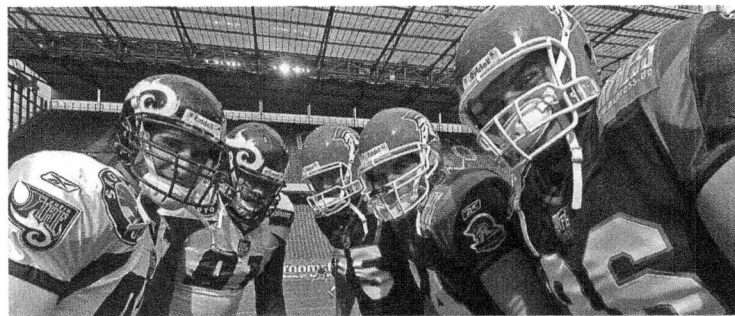

the amount of photography I was now doing I needed a full time editor with me. We would have to spend more time on the road in Germany and Holland but the economics made it worth while. Estelle was able to help game day with the computer work by sending out the pictures, bonus for me, there was no flying so the stress level was reduced. Just as well, I had discovered my blood pressure was running about 280 over 165, and that's dangerously high!

There was a down side, losing some of my additional PR work at home because I was only available midweek, but the bonus was to have some leisure time at last. Though I am not sure you would call travelling all over Germany, Switzerland, Holland, Luxembourg and Denmark taking photographs a break!

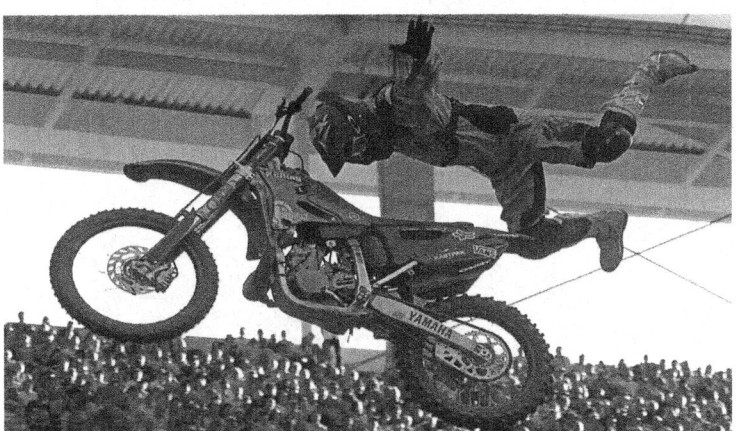

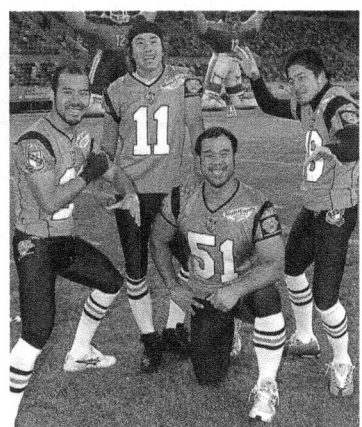

We pretty much lived out of a suitcase for the NFLE season driving from town to town. Estelle has her own thoughts on whether it was easier or not, given she had to work alongside me around the clock.

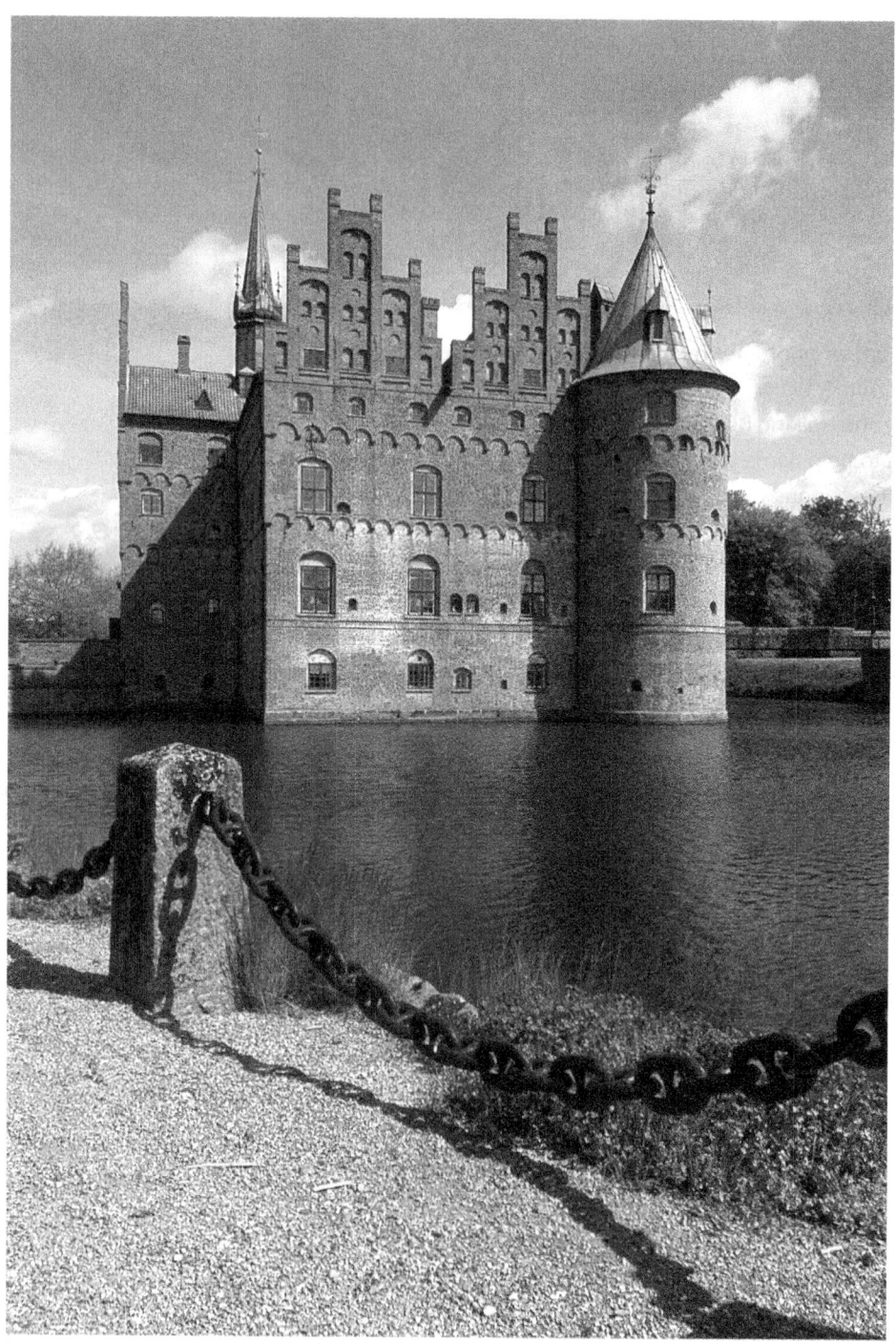

NEARLY FAMOUS

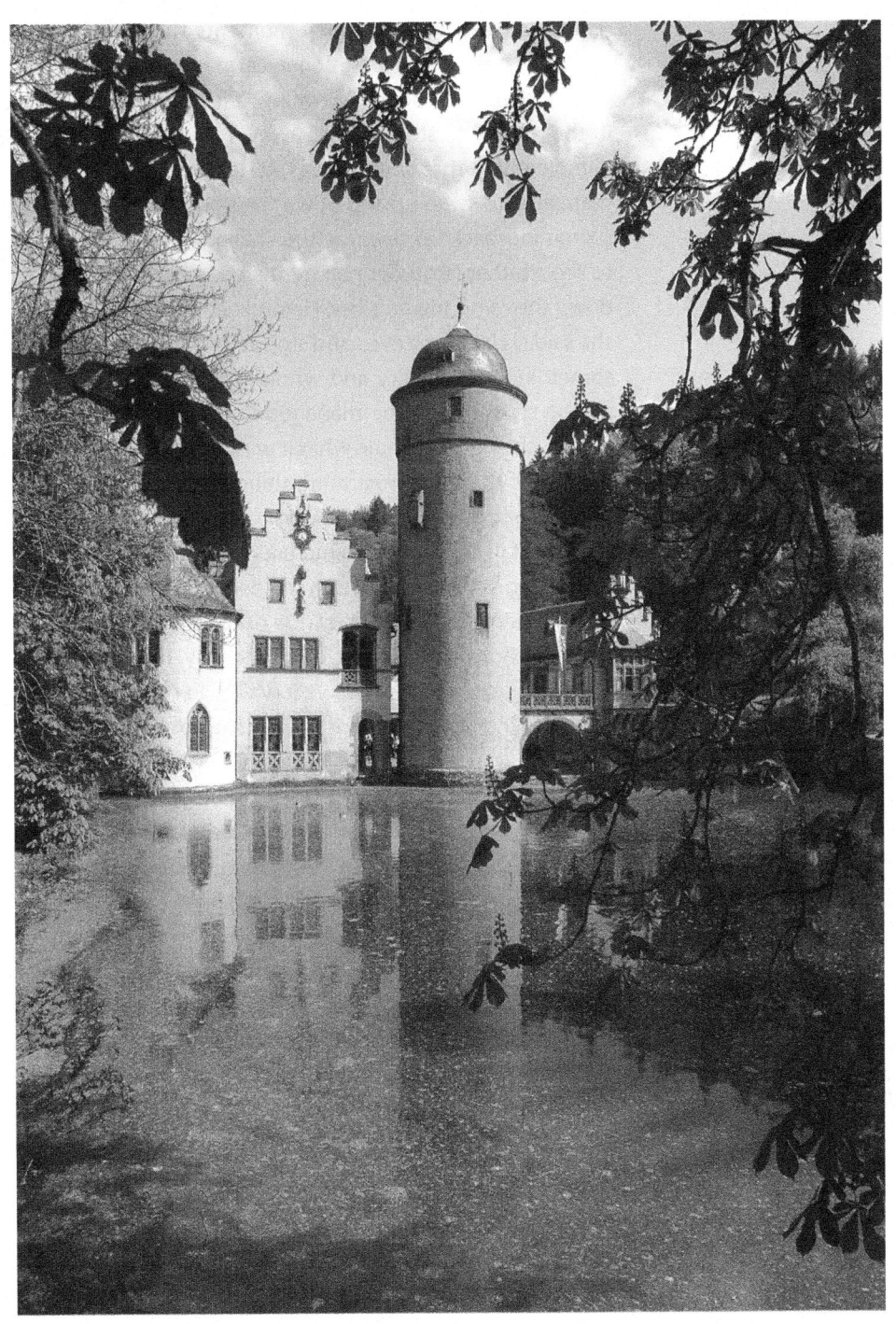

There were the odd funny moments though especially for her. We were staying in a traditional German hotel, it had a swimming pool and a sauna, now in Germany it is quite natural to take saunas in the nude, so Estelle stayed away from that room, she avoided it completely. At that time she was still learning to swim, slowly she was managing to swim up and down the pool. Well one day she was just swimming back up towards the shallow end, when she looked up to see a rather large German gentleman naked as a jay bird, coming down the ramp towards her. He proceeded to dive in straight at her, she said, "I closed my eye's and stopped swimming" she also muttered something about hairy and wrinkly, apparently as she went under for the second time she managed to grab on to something to save herself, she never told me what it was, but it took her breath away!

One of the most frustrating things I remember in the six years I worked for the league, was always having arguments with over eager security staff trying to stop me taking pictures, when I was standing on the edge of certain parts of the field that they felt wasn't allowed. Duh! I was the only official league photographer, I knew where I was allowed and where I might be in the way. It became so much of a problem I made up my own yellow vest so I stood out. I did get a bit of rib tickling from the office staff but at least it did the job.

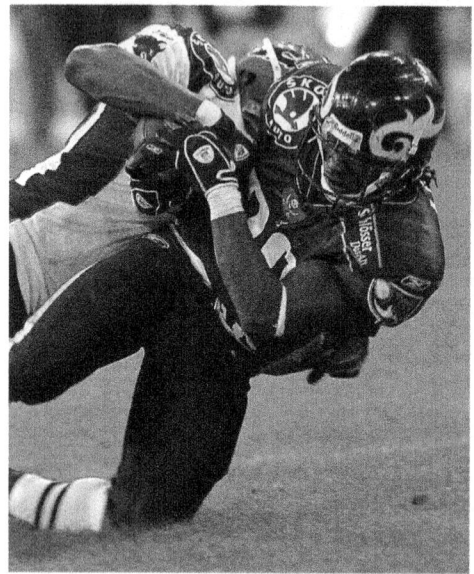

On one occasion I became the star of the week, everyone wanted to talk to me, did I see that? Did I get the picture? Well yes I did, a referee missed the play and called it wrong. The play had been called into question and I had the picture that showed what happened, even the action replay hadn't seen it, but my quickness had. It had no outcome on the game but the press jumped on it, I had to send pictures all over the place, because that one play had made Germany's press as the controversy of the week.

I even got a great quote on NFL.com by intrepid reporter and television personality Michael Carlson "NFLE's long time ace photographer, Wayne Paulo, was right on the spot and you'll see in the photo that Lewis's knee is firmly planted, while the ball is still a matter of joint custody." end quote. The story went world wide. Just call me Ace!

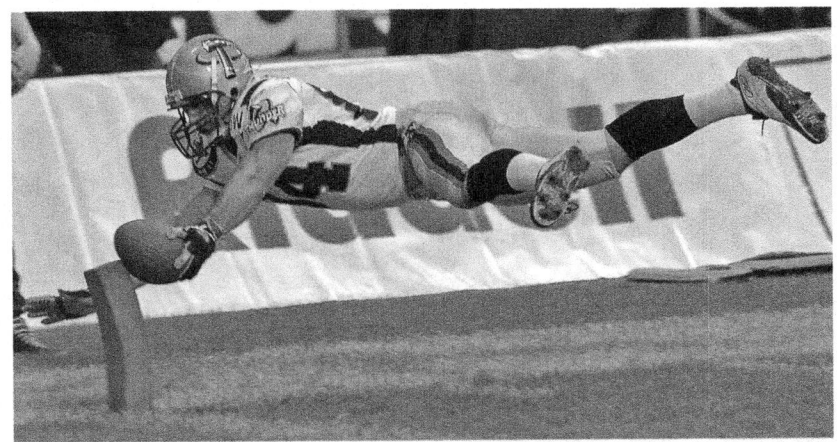
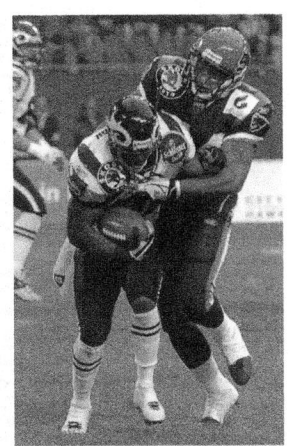
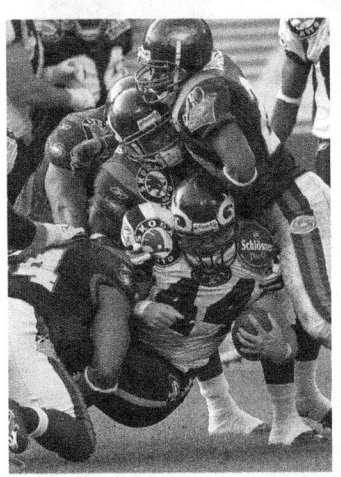
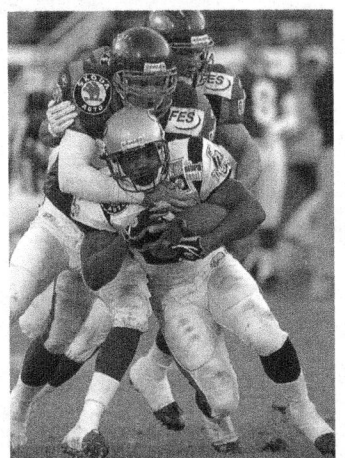
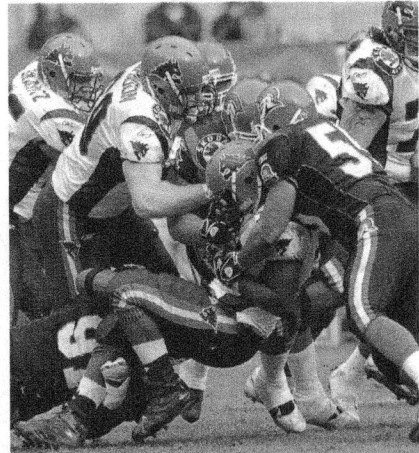
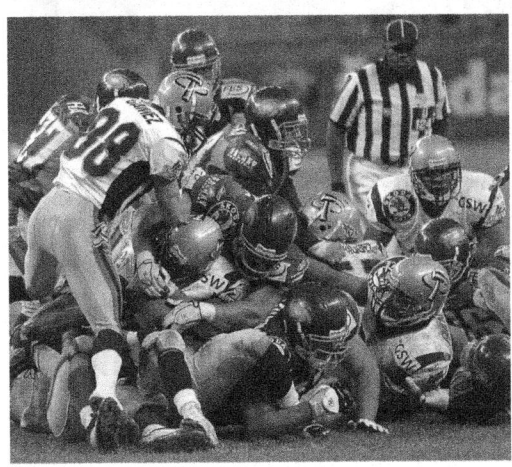
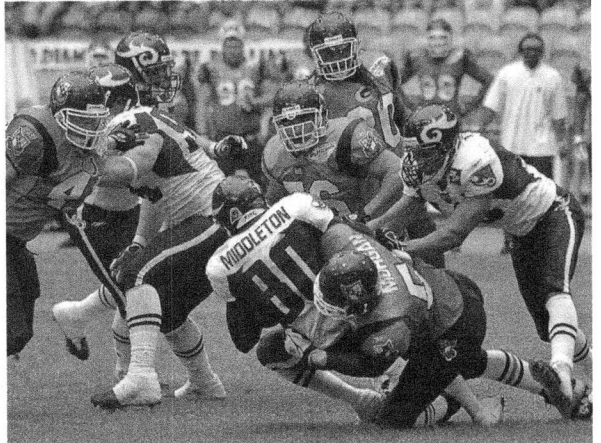

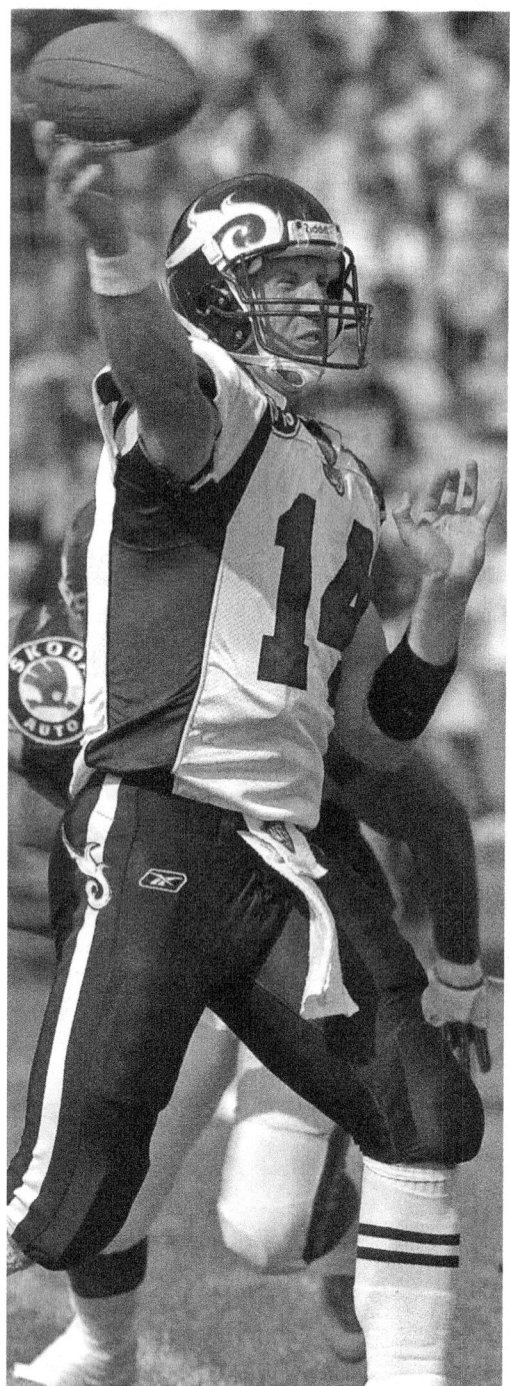

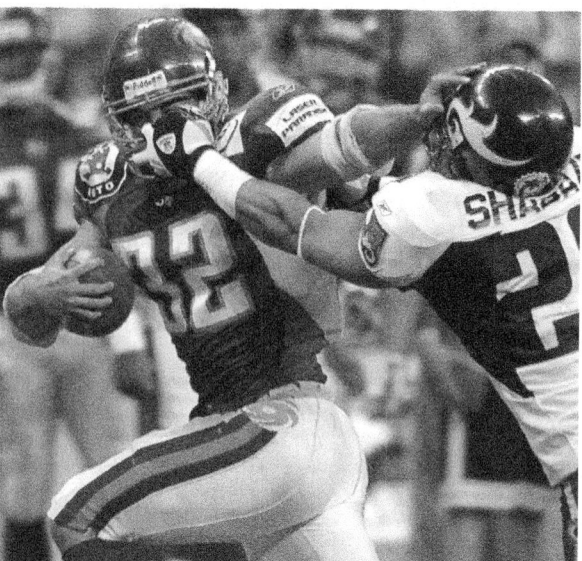

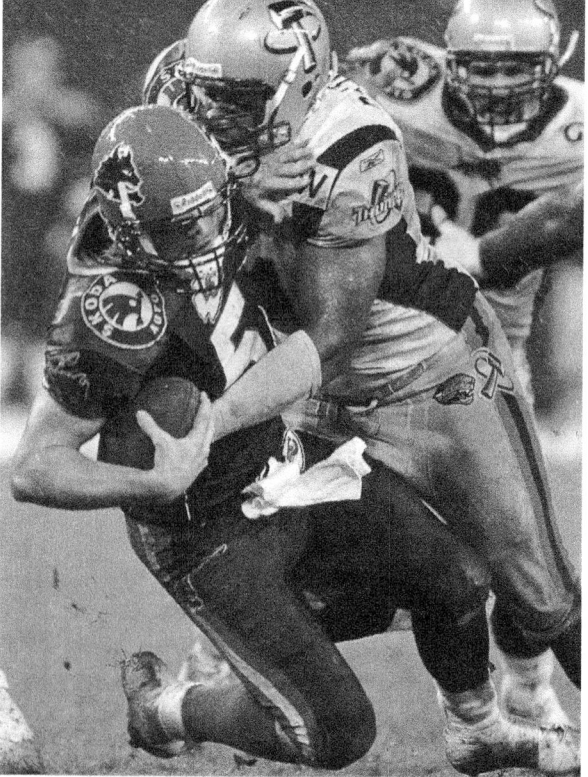

NEARLY FAMOUS

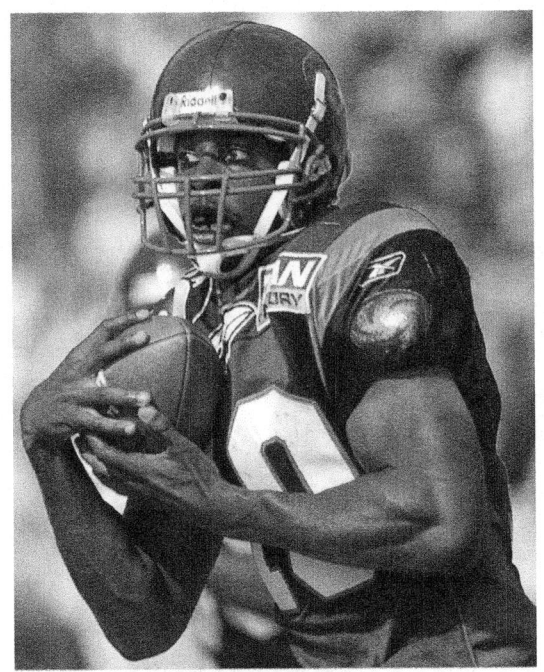

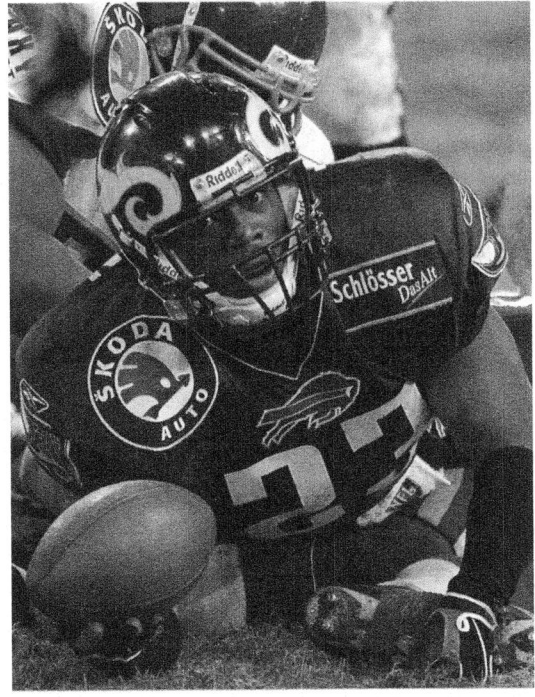

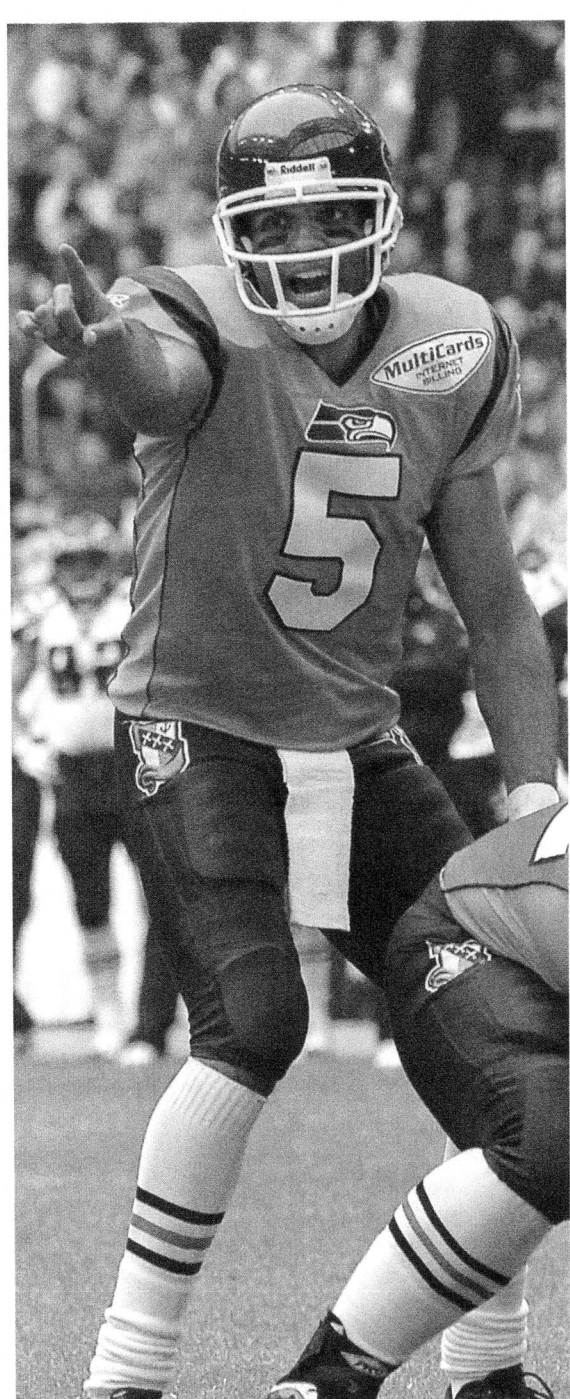

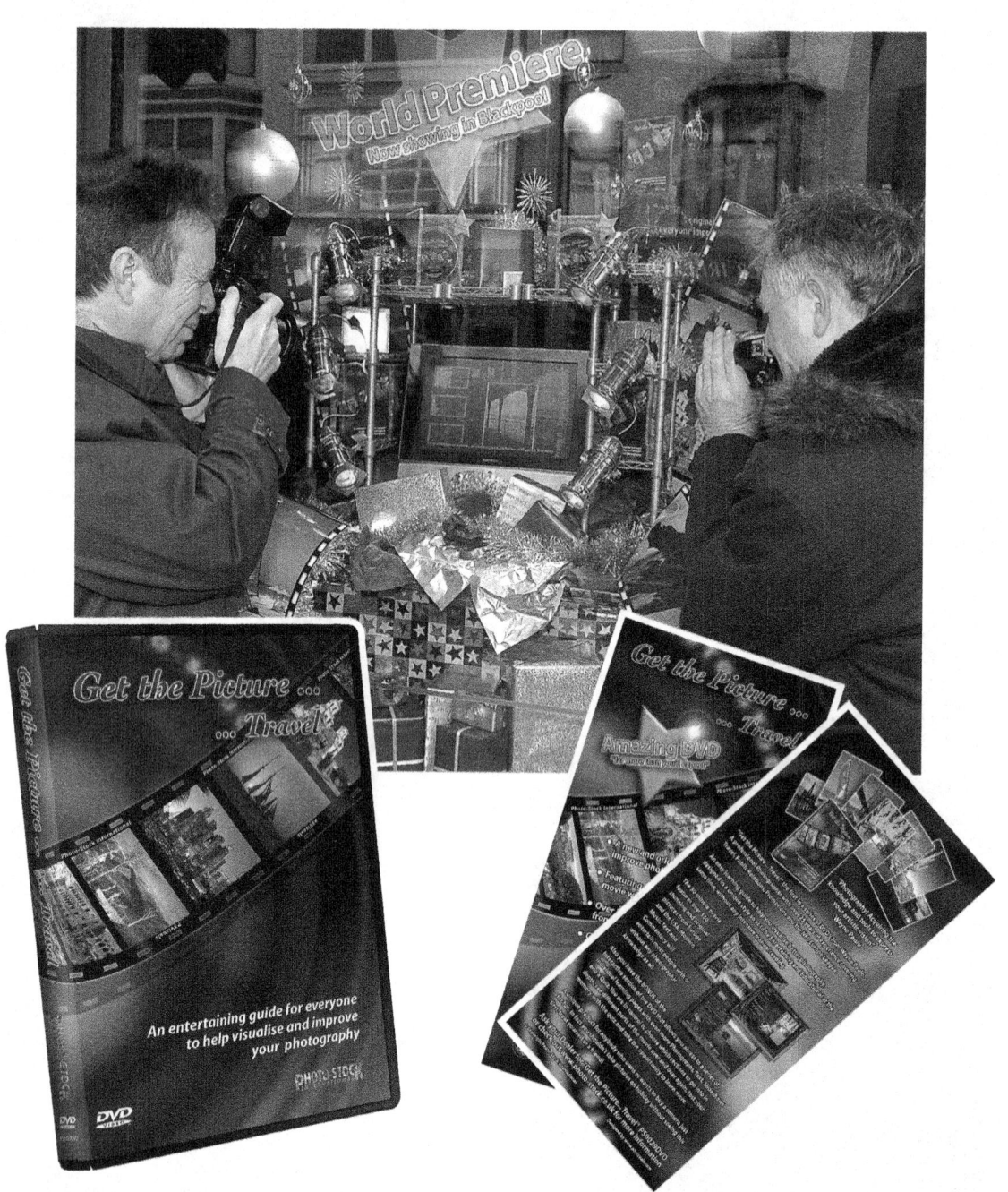

NEARLY FAMOUS

The world's smallest premier!

The "Get the Picture...Travel" Project started way back in 1996, when with a small Apple computer, a software programme called Supercard and very little knowledge I started my vision to produce an easy learning guide to photography. I called on my daughter Dani to help me produce the graphic interface and the interactive side of GTP...Travel was born. We managed to produce some great early betas despite my own development skills, but we couldn't quite 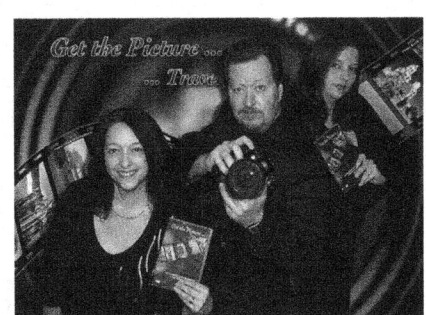 get it off the ground, with cross platform development required and limited funds, survival seemed to be a bigger priority and a need to earn a living eventually took over, the project was placed on the shelf for a long while as my work load increased.

Fortunately I continued to shoot stills at every opportunity on our travels, or should I say we, as Estelle was being coerced into being the videographer to record some of the events. We had foregone any normal vacations to take advantage of the time to shoot more footage for the project at every opportunity, stopping here and there on the way to and from jobs in Europe and the USA, so much so Estelle swears I have no idea what a real break is!

Then out of the blue Dani was made redundant when the design department of the company she worked for was moved to Hong Kong. Ironically after she helped set it up!

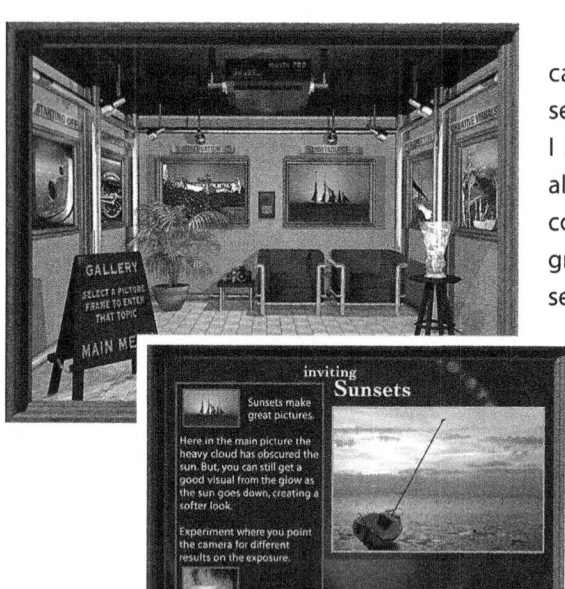

It must have been fate! I was once again able to call on her to help me, in her spare time, between job searches. I decided to revise "Get The Picture" fully. I became determined to complete the project, now almost 10 years later. I looked at the early betas, the concept was still good and the pictures were still great, plus my stock had grown enough to be more selective and add newer pictures. It was also time to move up a notch, move with the times and technology, the present DVD market offered more scope, my only dilemma was how not to be a 'boring ole fart', with a half hour programme just on me and photography, it needed more to encourage and show you how to improve your vision of photography!

Then one night I was sitting with Estelle watching television, channel hopping as impatient men do, I settled on one and it started to entertain us without a major sell or over zealous commentary, just music and graphics. We started to discuss, wouldn't it be great if we could blend photography, video and commentary with some modern music for the project, and that was it. Eureka! Our vision was complete, it would modernise the project, make it more visually entertaining and perhaps then the learning curve would be subliminally absorbed by the people watching it.

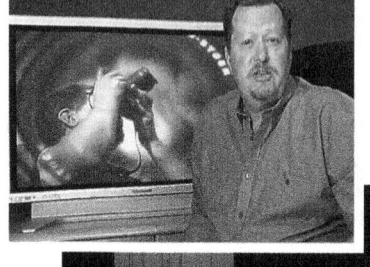

I was unable to curtail my euphoric excitement, selfishly as I look back, I placed the full burden squarely on the shoulders of Dani to creating my vision. I am pleased to say, as you read this, she rose to the challenge, Estelle and I fed her the materials, photographs, video clips, voice overs and what ever additional requirements were needed, and after a stressful period of development, computer crashes, changes in technology, inevitable cost outlays, hiccups and arguments (yes there were many), it finally matured into my DVD "Get The Picture ...Travel" and now more importantly could be your "Vision Of Photography". Did that sound like an advert? No, surely not! I even wrote a quote for the back cover -

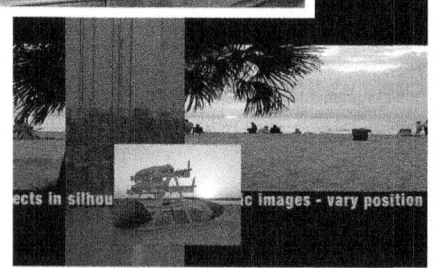

"Photography! Acquiring the knowledge and tools to express your artistic vision". I thought that was very appropriate to express my thoughts at the time.

We showed the finished beta version to all our neighbours and some of our friends, there is a stunning 30 minute narrated music video, it's entertaining and educational, featuring 100's of photographs taken across Europe and the USA, oops sorry, getting a bit carried away there. Seriously though, like I wasn't serious, reactions were positive across the board from all the different ages that watched accept one. A friend's wife suggested it would never work on her, she was hopeless at taking pictures, so I said what about the subliminal content that teaches you without knowing? "Oh," she said, "that doesn't work on me either, I would never remember the bit in the DVD about looking around before you takes pictures just in case there are any unwanted objects to spoil the view, like those pylons!" I rest my case!

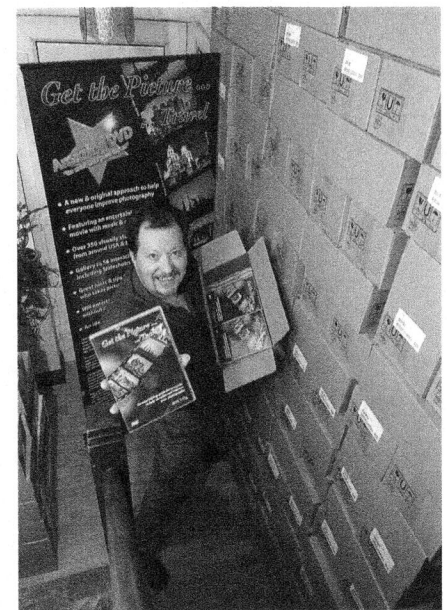

It was actually more successful than we had imagined, everyone said they would either buy one for themselves or as a present for a friend, perfect I thought and I jumped in with both feet. I ordered 5000 DVD's without realising I had nowhere to put them if they arrived, what do I mean if. They did arrive and ahead of schedule, my first ever commercial DVD release turned up on my doorstep, enough to fill a small van. The driver asked, "Where do you want them?". "Here I guess", was my reply as I rolled up my sleeves to help him carry them into my rather small hallway, a few hours later we had packed them into our tiny house. It is at times like these that you realise how much you love your wife for understanding!

A Story With An Abbey Ending! Yes it is a story with an Abbey ending. Well that was the name of the shop where we did our launch. The owners Mark and Tom allowed us to do a complete window display and launch the smallest movie premier in the world for Christmas 2004. We didn't have a budget to do it any bigger, it was always going to be a bit of a high risk venture without

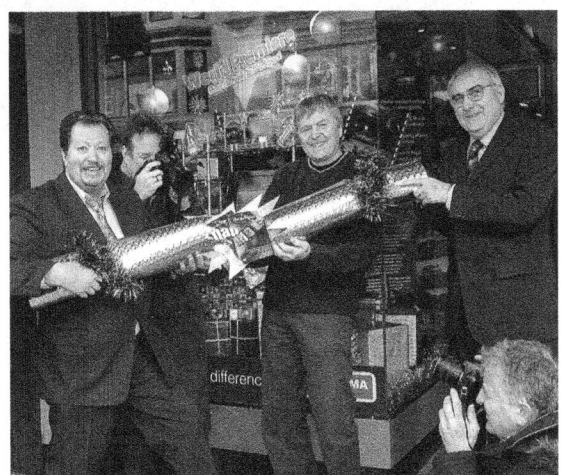

the support of a major company behind us, but as long as we had somewhere to keep the DVD's dry they would last forever. If you're interested I know where there are still a few left, right now they are a collectors item!

The whole concept of the DVD, photography for everyone, easy learning for all ages, gender and walks of life, sparked off the want to teach or pass on knowledge, I think? It could be an age thing or hormones, but as I get older I have become more passionate about it, I enjoy talking to people about photography.

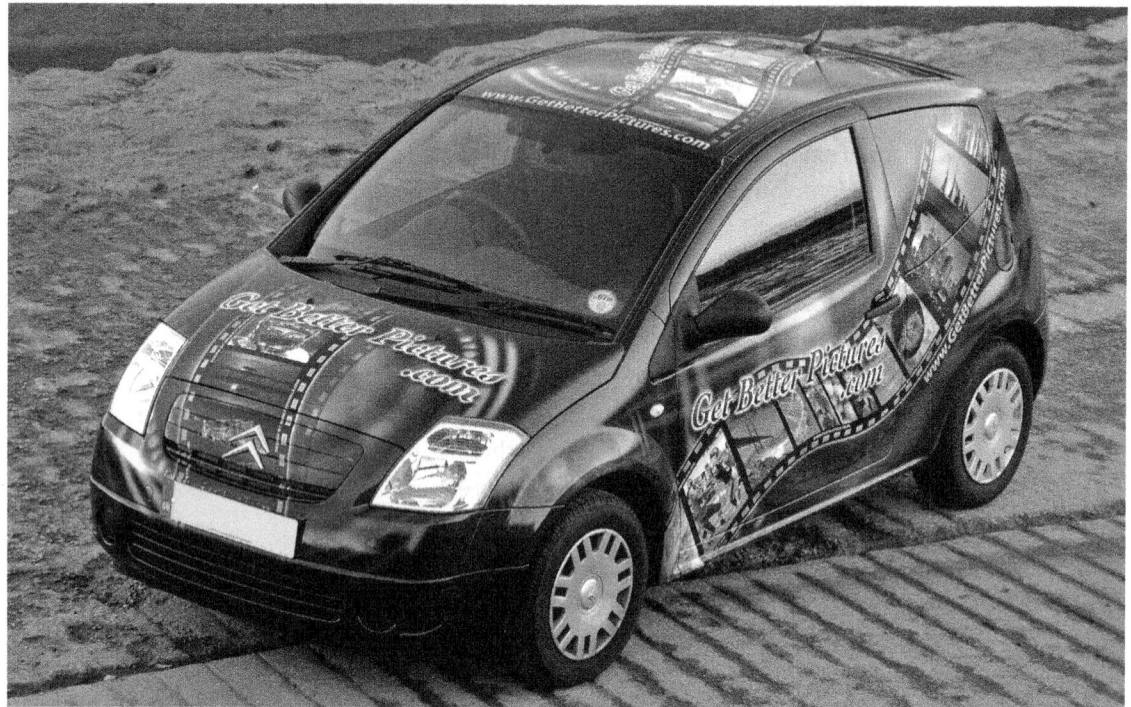

I launched the website, www.getbetterpictures.com for just that reason, something for everyone. Then on a whim I decided we needed a promotional vehicle to promote it, literally. I bought a small compact car, the same car we would eventually tour over a half of Europe in, though I didn't know it at the time. Once again I called on Dani to design the best promotional vehicle in Europe, and if I say so myself, when the wrap was complete, I think she made a pretty good job of it, well it became my mobile photographic exhibition!

NEARLY FAMOUS

Enrichment Talks

My first foray into lectures and guest speaking was at Blackburn Media college. My friend PR guru Darryl Freedman, for whom I had done an awful lot of work, asked if I would like to go along and talk to the media and photography students to give them a professional insight into PR photography. At the time I thought it was a daft idea, with no formal training or qualifications who would listen to me. It didn't dawn on me at the time, that people wanted to listen to an experienced photographer and hear real life stories, how I had actually taken my pictures and how I got there in the first place!

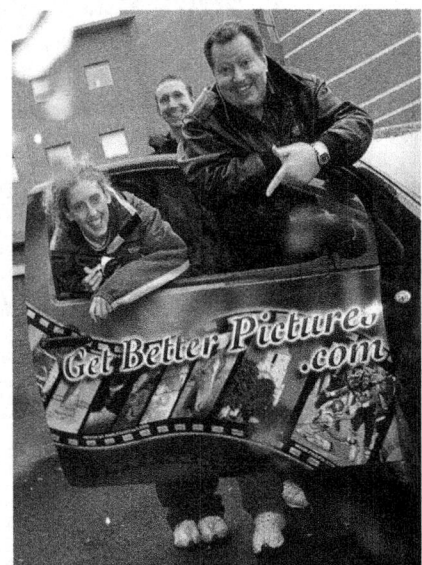

We put together a short video and some large prints, well you should know me by now, I don't do anything in half measures, we were still finalising what I would say in the car during the thirty five minute drive to Blackburn!

What should originally have been only a twenty minute talk on PR Photography, lasted two and a half hours by the time we had answered all the questions. It may have only been a small audience, but it was a resounding success. Even some of the students who had missed the talk due to a field trip, arrived back at the college, picked up on the thread of the talk and started joining in, asking questions about all areas of photography.

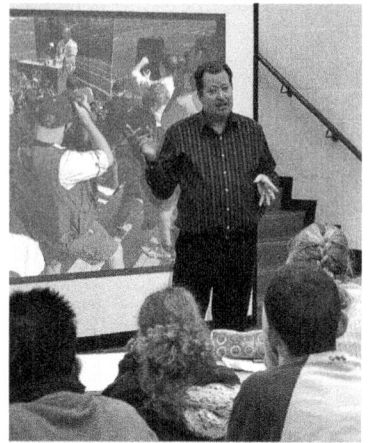

Hey wait a minute, now I had my video, lots of photographs, my patter and a satisfied audience, I felt a new career coming on!

Well it wasn't that easy. We spent the next 18 months working on a touring show, buying equipment and building a stage set. Yes I said a stage set, lights, stands, sound equipment, the lot, well the theatrical in me wanted to make it a show, plus we created a selection of large prints for a photographic display.

I thought we had cracked it with talks of a regular show touring a major store chain, but it never materialised, I was let down big time and several thousand pounds, or dollars if you like, worth of equipment and photographs were shelved!

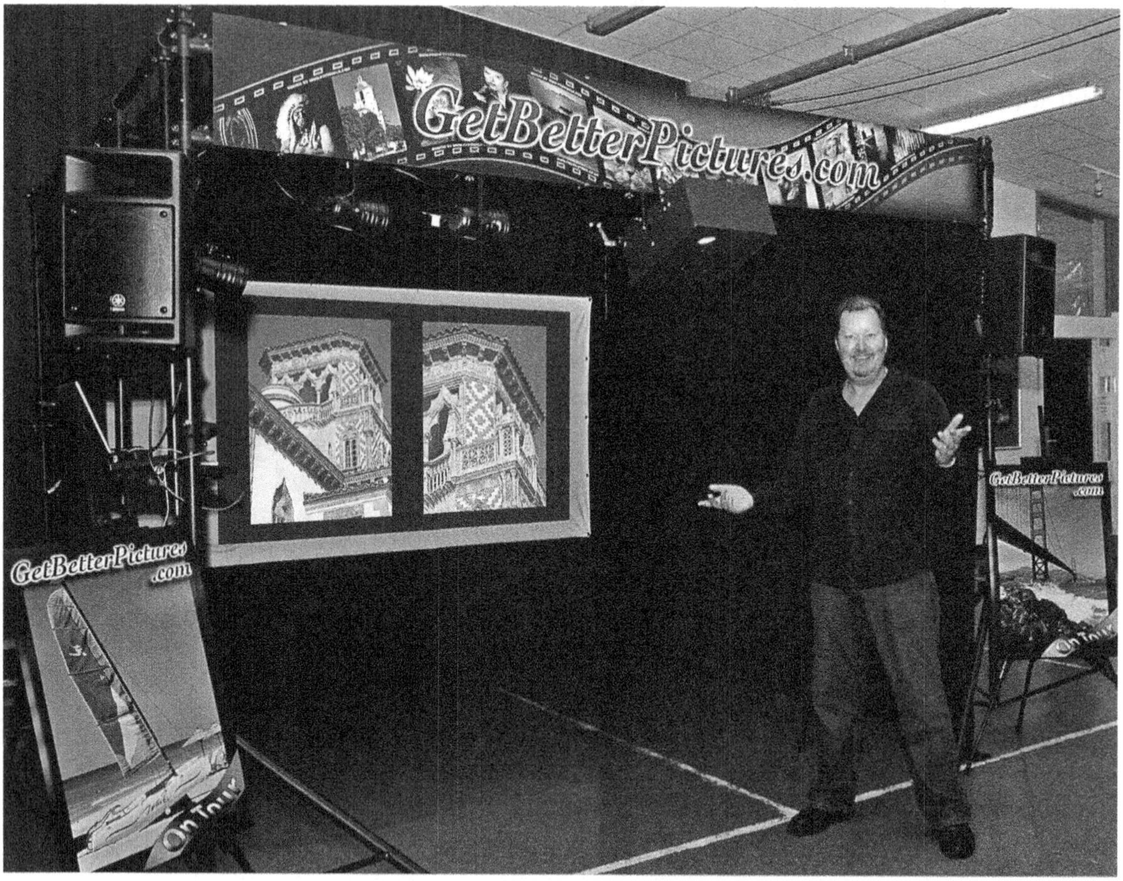

The End is Nigh!

Unfortunately there was more to come. My career as an American football photographer was also about to come to an end!

In 2006 the NFL Europe closed it's London office, transferred to Germany and became the NFL Europa, also my contract transferred as it ran until the end of January 2007, but without any PR Director for a few months while they looked for a German replacement. There was very little communication during that period while I waited to see what would happen to me, would I continue with the league? People I spoke to in the league said I had become part of the establishment, a fixture and nobody thought I would be cut. I was assured by the powers that be I would be able to negotiate a new contract soon. But I had a sense very early on about what was likely to happen.

Despite this we carried on with plans to cover the Super Bowl, after all as I was still under contract to the now NFL Europa, and you would expect them to make use of my services wouldn't you? They only had to pick up my expenses for the week and all the pictures supplied by me would be free to use, throughout the world!

The Super Bowl was in Miami, we had been invited by our American friends to visit them in Florida, so it seemed like the perfect excuse to go to Florida early in November for a vacation, after that be ready to cover the Southern Florida Super Bowl, then on to training camp when or if the league renewed my contract.

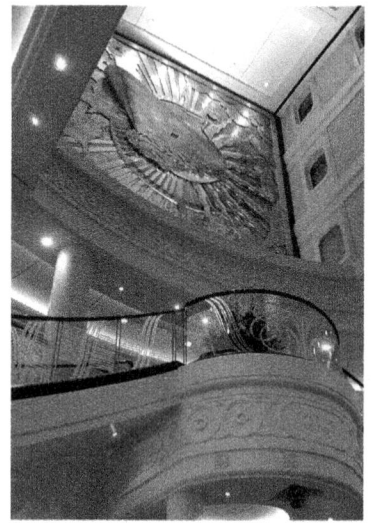
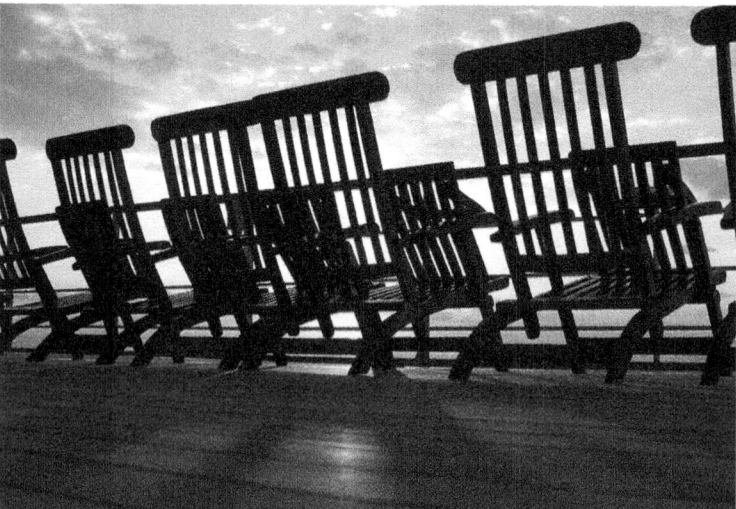

With my fear of flying getting worse, I decided that if I was paying to travel out there myself I would choose the transport. So we crossed transatlantic on the Queen Mary 2. I won't comment much on that accept to say that as a Brit I was disappointed, well it wasn't as opulent as I expected. Though I did receive some moral inspiration from the Cruise Director at the time on cruise lecturing.

Our friends Jack and Kathy Humphrey, two of the nicest Hillbilly's from Kentucky you could ever wish to meet, travelled 250 miles (350 km) down to the docks to pick us up, bless them, and in case you are wondering, yes, it was in a pick up truck. We were strapped in with our luggage in the back of the truck and caught flies and a suntan all the way back to their place. I'm kidding right? Or am I!

By the time we got to their place and I checked my email, my time with the NFL Europe was over, my emails confirmed it. What was supposed to be negotiations turned out to be a take it or leave it offer, less than half the money I had been earning, plus I would be expected to pay my own way out to the training camp in Florida, (so no refund on the travel expenses already incurred), my own accommodation and car hire. In fact it was starting to all look a little silly, I would have actually been paying for the privilege to photograph the league!

I can only assume they wanted to replace me with a local country man, to save on budget, I was prepared to compromise but there was no way I was going to be abused and that was that.

Not surprisingly they also declined my offer to work the Super Bowl for them in return for those expenses. I was a little hurt, these very people who had employed me for all those years, expecting me to be on call 24/7 supplying all kinds of pictures and at all times of the night, sending them to locations throughout the world at a moments notice, no longer had the time of day for me, with a few exceptions!

I guess that's business for you, the bigger they are the worse you are treated, loyalty doesn't count for much these days.

Given all that and the leagues approach, it was very apparent to me that the league wouldn't survive much longer anyway, even new management at the top didn't appear to turn it around. I'm not pleased to say I was right, but surprised I wasn't, when they closed it down five months later, a lot of hard working people like me who had given their all for the game were left stranded and out of work!

The NFL, apparently, from what I read at the time, wanted to concentrate in another direction by pursuing regular season games in Europe. They were about to bring a professional season game to Wembley in London for the first time.

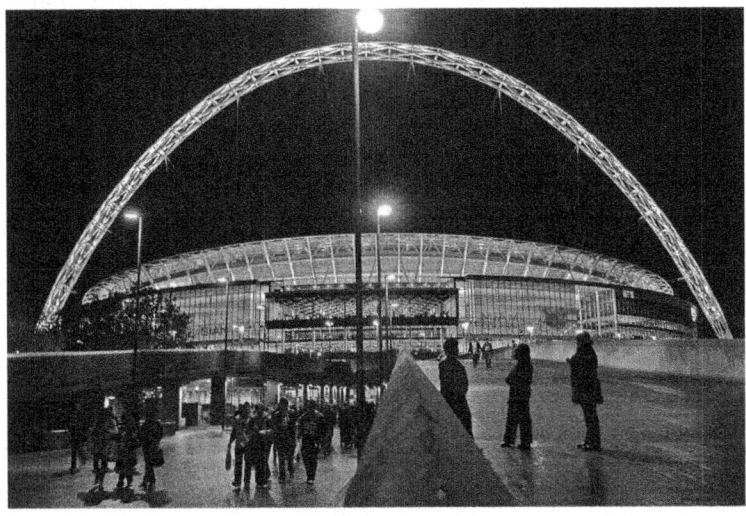
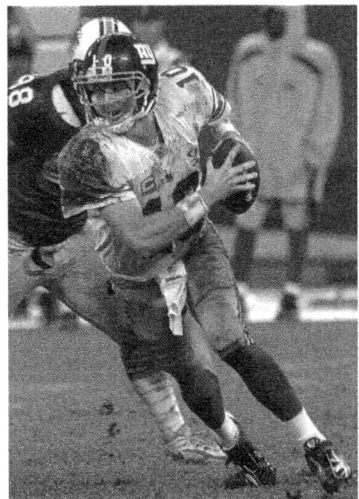

So there I was at the crossroads again. Not much future in American Football and starting to get a bit long in the tooth to return to the circus!

I was still in Florida and with another a couple of months to go until the Super Bowl in Miami, but now at a loose end and knowing nobody really wanted my services anymore!

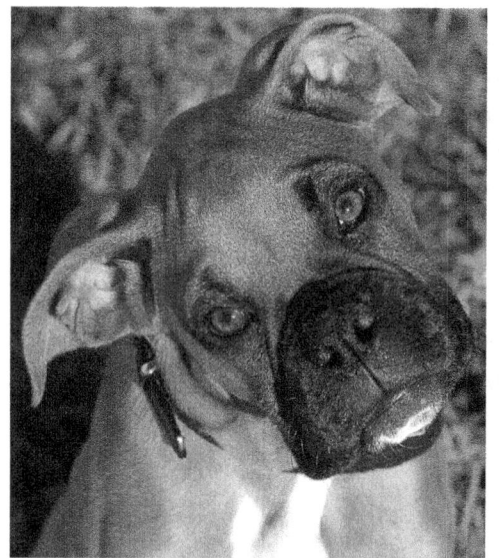

At that time I did have a bit of a down period, I say trying to play it down. Silly as it may sound I went through a dramatic withdrawal period, like a junky coming off of dope I suppose, American Football had become my life, all my friends were in it, I lived it 24/7 like I said earlier and now I was doing absolutely nothing. No demand for my pictures, no request for my services and worst of all no income. I don't think I was suicidal, but it did cross my mind a few times. But hey that would only have hurt my family, solving nothing for them and to be perfectly honest I was too much of a coward to do it, what if I only got it half right? What would I do then. I was definitely in a deep depression and I don't mean the weather!

I know I lost it a few times and said a lot of things I didn't mean. I am very grateful for the family and friends I had around me at the time. Oh and a puppy dog called Toby. Just look at that face how could you not smile? He wasn't mine, he belonged to our friends son JD and was staying at the house while he was away working. I played with him daily, took him for walks and just used my dog whispering skills to help house train him, it was very therapeutic.

Rather than let the world go by and just waste away I decided, with a little persistence from my family, that I should forget the sports for now and concentrate on other things. Producing a photographic exhibition for a tour was one of them. Fortunately, we had thought of the idea just before we were leaving home for the trip, so travelled with a 500 gb hard drive of my digital images, it allowed us to carry a vast amount of scenic, sport and creative pictures, photographs that had never seen the light of day before, we could create a rather exclusive and exciting exhibition in full colour.

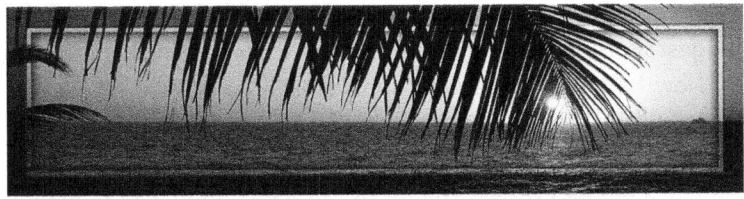

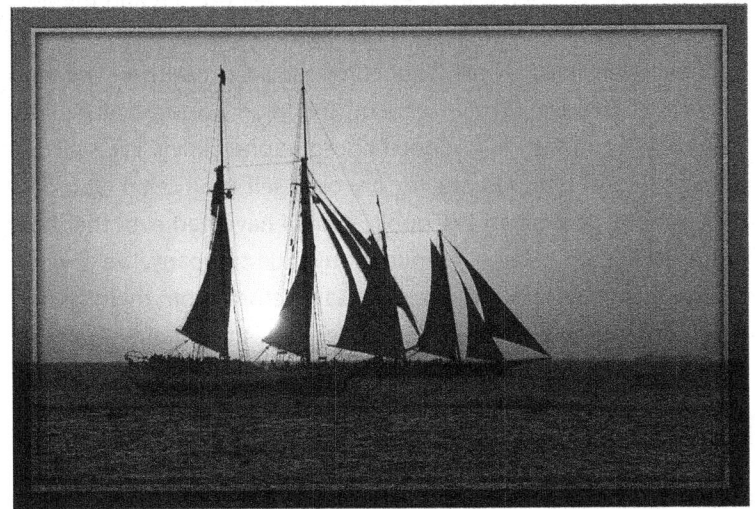

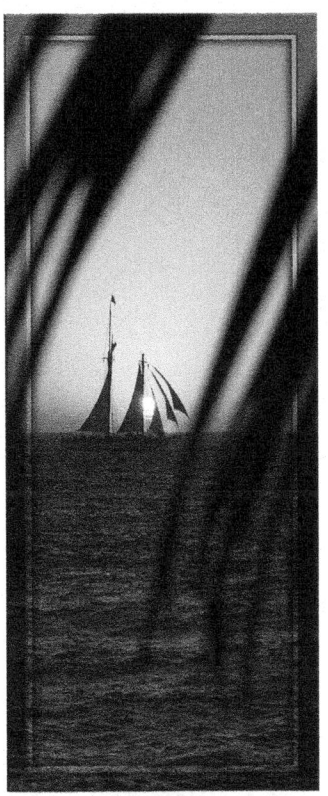

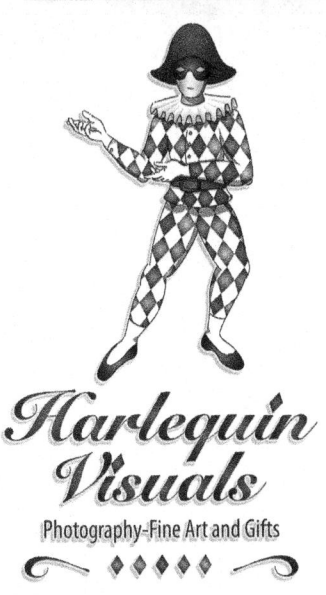

The next two months were spent searching through my files for the right pictures to use. Working with Estelle and Dani we produced some stunning images and picture sets, though I did get carried away a bit. Especially when I insisted, I could get them printed locally, and surely I could frame them up myself, wow, I was starting a new business! If you remember we were still staying with our friends in Florida, at times I had 24 x 36 inch (30x20cm) photographs and wood frames all over their place, there was about sixty as I ploughed into the new ideas each day. I also insisted Dani build a new web site for us just for the pictures and she did called www.harlequinvisuals. com, check it out and you can see what all the fuss was about, they are great, most importantly it served the purpose, mentally it kept me occupied and helped wean me off full time American Football. Unfortunately it's still a dream of mine yet to be realised. One photographic exhibition for rent. Any offers invited?

Harlequin Visuals
Photography-Fine Art and Gifts

Eventually the time came round for the big game, one of the biggest sporting events in the world the NFL Super Bowl.

Now here was a dilemma, should I still go or not? People will probably think I'm mad at this point, I had passes for the biggest game in the World and wasn't sure if I should go or not. I had to convince myself I should still go to the game and face the mental challenge, now I know I'm nuts, but I did, I really did, eventually I decided I should do it for myself, my own self esteem and my own web site photo library at Photo-Stock.co.uk.

There were still a whole lot of European press out there covering the event and some of them were my friends. It would be nice to see them again and they might need photographs. I knew I was always going to need photographs for my own self promotion, you only have to look at some of the publications I have had over the years to appreciate that. Hey, I'm proud of my little company, I've covered some great events and I'm proud to say pictures from them are still being published, just take a look at some of the Super Stars I have photographed in this book alone, including me!

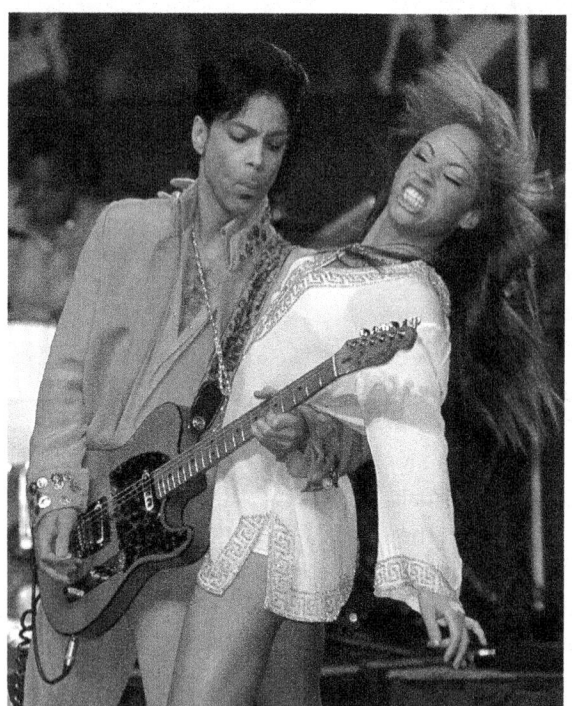

So I climbed back in the saddle and went to the pre game press conferences. Those events can usually be a little boring, but when Prince answered his questions by breaking into his act, literally, it was great. I followed that with the big game. My status had been downgraded slightly, not surprisingly I didn't get a sideline pass, well I was no longer working for the NFLE. It was a new approach for me, but probably just as well given Miami had one of the wettest Super Bowls I have ever seen, but I was still there and still working professionally, up to my neck in that wet and wonderful atmosphere. What an event!

So what was going to be next, in my somewhat life story of career changes? Hey I'm almost old enough to be a Country singer, I said jokingly at the time. Although the way my life has changed so often, you never know I still might return to it. Check for the CD on my web site!

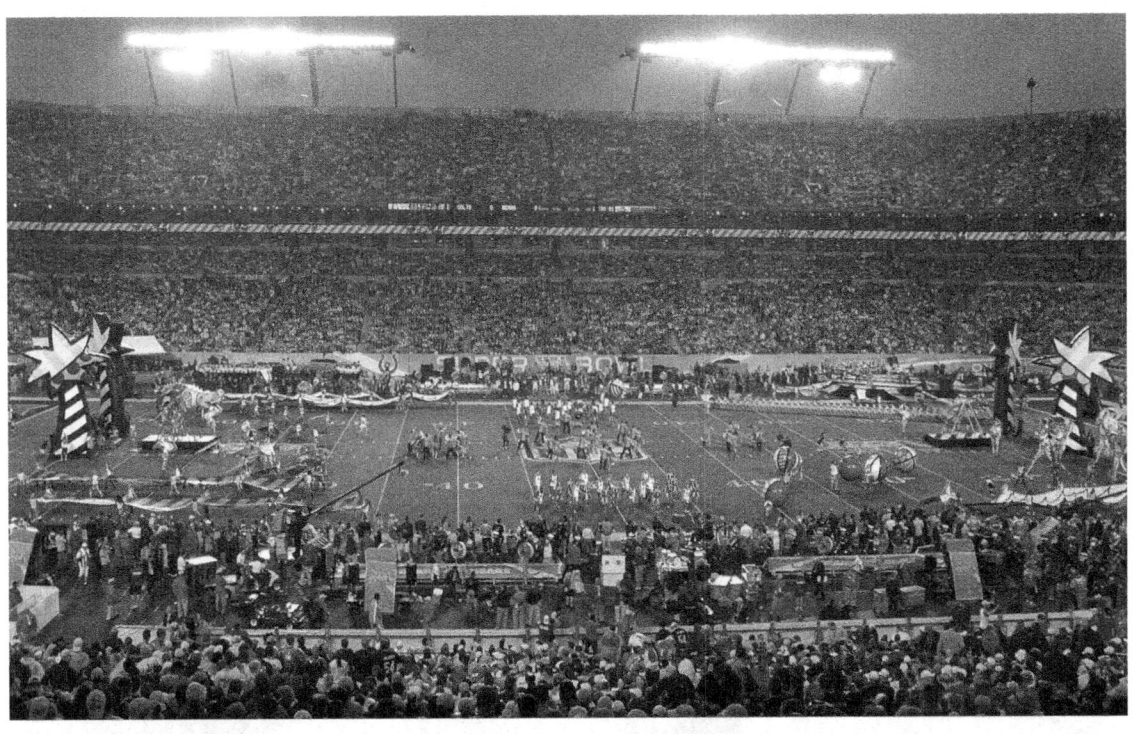

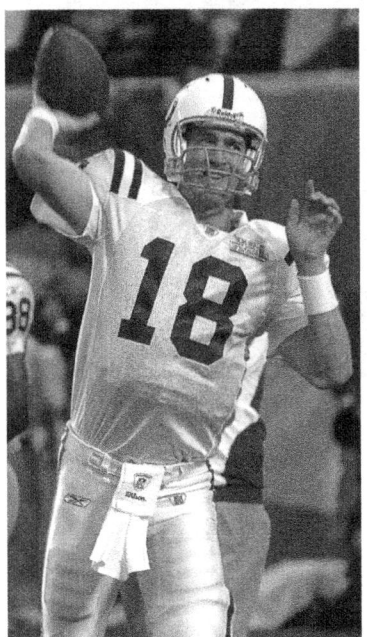

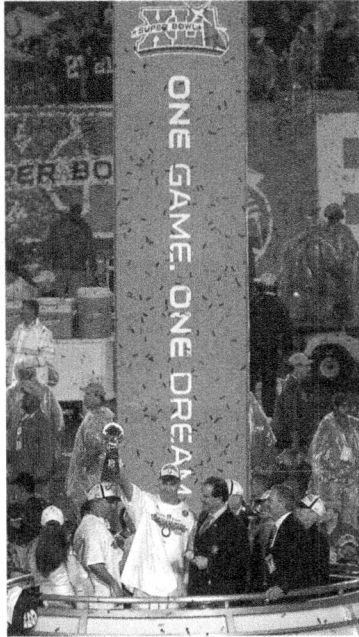

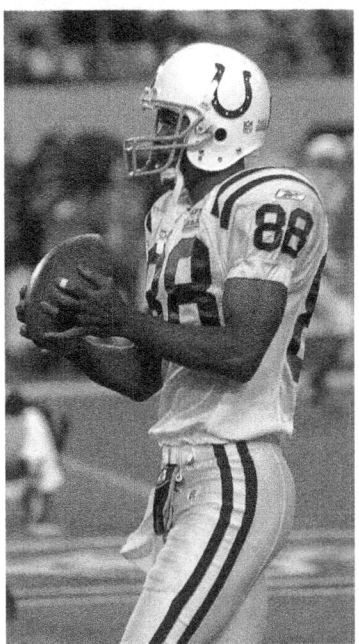

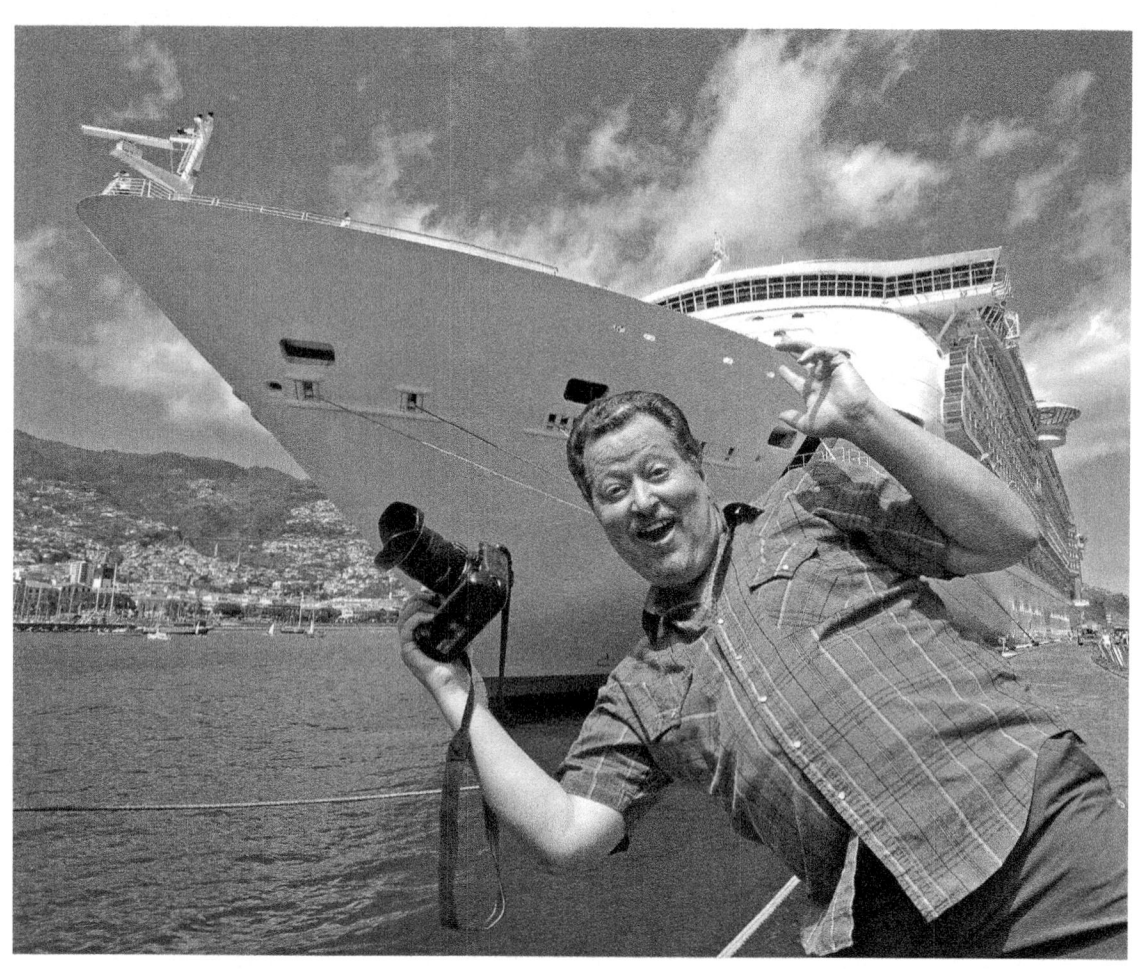

NEARLY FAMOUS

Guest Speaker

While we were still in America I decided to make a second foray into what the Americans call Enrichment speaking. This time I contacted the cruise lines, not only inspired by my memories of the successful college lecture I had done 18 months earlier, but by people everywhere, who interrupt me all the time when I get my camera out, they start asking photographic questions, they don't even know I am a professional photographer. Inspired, I contacted Royal Caribbean International (RCI) with my promo DVD and CV along with a photograph. Well it must have impressed someone, within 24 hours Estelle and I were offered a seven day cruise to Mexico if I could do two lectures while the ship was at sea, a sort of audition to see if I lived up to my own publicity if you like.

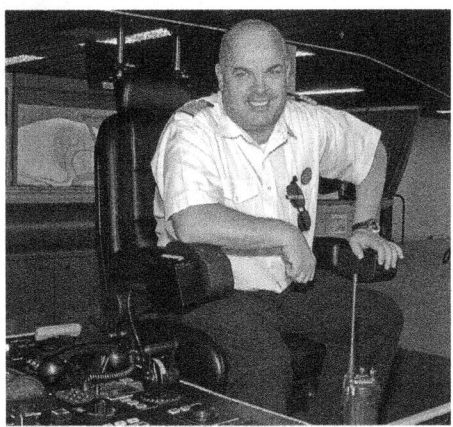

I'm remembering now just how dumb I must have sounded on the telephone. A lady with a lovely voice said, "We have a cruise available," Err yes, came my reply, "are you interested?" Err yes, I said again, "it sails from Tampa to Mexico," Err yes, I continued "would you like to take it?" Err yes. I don't think I was completely in shock, more trying to go through in my mind if I was ready this quick. Who did she think she was getting, not a man of many words that's for sure, I was a man of action. Fortunately for us it was leaving out of

Tampa and we could get there easily, our friends Justin and Crystal had a pick up truck, yes another pickup truck and boy did we need it!

Well it would have been easy if I hadn't decided to take 60 exhibition prints in frames of 24 x 36 inch (30x20cm) in size! I tracked down a car roof luggage pack to put them in, it was big and it was heavy, the porter nearly had a fit, but I did help him to lift it on his trolly. At this point I think I must have been off my trolly for even taking that many. Well a couple would have done, but I knew I desperately wanted to

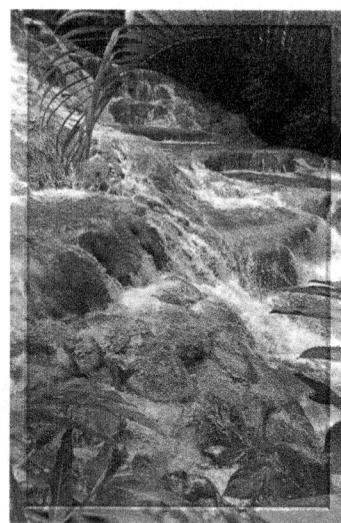
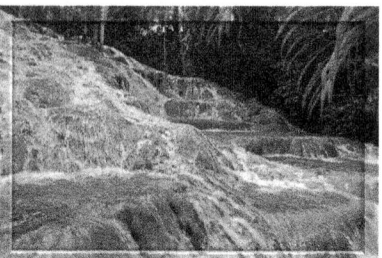
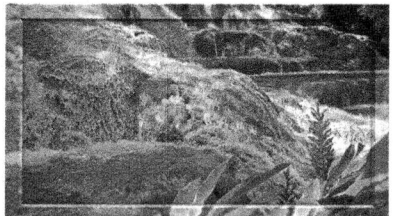

start selling photographs. More importantly, for some reason, I just wanted to impress people with my work and I was prepared to get a hernia proving it!

The crew on the ship were great and extremely helpful, and importantly, very friendly, we had a meeting as soon as we arrived, discussed my lecture times and requirements. I then met the Cruise Director and placed my Get The Picture DVDs in the shops, I had also taken about half a ton (that's a lot in kilos) of my own advertising posters and leaflets, but in reality they only needed a handful.

The next day Estelle and I nervously prepared for the presentation, by this time we had settled on displaying about a dozen of the exhibition prints I had taken on board, well the room wasn't big enough for many more. So with a series of relays back and forth from the cabin, I managed to get the easels, photographs and the equipment required for the talk. So there we were waiting in the hall outside the door early, scheduled to go in at 12.45pm and starting at 1pm, we had time to start putting the pictures on to the easels and then get the equipment out ready. Actually we ended up with enough time to do the whole presentation in the hallway as the previous lecture overran by 40 minutes. People turned up while we were standing there, but decided to skip the waiting and go on to

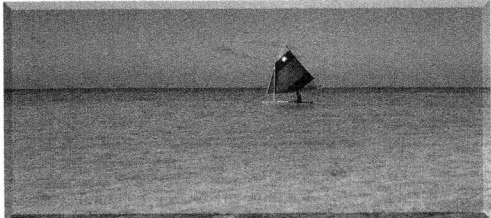
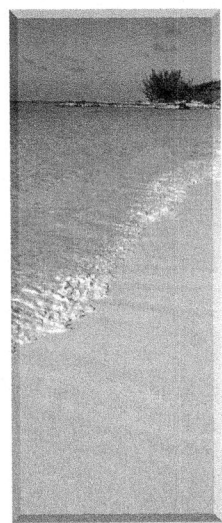
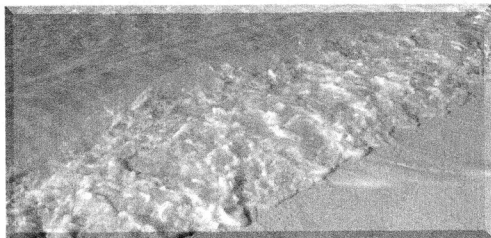

lunch and the other delights of the ship, who could blame them. At this point we were just going to give up, how could we suggest to the passengers that had just sat through one lecture, should now stay and watch me for another hour, it seemed fruitless as they came out, but we tried it anyway to no avail!

It was no surprise that by the time we had set up our presentation we were starring at an empty room. There was no lecture following me, how fortunate that was, excuse my sarcasm at this point. I decided not to miss the opportunity and to go through the motions as a rehearsal anyway. I started my first presentation off with an audio and visual sequence which lasted about 2 minutes, then as I looked up from the podium to start talking to Estelle a man walked into the room, my first reaction was he must have forgotten something from the previous lecture, he was carrying a bag perhaps he was here to repair something. But no! He came right up to the front and sat down right in front of me. I was so taken by surprise, I told him he had missed the intro and asked him if he wanted me to play it again. He said "I'm okay thank you" and I continued with what was the smallest audience I have ever performed for. He stayed for the whole presentation asking occasional questions even conversing with me in German, over one of my Bavarian pictures. It went really well and when I asked him afterwards if he had any more questions, he said I had answered all his questions in the actual presentation. So

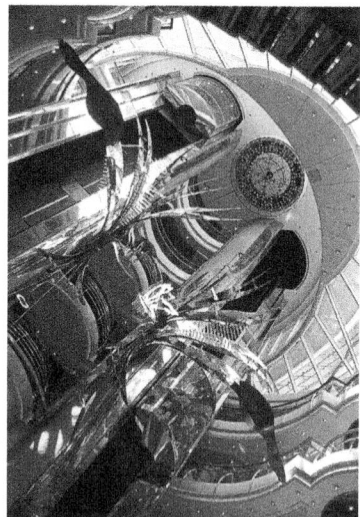
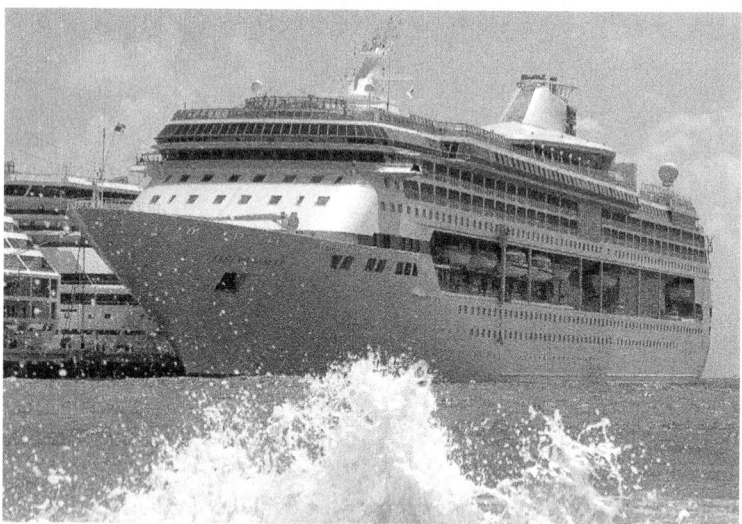

what more do you want, to all intensive purposes it was a successful lecture, I had entertained my audience of one to full satisfaction!

So what did we learn, there were a lot of activities happening on the cruise ship throughout the day and my lecture was only a very small part of it. So what did we do about it? We had another lecture to prepare for in four days!

Well not wanting to repeat the experience, Estelle and I set about a campaign of inviting our own audience, whenever we talked to anyone, at breakfast or in the bar, even in the swimming pool we would talk photography and about our personal lives, then we invited people to the next lecture which was due at the end of the week.

NEARLY FAMOUS

Now I think that was what RCI wanted all along, instead of a couple of lectures you are actually entertaining their guests all week! At this point we also asked the Cruise Director for a plug and offered our DVD for him to play over the internal television system, in fact we must have sounded a bit desperate at that point. Paranoid as I am, I also had a bit of a dilemma at that moment, as only one person had turned up, should we just do the same presentation?

Now come on you have read the book so far, what do you think? I don't do anything the easy way, being a true performer I decided against it, plus being quite mad, I also decided to rewrite the whole

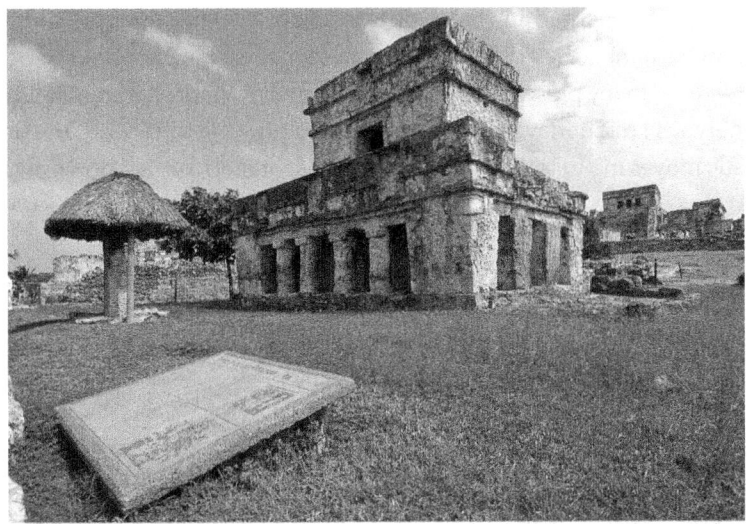 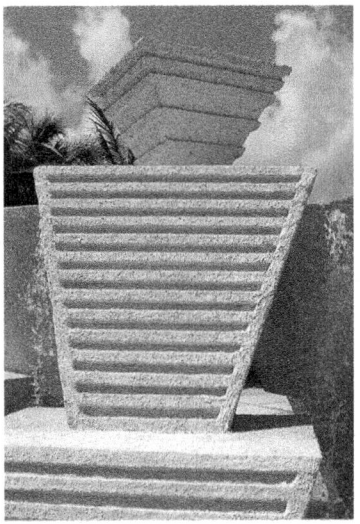

presentation based around the locations the ship went to, pictures of the ship itself and the people on it. Just a little crazy I know, especially given it can take a month or two to put together a good presentation with music, text and pictures. Remember I had only done one working lecture never mind the computer work on the program itself. Suffice to say we spent every day working on it, all but two hours a day when we took a break to swim, sunbathe, eat and oh, take the pictures of the ship.

We were still working on it, up to 5 minutes before setting up on the Friday. We headed out to the lecture room doing the same procedure as the first day, in relays with just as many exhibition pictures. I am nothing if not a professional, everyone gets the same treatment with me a 100% of my all in whatever I am trying to do, are you wondering if I was nervous again? Damn right I was. Would the people we invited turn up, would they even remember? After all they had been partying all week and surely they would want to eat lunch, yes we were on at lunch time again!

We went into the room, Estelle laid out the photographs and I started to connect the computer. I looked up after a few minutes and there she was, the lady we had invited while swimming. I turned away to adjust the screen and when I turned back there was a rush of people coming in the door, within minutes the room was full, everybody we had invited had turned up including jogger Randy and his family, they didn't know at the time but he was about to be featured in my presentation. At that moment if I hadn't been quite so nervous I might have cried, as I am doing now trying to write this, it still moves me to read it. I started the presentation, settled down and

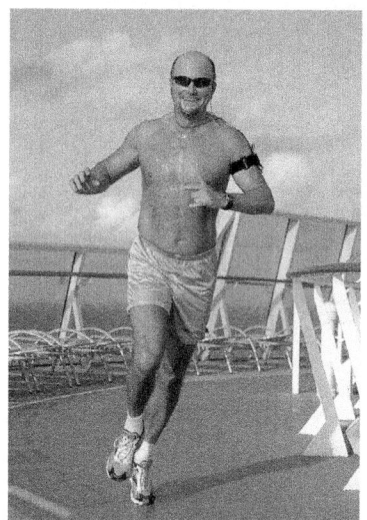 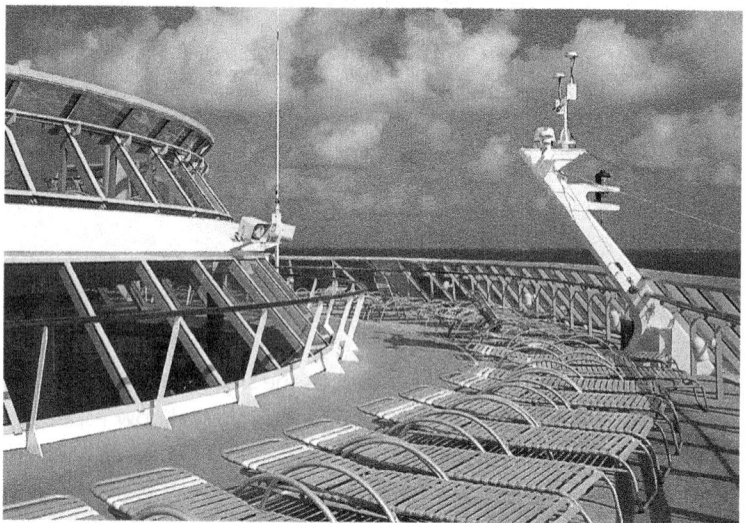

delivered what everyone said afterwards was, 'a great inspirational presentation,' I was just relieved somebody turned up and that I could answer all the questions satisfactorily. Nobody left early so I know it was a success, then Estelle unlocked the door. Only kidding!

On our return, correspondence with RCI suggested they would offer us more cruises in the future, and an email from Cunard to whom I also sent my CV, showed an interest in my lectures, quoting 'A unique subject matter' and requested further information. Did they follow through? Well Cunard declined, perhaps they thought I wasn't quite their cup of tea, who knows? Well they do of course!

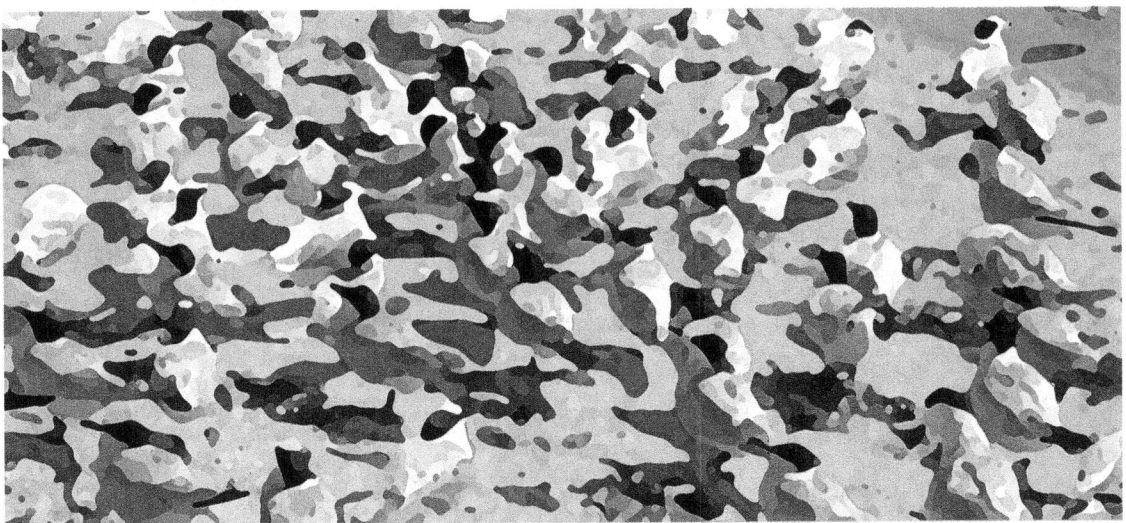

Fortunately to my joy, that lady with the lovely voice from Royal Caribbean International contacted me again, she booked me for another Cruise, this time on the biggest cruise ship in the world. I was torn between angst and excitement, but with more time to prepare this time I was confident. As I created four new lectures, I realised they didn't all have to teach photography. I created 'Is Photography Art?' to create a light hearted look at my work and the creative styles I have tried, best described as Fine Art and it did exactly what I expected. Everyone has their own opinion of Art so I set the scene and they pass their comments, good bad or indifferent, it's great fun to hear the opinions and contradictions in their comments. I still couldn't resist including new pictures of the ship and locations we were visiting in one presentation, which gave me additional work, but it worked really well, I went from strength to strength, there were more and more passengers at each lecture, because of this additional boost, I felt ready to launch my life story on them with excerpts from this book, the moving picture version which included playing my early musical compositions! If you haven't seen me live you need to book the show. By the end of the cruise, praises were coming in thick and fast, so much so by the time you read this I will have completed the next seven cruises I was also booked for. Making about thirty three lectures on completion and hopefully still doing more!

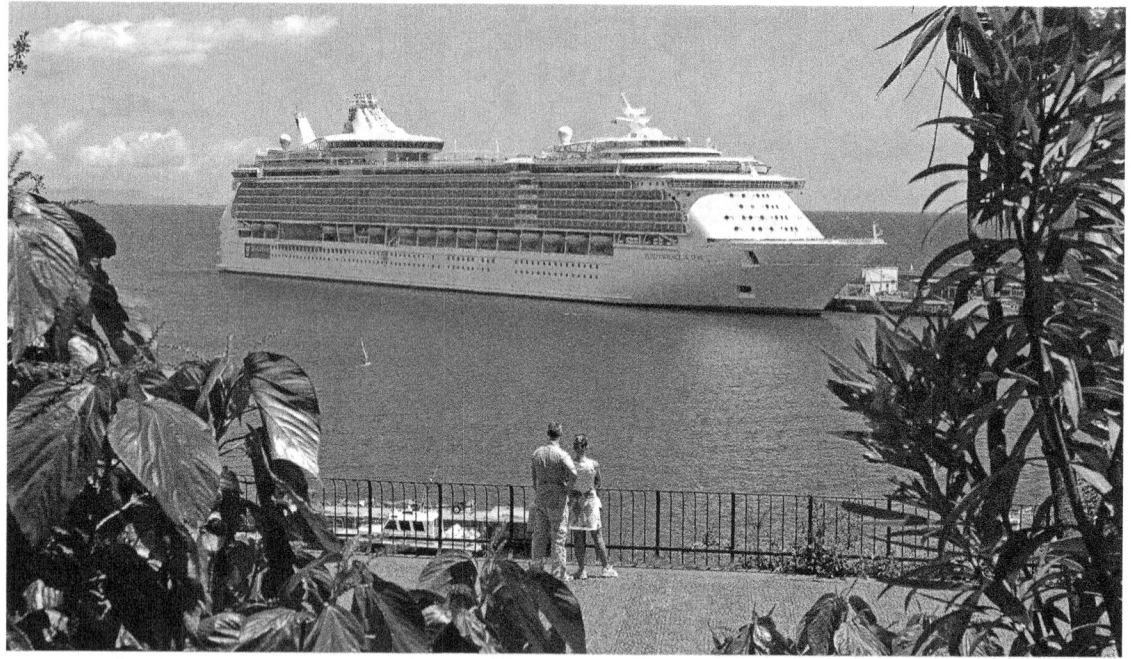

Getting the cruise lectures also created another requirement, some of them were out of Florida, so getting back to America was paramount and guess what, we went back to Jack and Kathy our friends in Florida. I couldn't believe they would have us back after everything they went through the last time I was there. Jack's like a brother to me, we banter back and forth on who had the poorest childhood background, he would tell me how he had to hunt with a bow and arrow for food, he had no shoes and had to wear hand me downs from his older sister, that explains a lot! Of course I have worked with too many comedians over the years so my circumstances were always worse. "Shoes, we never had shoes" I would say, "when I was young we were so poor, we had to go next door and dip our bread into our neighbours soup, my mum would blacken my feet and tie my toes up with laces so I could go to school", not true of course I didn't go to school, well not until the week before last when I started lecturing! Kathy, well I'm sure she thinks I'm nuts, well that's okay, I do too. I can put up with her love of freezing cold air conditioning, yes I said freezing. At their place in Florida we usually sat and watched television with a blanket around us, I laugh, thinking of wiping the icicles away. Though we come from very different backgrounds and lifestyles, we have an awful lot in common, we have the same dry sense of humour and laugh at the same things, a respect for our parents and people, importantly an appreciation for life and what it has given us. I have probably written half the book at their house, excuse me a minute while I put my coat on, as I write this chapter!

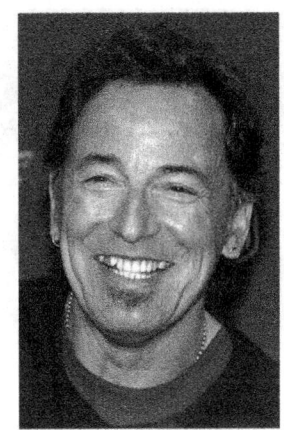

Estelle and I were in Florida gearing up for another Super Bowl, without the pressure this time. This will be number seven for me and Bruce Springsteen is doing the half time entertainment making a nice addition to my presentations and in particular for my live version of 'An Englishman's Road to the Super Bowl', 25 years of photographing American Football, not bad. I'm still getting publicity for the NFL in everything I do, so I was a pretty good investment for them, wasn't I?

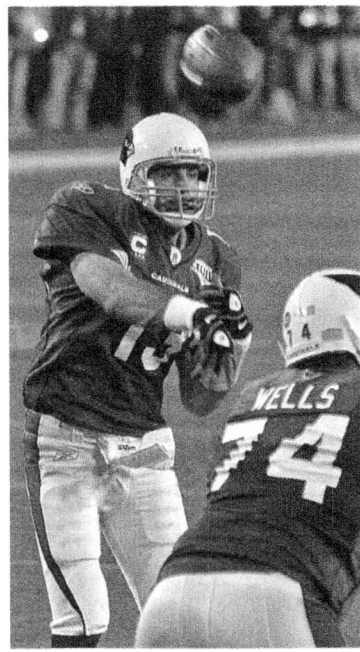
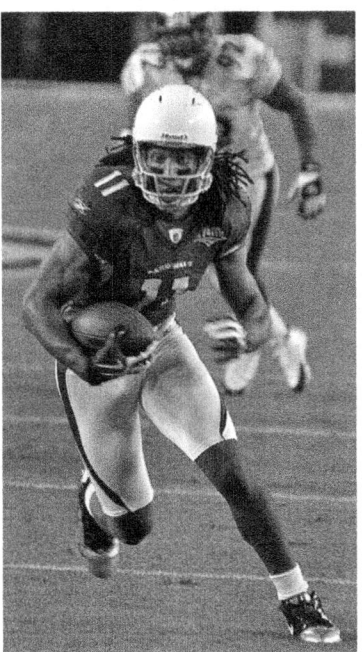
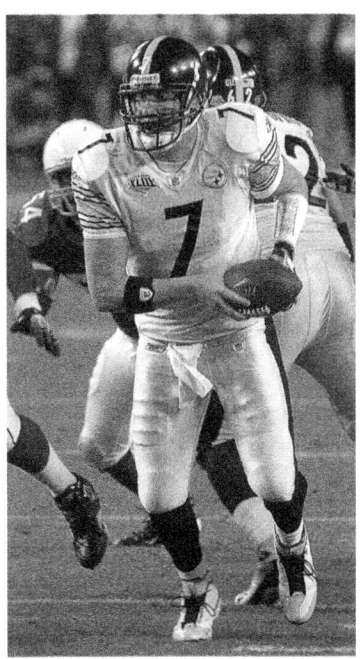

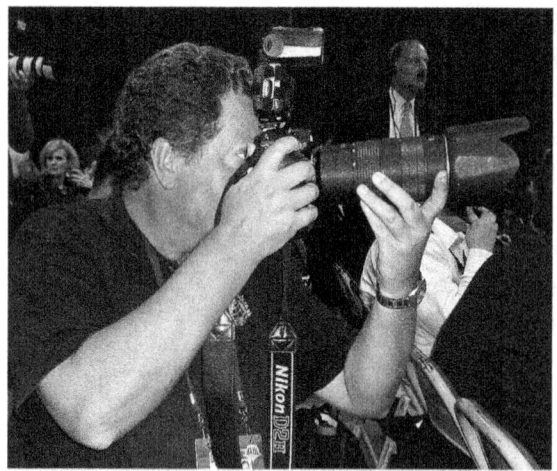

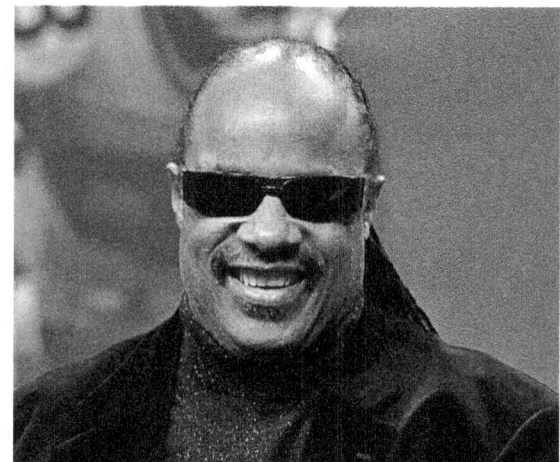

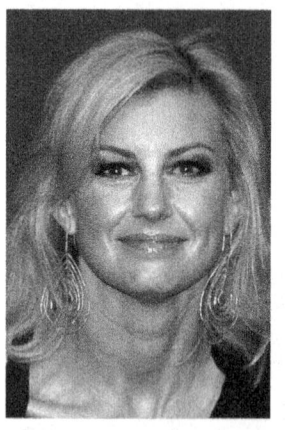

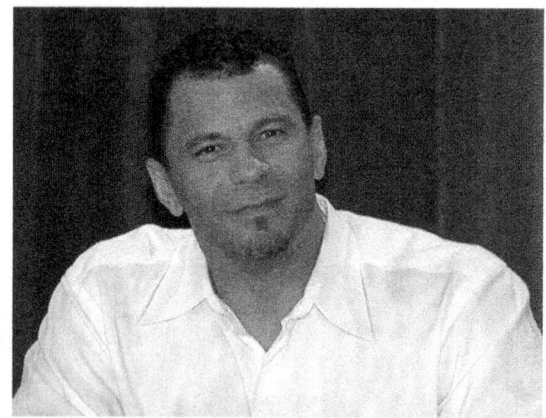

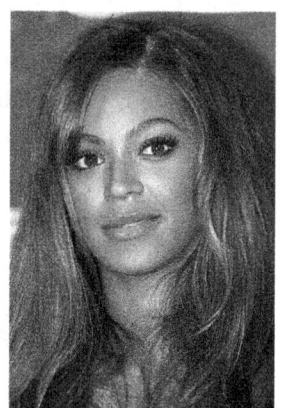

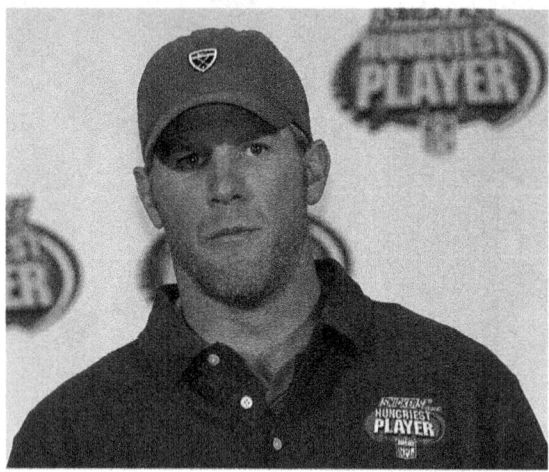

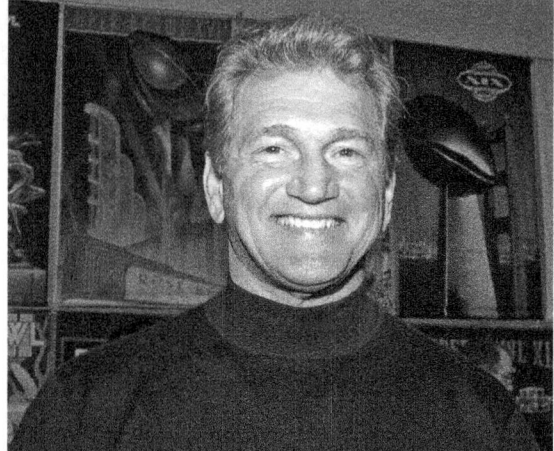

NEARLY FAMOUS

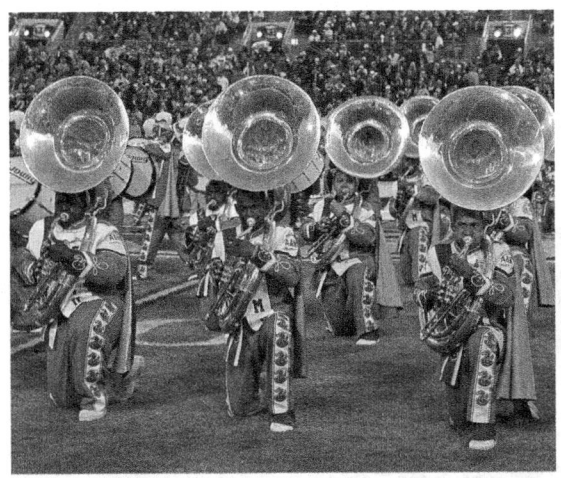
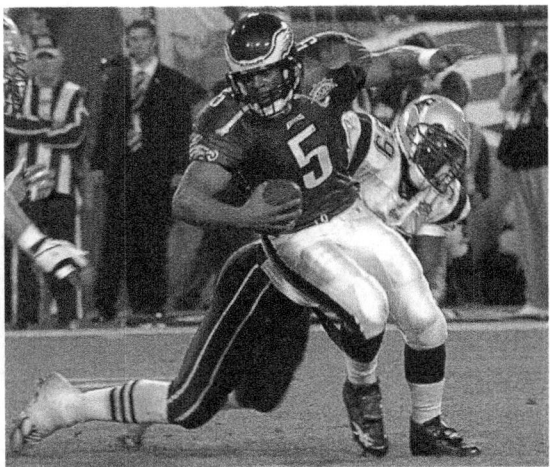
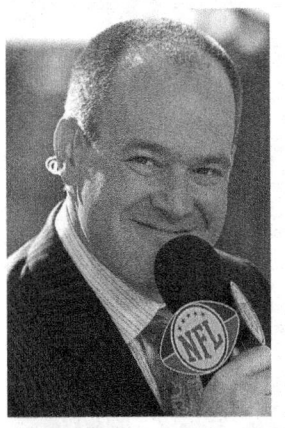
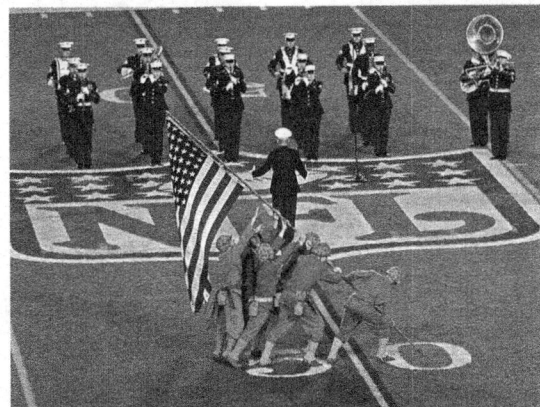
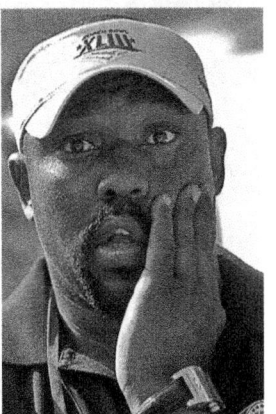
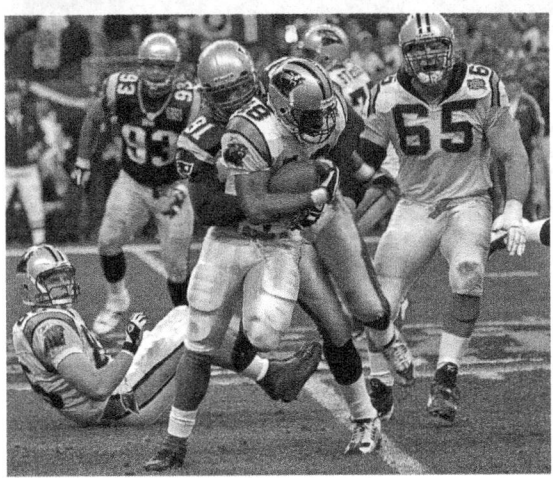
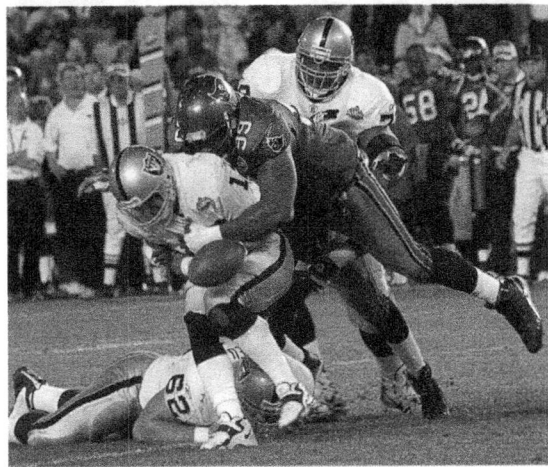

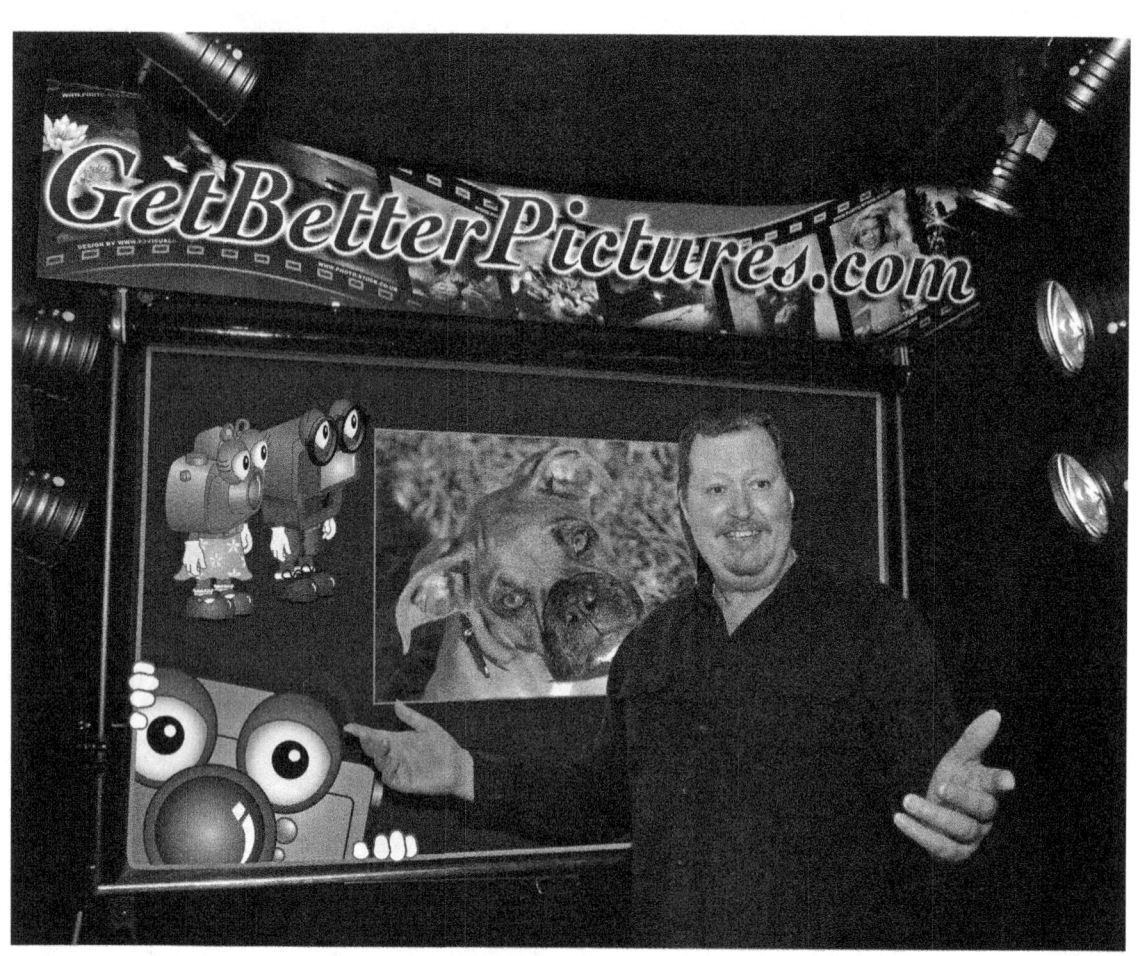

The Adventures Continue!

As I bring this book to a close, another side to the lectures has also developed, a children's touring show called 'GetBetterPictures.com On Tour', we completed the first one at a local Holiday school before I finished writing this book, it features an interactive show with the animated Camera Family characters, Calvin, Connie and Freddie, all designed by my daughter Dani.

It all sprang up from the idea I had to add a children's section to the Get Better Pictures web site. Once again I called on Dani to create some images, then I wanted them to walk and before you knew it they had to talk. As soon as we had got them that far, putting them into a lecture presentation was just a formality. Going public was the next stage and with some help and encouragement from friends, in particular Beverley and Ralph, we arranged a live test.

We used the stage set I had already bought for the roadshow idea that was shelved, it took a whole day to construct, remember we don't do things in half measures, we, I say we, the whole family worked on it, two car loads! When it was ready we put on three presentations over a week, it started by showing a sequence of pictorial photographs to music then followed by my introduction as the best presenter since sliced cake. The three characters appeared by surprise on the screen behind me and started to ask me questions on photography, I then

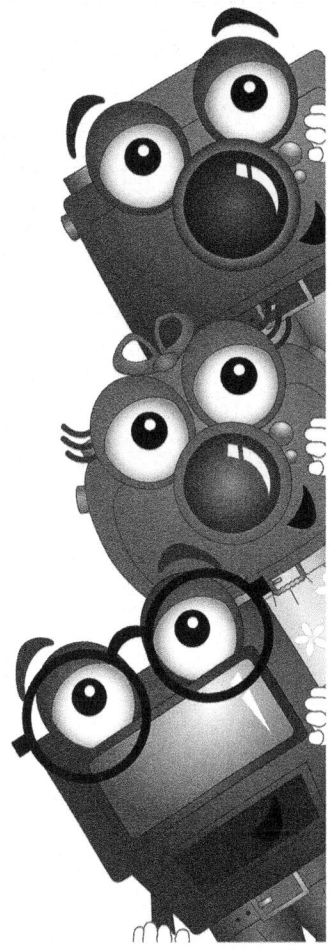

responded by answering them with the help of the children, creating a fun filled hour of easy learning. Afterwards we filmed the children's response to the show for the web site promo, check that out, it's funny. It provided us with a valuable insight, proved we had designed the appropriate characters to capture children's imagination and for us was a major success, a real moral booster, all we need now is a sponsor for the commercial tour, any offers!

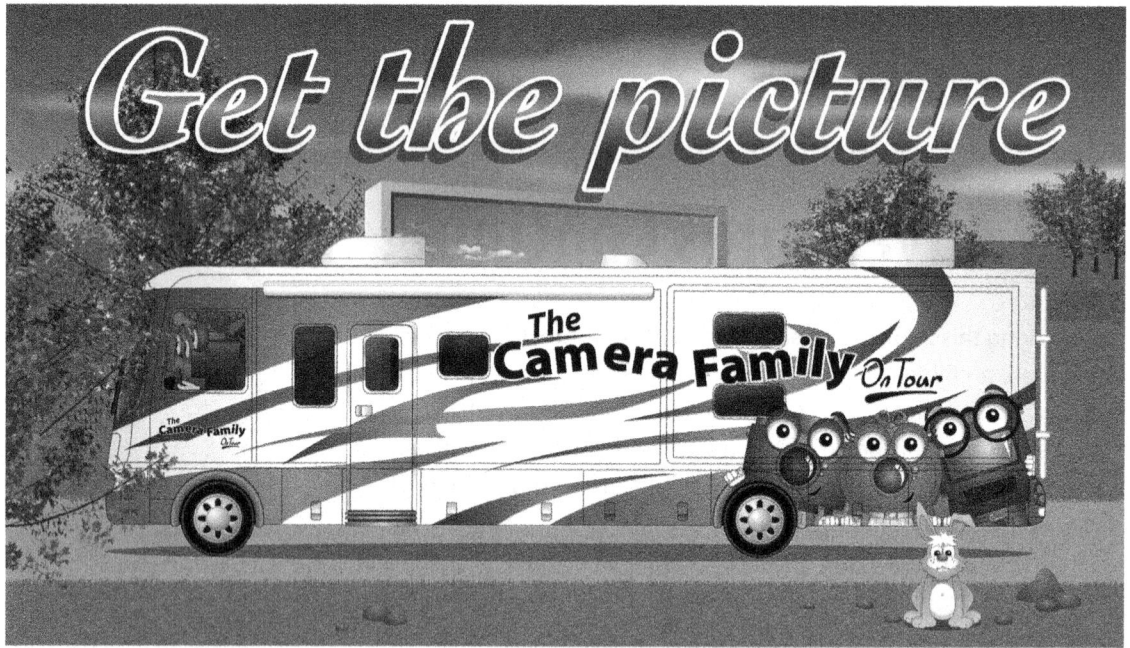

Now here is a little irony, as a result of this new venture I have gone full circle, I am now songwriting, composing and recording music again, even singing on the Camera Family theme song 'Get The Picture', well in fact the whole family sings!

www.GetBetterPictures.com is a web site close to my heart, I wanted to create an opportunity to give some free knowledge on photography back to the public, basically it is developing everyday. We are sharing and showing the work of other photography enthusiasts on the web site, while we develop a TV show with the Camera Family as an off shoot, potentially becoming the best thing since Disney. OK I'm getting carried away, yes I'm still dreaming!

As I do more and more lectures and presentations, I start to think it was my destiny, my youngest fan is just one year old, well she dances to my music and points at my pictures with a smile, and my oldest fan is about 86. I met him on one of my cruise lectures, a retired photographer who is thinking of taking it up again, he was inspired by my presentations and photographs, that is so flattering to me and the compliments just keep coming!

I have recently aspired to my first University appearance in the USA, now that is something I could never have foreseen or even have dreamt of, so I'm climbing back up the ladder one step at a time. I'm still entertaining and passing on the valuable knowledge I have learnt along the way. I know my life has been a series of bizarre and unsuccessful pursuits, some more than others, with a little bit of success along the way. You are obviously reading this book, whether you have paid good money for it or borrowed it from a friend doesn't really matter. I can now add you to my list, yes the list of people that know me is still growing, and as I look back over the years I can finally say one thing for sure, I'm known to a lot of people, and, in my own quiet and modest way, perhaps I was, just a little bit famous!

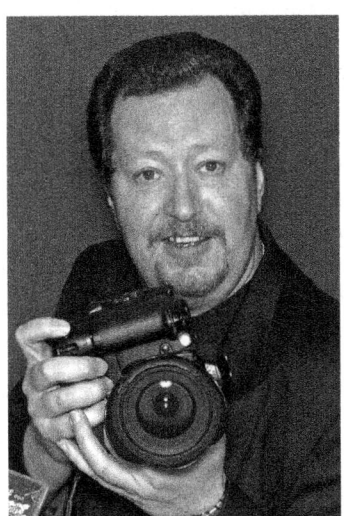

...It can't be the end I'm still here!

Check out my website,
www.waynepaulo.com
(yes, one last plug!) to see what I'm
doing next!

Photographic Index

LEGEND: P=Photograph T=Top L= Left M=Middle R=Right B=Bottom
AA=Amsterdam Admirals BD=Barcelona Dragons BT=Berlin Thunder
CS=Cologne Centurions RF=Rhein Fire FG=Frankfurt Galaxy HSD=Hamburg
Sea Devils SC=Scottish Claymores

Lightning Source UK Ltd.
Milton Keynes UK
UKOW07f1852100917

308920UK00005B/132/P